AF556039

Embroidery Techniques

Embroidery Techniques

Bhushan Tayal

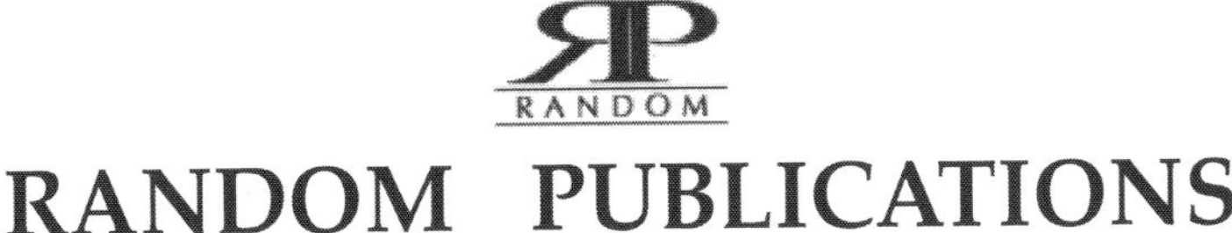

RANDOM PUBLICATIONS
NEW DELHI - 110 002 (INDIA)

Embroidery Techniques

ISBN 978-93-51112-64-8

Published in 2014 in India by

RANDOM PUBLICATIONS

4376-A/4B, Gali Murari Lal, Ansari Road
New Delhi-110 002
Phone: +9111-43580356, 23289044
E-mail: randomexports@gmail.com; sales@randompublications.com; info@randompublications.com

Reprinted 2025

Type Setting by: Friends Media, Delhi-110089
Digitally Printed at: Replika Press Pvt. Ltd.

Preface

Embroidery has been dated to the Warring States period in China (5th-3rd century BC). The process used to tailor, patch, mend and reinforce cloth fostered the development of sewing techniques, and the decorative possibilities of sewing led to the art of embroidery. In a garment from Migration period Sweden, roughly 300–700 CE, the edges of bands of trimming are reinforced with running stitch, back stitch, stem stitch, tailor's buttonhole stitch, and whipstitching, but it is uncertain whether this work simply reinforced the seams or should be interpreted as decorative embroidery. In the 16th century, in the reign of the Mughal Emperor Akbar, his chronicler Abu al-Fazl ibn Mubarak wrote in the famous Ain-i-Akbari: "His majesty (Akbar) pays much attention to various stuffs; hence Irani, Ottoman, and Mongolian articles of wear are in much abundance especially textiles embroidered in the patterns of Nakshi, Saadi, Chikhan, Ari, Zardozi, Wasli, Gota and Kohra. The imperial workshops in the towns of Lahore, Agra, Fatehpur and Ahmedabad turn out many masterpieces of workmanship in fabrics, and the figures and patterns, knots and variety of fashions which now prevail astonish even the most experienced travelers. Taste for fine material has since become general, and the drapery of embroidered fabrics used at feasts surpasses every description."

Embroidery was a very important art in the Medieval Islamic world. One of the most interesting accounts of embroidery were given by the 17th century Turkish traveller Evliya Çelebi, who called it the "craft of the two hands". Because embroidery was a sign of high social status in Muslim societies, it became a hugely popular art. In cities such as Damascus, Cairo and Istanbul, embroidery was visible on handkerchiefs, uniforms, flags, calligraphy, shoes, robes, tunics, horse trappings, slippers, sheaths, pouches, covers, and even on leatherbelts. Many craftsmen embroidered with gold and silver thread. A number of embroidery cottage industries, each employing over 800 people, grew to supply these items. Elaborately embroidered clothing, religious objects, and household items have been a mark of wealth and status in many cultures including ancient Persia, India, China, Japan, Byzantium, and medieval and Baroque Europe. Traditional folk techniques are passed from generation to generation in cultures as diverse as northern Vietnam, Mexico, and eastern Europe. Professional workshops and guilds arose in medieval England. The output of these workshops, called Opus Anglicanum or "English work," was famous throughout Europe. Embroidery can be classified according to whether the design is stitched on top of or through the foundation fabric, and by the relationship of stitch placement to the fabric. In free embroidery, designs are applied without regard to the weave of the underlying fabric. Examples include crewel and traditional Chinese and Japanese embroidery. Counted-thread embroidery patterns are created by making stitches over a predetermined number of threads in the foundation fabric. Counted-thread embroidery is more easily worked on an even-weave foundation fabric such as embroidery canvas, aida cloth, or specially woven cotton and linen fabrics although non-evenweave linen is used as well. Examples include needlepoint and some forms of blackwork embroidery. In canvas work threads are stitched through a fabric mesh to create a dense pattern that completely covers the foundation fabric. Traditional canvas work such as bargello is a counted-thread technique. Since the 19th century, printed and hand painted canvases, on which the printed or painted image serves as a guide to the placement of the various thread or yarn colours, have eliminated the need for counting threads. These are particularly suited to pictorial rather than geometric designs such as those deriving from the Berlin wool workcraze of the early 19th century. In drawn thread work and cutwork, the foundation fabric is deformed or cut away to create holes that are then embellished with embroidery, often with thread in the same colour as the foundation fabric. These techniques are the forerunners of needlelace. When created with white thread on white linen or cotton, this work is collectively referred to as whitework.

The book provides a clear, scientific and technical understanding of this subject. The information contained herein will equip the readers with latest and up-to-date knowledge.

I thank all members of my team who have helped in the preparation of the book. My special thanks go to "Random Publications" who have published the book.

—Bhushan Tayal

Contents

1

Introduction

Embroidery is the handicraft of decorating fabric or other materials with needle and thread or yarn. Embroidery may also incorporate other materials such as metal strips, pearls, beads, quills, and sequins. Embroidery is most often used on caps, hats, coats, blankets, dress shirts, denim, stockings, and golf shirts. Embroidery is available with a wide variety of thread or yarn colour.

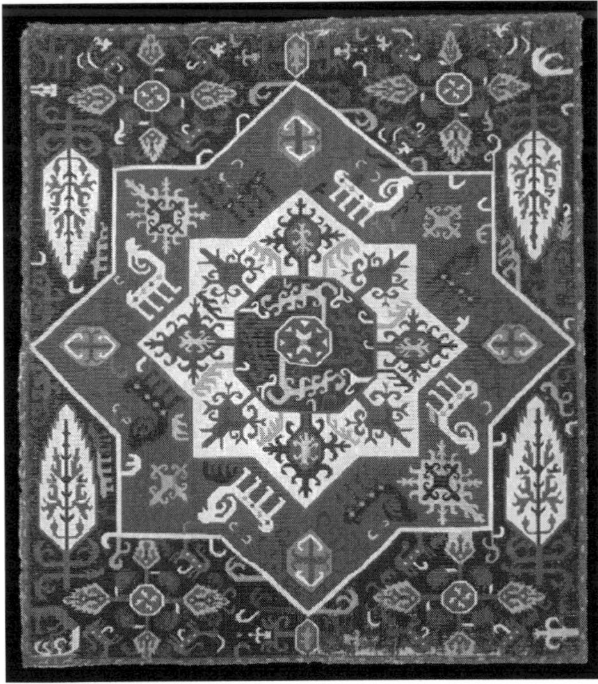

Figure: *Caucasus embroidery*

An interesting characteristic of embroidery is that the basic techniques or stitches on surviving examples of the earliest embroidery—chain stitch, buttonhole or blanket stitch, running stitch, satin stitch, cross stitch—remain the fundamental techniques of hand embroidery today.

Machine embroidery, which arose in the early stages of the Industrial Revolution, mimics hand embroidery, especially in the use of chain stitches, but the "satin stitch" and hemming stitches of machine work rely on the use of multiple threads and resemble hand work in their appearance but not their construction.

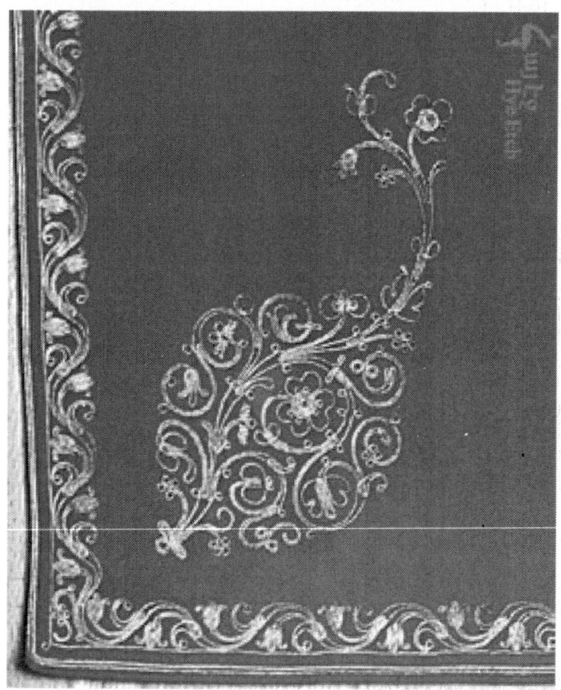

Figure: *Exquisite gold embroidery on the* gognots *(apron) of a 19th-century Armenian bridal dress from Akhaltsikhe.*

Embroidery is the handicraft of decorating fabric or other materials with needle and thread or yarn.

Embroidery may also incorporate other materials such as metal strips, pearls, beads, quills, and sequins.

Embroidery is most often used on caps, hats, coats, blankets, dress shirts, denim, stockings, and golf shirts. Embroidery is available with a wide variety of thread or yarn colour.

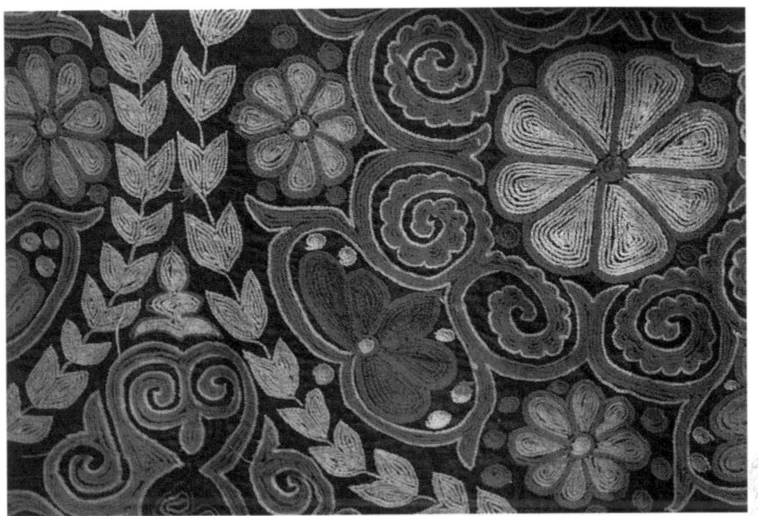

Figure: *Traditional embroidery in chain stitch on a Kazakh rug, contemporary.*

History

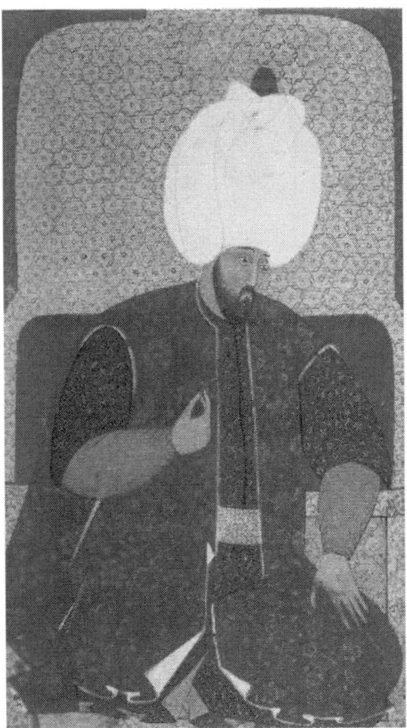

Figure: *The art of Embroidery became an important aspect of Ottoman culture.*

Embroidery has been dated to the Warring States period in China (5th-3rd century BC).

The process used to tailor, patch, mend and reinforce cloth fostered the development of sewing techniques, and the decorative possibilities of sewing led to the art of embroidery.

In a garment from Migration period Sweden, roughly 300–700 CE, the edges of bands of trimming are reinforced with running stitch, back stitch, stem stitch, tailor's buttonhole stitch, and whipstitching, but it is uncertain whether this work simply reinforced the seams or should be interpreted as decorative embroidery.

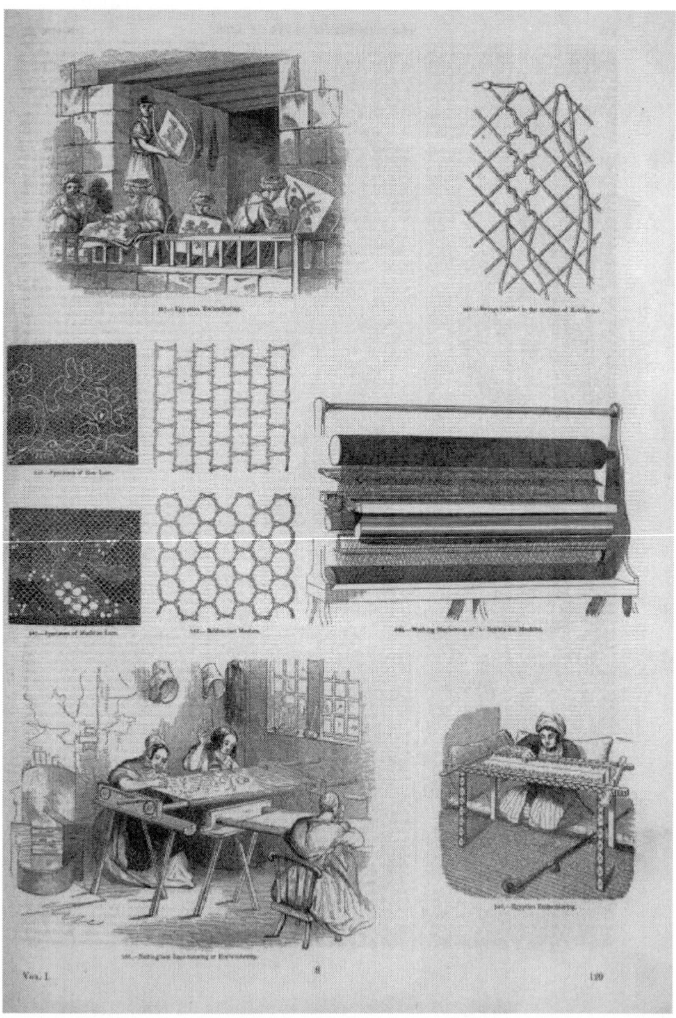

Figure: *Embroidering process in the textile industry in England, 1858.*

Basic Embroidery

The remarkable stability of basic embroidery stitches has been noted:

It is a striking fact that in the development of embroidery ... there are no changes of materials or techniques which can be felt or interpreted as advances from a primitive to a later, more refined stage. On the other hand, we often find in early works a technical accomplishment and high standard of craftsmanship rarely attained in later times.

In the 16th century, in the reign of the Mughal Emperor Akbar, his chronicler Abu al-Fazl ibn Mubarak wrote in the famous Ain-i-Akbari: "His majesty (Akbar) pays much attention to various stuffs; hence Irani, Ottoman, and Mongolian articles of wear are in much abundance especially textiles embroidered in the patterns of *Nakshi, Saadi, Chikhan, Ari, Zardozi, Wasli, Gota* and *Kohra*. The imperial workshops in the towns of Lahore, Agra, Fatehpur and Ahmedabad turn out many masterpieces of workmanship in fabrics, and the figures and patterns, knots and variety of fashions which now prevail astonish even the most experienced travellers. Taste for fine material has since become general, and the drapery of embroidered fabrics used at feasts surpasses every description."

Embroidery was a very important art in the Medieval Islamic world. One of the most interesting accounts of embroidery were given by the 17th century Turkish traveller Evliya Çelebi, who called it the "craft of the two hands". Because embroidery was a sign of high social status in Muslim societies, it became a hugely popular art. In cities such as Damascus, Cairo and Istanbul, embroidery was visible on handkerchiefs, uniforms, flags, calligraphy, shoes, robes, tunics, horse trappings, slippers, sheaths, pouches, covers, and even on leather belts. Many craftsmen embroidered with gold and silver thread. A number of embroidery cottage industries, each employing over 800 people, grew to supply these items.

Elaborately embroidered clothing, religious objects, and household items have been a mark of wealth and status in many cultures including ancient Persia, India, China, Japan, Byzantium, and medieval and Baroque Europe. Traditional folk techniques are passed from generation to generation in cultures as diverse as northern Vietnam, Mexico, and eastern Europe. Professional workshops and guilds arose in medieval England. The output of these workshops, called *Opus Anglicanum* or "English work," was famous throughout Europe.

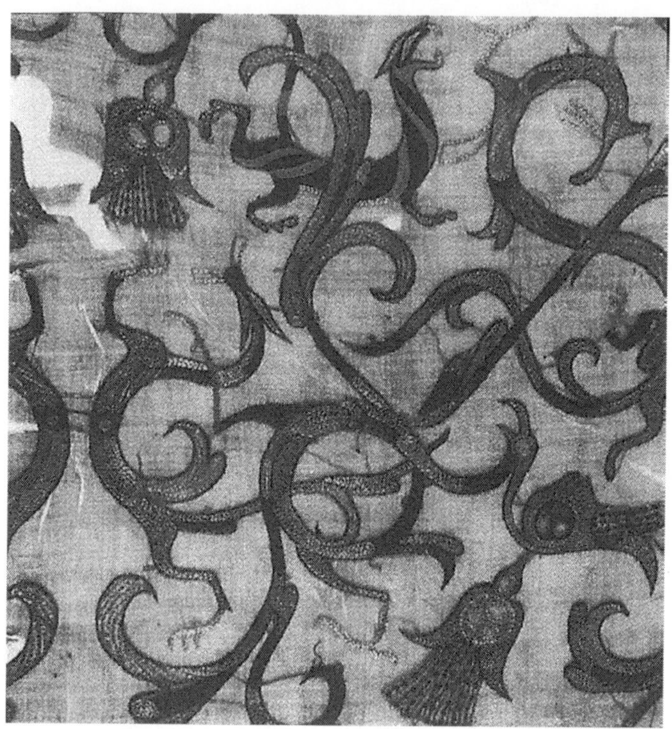

Figure: *Detail of embroidered silk gauze ritual garment. Rows of even, round chain stitch used for outline and colour. 4th century BC, Zhou tomb at Mashan, Hubei, China.*

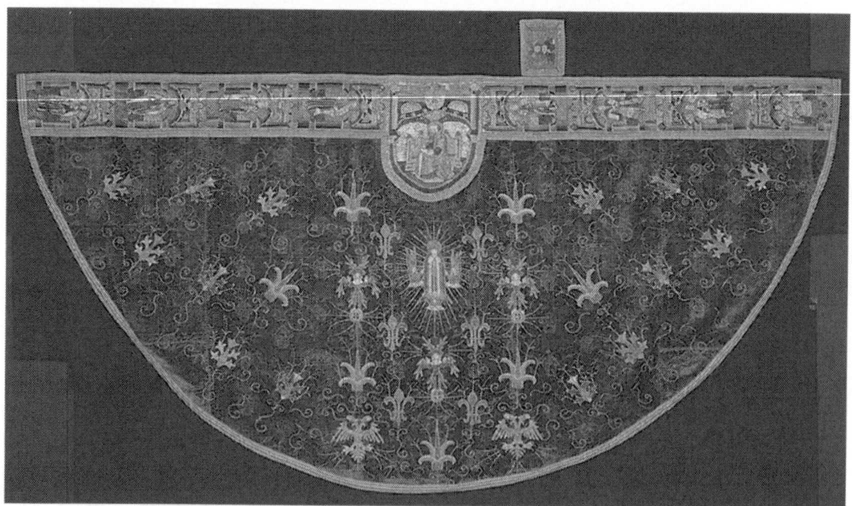

Figure: *English cope, late 15th or early 16th century. Silk velvet embroidered with silk and gold threads, closely laid and couched. Contemporary Art Institute of Chicago textile collection.*

Industrial Revolution

The development of machine embroidery on a mass production scale came about in stages. The earliest machine embroidery used a combination of machine looms and teams of women embroidering the textiles by hand. This was done in France by the mid-1800s.

The manufacture of machine-made embroideries in St. Gallen in eastern Switzerland flourished in the latter half of the 19th century.

Classification

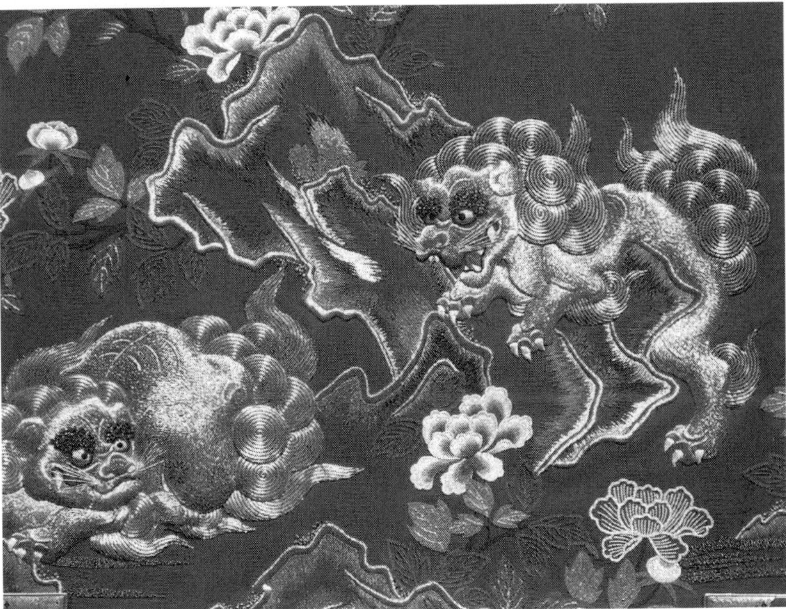

Figure: *Japanese free embroidery in silk and metal threads, contemporary.*

Embroidery can be classified according to whether the design is stitched *on top of* or *through* the foundation fabric, and by the relationship of stitch placement to the fabric.

In free embroidery, designs are applied without regard to the weave of the underlying fabric. Examples include crewel and traditional Chinese and Japanese embroidery.

Counted-thread embroidery patterns are created by making stitches over a predetermined number of threads in the foundation fabric. Counted-thread embroidery is more easily worked on an even-weave foundation fabric such as embroidery canvas, aida cloth, or specially woven cotton and linen fabrics although non-evenweave linen is used as well. Examples include needlepoint and some forms of blackwork embroidery.

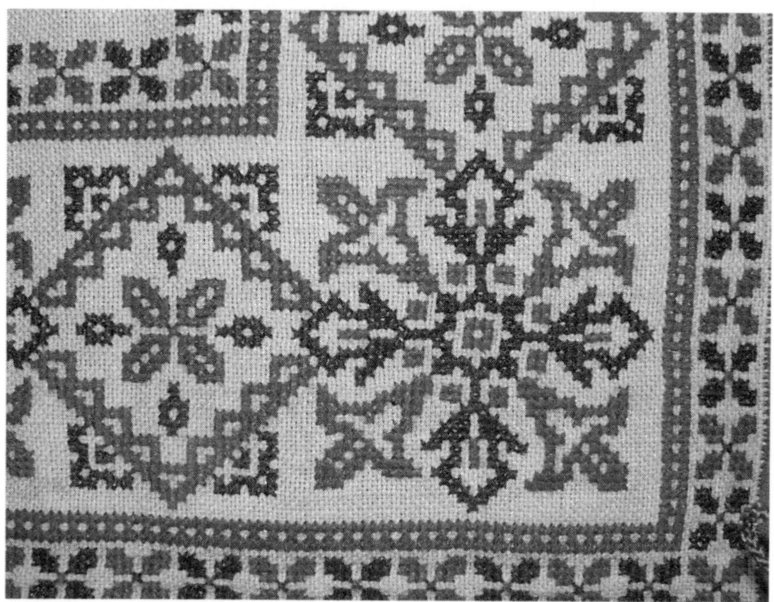

Figure: *Cross-stitch counted-thread embroidery. Tea-cloth, Hungary, mid-20th century*

In canvas work threads are stitched through a fabric mesh to create a dense pattern that completely covers the foundation fabric. Traditional canvas work such as bargello is a counted-thread technique. Since the 19th century, printed and hand painted canvases, on which the printed or painted image serves as a guide to the placement of the various thread or yarn colours, have eliminated the need for counting threads. These are particularly suited to pictorial rather than geometric designs such as those deriving from the Berlin wool work craze of the early 19th century.

In drawn thread work and cutwork, the foundation fabric is deformed or cut away to create holes that are then embellished with embroidery, often with thread in the same colour as the foundation fabric. These techniques are the forerunners of needlelace. When created with white thread on white linen or cotton, this work is collectively referred to as whitework.

Materials

The fabrics and yarns used in traditional embroidery vary from place to place. Wool, linen, and silk have been in use for thousands of years for both fabric and yarn. Today, embroidery thread is manufactured in cotton, rayon, and novelty yarns as well as in traditional wool, linen, and silk. Ribbon embroidery uses narrow ribbon in silk or silk/organza blend ribbon, most commonly to create floral motifs.

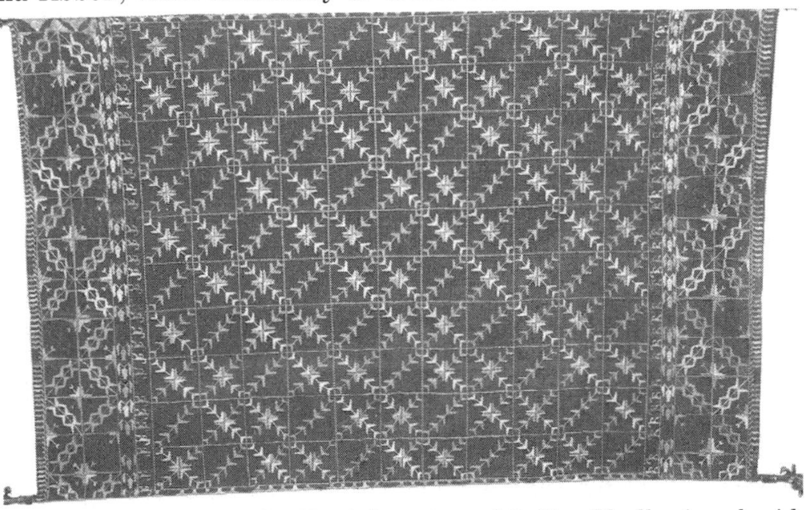

Figure: *Phulkari from the Punjab region of India. Phulkari embroidery, popular since at least the 15th century, is traditionally done on hand-spun cotton cloth with simple darning stitches using silk floss.*

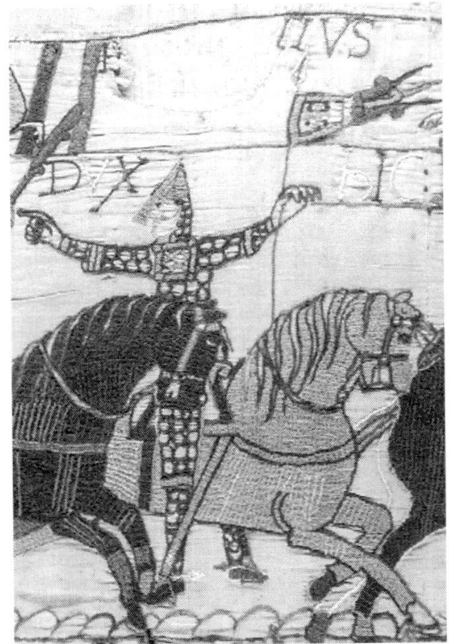

Figure: *Laid threads, a surface technique in wool on linen. The Bayeux Tapestry, 11th century.*

Surface embroidery techniques such as chain stitch and couching or laid-work are the most economical of expensive yarns; couching is generally used for goldwork. Canvas work techniques, in which large amounts of yarn are buried on the back of the work, use more materials but provide a sturdier and more substantial finished textile.

In both canvas work and surface embroidery an embroidery hoop or frame can be used to stretch the material and ensure even stitching tension that prevents pattern distortion.

Modern canvas work tends to follow symmetrical counted stitching patterns with designs emerging from the repetition of one or just a few similar stitches in a variety of hues. In contrast, many forms of surface embroidery make use of a wide range of stitching patterns in a single piece of work.

Machine

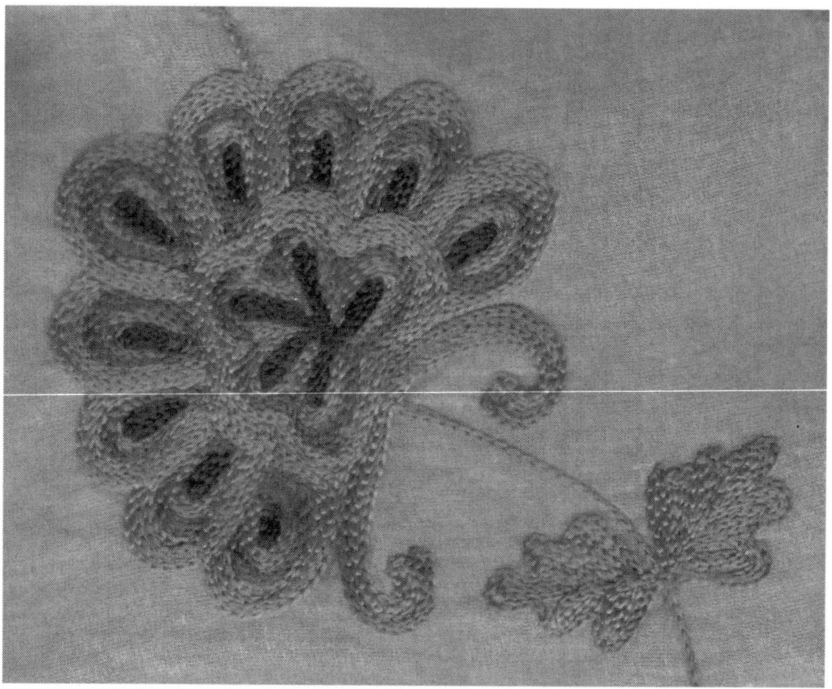

Figure: *Commercial machine embroidery in chain stitch on a voile curtain, China, early 21st century.*

Much contemporary embroidery is stitched with a computerized embroidery machine using patterns "digitized" with embroidery software. In machine embroidery, different types of "fills" add texture and design to the finished work. Machine embroidery is used to add logos and monograms to business shirts or jackets, gifts, and team apparel as well as to decorate household linens, draperies, and decorator fabrics that mimic the elaborate hand embroidery of the past.

Industrial Embroidery Machines

There are a number of brands available on the market; the top two are Tajima and Barudan, followed by Toyota & SWF

Chikan

Chikan is a traditional embroidery style from Lucknow, India. Literally translated, the word means embroidery. Believed to have been introduced by Nur Jehan, Mughal emperor Jahangir's wife, it is one of Lucknow's most famous textile decoration styles.

Origin

There are several theories about the origin of Chikankari. Chikankari - the process of chikan - was basically invented in Lucknow. It developed quickly during the period when the Mughals ruled and consisted of styles inspired by Persians. Lucknow grew into an international market for its renowned Chikankari work.

There are references to Indian Chikan work as early as 3rd century BC by Megasthenes, who mentioned the use of flowered muslims by Indians.

There is also a tale that mentions how a traveller taught Chikankari to a peasant in return of water to drink. However, the Noor Jahan story is the most popular of the lot. The name Chikan has been derived from the Persian word Chakin or Chikeen meaning a cloth wrought with needlework

Chikan began as a type of white-on-white (or whitework) embroidery.

Technique

The technique of creation of a chikan work is known as *chikankari.* Chikankari is a delicate and artfully done hand embroidery on a variety of textile fabric like muslin, silk, chiffon, organza, net etc. White thread is embroidered on cool, pastel shades of light muslin and cotton garments.

Nowadays *chikan* embroidery is also done with coloured and silk threads in different colours to meet the recent fashion trends and keep chikankari trendy with fashion. Lucknow is the heart of the *Chikankari* industry today and the variety is known as *Lucknawi chikan.*

The piece begins with the use of one or more pattern blocks that are used to block-print a pattern on the ground fabric. The embroiderer then stitches the pattern, and the finished piece is carefully washed to remove all traces of the printed pattern. Process of *Chikankari* includes following steps:

- Design
- Engraving
- Block printing
- Embroidery
- Washing & finishing

The patterns and effects created depend on the types of stitches and the thicknesses of the threads used in the embroidery. Some of the varieties of stitches used include backstitch, chain stitch and hemstitch.

The result is an open work pattern, *jali* (lace) or shadow-work. Often the embroiderer creates mesh-like sections in the design by using a needle to separate threads in the ground fabric, and then working around the spaces. It consists of 36 different stitches, which are:

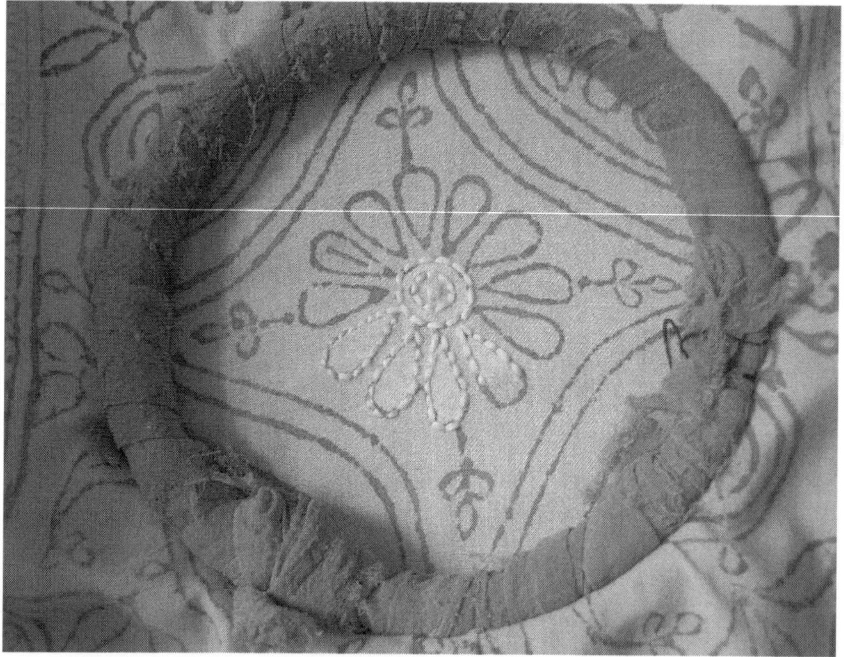

Figure: *Front view of Chikan embroidery being done over temporary block printed pattern*

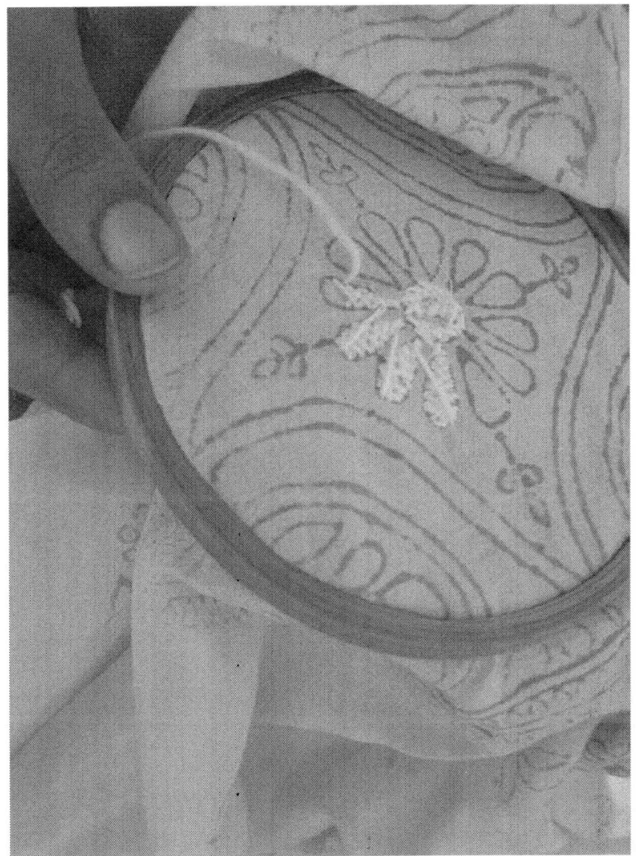

Figure: *Chikan embroidery from the back*

- *Tepchi*
- *Bakhiya*
- *Hool*
- *Zanzeera*
- *Rahet*
- *Banarsi*
- *Khatau*
- *Phanda"*
- *Murri*
- *Jali*
- *Turpai*
- *Darzdari*

- *Pechani*
- *Bijli*
- *Ghaspatti*
- *Makra*
- *Kauri*
- *Hathkadi*
- *Banjkali*
- *Sazi*
- *Karan*
- *Kapkapi*
- *Madrazi*
- *Bulbul-chasm*
- *Taj Mahal*
- *Janjeera*
- *Kangan*
- *Dhania-patti*
- *Rozan*
- *Meharki*
- *Chanapatti*
- *Baalda*
- *Jora*
- *Keel kangan*
- *bulbul*
- *sidhaul*
- *ghas ki patti*

GI Status

Geographical Indication Registry (GIR) accorded the Geographical Indication (GI) status for chikankari in December 2008, which recognised Lucknow as an exclusive hub of chikankari.

Couching

In embroidery, couching and laid work are techniques in which yarn or other materials are laid across the surface of the ground fabric and fastened in place with small stitches of the same or a different yarn.

The couching threads may be either the same colour as the laid threads or a contrasting colour.

When couching threads contrast with laid threads, patterns may be worked in the couching stitches.

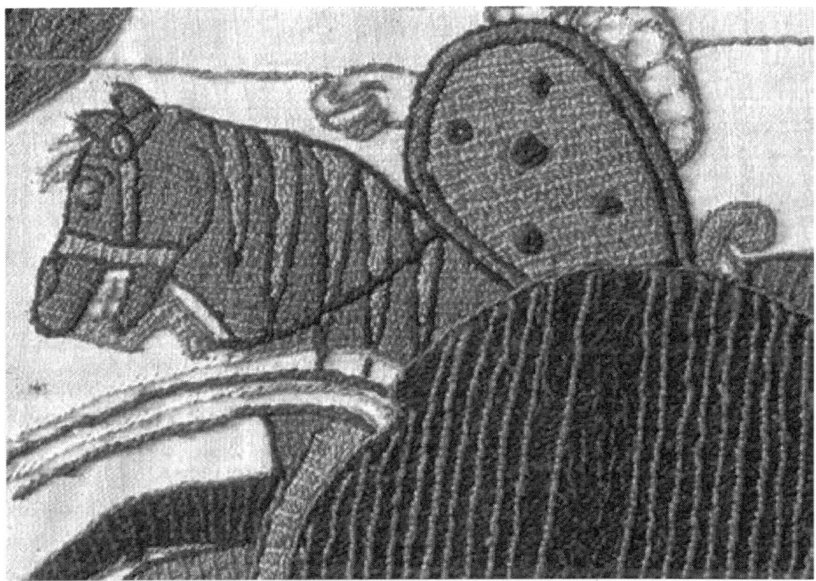

Figure: *Detail of the Bayeux Tapestry showing fillings in laid work.*

Applications

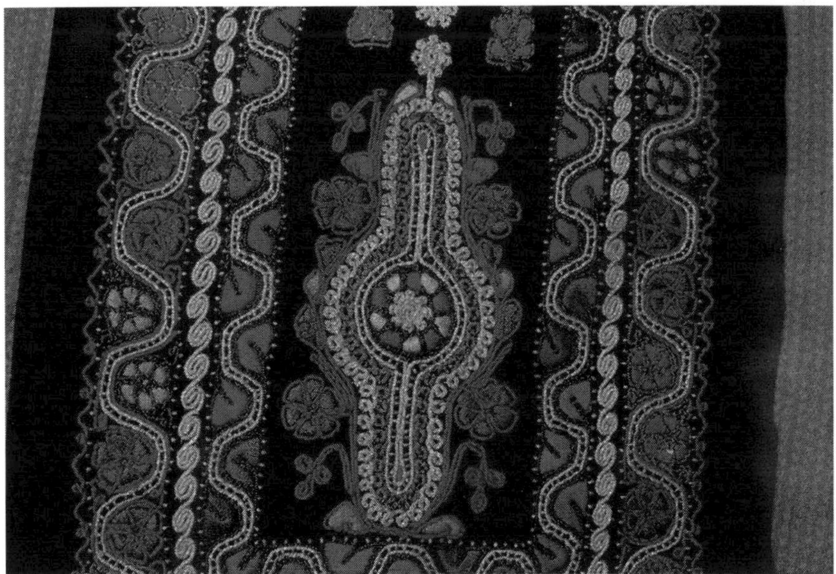

Figure: *Couching stitch from Beit Jalla. 2006.*

Laid work is one of two techniques used in the Bayeux Tapestry, an embroidered cloth probably dating to the later 1070s. (The other technique is stem stitch.)

Underside couching of metal thread was characteristic of earlier Opus Anglicanum in Medieval England and was also used historically in Sicily and rarely in other parts of Italy and France. Couching is also characteristic of Japanese metal-thread embroidery and Central Asian suzani work. There is a strong tradition of couching stitch in Palestine. Production centred on Bethlehem and its two neighbouring villages Beit Sahour and Beit Jalla; it was used for wedding dresses and formal wear.

Variants

- In couching, one or more threads are laid on the fabric surface and sewn to the fabric at regular intervals.
- In couched filling, threads are laid on the surface in a trellis pattern and sewn to the fabric at the intersections.
- In laid work or Bayeux stitch, threads are laid side-by-side to fill a shape, then held in place with a thread at right angles to the laid threads. This crossing thread is then couched to the fabric to hold the laid threads in place.
- In Bokhara couching or Bokhara stitch, the couched threads are held in place with many tiny crossing stitches, which may be aligned from row to row to produce patterns.,
- In Roumanian stitch, long satin stitches are each held in place with a small diagonal stitch made in the centre
- In Roumanian couching, bundles of laid threads are held in place with Roumanian stitches
- In Underside couching, a heavy couching thread (historically, a stout linen) is brought up from the wrong side of the work, looped over the laid thread, and returned to the wrong side. The couching thread is then given a sharp pull which draws a small loop of laid thread through to the wrong side of the fabric. Underside couching has the advantages that the couching thread is completely concealed from the front and is not subject to wear.

Butler-Bowden Cope

The Butler-Bowden Cope is a cope in the collection of the Victoria and Albert Museum. It derives its name from the family who owned it for several centuries. It dates from 1330–50 and shows scenes from the Life of the Virgin with Apostles and saints, embroidered with silver, silver-gilt thread and silk, on a rich crimson velvet.

This was the ideal base for the high quality English embroidery (called *Opus Anglicanum*, the Latin for "English work") which was much coveted by the most powerful people in Europe including kings and popes, and was used as a forceful visual statement of their wealth and status.

Many medieval church vestments were later cut up and re-used. This cope, as can be seen from its dismembered state, was made into a variety of ecclesiastical garments, but was re-assembled in the 19th century.

2

Bayeux Tapestry

The Bayeux Tapestry (French: *Tapisserie de Bayeux,* IPA: [tapis□i dY bajø], Norman: *La telle du conquest*) is an embroidered cloth—not an actual tapestry—nearly 70 metres (230 ft) long, which depicts the events leading up to the Norman conquest of England concerning William, Duke of Normandy, and Harold, Earl of Wessex, later King of England, and culminating in the Battle of Hastings.

According to Sylvette Lemagnen, conservator of the tapestry,

The Bayeux tapestry is one of the supreme achievements of the Norman Romanesque, ... Its survival almost intact over nine centuries is little short of miraculous, ... Its exceptional length, the harmony and freshness of its colours, its exquisite workmanship, and the genius of its guiding spirit combine to make it endlessly fascinating.

The tapestry consists of some fifty scenes with Latin *tituli* (captions), embroidered on linen with coloured woollen yarns. It is likely that it was commissioned by Bishop Odo, William's half-brother, and made in England—not Bayeux—in the 1070s. In 1729 the hanging was rediscovered by scholars at a time when it was being displayed annually in Bayeux Cathedral. The tapestry is now exhibited at *Musée de la Tapisserie de Bayeux* in Bayeux, Normandy, France.

Origins

The earliest known written reference to the tapestry is a 1476 inventory of Bayeux Cathedral, but its origins have been the subject of much speculation and controversy.

French legend maintained the tapestry was commissioned and created by Queen Matilda, William the Conqueror's wife, and her ladies-in-waiting. Indeed, in France it is occasionally known as "La Tapisserie de la Reine Mathilde" (Tapestry of Queen Matilda). However, scholarly analysis in the 20th century concluded it was probably commissioned by William's half-brother, Bishop Odo, who, after the Conquest, became Earl of Kent and, when William was absent in Normandy, regent of England.

The reasons for the Odo commission theory include: 1) three of the bishop's followers mentioned in the *Domesday Book* appear on the tapestry; 2) it was found in Bayeux Cathedral, built by Odo; and 3) it may have been commissioned at the same time as the cathedral's construction in the 1070s, possibly completed by 1077 in time for display on the cathedral's dedication.

Assuming Odo commissioned the tapestry, it was probably designed and constructed in England by Anglo-Saxon artists (Odo's main power base being by then in Kent); the Latin text contains hints of Anglo-Saxon; other embroideries originate from England at this time; and the vegetable dyes can be found in cloth traditionally woven there. Assuming this was the case, the actual physical work of stitching was most likely undertaken by skilled seamsters. Anglo-Saxon needlework, or Opus Anglicanum, was famous across Europe.

Alternative theories exist. Carola Hicks has suggested it could possibly have been commissioned by Edith of Wessex. Wolfgang Grape has challenged the consensus that the embroidery is Anglo-Saxon, distinguishing between Anglo-Saxon and other Northern European techniques; Medieval material authority Elizabeth Coatsworth contradicted this:

> *"The attempt to distinguish Anglo-Saxon from other Northern European embroideries before 1100 on the grounds of technique cannot be upheld on the basis of present knowledge."*

George Beech suggests the tapestry was executed at the Abbey of St. Florent in the Loire Valley, and says the detailed depiction of the Breton campaign argues for additional sources in France. Andrew Bridgeford has suggested that the tapestry was actually of English design and encoded with secret messages meant to undermine Norman rule.

Construction, Design and Technique

In common with other embroidered hangings of the early medieval period, this piece is conventionally referred to as a "tapestry", although it is not a true tapestry in which the design is woven into the cloth; it is in fact an embroidery.

The Bayeux tapestry is embroidered in wool yarn on a tabby-woven linen ground 68.38 metres long and 0.5 metres wide (224.3 ft × 1.6 ft) and using two methods of stitching: outline or stem stitch for lettering and the outlines, and couching or laid work for filling. Nine linen panels, between fourteen and three metres in length, were sewn together after each was embroidered and the joins were disguised with subsequent embroidery.

At the first join (start of scene 14) the borders do not line up properly but the technique was improved so that the later joins are practically invisible. The design involved a broad central zone with narrow decorative borders top and bottom.

By inspecting the woollen threads behind the linen it is apparent all these aspects were embroidered together at a session and the awkward placing of the *tituli* is not due to them being added later. Later generations have patched the hanging in numerous places and some of the embroidery (especially in the final scene) has been reworked. The tapestry may well have maintained much of its original appearance—it now compares closely with a careful drawing made in 1730.

The main yarn colours are terracotta or russet, blue-green, dull gold, olive green, and blue, with small amounts of dark blue or black and sage green. Later repairs are worked in light yellow, orange, and light greens. Laid yarns are couched in place with yarn of the same or contrasting colour.

The tapestry's central zone contains most of the action, which sometimes overflows into the borders either for dramatic effect or because depictions would otherwise be very cramped (for example at Edward's death scene). Events take place in a long series of scenes which are generally separated by highly stylised trees. However, the trees are not placed consistently and the greatest scene shift, between Harold's audience with Edward after his return to England and Edward's burial scene, is not marked in any way at all.

The *tituli* are normally in the central zone but occasionally use the top border. The borders are otherwise mostly purely decorative and only sometimes does the decoration complement the action in the central zone. The decoration consists of birds, beasts, fish and scenes from fables, agriculture and hunting. There are frequent oblique bands separating the vignettes.

The end of the tapestry has been missing from time immemorial and the final *titulus* "Et fuga verterunt Angli" ("and the English left fleeing") is said to be "entirely spurious", added shortly before 1814 at a time of anti-English sentiment. Musset speculates the hanging was originally about 1.5 metres longer. At the last section still remaining the embroidery has been almost completely restored but this seems to have been done with at least some regard to the original stitching. The stylised tree is quite unlike any other tree in the tapestry. The start of the tapestry has also been restored but to a much lesser extent.

In 1724 a linen backing cloth was sewn on comparatively crudely and, in around the year 1800, large ink numerals were written on the backing which broadly enumerate each scene and which are still commonly used for reference.

Background to the Events Depicted

In a series of pictures supported by a written commentary the tapestry tells the story of the events of 1064–1066 culminating in the Battle of Hastings. The two main protagonists are Harold Godwinson, recently crowned King of England, leading the Anglo-Saxon English, and William, Duke of Normandy, leading a mainly Norman army, sometimes called the companions of William the Conqueror.

William was the illegitimate son of Robert the Magnificent, Duke of Normandy, and Herleva (or Arlette), a tanner's daughter. William became Duke of Normandy at the age of seven and was in control of Normandy by the age of nineteen. His half brother was Bishop Odo of Bayeux. King Edward the Confessor, king of England and about sixty years old at the time the tapestry starts its narration, had no children or any clear successor. Edward's mother, Emma of Normandy, was William's great aunt. At that time succession to the English throne was not by primogeniture but was decided jointly by the king and by an assembly of nobility, the Witenagemot.

Harold Godwinson, earl of Wessex and the most powerful noble in England, was Edward's brother-in-law. The Norman chronicler William of Poitiers recorded that Edward sent Harold to tell William that Edward had decided William should succeed him as king of England upon his (Edward's) death. However, other sources dispute this claim.

Events Depicted in the Tapestry

The tapestry begins with a panel of Edward the Confessor sending Harold to Normandy. Later Norman sources say that the mission was for Harold to pledge loyalty to William but the tapestry does not suggest any specific purpose. By mischance, Harold arrives at the wrong location in France and is taken prisoner by Guy, Count of Ponthieu. After exchanges of messages borne by mounted messengers, Harold is released to William who then invites Harold to come on a campaign against Conan II, Duke of Brittany.

On the way, just outside the monastery of Mont Saint-Michel, the army become mired in quicksand and Harold saves two Norman soldiers. William's army chases Conan from Dol de Bretagne to Rennes, and Conan finally surrenders at Dinan. William gives Harold arms and armour (possibly knighting him) and Harold takes an oath on saintly relics. Although the writing on the tapestry explicitly states an oath is taken there is no clue as to what is being promised.

Harold leaves for home and meets again with the old king Edward, who appears to be remonstrating with him. Harold is in a somewhat submissive posture and seems to be in disgrace.

However, possibly deliberately, the king's intentions are not made clear. The scene then shifts by about one year to when Edward has become mortally ill and the tapestry strongly suggests that, on his deathbed, he bequeaths the crown to Harold. What is probably the coronation ceremony is attended by Stigand, whose position as Archbishop of Canterbury was controversial. Stigand is performing a liturgical function, possibly not the crowning itself. The tapestry labels the celebrant as "Stigant Archieps" (Stigand the archbishop) although by that time he had been excommunicated by the papacy who considered his appointment unlawful.

A star with a streaming tail then appears: Halley's Comet. Comets, in the beliefs of the Middle Ages, were a bad omen. At this point the lower border of the tapestry shows a fleet of ghost-like ships thus hinting at a future invasion. The news of Harold's coronation is taken to Normandy, whereupon we are told that William is ordering a fleet of ships to be built although it is Bishop Odo shown issuing the instructions.

The invaders reach England, and land unopposed. William orders his men to find food, and a meal is cooked. A house is burnt, which may indicate some ravaging of the local countryside on the part of the invaders. News is brought to William. The Normans build a motte and bailey at Hastings to defend their position. Messengers are sent between the two armies, and William makes a speech to prepare his army for battle.

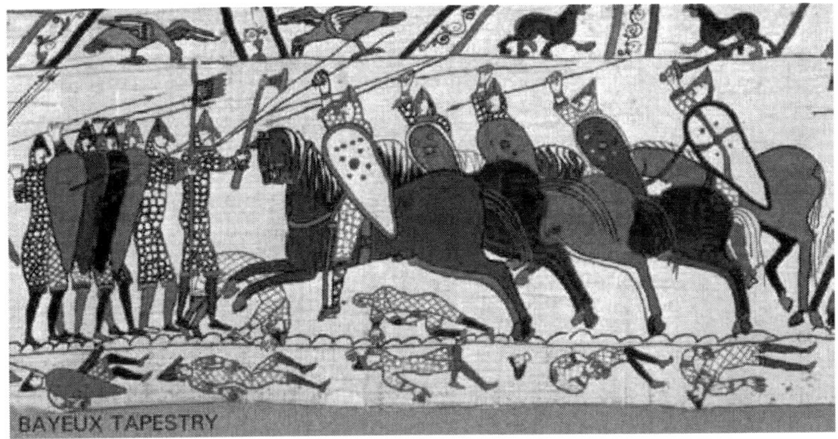

Figure: *Battle of Hastings*

The Battle of Hastings was fought on 14 October 1066 less than three weeks after the Battle of Stamford Bridge but the tapestry does not provide this context.

The English fight on foot behind a shield wall, whilst the Normans are on horses. Two fallen knights are named as Leofwine and Gyrth, Harold's brothers, but both armies are shown fighting bravely. Bishop Odo brandishes his baton or mace and rallies the Norman troops in battle.

To reassure his knights that he is still alive and well, William raises his helmet to show his face. The battle becomes very bloody with troops being slaughtered and dismembered corpses littering the ground. King Harold is killed. This scene can be interpreted in different ways, as the name "Harold" appears above a number of knights, making it difficult to identify which character is Harold. The final remaining scene shows unarmoured English troops fleeing the battlefield. The last part of the tapestry is missing but it is thought that story never continued for very much further.

Latin Text

Tituli are included on many scenes to point out names of people and places or to explain briefly the event being depicted. The text is in Latin but at times the style of words and spelling shows an English influence. A dark blue wool, almost black, is mostly used but towards the end of the tapestry other colours are used, sometimes for each word and other times for each letter. The complete text and an English translations are displayed beside images of each scene at Bayeux Tapestry tituli.

History of the Tapestry

The first reference to the tapestry is from 1476 when it was listed in an inventory of the treasures of Bayeux Cathedral. It survived the sack of Bayeux by the Huguenots in 1562; and the next certain reference is from 1724.

Antoine Lancelot sent a report to the *Académie Royale des Inscriptions et Belles-Lettres* concerning a sketch he had received about a work concerning William the Conqueror. He had no idea whether the original was a sculpture or painting though he mooted it could be a tapestry.

Despite his further enquiries he discovered no more. However, the Benedictine scholar Bernard de Montfaucon made more successful investigations and found that the sketch was of a small portion of a tapestry preserved at Bayeux Cathedral.

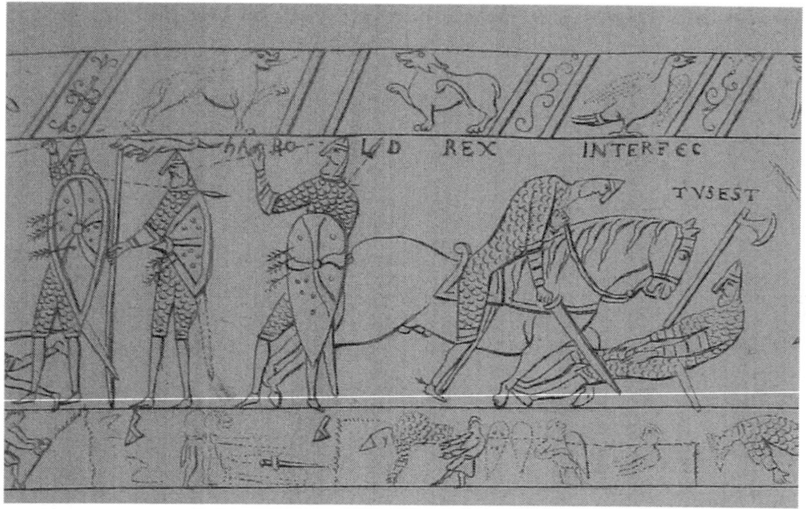

Figure: *Montfaucon / Benoît drawing showing Harold's death*

In 1729 and 1730 he published drawings and a detailed description of the complete work in the first two volumes of his *Les Monuments de la Monarchie française*. The drawings were by Antoine Benoît, one of the ablest draughtsmen of that time.

The tapestry was first briefly noted in English in 1743 by William Stukeley, in his *Palaeographia Britannica*. The first detailed account in English was written by Smart Lethieullier, who was living in Paris in 1732–3, and was acquainted with Lancelot and de Montfaucon: it was not published, however, until 1767, as an appendix to Andrew Ducarel's *Anglo-Norman Antiquities*.

During the French Revolution, in 1792, the tapestry was confiscated as public property to be used for covering military wagons. It was rescued from a wagon by a local lawyer who stored it in his house until the troubles were over when he sent it to the city administrators for safekeeping. After the Terror the Fine Arts Commission, set up to safeguard national treasures, in 1803 required it to be removed to Paris for display at the Musée Napoléon. When Napoleon abandoned his planned invasion of Britain its propaganda value was lost and it was returned to Bayeux where the council displayed it on a winding apparatus of two cylinders. Despite scholars' concern that the tapestry was becoming damaged the council refused to return it to the Cathedral.

In 1816 the Society of Antiquaries of London commissioned its historical draughtsman, Charles Stothard, to visit Bayeux to make an accurate hand-coloured facsimile of the tapestry. His drawings were subsequently engraved by James Basire jr., and published by the Society in 1819-23. Stothard's images are still of value as a record of the tapestry as it was before 19th-century restoration.

By 1842 the tapestry was displayed in a special-purpose room in the Bibliothèque Publique. It required special storage in 1870 with the threatened invasion of Normandy in the Franco-Prussian War and again in 1939–1944 by the Ahnenerbe during the German occupation of France and the Normandy landings. On 27 June 1944 the Gestapo took the tapestry to the Louvre and on 18 August, three days before the Wehrmacht withdrew from Paris, Himmler sent a message (intercepted by Bletchley Park) ordering it to be taken to "a place of safety", thought to be Berlin. It was only on 22 August that the SS attempted to take possession of the tapestry by which time the Louvre was again in French hands. After the liberation of Paris, on 25 August, the tapestry was again put on public display in the Louvre and in 1945 it was returned to Bayeux where it is exhibited at *Musée de la Tapisserie de Bayeux.*

Critical Reception

The inventory listing of 1476 shows that the tapestry was being hung annually in Bayeux Cathedral for the week of the Feast of St. John the Baptist and this was still the case in 1728 although by that time the purpose was merely to air the hanging which was otherwise stored in a chest. Clearly, the work was being well cared for. In the eighteenth century the artistry was regarded as crude or even barbarous — red and yellow multi-coloured horses upset some critics. It was thought to be unfinished because the linen was not covered with embroidery. However, its exhibition in the Louvre in 1797 caused a sensation with *Le Moniteur*, which normally dealt with foreign affairs, reporting on it on its first two pages. It inspired a popular musical *La Tapisserie de la Reine Mathilde.* It was because the tapestry was regarded as an antiquity, rather than a work of art, that in 1804 it was returned to Bayeux where in 1823 one commentator, A. L. Léchaudé d'Anisy, reported "there is a sort of purity in its primitive forms, especially considering the state of the arts in the eleventh century".

The tapestry was becoming a tourist attraction with Robert Southey complaining of the need to queue to see the work In the 1843 *Hand-book for Travellers in France* by John Murray III a visit was included on *Recommended Route 26 (Caen to Cherbourg via Bayeux)* and this guidebook led John Ruskin to go there describing it as "the most interesting thing in its way conceivable". Charles Dickens was not impressed: "It is certainly the work of amateurs; very feeble amateurs at the beginning and very heedless some of them too".

During the Second World War Heinrich Himmler coveted the work regarding it as "Important for our glorious and cultured Germanic history".

Mysteries

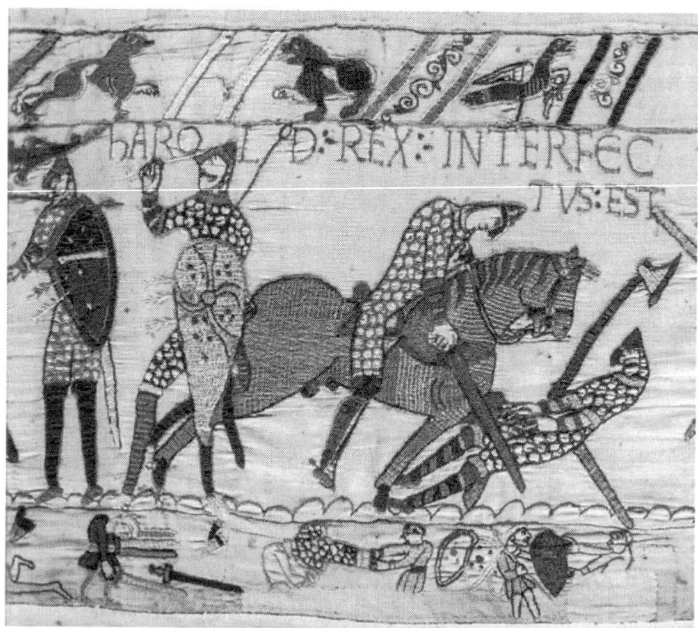

Figure: *Harold's death. Legend above:* Harold Rex Interfectus Est, *"Harold the King is killed"*

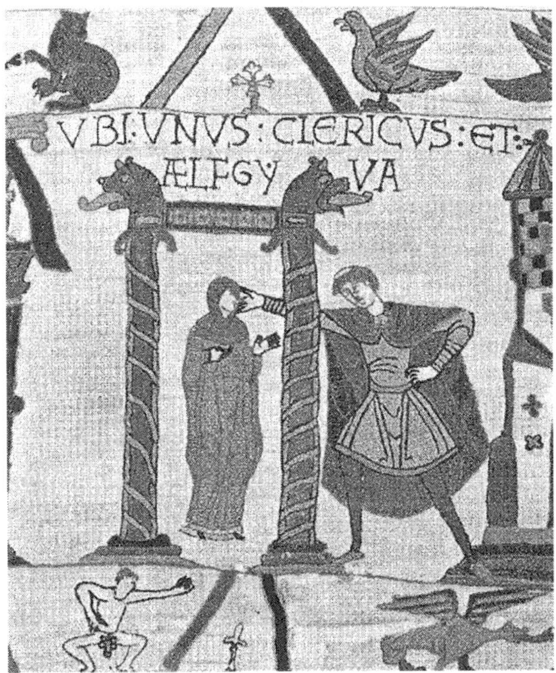

Figure: *Ubi unus clericus et Ælfgyva*

The tapestry contains several mysteries:

- The identity of Harold II of England in the vignette depicting his death is disputed. Some recent historians disagree with the traditional view that Harold II is the figure struck in the eye with an arrow. The view that it is Harold is supported by the fact that the words *Harold Rex* (King Harold) appear right above the figure's head. However, the arrow is a later addition following a period of repair. Evidence of this can be found in a comparison with engravings of the tapestry in 1729 by Bernard de Montfaucon, in which the arrow is absent. However, needle holes in the linen suggest that there had been something previously in this place: though possibly a lance.

  A figure is slain with a sword in the subsequent plate and the phrase above the figure refers to Harold's death (*Interfectus est*, "he is slain"). This would appear to be more consistent with the labelling used elsewhere in the work. It was common medieval iconography that a perjurer was to die with a weapon through the eye.

  Therefore, the tapestry might be said to emphasize William's rightful claim to the throne by depicting Harold as an oath breaker. Whether he actually died in this way remains a mystery and is much debated.

- There is a panel with what appears to be a clergyman touching or possibly striking a woman's face. No one knows the meaning of the caption above this scene *ubi unus clericus et Ælgyva*, "where [or *in which/during which*] a certain cleric and Ælfgyua", a Latinised version of Ælfgifu, a popular Anglo-Saxon woman's name. The elided AE shows familiarity with English spelling.
- At least two panels of the tapestry are missing, perhaps even another 6.4 m (7.0 yd) worth. This missing area would probably have included William's coronation.

Reliability

The Bayeux Tapestry was probably commissioned by the House of Normandy and essentially depicts a Norman viewpoint. However, Harold is shown as brave and his soldiers are not belittled. Throughout, William is described as "dux" (duke) whereas Harold, also called dux up to his coronation, is subsequently called "rex" (king). The fact that the narrative extensively covers Harold's activities in Normandy (in 1064) indicates that the intention was to show a strong relationship between that expedition and the Norman Conquest starting two years later. It is for this reason that the tapestry is generally seen by modern scholars as an apologia for the Norman Conquest.

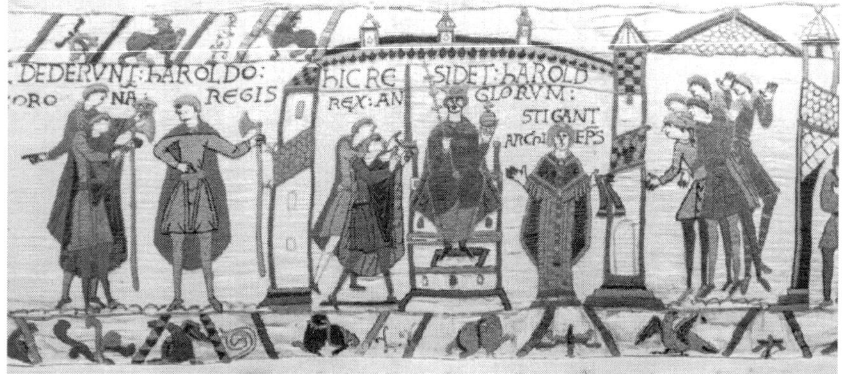

***Figure:** Coronation of Harold*

The tapestry's narration seems to place stress on Harold's oath to William although its rationale is not made clear. Norman sources claimed that the English succession was being pledged to William but English sources gave varied accounts. Today it is thought the Norman sources are to be preferred. Both the tapestry and Norman sources named Stigand, the excommunicated Archbishop of Canterbury, as the man who crowned Harold, possibly to discredit Harold's kingship; English sources suggested that he was crowned by Ealdred, Archbishop of York and favoured by the papacy, making Harold's position as legitimate king more secure. Contemporary scholarship has not decided the matter although it is generally thought Ealdred performed the coronation.

While political propaganda or personal emphasis may have somewhat distorted the historical accuracy of the story, the Bayeux tapestry presents a unique visual document of medieval arms, apparel, and other objects unlike any other artifact surviving from this period. There is no attempt at continuity between scenes either for individuals' appearance or clothing. The knights carry shields, but show no system of hereditary coats of arms—the beginnings of modern heraldic structure were in place, but would not become standard until the middle of the 12th century. It has been noted that the warriors are depicted fighting with bare hands, while other sources indicate the general use of gloves in battle and hunt.

Artistic Context

Tapestry fragments have been found in Scandinavia dating from the ninth century and it is thought that Norman and Anglo-Saxon embroidery developed from this sort of work. Examples are to be found in the grave goods of the Oseberg ship and the Överhogdal tapestries.

A monastic text from Ely, the *Liber Eliensis*, mentions a woven narrative wall-hanging commemorating the deeds of Byrhtnoth, killed in 991. Wall-hangings were common by the tenth century with English and Norman texts particularly commending the skill of Anglo-Saxon seamstresses. Mural paintings imitating draperies still exist in France and Italy and there are twelfth century mentions of other wall-hangings in Normandy and France. A poem by Baldric of Dol might even be describing the Bayeux Tapestry itself. Therefore, the Bayeux Tapestry was not unique at the time it was created—rather it is remarkable for being the sole surviving example of Middle Ages' narrative needlework.

Replicas & Continuations

There are a number of replicas of the Bayeux Tapestry in existence. Through the collaboration of William Morris with textile manufacturer

Thomas Wardle, Wardle's wife Elizabeth, who was an accomplished seamstress, embarked on creating a reproduction in 1885. She organised some 37 women in her *Leek School of Art Embroidery* to collaborate working from a full-scale water-colour facsimile drawing provided by the South Kensington Museum The full-size replica was finished in 1886 and is now exhibited in the Museum of Reading in Reading, Berkshire, England. The naked figure in the original tapestry (in the border below the Ælfgyva figure) is depicted wearing a brief garment because the drawing which was worked from was similarly bowdlerised.

Ray Dugan of University of Waterloo, Ontario, Canada, completed a stitched replica in 1996. Since its completion, it has been displayed in various museums and galleries in Canada and the United States.

Starting in 2000, the Bayeux Group, part of the Viking Group Lindholm Høje, has been making an accurate replica of the Bayeux Tapestry in Denmark, using the original sewing technique.

A hand-painted full-size replica of the Bayeux Tapestry is at the University of West Georgia, Carrollton, Georgia, United States. It is displayed in the third floor atrium of the Humanities building as part of an art gallery. Dr. E. D. Wheeler, former judge and former dean at Oglethorpe University, commissioned the work and donated it to the university in 1997.

An approximately half scale mosaic version of the Bayeux Tapestry is on display at Geraldine, New Zealand. It was created by Michael Linton over a period of twenty years from 1979. The work includes a hypothetical reconstruction of the missing final section of the Tapestry up to William The Conqueror's coronation at Westminster Abbey on Christmas Day, 1066.

Similarly, other modern artists have attempted to complete the work by creating panels depicting subsequent events up to William's coronation, though the actual content of the missing panels is unknown. In 1997, the embroidery artist Jan Messent completed a reconstruction showing William accepting the surrender of English nobles at Berkhamsted (*Beorcham*), Hertfordshire, and his coronation. In early 2013, 416 residents of Alderney in the Channel Islands finished a continuation including William's coronation and the building of the Tower of London.

In Popular Culture

The tapestry was cited by Scott McCloud in *Understanding Comics* as an example of early narrative art and Bryan Talbot, a British comic book artist, has called it "the first known British comic strip". Because it resembles a movie storyboard, is widely recognised and, by modern standards at least, is so distinctive in its artistic style, the Bayeux Tapestry has frequently been used or reimagined in a variety of different popular culture contexts.

It has inspired many modern political and other cartoons, including the 15 July 1944 cover of the *New Yorker* magazine marking D-Day; and George Gale's pastiche chronicling the saga leading up to Britain's entry into the European Economic Community, published across six pages in *The Times*'s "Europa" supplement on 1 January 1973.

The tapestry has also inspired modern embroideries, notably the Overlord embroidery commemorating the Normandy landings invasion, now at Portsmouth; and the Prestonpans Tapestry, which chronicles the events surrounding the Battle of Prestonpans in 1745.

A number of films have used sections of the tapestry in their opening credits or closing titles, including: the Disney film *Bedknobs and Broomsticks*, Anthony Mann's *El Cid*, Zeffirelli's *Hamlet*, Frank Cassenti's *La Chanson de Roland*, *Robin Hood: Prince of Thieves*, and Richard Fleischer's *The Vikings*.

The tapestry is referenced in Tony Kushner's play *Angels in America*. The apocryphal account of Queen Matilda's creation of the tapestry is used, perhaps in order to demonstrate that Louis, one of the main characters, holds himself to mythological standards.

Bradford Carpet

The Bradford Carpet is a canvas work embroidery made in the early 17th century (ca. 1600–1615) that originally belonged to the Earl of Bradford at Castle Bromwich.

The carpet measures 16 by 6 feet (4.9 m × 1.8 m). In the Victoria and Albert Museum it covers an entire wall. However, it was made neither for wall nor floor, but as a table covering. Its 17-inch-wide (430 mm) border was designed to hang down over the edges of a table, and it would have been removed or covered with a linen cloth when the table was used.

The carpet is worked with silk embroidery thread in tent stitch on a linen ground. The stitching is very fine (400 stitches/inch, 62 stitches/cm) and was worked in at least 23 different colours. The tension of the tent stitches over time has distorted the shape of the carpet. It is characteristic of professional canvas work popular for furnishings in the Elizabethan era. The field design is a grape vine trellis. The border, thought to represent human progression from a wild state to civilisation, depicts a variety of country pursuits set against a pastoral landscape, described as "perhaps the finest range of genre scenes to come down to us from Elizabethan times". A manor house, shepherd, travelling vendor with his packhorse, lords and ladies, hunting scenes, milkmaids, millers, water mills and windmills are all shown.

Hastings Embroidery

The Hastings Embroidery was commissioned by Group Captain Ralph Ward and made by the Royal School of Needlework in 1965 to celebrate the 900th anniversary of the Battle of Hastings the following year. Intended to be a modern day equivalent of the Bayeux Tapestry, the embroidery consists of 27 panels, each 9 × 3 ft, and shows 81 great events in British history during the 900 years from 1066 to 1966. It took 22 embroiderers 10 months to finish.

The Hastings Embroidery is worked in applique by hand, with the addition of couched threads and cords, tweed from Scotland, fabrics from the Victoria and Albert Museum, and feathers from London Zoo.

The Embroidery was on public display in Hastings, firstly in the Town Hall and then on the pier in a domed shaped building.

The Hastings Embroidery is currently in storage, and apart from two panels on permanent display in the Town Hall, can not be viewed, despite local campaigns to protest. It has been said that to preserve the cloth and applique that special storage displays would have to constructed and that these would cost too much to provide.

Hestia Tapestry

The Hestia Tapestry is a Byzantine tapestry woven from wool and linen in 6th century AD in Egypt. It is a late representation of Hestia the Greek goddess of the hearth. The tapestry measures 44 x 53 inches and is labelled in Greek "Hestia Polyolbos" (Hestia full of Blessings). In 1945 a book discussing the symbolism and history of the tapestry was published by Paul Friedlander titled *Documents of Dying Paganism*. It is in the Dumbarton Oaks Collection in Washington D.C.

Margaret Laton's Jacket

Margaret Laton's jacket is a surviving example of English Jacobean embroidery, significant because it appears in a portrait which has also survived. The jacket was originally owned and worn by Margaret Laton (1579–1641), wife of Francis Laton (1577–1661) who was one of the Yeomen of the Jewel House during the reigns of James I, Charles I and, briefly, Charles II.

Embroidered linen jackets were worn as informal dress, and were particularly popular among wealthy women in the late sixteenth and early seventeenth centuries. This jacket is exquisitely decorated with flowers, birds and butterflies, embroidered in coloured silks, coiled tendrils of silver-gilt plaited braid stitch and silver-gilt sequins. The edges of the jacket are trimmed with silver and silver-gilt bobbin lace and silver-gilt spangles.

This jacket appears in a portrait of Margaret Laton which probably dates from around 1620 and is painted in oils on oak boards. The painter is not known, but the style of portraiture is similar to that of Marcus Gheeraerts the Younger (1561?–1635) who was the most fashionable portrait painter of the period.

Both the jacket and the portrait are in the Victoria and Albert Museum.

New World Tapestry

The New World Tapestry is the largest stitched embroidery in the world, larger than the Bayeux Tapestry. It depicts English colonisation attempts in Newfoundland, North America, the Guyanas and Bermuda between the years 1583 and 1642, when the English Civil War began.

Work began on the tapestry in 1980 and continued for twenty years. When it is not on tour, the tapestry's home is the British Empire and Commonwealth Museum in the original 1840s terminal station designed by Brunel near the modern Bristol Temple Meads railway station in central Bristol, England.

The Creation of the Tapestry

The designer was Tom Mor, who also designed the Plymouth Tapestry at Prysten House, Plymouth, the Adventurers for Virginia (London) Tapestry, and was the consultant on the Jersey Liberation Tapestry (St Helier, Channel Islands) and the Plympton Tapestry (Plympton, Devon). The panel was researched by Tom Mor, Tom Maddock, Paul Presswell and Freda Simpson. Chief tapissiers were Joan Roncarelli and Renée Harvey. A New World Tapestry Website has been developed as of December 2008 and will soon include 120 pages, showing all complete panels.

Research for the New World Tapestry's twenty four panels began in 1980. Tom Mor was joined by Tom Maddock, a retired friend from Ivybridge. Over the months they travelled hundreds of miles together, researching the two hundred sixty four people who would be named on the tapestry. Heraldic expert Paul Presswell of Buckfastleigh identified all the Coats of Arms of the people, colleges and companies involved. The result has been the creation alongside the tapestry of a library of files on each person and a collection of reference books of great use to researchers, scholars and teachers.

Two hundred sixty four armorial shields run along the top and bottom tapestry borders throughout its length, alternating with illustrations of the same number of flowers of herbs, medicinal plants, trees and shrubs. The latter are shown because the colonists took ointments and cure-alls with them on their voyages and plant hunters returned with such things as the potato and tobacco.

All the flowers and florets depicted were drawn from nature by Tom Mor, who studied them under a watchmaker's glass. He was helped from the very early days by Freda Simpson of Plymouth, who was passionately interested in herbs and old herbal remedies. She identified and gave him over 230 flower specimens in the years that Mor lived with his wife and family in Plymouth. Later they moved to Cambridge were he was able to complete the set of 264 drawings with the help of Clive King and Caroline Lawes of the Cambridge University Botanic Garden, Lady Jane Renfrew of Lucy Cavendish College and Alison Davies, Monica Stokes and Edna Norman.

The Stitchers

Tom Mor could not have seen his canvasses brought to life without the help of his friends and the expertise of the dedicated tapissiers. When the very first stitch was made in the New World Tapestry in 1980, the team working in Prysten House numbered twenty. By the time the last stitch was made in March 2000, the number of tapissiers had increased to two hundred fifty-six with the addition of another eight centres. In Devon there was a second in Plymouth at HMS Drake (the Royal Navy's panel), Ivybridge, Chillington, Exeter, Bideford, Totnes and Tiverton Castle. Dorset's Tapestry centre was in the Guildhall at Lyme Regis and it was there that the Great Gardeners and Herbalists panel was stitched.

The first Oblique Gobelin stitch was made on 26 September 1980 in Prysten House in Plymouth, by U.S. Ambassador the Hon. Kingman Brewster.

The coat of arms of His Excellency's ancestor, Pilgrim leader William Brewster, appears on the 1620 Mayflower Panel.

The last Oblique Gobelin stitch was made by HRH The Prince of Wales on 3 March 2000 in the Orchard Room of his home at Highgrove House in Gloucestershire. Most fittingly, with his interest in history and a keen gardener himself, the Prince put his golden wool stitch in the date of the 1642 Great Gardeners and Herbalists' Panel.

Stitches have also been added by HM The Queen, HM Queen Elizabeth The Queen Mother, HRH The Duke of Edinburgh, HRH The Princess Royal and HRH The Duchess of Gloucester.

The Library

The New World Tapestry Library material includes histories of the years 1583-1642, much of it original research, files on the two hundred sixty four people named on the tapestry, plus heraldic information on over three hundred individuals, companies, towns, counties and universities.

Supporters

Supporters of the New World Tapestry include the Adventurers for Virginia patrons of the New World Tapestry and Library. Their names are inscribed for posterity in the Adventurers for Virginia Record Book. Supporters who join the Adventurers for Virginia may also:

- In London, celebrate the Adventurers for Virginia Day every 10 April to commemorate the granting of Royal Charters by James II of England to the London Company and the Plymouth Adventurers (Plymouth Company) in 1606 to establish colonies in Virginia
- Help fund the production of the book, *The Jamestown, Sagadahoc and Bermuda Story,* for schools and researchers.
- Help fund the production of the Yeardley/Flowerdew Brasses for presentation in England and America.
- Help make grants to the British Empire and Commonwealth Museum at Temple Meads in Bristol to create the permanent exhibition of the New World Tapestry, expand and enhance the New World Tapestry Library and help the development of three-way educational research between England, the Americas and Bermuda.
- Receive a tie showing the Adventurers' badge plus a lifetime pass to view the tapestry at the museum in Bristol.

Overlord Embroidery

The Overlord embroidery was commissioned by Lord Dulverton in 1968 and made by the Royal School of Needlework from designs by artist Sandra Lawrence. It commemorates the D-Day invasion of France during World War II.

It tells the story of Operation Overlord which was the code name for the Allied invasion of Normandy in June 1944. The embroidery begins telling the story well before the invasion, with war-time production and The Blitz. It continues through the entry of the United States into the war, and the planning and preparation of the invasion. The majority of the work covers the crossing of the English Channel by the invasion fleet and the combat once the troops landed on the French coast. The embroidery ends with a scene of British infantry advancing as German troops retreat across the Seine.

There are 34 panels which together measure 83 metres (272 feet) in length. The Overlord embroidery is the longest work of its kind in the world and is 10 metres (33 feet) longer than the Bayeux tapestry. Twenty embroiderers worked for five years to create the embroidery. Battledress khaki and gold braid were appliqued onto the panels.

Since 1984 the embroidery has been housed in the D-Day museum in Southsea, Portsmouth.

Quaker Tapestry

The Quaker Tapestry consists of 77 panels illustrating the history of Quakerism from the 17th century up to the present day. The idea of Quaker Anne Wynn-Wilson, the tapestry has a permanent home at the Friends Meeting House at Kendal, Cumbria, England.

The design was heavily influenced by the Bayeux Tapestry, and includes similar design choices, including three horizontal divisions within panels, embroidered outlines for faces and hands, and solid infilling of clothing, which is embroidered in the Bayeux Technique. The tapestry is worked in crewel embroidery using woolen yarns on a handwoven woolen background. In addition to using four historic and well-known stitches (*Split Stitch*, *Stem Stitch*, *Chain Stitch*, and *Peking Knot*), Wynn-Wilson invented a new corded stitch, known as *Quaker Stitch*, to allow for tight curves on the lettering.

Each panel measures 25 inches wide by 21 inches tall.

4,000 men, women and children from 15 countries worked on the panels between 1981 and 1989.

Panels have been toured in travelling exhibitions including a North American tour in 1993/1994. An exhibition of 39 panels in Ely Cathedral in 2012 attracted 11,273 visitors during its 27 day stay.

St. Gallen Embroidery

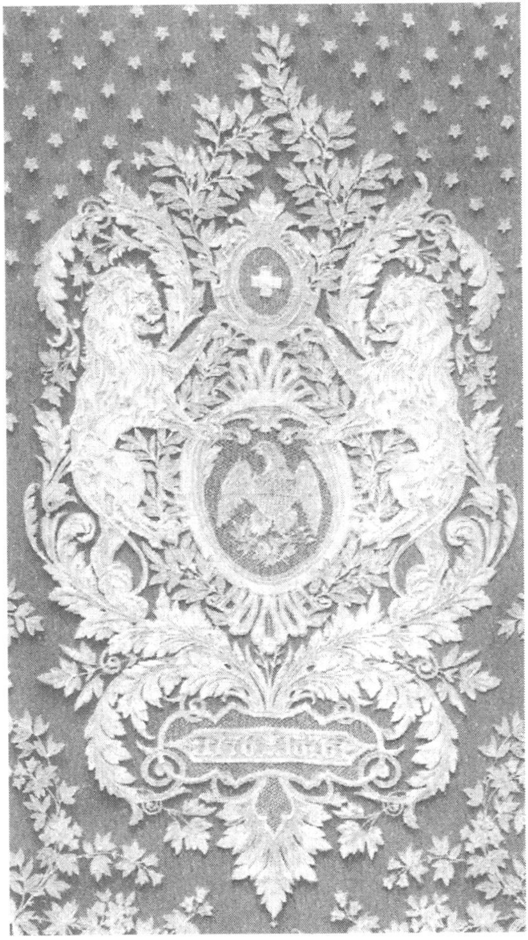

Figure: *An excerpt from the World Expo 1876 in Philadelphia: the motif comemorizes the 100-year anniversary of the U.S. Constitution. Coat of Arms with lions and the flags of Switzerland and the United States.*

St. Gallen embroidery refers to embroidery products from the city and the region of St. Gallen, Switzerland. The region was once the largest and most important export area for embroidery. Around 1910 the embroidery production was the largest export branch of the Swiss economy with 18 percent of the overall export value. More than 50 percent of the world production came from St. Gallen. With the advent of the First World War, the demand for the luxury dropped suddenly and significantly and so a lot of people were unemployed, which resulted in the biggest economic crisis in the region. Today, the embroidery industry has somewhat recovered, but it will probably never again reach its former size. Nevertheless, the *St. Galler Spitzen* (as the embroidery is also called) are still very popular as a raw material for expensive haute couture creations in Paris and count among the most famous textiles in the world.

Beginnings

Initial figures state that there were already up to 100,000 employees in the St. Gallen embroidery industry at the end of the 18th century, long before the invention of the hand embroidery machine. This figure is probably somewhat exaggerated, but it is an indication of the importance of embroidery in eastern Switzerland. The strengthening of the embroidery industry was accompanied by the decline of the canvas industry, especially in the city of St. Gallen itself. It had already been weakened sustantially by the production of cotton started by Peter Bion, and by foreign competition. Those without livelihood in the cotton industry changed to embroidery. Later during the Continental Blockade around 1810 the cotton industry too suffered. The *General-Societät der englischen Baumwollspinnerei in St. Gallen*, the first Swiss stock company founded in 1801, had to close in 1817 due to lack of money.

First Embroidery Machines

The expansion of the embroidery industry began with the invention of the (hand-) embroidery machine by Joshua Heilmann of Mulhouse in 1828. Just one year later, *Franz Mange* (1776-1846) ordered two such machines from Heilmann, under the condition that he sold no other machine in Switzerland or its immediate surroundings without Mange's consent. However, Mange allowed the *Maschinen-Werkstätte und Eisengießerey*, that Michael Weniger had recently opened in St. Georgen (city district of St. Gallen), the production of such machines. He himself had improved the design and several machines were exported abroad, but without lasting success for the local industry.

Mange's company passed in 1839 to his son-in-law *Bartholome Rittmeyer* (1786-1848), but shortly afterwards to Rittmeyer's son *Franz Rittmeyer* (1819-1892). Together with his mechanic and thanks to the support of Anton Saurer he improved the machinery such that the quality was now nearly equal to that of hand-embroidery. Thus, from

1852 the hand embroidery machines were manufactured in series, including at the already mentioned Maschinenfabrik in St. Georgen. Production amounted to more than 1,500 machines until 1875. The machines had the disadvantage that they were only able to do band-like embroidery.

The simultaneous invention of the sewing machine could, however, fix the problem, because now even smaller pieces could be sewn in great numbers on towels. A businessman from Hamburg called these new products *Hamburghs* to deceive the competitors as to the real origin of the article. Rittmeyer had to relocate and expand his factory several times because the ever increasing demand could no longer be covered. Just by itself, the 1856-completed embroidery factory in Bruggen (later relocated to Sittertal) worked temporarily 120 machines.

Rapid Ascent

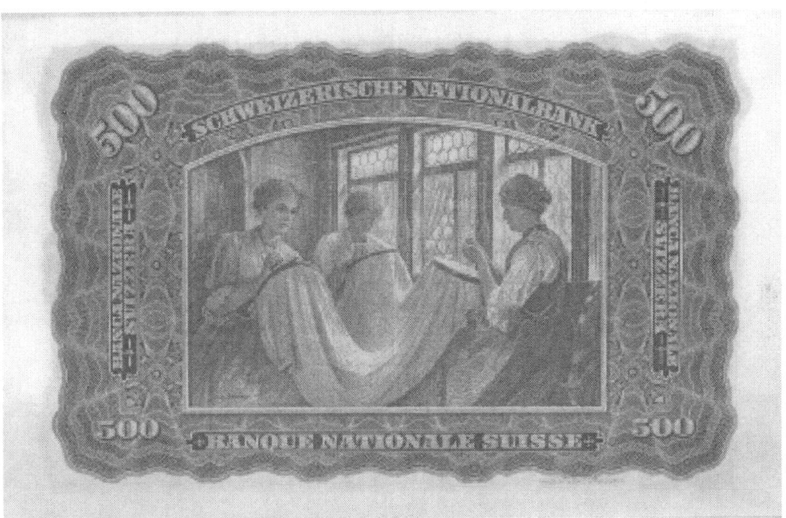

Figure: *Swiss 500 - franc note from the series of 1911, according to a draft of Eugène Burnand. The big economic weight of the St. Gallen embroidery shows the choice as a motive for the banknote with the second highest nominal price.*

The meteoric rise of St. Gallen embroidery can only be explained by a combination of economic, political, and technical conditions in the second half of the 19th century. In the political environment, it was the end of the American Civil War and the onset of free trade politics; economically, inter alia, the very popular mode of the second Rococo at the French court; and in the technical conditions the development of the machines. In the years after 1860, the demand for embroidered products rose so sharply that embroidery companies sprang up like mushrooms. Many farmers, artisans, and former weavers had an embroidery machine installed in their houses for credit.

Thus, embroidery had soon become in large part homework and a major addition to the income of the peasants and craftsmen, mainly in winter, as it had partially been before in the linen or spinning time. For the former, it was particularly the bad reputation of the factory and the dependence on a single employer, which let them decide for this kind of economic model; for the latter it was the capability to benefit from the possibility to increase and decrease the capacities very quickly and to let the entire economic risk remain with the workers.

The embroiders also appreciated the freedom to schedule their working hours and the unlimited use of child labour, especially since the introduction of the federal factory labour law in 1877, which denied young people under 14 years of age work in factories. Particularly benefiting from the development of home embroidery were the traders, who imported the commondies for the embroiders and distributed the finished products back around the world. In the period from 1872 to 1890, the number of installed embroidery machines in the cantons of St. Gallen, Appenzell and Thurgau rose from 6,384 to 19,389, but at the same time, the number of machines installed in factories decreased from 93% to 53%.

The value of goods exported to the Americas alone increased between 1867 and 1880 from 3.1 to over 21 million Swiss francs. Representatives of trading companies from overseas visited St. Gallen regularly to select patterns and to place new orders. The shipping company Danzas advertised in newspapers and praised itself as a "special agency for the embroidery traffic in St. Gallen" with postal ships to North America, East India, China, Japan, Australia and several other locations around the world. In this context we must also mention the *Kaufmännische Corporation,* which kept improving the framework conditions for the export trade. They built a duty-free storehouse in the city and opened a school for pattern designers; they also started today's Textile Museum.

Further Developments

To the next thrust, the embroidery industry rose in 1863 with the invention of the *Schifflistickmaschine* by Isaak Gröbli. An experimental machine was first built in Winterthur, and later went into series production at the Adolph Saurer AG in Arbon. In 1869 a new factory with 210 of these machines opened. A temporary setback affected the embroidery industry in 1885 due to its own overproduction in a time of economic crises. Orders suddenly declined significantly, resulting in wages dropping substantially. Only around 1898 did the embroidery industry recover through various internal reforms, restrictions on maximum working hours and minimum wages, and the rise of the global economy.

The last crucial step in the technical development of embroidery, the invention of the so-called *automatic* machines, in which the design is no longer entered using the pantographs but by punched card. The first of these machines came from Plauen. In 1911, Arnold Groebli, the son of Isaac, improved the machine at Saurer (in Arbon) so that they were in almost all respects superior to the German ones. The Schiffli- and hand embroidery machines were not removed completely, despite the now much higher speed, because the preparation of punched cards was often not worth the effort for small jobs. Since the various products of the industry had very different requirements, even in 1945, some orders were fulfilled with hand embroidery machines, or it was even embroidered entirely by hand.

The Big Crisis and the Recovery

The decline of the embroidery industry began in 1914 with the outbreak of the First World War. The demand for luxury products–and embroidery counted among these–collapsed suddenly, and also the free trade zones were disrupted. Partially neutral countries were still customers, but they could only compensate in the short term.

To preserve wages somewhat from the free-fall, maximum working hours and minimum wages were now also fixed. In fact, these measures were rather counter-productive–only workers who demanded less than the minimum wage got a job. The year 1917, still in the middle of WWI, temporarily brought a surprising turn: the Entente forbade the export of cotton products to Germany, but not the export of embroidery. Therefore, every cloth to be sold to Germany was embroidered in some way, as embroidery could be sold.

A year later, the sale of embroidery to Germany was forbidden, too, and this meant the end of the brief upturn. The last little flurry of exports came in 1919 after the end of the war, when the reconstruction of the war-stricken countries brought another short rise. With the start of the economic crisis, the heyday for the St. Gallen embroidery was finally ended. One sign of the extent of the crisis, is that from 1910 to 1930, the population of St. Gallen was reduced by emigration (as a result of unemployment) from 75,482 to 64,079.

Although embroidery exports rose again after the war, the time of the biggest economic crisis for the city began no later than the 1920s. Between 1920 and 1937, the number of embroidery machines was reduced from about 13,000 to less than 2,000. In 1929 the federal government subsidized a reduction of machines–compared with 1905, the number of people employed in industry declined by 65%. The absolute low point was reached in 1935 with an embroidery export of 640 tonnes (compared to 5,899 tons in 1913). In 1937, however, exports rose again for the first time to over 20 million Swiss francs, and the majority of the 97 newly opened facilities in the area were in the textile industry.

Working Conditions

Initially, embroidery was primarily or even almost exclusively women's work, this changed abruptly with the introduction of embroidery machines. The work on the machine was exclusively men's work, the woman was, however, still required as a helper-she took care of the replacement of broken needles and the threading, if a thread had ended.

In traditional historiography, the above-mentioned advantages of home work were accentuated-in 1877 Dr. Wagner from the *Schweizerische Gemeinnützige Gesellschaft* wrote about factory work that "The greatest misery of our time is the dissolution of the family"-so it is now generally judged more critically. First, the earnings of homeworkers were at times very low, and secondly, many children and even grandparents had to work at the embroidery machines, in order to earn enough to survive.

While the majority of the home-workers lived in a reasonable housing with a comfortable quality of life, the workrooms were often bad, because these were in damp, poorly heated and poorly ventilated rooms (which was, for the quality of the produced textile, an advantage). The traditional historiography always emphasized the interaction between the textile industry and agriculture. The farmers, ideally would use their free time productively, have job variation, and a supplement to their poor income. Undeniably, this was actually true for a few farms. However, the competition was fierce and the loan for the machine would have to be paid back, so that often little time was left for agriculture.

Also, the rough work of a farmer was not conducive for the fine embroidery work, so that many of these agricultural enterprises could only perform coarser embroidery works. Excluded from this was the pure hand embroidery by women, as it was predominantly done in Appenzell-Innerrhoden until well into the 20th century.

The earnings of the embroiderers were generally quite good, especially for the self-employed homeworkers. It was worse for the auxiliaries, who often lived from hand to mouth. The working days, notably in times of great demand, were very long. The workday lasted 10–14 hours, which caused health damage because of straining of the muscles-most embroidery machines were still operated by hand-and anemia or pulmonary tuberculosis. Moreover, the position of the embroiderers in front of the pantographs was, from an ergonomic point of view, extremely bad-the chest was severely compressed in its development and the spine was crooked. A full 25% of all embroiderers were already classified "unfit for service" at their mustering.

Also, the infant mortality in the northern, industrialized districts of the canton of St. Gallen was extraordinarily high. Various doctors tried to counteract this problem with studies and public education in the areas of health, nutrition counselling, and child care-with measurable success. Through the awareness especially of the teachers for hygiene and in the hiring of specific medics for schools, the hygiene awareness of the population improved considerably. Since 1895, the soldiers in the barracks were also supposed to shower regularly . In addition to external cleanliness the attention of the doctors also came to the "hygiene of the stomach"-the diet. Dairy and meat products were advertised as healthy and tobacco and carbohydrates came into disrepute. This benefitted the agricultural sector, which also increasingly focused on the livestock industry. Even the hitherto totally normal consumption of large amounts of alcohol was discouraged.

Embroidery Today

Although embroidery no longer has the significance for the region as at the beginning of the last century, it is still an economic factor. Embroidery machine producing companies such as Benninger AG are among the larger employers in the region. Big names such as Akris, Pierre Cardin, Chanel, Christian Dior, Giorgio Armani, Emanuel Ungaro Hubert de Givenchy, Christian Lacroix, Nina Ricci, Hemant and Yves Saint Laurent work with embroidered fabrics from St. Gallen. In the city itself embroidery products are, in addition to the traditional fashion show on the CSIO and the "OFFA Frühlings- und Trendmesse St. Gallen" presented during the St. Gallen Kinderfest. This festival owes a large part of its importance and its character to the embroidery on display. The great boom of embroidery and the associated wealth of the city also has influenced its development. From today's perspective, one can say that the city was built around 1920 - apart from the later extensions at the edge of the city. The Art Nouveau and Neu-Renaissance buildings constructed from 1880 to 1930 define the image of the commercial districts built around the old city. The names of these former business places suggest the past significance of world trade for the city: Pacific, Oceanic, Atlantic, Chicago, Britannia, Washington, Florida, and so forth.

Phulkari

Phulkarian embroidery technique from the Punjab region (divided between India and Pakistan) literally means *flower working*, which was at one time used as the word for embroidery, but in time the word "Phulkari" became restricted to embroidered shawls and head scarfs. Simple and sparsely embroidered *odini* (head scarfs), dupatta and shawls, made for everyday use, are called *Phulkaris*, whereas garments that cover the entire body, made for special and ceremonial occasions, are known as *Baghs* ("garden").

The word *phul* means flower and *kari* means craft, thus its name, literally means floral work or floral craft.

Overview

Phulkaris and Baghs were worn by women all over Punjab during marriage festivals and other joyous occasions. They were embroidered by the women for their own use and use of other family members and were not for sale in the market. Thus, it was purely a domestic art which not only satisfied their inner urge for creation but brought colour into day to day life. In a way, it was true folk art. Custom had grown to give Phulkaris and Baghs to brides at the time of marriages. Some best Phulkaris and Baghs are known to have been made in Hazara and Chakwal, areas of Northern Punjab in Pakistan.

Some scholars feel that the art of Phulkari came from Iran where it is known as "Gulkari". Some feel it came from Central Asia along with Jat tribes who migrated to India and settled in Punjab, Haryana and Gujarat. There is reference of Phulkari in Vedas, Mahabharat, Guru Granth Sahib and folk songs of Punjab. In its present form, phulkari embroidery has been popular since the 15th century.

The main characteristics of Phulkari embroidery are use of darn stitch on the wrong side of coarse cotton cloth with coloured silken thread. Punjabi women created innumerable alluring and interesting designs and patterns by their skilful manipulation of the darn stitch. The base khaddar cloth used in Western Punjab is finer from those of Central Punjab. Black/blue are not preferred in Western Punjab, whereas white is not used in East Punjab. In West Punjab, 2 or 3 pieces of cloth are first folded and joined together. In East Punjab, they are joined together first and then embroidered.

In Phulkari embroidery ornaments the cloth, whereas in *Bagh*, it entirely covers the garment so that the base cloth is not visible. The end portion of pallav of Phulkari have separate panels of exquisite workmanship of striking design.

The most favoured colour is red and its shades, because Bagh and Phulkari are used during marriage and other festivals. Red is considered auspicious by Hindus and Sikhs. Other colours are brown, blue, black, white. White was used in Bagh by elderly ladies. Silk thread in strands came from Kashmir, Afghanistan and Bengal. The best quality silk came from China.

No religious subject or darbar scenes were embroidered. Phulkari encompassed life in the villages. Creative ability of Punjabi women has produced innumerable and intricate geometrical patterns. However, most motifs were taken from everyday life. Wheat and barley stalk with ears are a common motif.

Revival and Modern Applications

Traditionally, phulkari garments were part of a girl's wedding trousseau, its motifs expressive of her emotions and the number of phulkari pieces defined the status of the family. Over the years, government has been working towards promotion of phulkari embroidery, by organising special training programs, fairs, and exhibitions. Since most of women artisan creating phulkari are in the unorganised sector or work through agents, they do not make much money compared to an actual market price of their product, to avoid this lacuna Punjab Small Industries and Export Corporation (PSIEC) has formed women self-help groups and cooperatives to sell directly and make more profits.

Indira Gandhi National Centre for the Arts (IGNCA) acquired a collection of selected phulkari for its archives in 1994. Some modern fashion designers are incorporating this embroidery into their garments, and its use has spread beyond *salwar kameez* and *dupatta* to objects and garments as varied, as jackets, bags, cushion covers, table-mats, shoes, slipper, *juttis*, and kids garments.

In 2011, after a five-year long legal case, Phulkari was awarded the geographical indication (GI) status in India, which means that after that only registered traders and manufacturers, from Punjab Haryana and Rajasthan states would be able to use the term for the traditional craft, and the patent information centre (PIC) of Punjab State Council for Science and Technology would issue a logo or hologram to distinguish the product.

Working with Metal Thread and Spangles

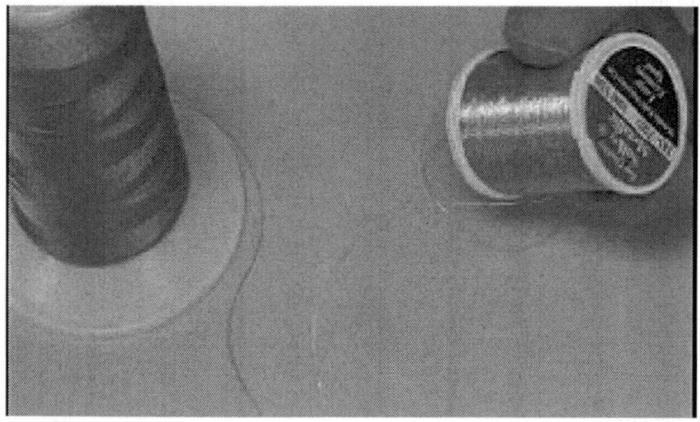

Metallic thread is fun to use to add sparkle and shimmer to holiday projects. It's also great for adding a bit of "bling" to garments, too!Metallic thread can be a little tricky to work with. Sometimes you can have repetitive thread breaks, or thread nests. The following information will help you to avoid those "threadaches," and have a successful and enjoyable time working with metallic thread.

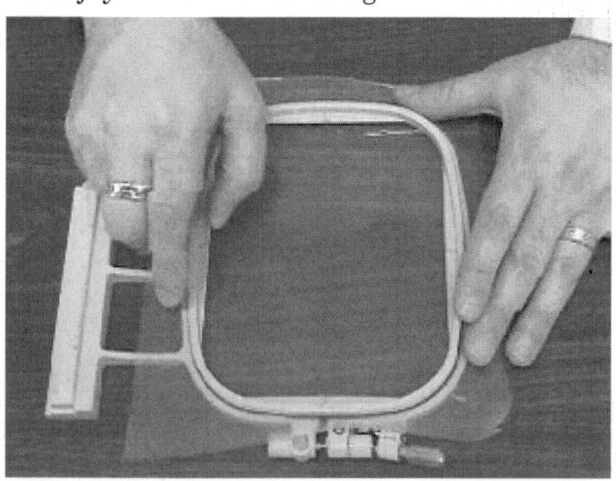

Metallic thread is thinner than rayon or polyester thread. It has a polyester core, so it has more stretch, too.

Because metallic thread is thinner than other types of thread, it should be used in small areas of a design, a freestanding lace design, or with designs that are specifically digitized for metallic thread.

For this example, we stitched a freestanding lace snowflake with metallic thread. To do this, we hooped a piece of heavy weight water-soluble stabilizer.

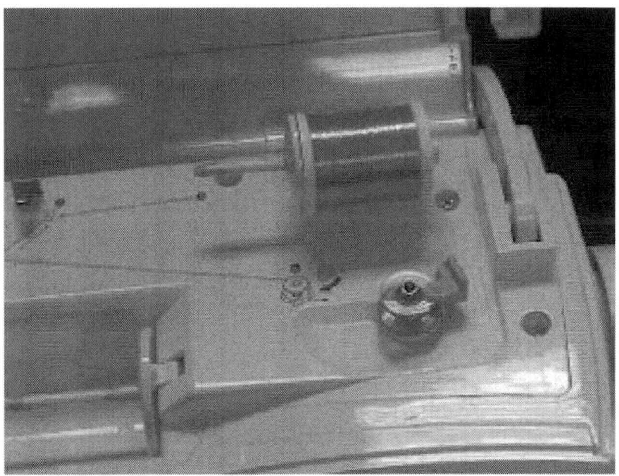

Because freestanding lace is double-sided, we wound a bobbin with metallic thread.

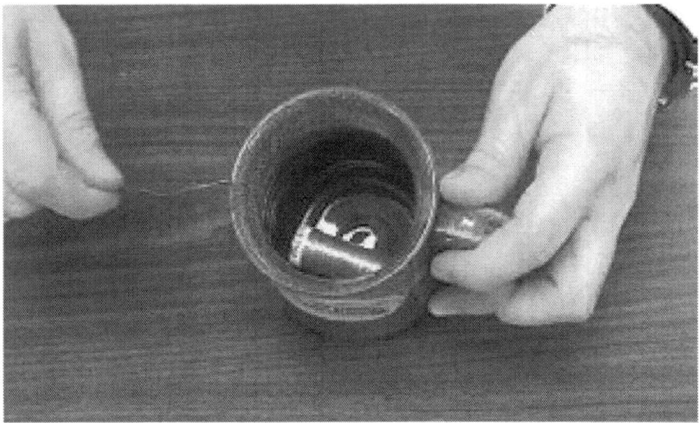

One of the tricks for getting great results when working with metallic thread is to let the thread relax before it goes through the tension discs and take-up lever. We placed the spool of metallic thread in a cup. This trick works with smaller spools; larger spools and cones may be too heavy. The thread will unwind in the cup, and relax a bit before going through the tension discs.

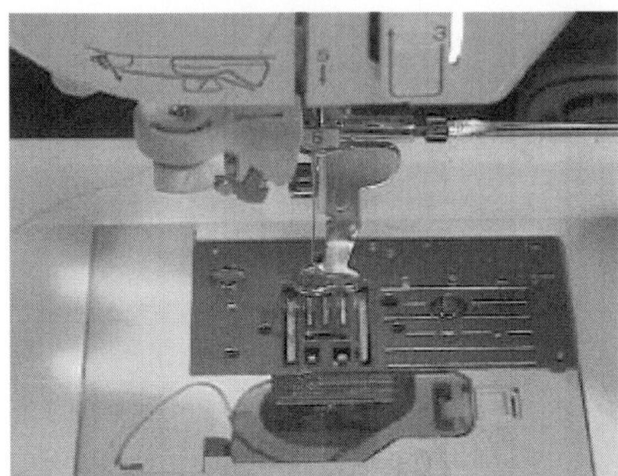

Metallic thread is sensitive to friction, resulting in shredding and breaks. There are special needles made to work with metallic thread. Those types of needles have larger eyes to ease the amount of friction.

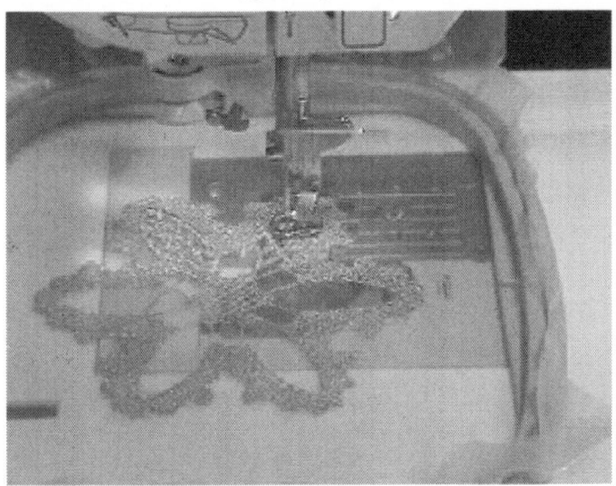

Normally we run the machine at about 600 stitches per minute. When working with metallic thread, we run the machine at about 400 stitches per minute.

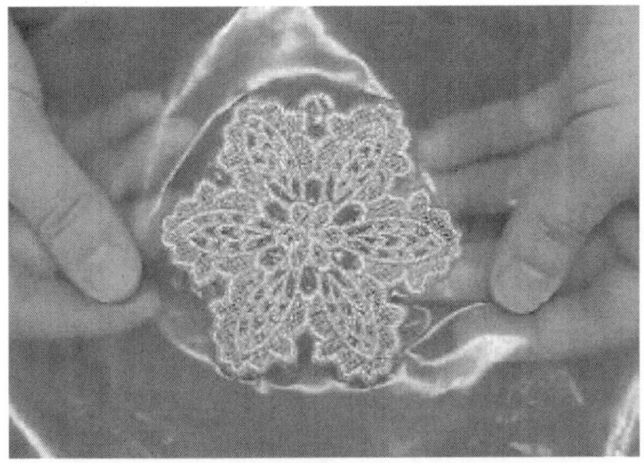

Those three tricks — relaxing the thread, using a special needle with a larger eye, and running the machine at a slower speed — means that this 20,000 stitch snowflake was embroidered without one thread break!

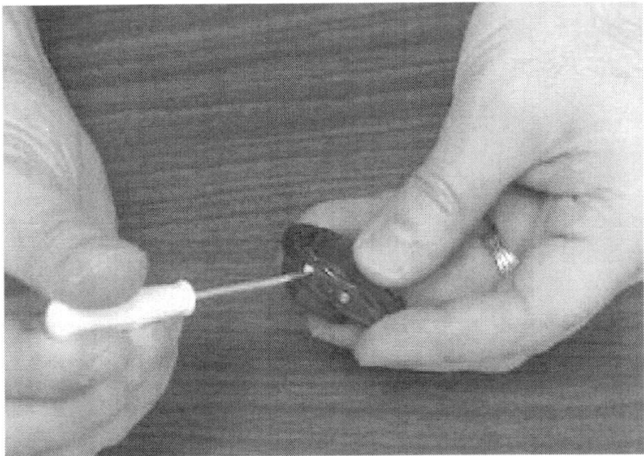

If you're doing all of the above and still getting thread breaks, try loosening your bobbin tension just a tiny bit.

A small turn to the left will loosen the tension; a small turn to the right will tighten it. You can mark the "default" or starting point with a bit of nail polish so that it's easy to change back to the preset tension after you've finished working with the metallic thread.

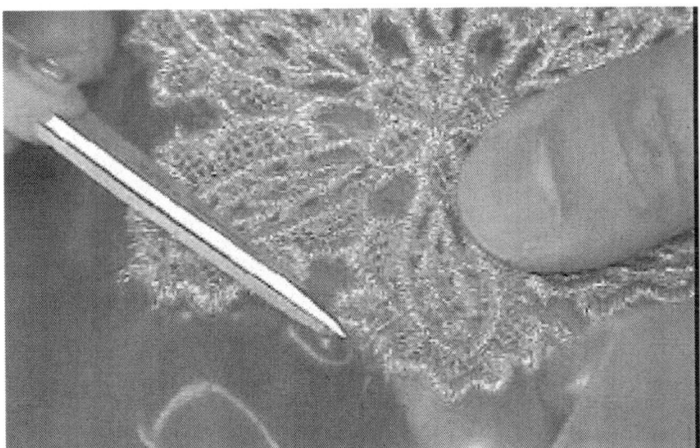

If you see the thread looping when working with metallic thread, that's an indication that the top or bobbin tension is too loose. It can also mean that one of the settings is too loose, and the other is too tight.

For that, you'll need to adjust both thread tensions to eliminate the looping.

Gold-Work

Goldwork is the art of embroidery using metal threads. It is particularly prized for the way light plays on it. The term "goldwork" is used even when the threads are imitation gold, silver, or copper. The metal wires used to make the threads have never been entirely gold; they have always been gold-coated silver (*silver-gilt*) or cheaper metals, and even then the "gold" often contains a very low percent of real gold. Most metal threads are available in silver and sometimes copper as well as gold; some are available in colours as well.

Goldwork is always surface embroidery and free embroidery; the vast majority is a form of laid work or couching; that is, the gold threads are held onto the surface of the fabric by a second thread, usually of fine silk. The ends of the thread, depending on type, are simply cut off, or are pulled through to the back of the embroidery and carefully secured with the couching thread. A tool called a mellore or a stilleto is used to help position the threads and create the holes needed to pull them through.

History

Goldwork was originally developed in Asia, and has been used for at least 2000 years. Its use reached a remarkable level of skill in the Middle Ages, when a style called Opus Anglicanum was developed in England and used extensively in church vestments and hangings. After this period it was also used frequently in the clothing and furnishings of the royalty and nobility throughout Europe, and still later on military and other regalia.

Goldwork is currently a fairly uncommon skill, even among embroiderers who work in other free embroidery styles; it is now most commonly used for the highest-quality church vestments and art embroidery. It has always been reserved for occasional and special use only, due to both the expense of the materials and the time to create the embroidery, and because the threads - no matter how expertly applied - will not hold up to frequent laundering of any kind.

Types of Metal Thread

A variety of threads exists, in order to create differing textures.

Passing is the most basic and common thread used in goldwork; it consists of a thin strip of metal wound around a core of cotton or silk. For gold thread this is typically yellow, or in older examples orange; for silver, white or gray. This is always attached by couching, either one or two threads at a time, and pulled through to the back to secure it. When multiple threads must be laid next to each other, a technique called *bricking* is used: the position of the couching stitches is offset between rows, producing an appearance similar to a brick wall. This same type of thread is used in making cloth of gold.

Japan thread, sometimes called jap, is a cheaper replacement for passing, and is far more commonly used in modern goldwork. It appears nearly identical, but rather than a strip of metal, a strip of foil paper is wrapped around the core.

Bullion or Purl is structurally a very long spring, hollow at the core; it can be stretched apart slightly and couched between the wraps of wire, or cut into short lengths and applied like beads. This thread comes in both shiny and matte versions.

Jaceron or Pearl purl is similar to buillion, but with a much wider piece of metal which has been shaped (rounded) prior to purling it, such that it looks like a string of pearl-like beads when couched down between the wraps of metal. Lizerine is a similar thread that has a flat appearance having not been shaped prior to purling.

Freize or Check purl is again similar, but the metal used is shaped differently, producing a faceted, sparkly look.

Faconnee or Crimped purl is almost identical to buillion, but has been crimped at intervals.

Roccoco and the similar Crinkle cordonnet are made of wire tightly wrapped around a cotton core, with a wavy or kinked appearance.

Milliary wire is a stretched pearl purl laced to a base of passing thread.

Broad Plate is a strip of metal a 2 millimetres wide; often this is used to fill small shapes by folding it back and forth, hiding the couching stitches under the folds. This is also available as 11's plate which is 1mm wide and whipped plate where the broad plate has a fine wire wrapped around it.

Flat Worm or simply Oval thread is a thin plate wrapped around a yarn core and flattened slightly. This is used like plate, but is considerably easier to work with.

Twists or Torsade, threads made of multiple strands of metal twisted together are also sometimes used, some of which, such as Soutache, sometimes have different coloured metals or coloured non-metal threads twisted together. These are either couched like passing, with the couching thread visible, or with the thread angled with the twist to make it invisible. In addition, paillettes or spangles (sequins of real metal), small pieces of appliqued rich fabric or kid leather, pearls, and real or imitation gems are commonly used as accents, and felt or string padding may be used to create raised areas or texture.

Silk thread work in satin stitch or other stitches is often combined with goldwork, and in some periods goldwork was combined with blackwork embroidery as well.

Or Nué

'Or nué' is a special technique invented in the 15th century, wherein many threads of passing or Japan thread are laid down parallel and touching. By varying the spacing and colour of the couching stitches, elaborate, gleaming images can be created. This is not uncommonly used to depict the garments of saints in church embroidery.

Sequin

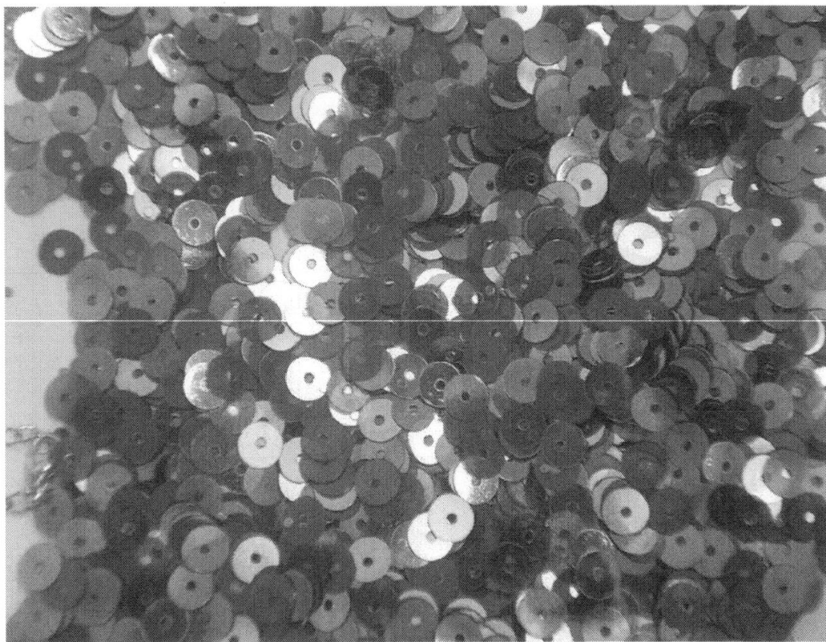

Sequins are disk-shaped beads used for decorative purposes. In earlier centuries they were made from shiny metals. Today sequins are most often made from plastic. Today they are available in a wide variety of colours and geometrical shapes. Sequins are commonly used on clothing, jewelry, bags, shoes and lots of other accessories.

Sequins are sometimes also referred to as spangles, paillettes, or diamantes. Paillettes themselves are commonly very large and flat. Sequins may be stitched flat to the fabric, so that they do not move, and are less likely to fall off; or they may be stitched at only one point, so that they dangle and move easily, to catch more light. Some sequins are made with multiple facets, to increase their reflective ability.

History

Evidence exists that gold sequins were being used as decoration on clothing or paraphernalia in the Indus Valley as early as 2500BC, during the Kot Diji phase.

The word "sequin" is from a rendition into French of the Italian word *zecchino,* which was a gold coin that was issued in the late medieval and early post-medieval centuries in Republic of Venice and also issued in Ottoman Turkey. By the early 19th century the sequin coins were no longer being issued, and the name sequin was falling out of use in its original sense. It was then that the name was taken up in France to designate what it means today. The 19th century sequins were made of shiny metal.

Large sequins, fastened only at the top, have been used on billboards and other signage, particularly prior to the development of lighted and neon signs.

3

Silk Embroidery

Silk is a natural protein fibre, some forms of which can be woven into textiles. The protein fibre of silk is composed mainly of fibroin and produced by certain insect larvae to form cocoons. The best-known type of silk is obtained from the cocoons of the larvae of the mulberry silkworm *Bombyx mori* reared in captivity (sericulture). The shimmering appearance of silk is due to the triangular prism-like structure of the silk fibre, which allows silk cloth to refract incoming light at different angles, thus producing different colours.

Silks are produced by several other insects, but generally only the silk of moth caterpillars has been used for textile manufacturing. There has been some research into other silks, which differ at the molecular level. Many silks are mainly produced by the larvae of insects undergoing complete metamorphosis, but some adult insects such as webspinners produce silk, and some insects such as raspy crickets produce silk throughout their lives. Silk production also occurs in Hymenoptera (bees, wasps, and ants), silverfish, mayflies, thrips, leafhoppers, beetles, lacewings, fleas, flies and midges. Other types of arthropod produce silk, most notably various arachnids such as spiders.

History of Silk

According to Chinese tradition, the history of silk began in the 27th century BCE. Its use was confined to China until the Silk Road opened at some point during the later half of the first millennium BCE. China maintained its virtual monopoly over silk for another thousand years. Not confined to clothing, silk was also used for a number of other applications, including writing, and the colour of silk worn was an important indicator of social class during the Tang Dynasty.

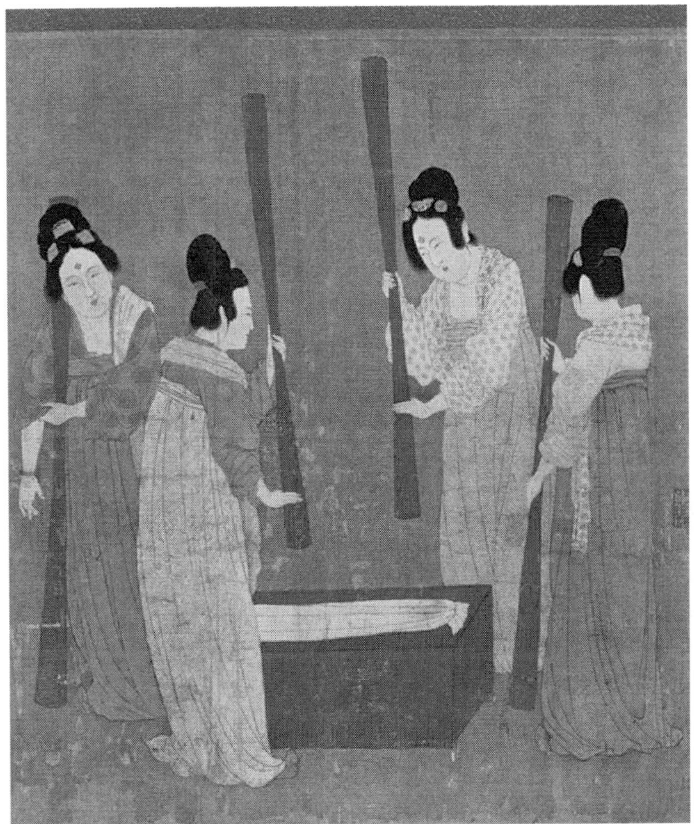

Figure: *Women preparing silk, painting by Emperor Huizong of Song, early 12th century.*

Silk cultivation spread to Japan in around 300 CE, and by 522 the Byzantines managed to obtain silkworm eggs and were able to begin silkworm cultivation. The Arabs also began to manufacture silk during this same time. As a result of the spread of sericulture, Chinese silk exports became less important, although they still maintained dominance over the luxury silk market. The Crusades brought silk production to Western Europe, in particular to many Italian states, which saw an economic boom exporting silk to the rest of Europe. Changes in manufacturing techniques also began to take place during the Middle Ages, with devices such as the spinning wheel first appearing. During the 16th century France joined Italy in developing a successful silk trade, though the efforts of most other nations to develop a silk industry of their own were unsuccessful.

The Industrial Revolution changed much of Europe's silk industry. Due to innovations in spinning cotton, cotton became much cheaper to manufacture and therefore caused more expensive silk production to become less mainstream. New weaving technologies, however, increased the efficiency of production. Among these was the Jacquard loom, developed for silk embroidery. An epidemic of several silkworm diseases caused production to fall, especially in France, where the industry never recovered.

In the 20th century Japan and China regained their earlier role in silk production, and China is now once again the world's largest producer of silk. The rise of new fabrics such as nylon reduced the prevalence of silk throughout the world, and silk is now once again a rare luxury good, much less important than in its heyday.

Early History

The appearance of silk:

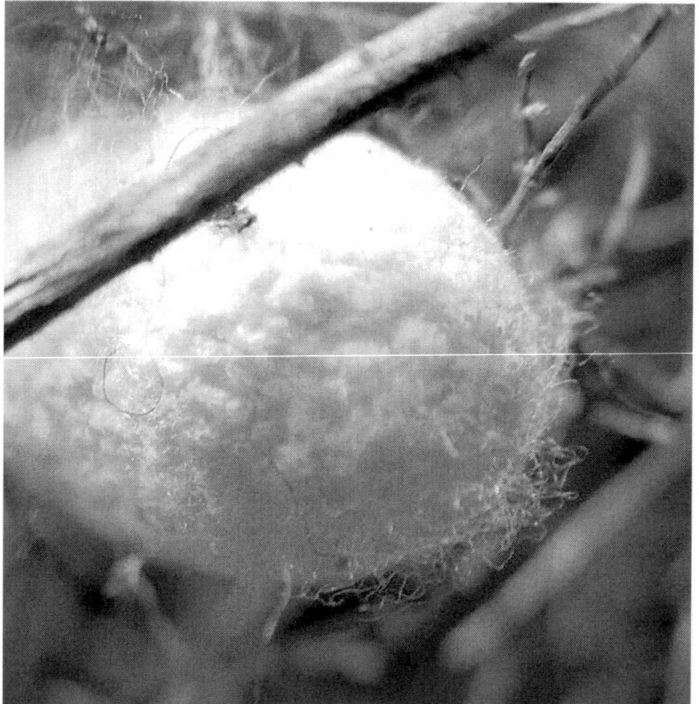

Figure: *The silkworm cocoon*

The earliest evidence of silk was found at the sites of Yangshao culture in Xia County, Shanxi, where a silk cocoon was found cut in half by a sharp knife, dating back to between 4000 and 3000 BCE.

The species was identified as bombyx mori, the domesticated silkworm. Fragments of primitive loom can also be seen from the sites of Hemudu culture in Yuyao, Zhejiang, dated to about 4000 BCE. Scraps of silk were found in a Liangzhu culture site at Qianshanyang in Huzhou, Zhejiang, dating back to 2700 BCE. Other fragments have been recovered from royal tombs in the Shang Dynasty (c. 1600 - c. 1046 BCE).

During the later epoch, the Chinese lost their secret to the Koreans, the Japanese, and later the Indians, as they discovered how to make silk. Allusions to the fabric in the Old Testament show that it was known in western Asia in biblical times. Scholars believe that starting in the 2nd century BCE the Chinese established a commercial network aimed at exporting silk to the West. Silk was used, for example, by the Persian court and its king, Darius III, when Alexander the Great conquered the empire. Even though silk spread rapidly across Eurasia, with the possible exception of Japan its production remained exclusively Chinese for three millennia.

Myths and Legends

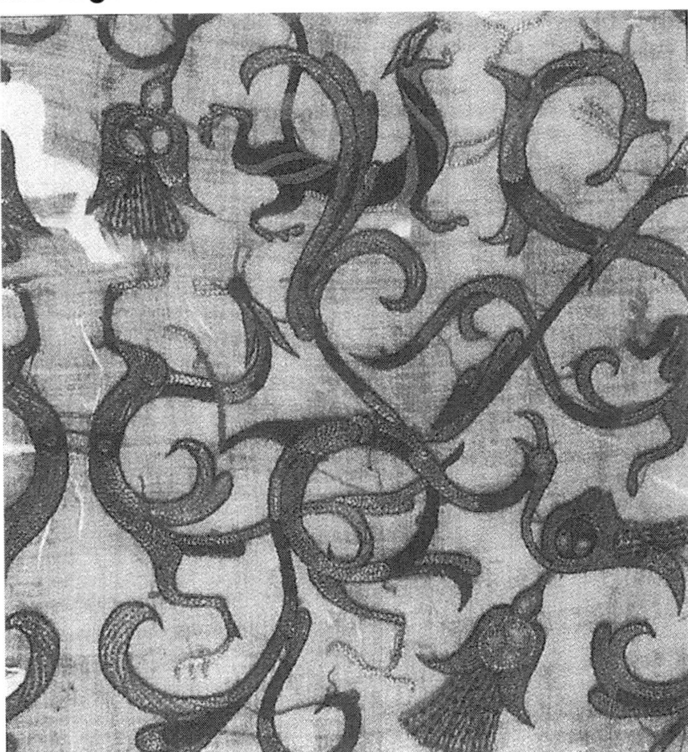

Figure: *Detail of an embroidered silk gauze ritual garment from a 4th-century BCE, Zhou era tomb at Mashan, Hubei province, China.*

The writings of Confucius and Chinese tradition recount that in the 27th century BCE a silk worm's cocoon fell into the tea cup of the empress Leizu. Wishing to extract it from her drink, the young girl of fourteen began to unroll the thread of the cocoon. She then had the idea to weave it. Having observed the life of the silk worm on the recommendation of her husband, the Yellow Emperor, she began to instruct her entourage the art of raising silk worms, sericulture. From this point on, the girl became the goddess of silk in Chinese mythology. Silk eventually left China in the heir of a princess promised to a prince of Khotan. This probably occurred in the early 1st century CE. The princess, refusing to go without the fabric she loved, would finally break the imperial ban on silk worm exportation.

Though silk was exported to foreign countries in great amounts, sericulture remained a secret that the Chinese guarded carefully. Consequently, other peoples invented wildly varying accounts of the source of the incredible fabric. In classical antiquity, most Romans, great admirers of the cloth, were convinced that the Chinese took the fabric from tree leaves. This belief was affirmed by Seneca the Younger in his Phaedra and by Virgil in his Georgics. Notably, Pliny the Elder knew better. Speaking of the *bombyx* or silk moth, he wrote in his *Natural History* "They weave webs, like spiders, that become a luxurious clothing material for women, called silk."

Silk Usage in Ancient and Medieval China

In China, silk worm farming was originally restricted to women, and many women were employed in the silk-making industry. Even though some saw the development of a luxury product as useless, silk provoked such a craze among high society that the rules in the *Li Ji* were used to regulate and limit its use to the members of the imperial family. For approximately a millennium, the right to wear silk was reserved for the emperor and the highest dignitaries. Later, it gradually extended to other classes of Chinese society. Silk began to be used for decorative means and also in less luxurious ways: musical instruments, fishing, and bow-making. Peasants did not have the right to wear silk until the Qing dynasty (1644–1911).

Paper was one of the greatest discoveries of ancient China. Beginning in the 3rd century BCE paper was made in all sizes with various materials. Silk was no exception, and silk workers had been making paper since the 2nd century BCE. Silk, bamboo, linen, wheat and rice straw were all used differently, and paper made with silk became the first type of luxury paper. Researchers have found an early example of writing done on silk paper in the tomb of a Marchioness who died around 168, in Mawangdui, Hunan. The material was certainly more expensive, but also more practical than bamboo slips. Treatises on many subjects, including meteorology, medicine, astrology, divinity, and even maps written on silk have been discovered.

During the Han Dynasty, silk became progressively more valuable in its own right, and became more than simply a material. It was used to pay government officials and compensate citizens who were particularly worthy. By the same token that one would sometimes estimate the price of products according to a certain weight of gold, the length of the silk cloth became a monetary standard in China (in addition to bronze coins). The wealth that silk brought to China stirred up envy in neighbouring peoples. Beginning in the 2nd century BCE the Xiongnu, regularly pillaged the provinces of the Han Chinese for around 250 years. Silk was a common offering by the emperor to these tribes in exchange for peace.

> *". . . the military payrolls tell us that soldiers were paid in bundles of plain silk textiles, which circulated as currency in Han times. Soldiers may well have traded their silk with the nomads who came to the gates of the Great Wall to sell horses and furs."*

For more than a millennium, silk remained the principal diplomatic gift of the emperor of China to his neighbours or to his vassals. The use of silk became so important that "silk" (ø|) soon constituted one of the principal radicals of Chinese script.

Broadly speaking, the use of silk was regulated by a very precise code in China. For example, the Tang Dynasty and Song Dynasty imposed upon bureaucrats the use of a particular colour according to their different functions in society. Under the Ming, silk began to be used in a series of accessories: handkerchiefs, wallets, belts, or even an embroidered piece of fabric displaying dozens of animals, real or mythical. These fashion accessories remained associated with a particular position: there was a specific bonnet for warriors, for judges, for nobles, and others for religious use. The women of high Chinese society heeded codified practices and used silk in their garments to which they added countless motifs. A 13th-century work, the *Jinpingmei*, gives a description of one such motif:

> *"Golden lotus having a quilted backgammon pattern, double-folded, adorned with savage geese pecking at a landscape of flowers and roses; the dress' right figure*

had a floral border with buttons in the form of bees or chrysanthemums."

Chinese Silk and its Commerce

A number of archaeological discoveries showed that silk had become a luxury material appreciated in foreign countries well before the opening of the Silk Road by the Chinese. For example, silk has been found in the Valley of the Kings in a tomb of a mummy dating from 1070 BCE. First the Greeks, then the Romans began to speak of the Seres (people of silk), a term to designate the inhabitants of the far-off kingdom, China. According to certain historians, the first Roman contact with silk was that of the legions of the governor of Syria, Crassus. At the Battle of Carrhae, near to the Euphrates, the legions were said to be so surprised by the brilliance of the banners of Parthia that they fled.

The silk road toward the west was opened by the Chinese in the 2nd century CE. The main road left from Xi'an, going either to the north or south of the Taklamakan desert, one of the most arid in the world, before crossing the Pamir Mountains. The caravans that employed this method to exchange silk with other merchants were generally quite large, including from 100 to 500 people as well as camels and yaks carrying around 140 kg (300 lb) of merchandise. They linked to Antioch and the coasts of the Mediterranean, about one year's travel from Xi'an. In the South, a second route went by Yemen, Burma, and India before rejoining the northern route.

Not long after the conquest of Egypt in 30 BCE regular commerce began between the Romans and Asia, marked by the Roman appetite for silk cloth coming from the Far East, which was then resold to the Romans by the Parthians. The Roman Senate tried in vain to prohibit the wearing of silk, for economic reasons as well as moral ones. The import of Chinese silk resulted in vast amounts of gold leaving Rome, to such an extent that silk clothing was perceived as a sign of decadence and immorality.

> *"I can see clothes of silk, if materials that do not hide the body, nor even one's decency, can be called clothes. ... Wretched flocks of maids labour so that the adulteress may be visible through her thin dress, so that her husband has no more acquaintance than any outsider or foreigner with his wife's body."*
>
> *Seneca the Younger,* Declamations *Vol. I.*

Spread of Production

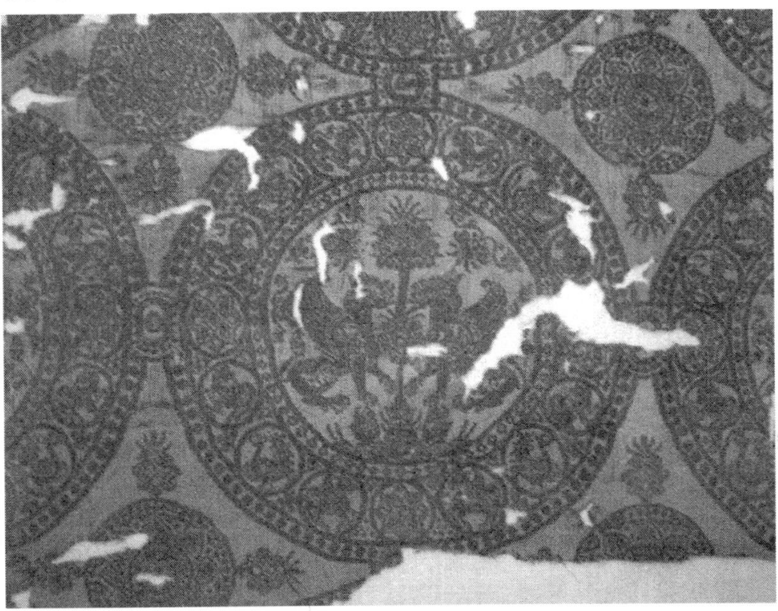

Figure: *Sassanid inspired two-sided silk cloth, with winged lions and tree of life, from the early Islamic period in Iran, National Museum of Iran.*

Although silk was well known in Europe and most of Asia, China was able to keep a near monopoly on silk production. The monopoly was defended by an imperial decree, condemning to death anyone attempting to export silkworms or their eggs. Only around the year 300 CE did a Japanese expedition succeed in taking some silkworm eggs and four young Chinese girls, who were forced to teach their captors the art of sericulture. Techniques of sericulture were subsequently introduced to Japan on a larger scale by frequent diplomatic exchanges between the 8th century and 9th centuries.

Starting in the 4th century BCE silk began to reach the West by merchants who would exchange it for gold, ivory, horses or precious stones. Up to the frontiers of the Roman Empire, silk became a monetary standard for estimating the value of different products. Hellenistic Greece appreciated the high quality of the Chinese goods and made efforts to plant mulberry trees and breed silkworms in the Mediterranean basin. Sassanid Persia controlled the trade of silk destined for Europe and Byzantium.

According to story by Procopius, it was not until 552 CE that the Byzantine emperor Justinian obtained the first silkworm eggs. He had sent two Nestorian monks to Central Asia, and they were able to smuggle silkworm eggs to him hidden in rods of bamboo. While under the monks' care, the eggs hatched, though they did not cocoon before arrival. The Byzantine church was thus able to make fabrics for the emperor, with the intention of developing a large silk industry in the Eastern Roman Empire, using techniques learned from the Sassanids. These gynecia had a legal monopoly on the fabric, but the empire continued to import silk from other major urban centres on the Mediterranean. The magnificence of the Byzantine techniques was not a result of the manufacturing process, but instead of the meticulous attention paid to the execution and decorations. The weaving techniques they used were taken from Egypt. The first diagrams of semple looms appeared in the 5th century.

The Arabs, with their widening conquests, spread sericulture across the shores of the Mediterranean. Included in these were Africa, Spain and Sicily, all of which developed an important silk industry. The mutual interactions among Byzantine and Muslim silk-weaving centres of all levels of quality, with imitations made in Andalusia and Lucca, among other cities, have made the identification and date of rare surviving examples difficult to pinpoint.

While the Chinese lost their monopoly on silk production, they were able re-established themselves as major silk supplier (during the Tang dynasty) and industrialize their production in a large scale (during the Song dynasty). China continued to export high-quality fabric to Europe and the Near East along the silk road.

Much later, following the Crusades, techniques of silk production began to spread across Western Europe. In 1147 while Byzantine emperor Manuel I Komnenos was focusing all his efforts on the Second Crusade, the Norman king Roger II of Sicily attacked Corinth and Thebes, two important centres of Byzantine silk production. They took the crops and silk production infrastructure, and deported all the workers to Palermo, thereby causing the Norman silk industry to flourish. The sack of Constantinople by the Fourth Crusade in 1204 brought decline to the city and its silk industry, and many artisans left the city in the early 13th century. Italy developed a large domestic silk industry after 2000 skilled weavers came from Constantinople. Many also chose to settle in Avignon to furnish the popes of Avignon.

The sudden boom of the silk industry in the Italian state of Lucca, starting in the 11th and 12th centuries was due to much Sicilian, Jewish, and Greek settlement, alongside many other immigrants from neighbouring cities in southern Italy. With the loss of many Italian trading posts in the Orient, the import of Chinese styles drastically declined. Gaining momentum, in order to satisfy the rich and powerful bourgeoisie's demands for luxury fabrics, the cities of Lucca, Genoa, Venice and Florence were soon exporting silk to all of Europe. In 1472 there were 84 workshops and at least 7000 craftsmen in Florence alone.

Reciprocal Influences

Silk was made using various breeds of lepidopterans, both wild and domestic. While wild silks were produced in many countries, there is no doubt that the Chinese were the first to begin production on such a large scale, having the most effective species for silk production, the *Bombyx mandarina* and its domesticated descendent *B. mori*. Chinese sources claim the existence of a machine to unwind silkworm cocoons in 1090.

The cocoons were placed in a large basin of hot water, the silk would leave the cauldron by tiny guiding rings, and would be wound onto a large spool, thanks to a backwards and forward motion. Little information exists about spinning techniques in use in China. The spinning wheel, in all likelihood moved by hand, was known by the beginning of the Christian era. The first accepted image of a spinning wheel appears in 1210. There is an image of a silk spinning machine powered by a water wheel that dates to 1313.

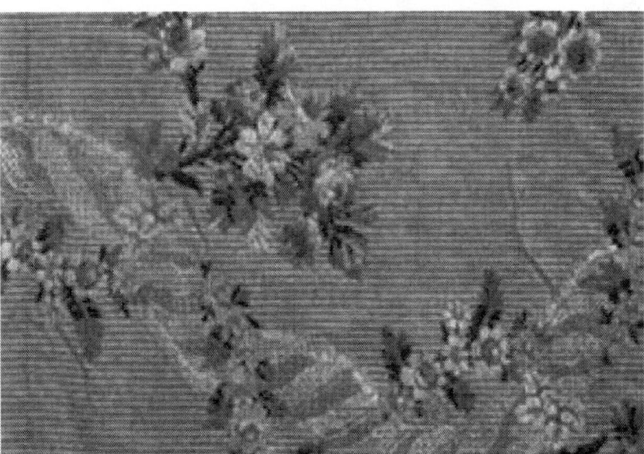

Figure: *French silk brocade - Lyon 1760-1770*

More information is known about the looms used. The *Nung Sang Chi Yao*, or *Fundamentals of Agriculture and Sericulture*, compiled around 1210, is rich with pictures and descriptions, many pertaining to silk. It repeatedly claims the Chinese looms to be far superior to all others. It speaks of two types of loom that leave the worker's arms free: the draw loom, which is of Eurasian origin, and the pedal loom which is attributed to East Asian origins. There are many diagrams originate in the 12th and 13th centuries. When examined closely, many similarities between Eurasian machines can be drawn. Since the Jin dynasty, the existence of silk damasks has been well recorded, and since the 2nd century BCE, four-shafted looms and other innovations allowed the creation of silk brocades.

Silk in the Medieval World

A more abundant luxury:

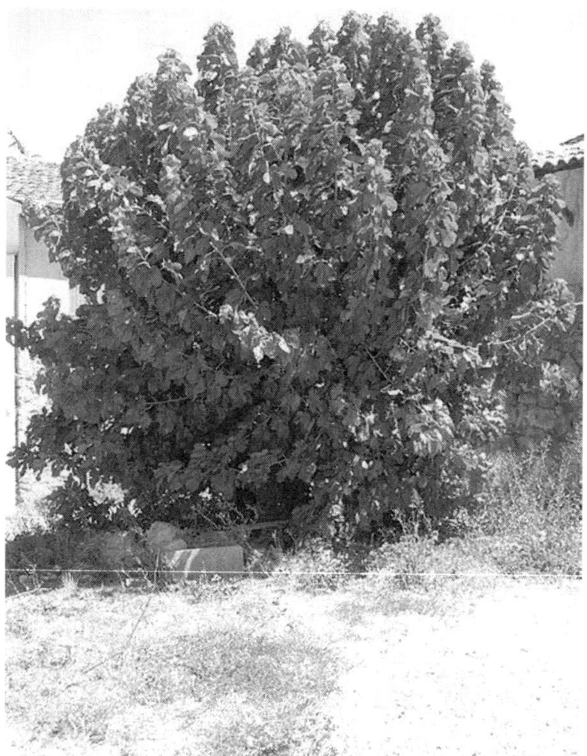

Figure: *A mature mulberry tree in Provence.*

The high Middle Ages saw continued use of established techniques for silk manufacture without any changes to speak of, neither in materials nor in tools used. Between the 10th and 12th centuries, small changes began to appear, though the changes of the 13th century were much larger and more radical. In a short time, new fabrics began to appear; hemp and cotton each also had their own particular techniques of manufacture. Known since Roman times, silk remained a rare and expensive material. Byzantine magnaneries in Greece and

Syria (6th to 8th century), and those of the Arabs in Sicily and Spain (8th to 10th century) were able to supply the luxury material in a much greater abundance.

Improved Technology

The 13th century saw an already changing technology undergo many dramatic changes. It is possible that, as with in England at the end of the 18th century, advances in the textile industry were a driving force behind advances in technology as a whole. Silk indeed occupies a privileged place in history on account of this.

At the start of the 13th century, a primitive form of milling the silk threads was already in use. In 1221 Jean de Garlande's dictionary, and in 1226, Étienne Boileau's *Livre des métiers* (*Tradesman's Handbook*) enumerated many types of devices which can only have been doubling machines. The instruments used were further perfected in Bologna between 1270 and 1280. From the start of the 14th century, many documents allude to the use of devices that were quite complex.

The reel, originally developed for the silk industry, now has multiple uses. The earliest surviving depiction of a spinning wheel is a panel of stained glass in the Cathedral of Chartres. Bobbins and warping machines appear together in the stained glass at Chartres and in a fresco in the Cologne Kunkelhaus (ca 1300). It is possible that the toothed warping machine was created by the silk industry; it allowed the warp to be more uniform and allowed the warp to be of a longer length.

Starting at the end of the 14th century, no doubt on account of the devastation caused mid-century by the Black Death, there was a general shift towards less expensive techniques. Many things which would have earlier been completely forbidden by the guilds were now commonplace (using low quality wool, carding, etc.). In the silk industry, the use of water-powered mills grew, and by the 15th century, the loom designed by Jean le Calabrais saw nearly universal use.

The Silk Industry in France

Italian silk cloth was very expensive, as much a result of the cost of the raw material as of the production costs. The craftsmen in Italy proved unable to keep up with the exigencies of French fashion, which continuously demanded lighter and less expensive materials. These materials were used for clothing, and garment production began to be done locally. Nevertheless, Italian silk long remained among the most prized, mostly for furnishings and the brilliant colours of the dyes.

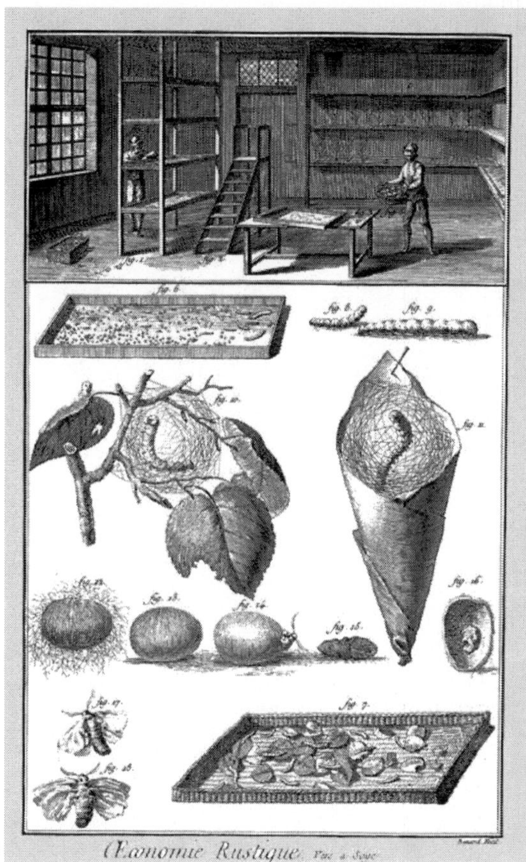

***Figure:** A picture from the* Encyclopédie *of Diderot and d'Alembert, showing the different steps in sericulture and the manufacture of silk.*

Following the example of the wealthy Italian city-states of the era (Venice, Florence, Lucca, etc.), which had become the centre of the luxury textile industry, Lyon obtained a similar function in the French market. In 1466 King Louis XI decided to develop a national silk industry in Lyon. In the face of protests by the Lyonnais, he conceded and moved the silk fabrication to Tours, but the industry in Tours stayed relatively marginal. His main objective was to reduce France's trade deficit with Italy, which caused France to lose 400,000 to 500,000 golden écus a year.

It was under Francis I in around 1535 that a royal charter was granted to two merchants, Étienne Turquet and Barthélemy Naris, to develop a silk trade in Lyon. In 1540 the king granted a monopoly on silk production to the city of Lyon. Starting in the 16th century Lyon became the capital of the European silk trade, notably producing many reputable fashions. Gaining confidence, the silks produced in the city little by little began to abandon the original oriental styles and moved towards their own distinctive style, with an emphasis on landscapes. Thousand of workers, the canuts, devoted themselves to the flourishing industry. In the middle of the 17th century over 14,000 looms were in use in Lyon, and the silk industry fed a third of the city's population.

In the 18th and 19th centuries Provence experienced a boom in sericulture that would last until the First World War, with much of the silk produced being shipped north to Lyon. Viens and La Bastide-des-Jourdans are two of the *communes* of Luberon that profited the most from mulberry plantations that have since disappeared. Working at home under the domestic system, silk spinning and silk treatment employed many people and increased the income of the working class.

Spread to Other Countries

England under Henry IV was also looking to develop a silk industry, but no opportunity arose until the revocation of the Edict of Nantes in the 1680s when hundreds of thousands of French Huguenots, many of which were skilled weavers and experts in sericulture, began immigrating to England to escape religious persecution. Some areas, including Spitalfields saw many high-quality silk workshops spring up, their products distinct from continental silk largely by the colours used. Nonetheless, the British climate prevented England's domestic silk trade from becoming globally dominant.

Many envisioned starting a silk industry in the British colonies in America starting in 1619 under the reign of King James I of England. The silk industry in the Colonies never became very large. Likewise, silk was introduced to numerous other countries, including Mexico, where it was brought by Cortez in 1522. Only rarely did these new silk industries grow to any significant size.

Silk Since the Industrial Revolution

The Start of the Industrial Revolution

The start of the Industrial Revolution was marked by a massive boom in the textile industry, with remarkable technological innovations made, led by the cotton industry of Great Britain. In its early years, there were often disparities in technological innovation between different stages of fabric manufacture, which encouraged complementary innovations. For example, spinning progressed much more rapidly than weaving.

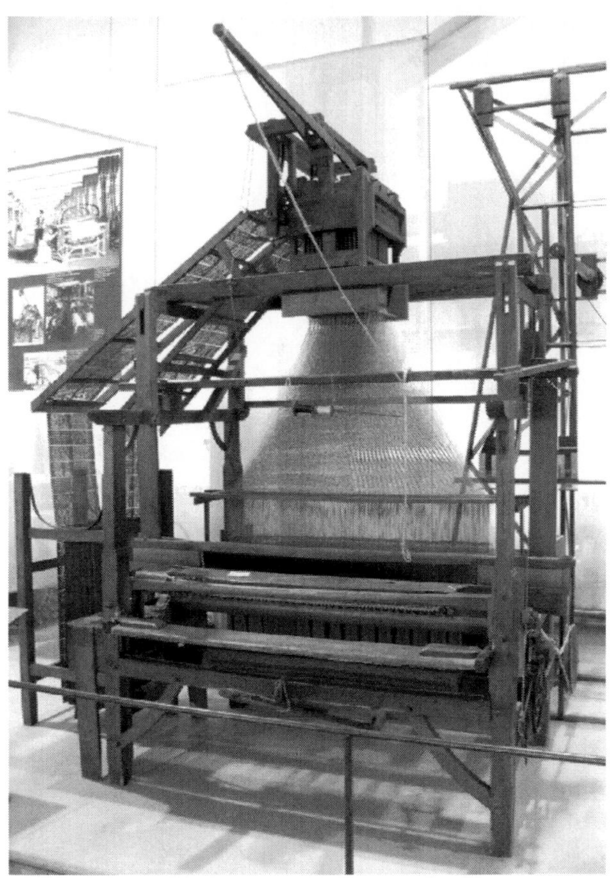

Figure: *A Jacquard loom.*

The silk industry, however, did not gain any benefit from innovations in spinning, as silk is naturally already a thread. Making silk, silver, and gold brocades is a very delicate and precise process, with each colour needing its own dedicated shuttle. In the 17th century and 18th centuries progress began to be made in the simplification and standardization of silk manufacture, with many advances following one after another. Bouchon and Falcon's punched card loom appeared in 1775, later improved on by Jacques de Vaucanson. Later, Joseph-Marie Jacquard improved on the designs of Falcon and Vaucanson, introducing the revolutionary Jacquard loom, which allowed a string of punched cards to be processed mechanically in the correct sequence. The punched cards of the Jacquard loom were a direct precursor to the modern computer, in that they gave a (limited) form of programmability. Punched cards themselves were carried over to computers, and were ubiquitous until their obsolescence in the 1970s.

From 1801 embroidery became highly mechanized due to the effectiveness of the Jacquard loom. The mechanism behind the Jacquard loom even allowed complex designs to be mass-produced.

The Jacquard loom was immediately denounced by workers, who accused it of causing unemployment, but soon it had become vital to the industry. The loom was declared public property in 1806, and Jacquard was rewarded with a pension and a royalty on each machine. In 1834 there were a total of 2885 Jacquard looms in Lyon alone.

The Canut revolt in 1831 foreshadowed many of the larger worker uprisings of the Industrial Revolution. The canuts occupied the city of Lyon, and would not relinquish it until a bloody repression by the army, led by Marshal Soult. A second revolt, similar to the first, took place in 1834.

Decline in the European Silk Industry

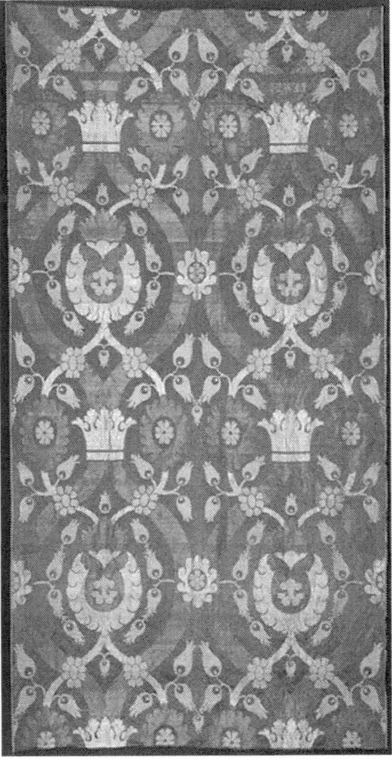

Figure: *Silk, cotton and gilt-metal-strip-wrapped cotton panel, machine-woven in Scotland c. 1887. Tulip motif is inspired by Turkish textiles.*

The first silkworm diseases began to appear in 1845, creating an epidemic. Among them are pébrine, caused by the microsporidia

Nosema bombycis, grasserie, caused by a virus, flacherie, caused by eating infected mulberry leaves or white muscardine disease, caused by the fungus *Beauveria bassiana*. The epidemic grew to a massive scale, and after having attacked the silkworms, other viruses began to infect the mulberry trees.

The chemist Jean-Baptiste Dumas, French minister of agriculture, was charged with stopping the epidemic. In face of sericulturers' call for help, he asked Louis Pasteur to study the disease, starting in 1865. For many years, Pasteur thought that pébrine was not a contagious disease. In 1870 he changed his view, and measures were enacted that caused the disease to decline.

Nevertheless, the increase in the price of silkworm cocoons and the reduction in importance of silk in the garments of the bourgeoisie in the 19th century caused the decline of the silk industry in Europe. The opening of the Suez Canal in 1869 and the silk shortage in France reduced the price of importing Asian silk, particularly from China and Japan.

Starting from the Long Depression (1873 – 1896), Lyonnais silk production had become totally industrialized, and hand looms were rapidly disappearing. The 19th century saw the textile industry's progress caused by advances in chemistry. The synthesis of aniline was used to make mauveine (aniline purple) dye and the synthesis of quinine was used to make indigo dye. In 1884 Count Hilaire de Chardonnet invented artificial silk and in 1891 opened a factory dedicated to the production of artificial silk (viscose), which cost much less and in part replaced natural silk.

Silk in Modern Times

Following the crisis in Europe, the modernisation of sericulture in Japan made it the world's foremost silk producer. Italy managed to rebound from the crisis, but France was never able to. Urbanization in Europe saw many French and Italian agricultural workers leave silk growing for more lucrative factory work. Raw silk was imported from Japan to fill the void. Asian countries, formerly exporters of raw materials (cocoons and raw silk), progressively began to export more and more finished garments.

During the Second World War, silk supplies from Japan were cut off, so western countries were forced to find substitutes. Synthetic fibres such as nylon were used in products such as parachutes and stockings, replacing silk. Even after the war, silk was not able to regain many of the markets lost, though it remained an expensive luxury product. Postwar Japan, through improvements in technology and a protectionist market policy, became the world's foremost exporter of raw silk, a position it held until the 1970s. The continued rise in importance of synthetic fibres and loosening of the protectionist economy contributed to the decline of Japan's silk industry, and by 1975 it was no longer a net exporter of silk.

With its recent economic reforms, the People's Republic of China has become the world's largest silk producer. In 1996 it produced 58,000 tonnes out of a world production of 81,000, followed by India at 13,000 tonnes. Japanese production is now marginal, at only 2500 tonnes. Between 1995 and 1997 Chinese silk production went down 40% in an effort to raise prices, reminiscent of earlier shortages.

In December 2006 the General Assembly of the United Nations proclaimed 2009 to be the International Year of Natural Fibres, so as to raise the profile of silk and other natural fibres.

Chinese Embroidery

Chinese embroidery refers to embroidery created by any of the cultures located in the area that makes up modern China. It is some of the oldest extant needlework. The four major regional styles of Chinese embroidery are Suzhou embroidery (Su Xiu), Hunan embroidery (Xiang Xiu), Guangdong embroidery (Yue Xiu) and Sichuan embroidery (Shu Xiu). All of them are nominated as Chinese Intangible Cultural Heritage.

Chinese embroidery has a long history since Neolithic age. Because of the quality of silk fibre, most Chinese fine embroideries are made in silk. Some ancient vestiges of silk production have been found in various Neolithic sites dating back 5,000-6,000 years in China. Currently the earliest real sample of silk embroidery discovered in China is from a tomb in Mashan in Hubei province identified with the Zhanguo period (5th-3rd centuries BC). After the opening of Silk Route in Han Dynasty, the silk production and trade became flourishing. In 14th century, the Chinese silk embroidery production reached its high peak. Several major silk embroidery styles had been developed, like Song Jin (‹[& • Song embroidery) in Suzhou, Yun Jin ('N& • Cloud embroidery) in Nanjing and Shu Jin (‡& • Shu embroidery) in Sichuan.

Today most handwork had been replaced by machinery, but some very sophisticated production are still hand-made. The modern Chinese silk embroidery still prevails in southern China.

Genres

Major Styles

- Su Xiu (Ï,ã~) — Suzhou embroidery is crafted in areas around Suzhou, Jiangsu Province, having a history dating back 2,000 years. It is famous for its beautiful patterns, elegant colours, variety of stitches, and consummate craftsmanship. Its stitching is meticulously skillful, colouration subtle and refined. Suzhou artists are able to use more than 40 needlework and a 1,000 different types of threads to make embroidery, typically with nature and environment themes such as flowers, birds, animals and even gardens on a piece of cloth.
  - o A rare subset is Su double-sided embroidery which requires ultimate skill and artistry. The front and back of the piece may have different designs, but the ends are not knotted but woven in so the back can't be distinguished.
- Xiang Xiu (Xnã~) — Hunan embroidery comes from areas around Changsha, Hunan Province. It is distinct for its starkly elegant black, white and gray colouration. Its emphasis is on contrasts of light and shade that highlight the pattern texture to give a three-dimensional effect. Xiang embroidery composition combines void and solid imagery, utilising empty space in the same way as Chinese ink and wash paintings.
- Yue Xiu/Guang Xiu (£ | ã~/n^Ày) — Guangdong embroidery is crafted in Chaozhou, Guangdong Province. It is composed of intricate but symmetrical patterns, vibrant colours, varied stitches and a defined weave. Its use of primary colours, light and shade are reminiscent of western paintings.
- Shu Xiu (‡ã~) — Sichuan embroidery comes from areas around Chengdu, Sichuan Province. It is oldest known embroidery style in Chinese embroidery history. Its raw materials are satin and coloured silk, its craftsmanship painstaking and refined. The emphasis is on even stitching, delicate colouration, and local flavour. Sichuan embroidery is used to decorate quilt covers, pillowcases, garments, shoes and painted screens.

Other Styles

- Gu Xiu (~˜ã~) — Gu embroidery is rather a family style than a local style originated from Gu Mingshi's family during the Ming Dynasty in Shanghai. Gu embroidery is also named Lu Xiang Yuan embroidery after the place where the Gu family lived. Gu embroidery ss different from other styles as it specialised in painting and calligraphy. The inventor of Gu embroidery was a concubine of Gu Mingshi's first son, Gu Huihai. Later, Han Ximeng, the wife of the second grandson of Gu Mingshi developed the skill and was reputed as "Needle Saint" (^"#W). Some of her masterpieces are kept in the Forbidden City. Today Gu embroidery has become a special local product in Shanghai.

Ethnic Styles

Other Chinese ethnic groups, like Bai, Miao, Zhuang and Tibetan people also have their own style of embroidery, which usually depicts a mythical or religious topic.

Tambour

Embroidery hoops and frames are tools used to keep fabric taut while working embroidery or other forms of needlework.

Tambour embroidery, introduced to the Western world by France, is a continuous worked chain stitch formed with a tambour hook, which forms a loop similar to a crochet chain. The stitch is formed on the fabric with the thread held underneath in one hand while the other hand inserts the hook down through the fabric to catch the thread. The needle is brought back through the same hole, forming a loop. The following stitches are formed a short distance from the previous stitch, catching the loop of the last stitch at the beginning of the next.

The Chinese introduced this embroidery technique to the French during the later part of the 18th century. The French term "tambour: (meaning) a drum" best described the technique that required the ground fabric to be first stretched taught in a frame before the stitching was begun. The embroidery yarns used for a tambour stitch could be: a single strands of floss, twisted silk, metal or fine silk chenille threads. Even though the stitch itself was simple, the elegant yarns coupled with the intricate shading and elaborate designs tended to create extraordinary thread painted works of art.

The Forgotten Arts of Hollie Point

Hollie Point is an English needle lace noted for its use in baby clothes in the 18th and 19th century.

It is found in English needleworks such as samplers, stump-work embroideries and tape laces from second half of 17th century, its use in the form known as *hollie point* dates from early 18th century. Hollie Point is a flat needlepoint lace with rows of knotted buttonhole stitches worked over stretched threads. Simple designs are created by holes left in otherwise plain cloth work formed by the buttonhole stitches. Noted for its appearance in baby clothes in the 18th and early 19th century, particularly in caps, the shoulder seams of shirts, bibs and detachable sleeves worn over babies swaddling bands.

Early 18th century bonnets tend to be plain but the second half of the century saw the introduction of a band of lace extending from centre front of bonnet to the nape of the neck, sometimes with a circle in the back. This band was later accompanied by parallel line of pulled-thread embroidery while in early 19th century the circular cap back reappeared.

Items decorated with hollie point were often made for christenings, it is probable that this type of work was done by ladies of a household or the nanny

Kneetting

Knitting is a method by which thread or yarn is used to create a cloth. Knitted fabric consists of a number of consecutive rows of loops, called stitches. As each row progresses, a new loop is pulled through an existing loop. The active stitches are held on a needle until another loop can be passed through them. This process eventually results in a fabric, often used for garments.

Knitting may be done by hand or by machine. There exist numerous styles and methods of hand knitting.

Different types of yarns and needles may be used to achieve a plethora of knitted materials; these tools give the final piece a different colour, texture, weight, and/or integrity. Other factors that affect the end result include the needle's shape, thickness and malleability, as well as the yarn's fibre type, texture and twist.

Structure

Courses and wales: Like weaving, knitting is a technique for producing a two-dimensional fabric made from a one-dimensional yarn or thread. In weaving, threads are always straight, running parallel either lengthwise (warp threads) or crosswise (weft threads). By contrast, the yarn in knitted fabrics follows a meandering path (a *course*), forming symmetric loops (also called bights) symmetrically above and below the mean path of the yarn.

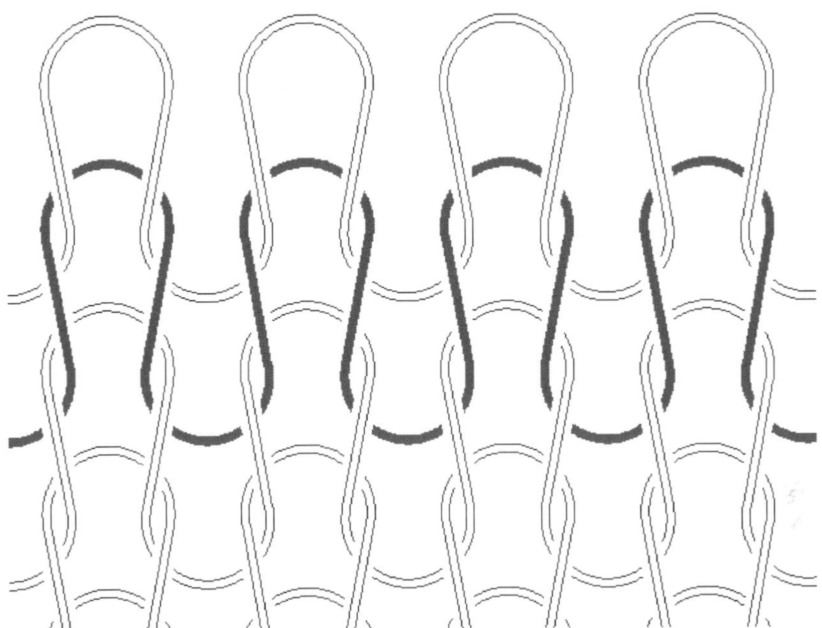

Figure: *Structure of stockinette, a common knitted fabric. The meandering red path defines one* course, *the path of the yarn through the fabric. The uppermost white loops are unsecured and "active", but they secure the red loops suspended from them. In turn, the red loops secure the white loops just below them, which in turn secure the loops below them, and so on.*

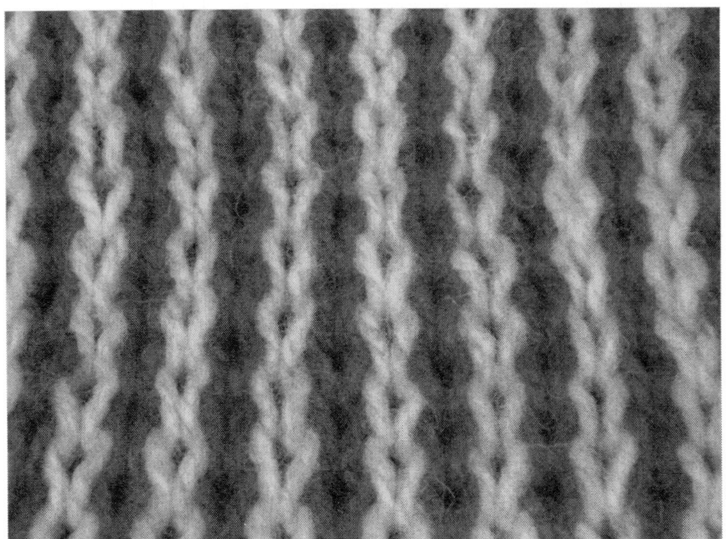

Figure: *Alternating wales of red and white knit stitches. Each stitch in a wale is suspended from the one above it.*

These meandering loops can be stretched easily in different directions, which gives knitting much more elasticity than woven fabrics; depending on the yarn and knitting pattern, knitted garments can stretch as much as 500%. For this reason, knitting was initially developed for garments that must be elastic or stretch in response to the wearer's motions, such as socks and hosiery.

For comparison, woven garments stretch mainly along one direction (the *bias*) and are not very elastic, unless they are woven from stretchable material such as spandex. Knitted garments are often more form-fitting than woven garments, since their elasticity allows them to contour to the body's outline more closely; by contrast, curvature is introduced into most woven garments only with sewn darts, flares, gussets and gores, the seams of which lower the elasticity of the woven fabric still further.

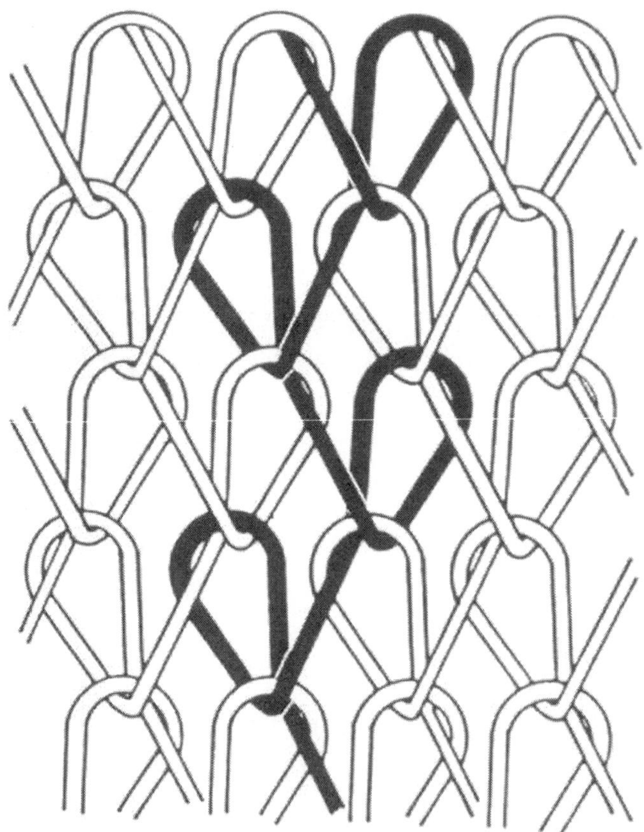

Figure: *Basic pattern of warp knitting. Parallel yarns zigzag lengthwise along the fabric, each loop securing a loop of an adjacent strand from the previous row.*

Extra curvature can be introduced into knitted garments without seams, as in the heel of a sock; the effect of darts, flares, etc. can be obtained with short rows or by increasing or decreasing the number of stitches. Thread used in weaving is usually much finer than the yarn used in knitting, which can give the knitted fabric more bulk and less drape than a woven fabric.

If they are not secured, the loops of a knitted course will come undone when their yarn is pulled; this is known as *ripping out*, *unravelling* knitting, or humorously, *frogging* (because you 'rip it', this sounds like a frog croaking: 'rib-bit'). To secure a stitch, at least one new loop is passed through it.

Although the new stitch is itself unsecured ("active" or "live"), it secures the stitch(es) suspended from it. A sequence of stitches in which each stitch is suspended from the next is called a *wale*. To secure the initial stitches of a knitted fabric, a method for casting on is used; to secure the final stitches in a wale, one uses a method of binding off. During knitting, the active stitches are secured mechanically, either from individual hooks (in knitting machines) or from a knitting needle or frame in hand-knitting.

Weft and Warp Knitting

There are two major varieties of knitting: weft knitting and warp knitting. In the more common *weft knitting*, the wales are perpendicular to the course of the yarn. In warp knitting, the wales and courses run roughly parallel. In weft knitting, the entire fabric may be produced from a single yarn, by adding stitches to each wale in turn, moving across the fabric as in a raster scan. By contrast, in warp knitting, one yarn is required for every wale. Since a typical piece of knitted fabric may have hundreds of wales, warp knitting is typically done by machine, whereas weft knitting is done by both hand and machine. Warp-knitted fabrics such as tricot and milanese are resistant to runs, and are commonly used in lingerie.

Weft-knit fabrics may also be knit with multiple yarns, usually to produce interesting colour patterns. The two most common approaches are intarsia and stranded colourwork. In intarsia, the yarns are used in well-segregated regions, e.g., a red apple on a field of green; in that case, the yarns are kept on separate spools and only one is knitted at any time. In the more complex stranded approach, two or more yarns alternate repeatedly within one row and all the yarns must be carried along the row, as seen in Fair Isle sweaters. Double knitting can produce two separate knitted fabrics simultaneously, e.g., two socks; however, the two fabrics are usually integrated into one, giving it great warmth and excellent drape.

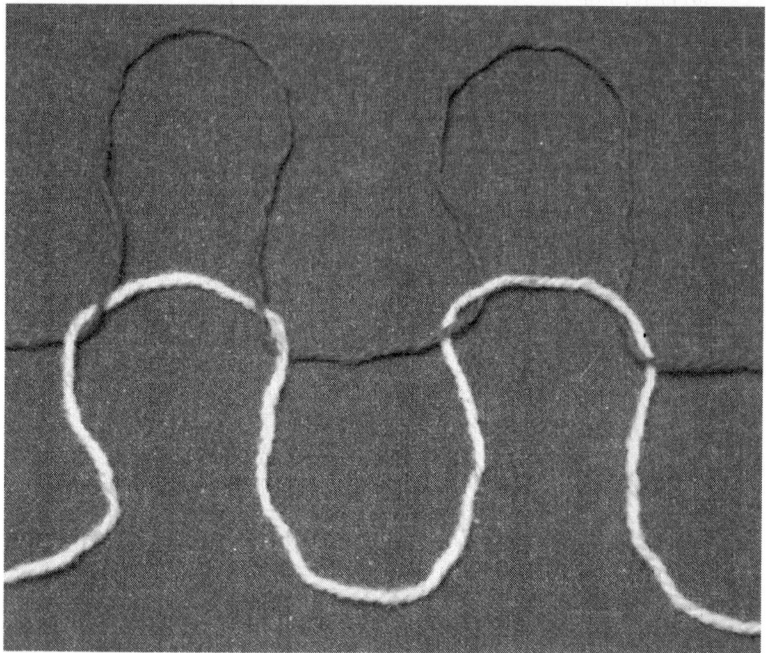

Figure: *In the knit stitch on the left, the next (red) loop passes through the previous (white) loop from* below, *whereas in the purl stitch (right), the next stitch enters from above. Thus, a knit stitch on one side of the fabric appears as a purl stitch on the other, and vice versa.*

Warp Knitting

Warp knitting is a family of knitting methods in which the yarn zigzags along the length of the fabric, i.e., following adjacent columns ("wales") of knitting, rather than a single row ("course"). For comparison, knitting across the width of the fabric is called weft knitting. Since warp knitting requires that the number of separate strands of yarn ("ends") equals the number of stitches in a row, warp knitting is almost always done by machine, not by hand.

Types

Warp knitting comprises several types of knitted fabrics, including tricot, raschel knits, milanese knits and stitch-bonding. All warp-knit fabrics are resistant to runs and relatively easy to sew. Raschel lace—the most common type of lace—is a warp knit fabric but using many more guide-bars (12+) than the usual machines which mostly have three or four bars.

- Tricot is very common in lingerie. The right side of the fabric has fine lengthwise ribs while the reverse has crosswise ribs. The properties of these fabrics include having a soft and 'drapey' texture with some lengthwise stretch and almost no crosswise stretch.
- Milanese is stronger, more stable, smoother and more expensive than tricot and, hence, is used in better lingerie. These knit fabrics are made from two sets of yarn knitted diagonally, which results in the face fabric having a fine vertical rib and the reverse having a diagonal structure, and results in these fabrics being lightweight, smooth, and run-resistant. Milanese is now virtually obsolete.
- Raschel knits do not stretch significantly and are often bulky; consequently, they are often used as an unlined material for coats, jackets, straight skirts and dresses. These fabrics can be made out of conventional or novelty yarns which allows for interesting textures and designs to be created. The qualities of these fabrics range from "dense and compact to open and lofty [and] can be either stable or stretchy, and single-faced or reversible. The largest outlet for the Raschel Warp Knitting Machine is for lace fabric and trimmings.
- Stitch-Bonding is a special form of warp knitting and is commonly used for the production of composite materials and technical textiles. As a method of production, stitch-bonding is efficient, and is one of the most modern ways to create reinforced textiles and composite materials for industrial use. The advantages of the stitch-bonding process includes its high productivity rate and the scope it offers for functional design of textiles, such as fibre-reinforced plastics. Stitch-bonding involves layers of threads and fabric being joined together with a knitting thread, which creates a layered structure called a multiply. This is created through a warp-knitting thread system, which is fixed on the reverse side of the fabric with a sinker loop, and a weft thread layer. A needle with the warp thread passes through the material, which requires the warp and knitting threads to be moving both parallel and perpendicular to the vertical/warp direction of the stitch-bonding machine. Stitch-bonded fabrics are currently being used in such fields as wind energy generation and aviation. Research is currently being conducted into the usage and benefits of stitch-bonded

fabrics as a way to reinforce concrete. Fabrics produced with this process offer the potential of using "sensitive fibre materials such as glass and carbon with only little damage, non-crimp fibre orientation and variable distance between threads".

- Needle shift technique is when "Both outer warp layers [are] secured in one procedure by incorporating a shift of the needle bar during the stitching process, creating endless possibilities for the arrangement and patterns in the stitch-bonding process.
- Extended Stitch-Bonding process (or the extended warp-knitting process): the compound needle that pierces the piles is shifted laterally according to the yarn guides. This then makes it possible for the layers of the stitch-bonded fabric to be arranged freely and be made symmetrical in one working step. This process is advantageous to the characteristics of the composite as the "residual stresses resulting from asymmetric alignment of the layers are avoided, [while] the tensile strength and the impact strength of the composite are improved".

Advantages

Producing textiles through the warp knitting process has the following advantages

- higher productivity rates than weaving
- variety of fabric constructions
- large working widths
- low stress rate on the yarn that allows for use of fibres such as glass, aramide and carbon
- the creation of three-dimensional structures that can be knitted on double needle bar raschels

Applications

Warp knitted fabrics have several industrial uses, including producing mosquito netting, tulle fabrics, sports wear, shoe fabric, fabrics for printing and advertising, coating substrates and laminating backgrounds. Research is also being conducted into the use of warp knitted fabrics for industrial applications (for example, to reinforce concrete), and for the production of biotextiles.

Warp Knitting and Biotextiles

The warp knitting process is also being used to create biotextiles. For example, a warp knitted polyester cardiac support device has been created to attempt to limit the growth of diseased hearts by being installed tightly around the diseased heart. Current research on animals "have confirmed that...the implantation of the device reverses the disease state, which makes this an alternative innovative therapy for patients who have side effects from traditional drug regimes".

Knit and Purl Stitches

In securing the previous stitch in a wale, the next stitch can pass through the previous loop from either below or above. If the former, the stitch is denoted as a *knit stitch* or a *plain stitch*; if the latter, as a *purl stitch*. The two stitches are related in that a knit stitch seen from one side of the fabric appears as a purl stitch on the other side.

The two types of stitches have a different visual effect; the knit stitches look like "V"'s stacked vertically, whereas the purl stitches look like a wavy horizontal line across the fabric. Patterns and pictures can be created in knitted fabrics by using knit and purl stitches as "pixels"; however, such pixels are usually rectangular, rather than square, depending on the gauge of the knitting. Individual stitches, or rows of stitches, may be made taller by drawing more yarn into the new loop (an elongated stitch), which is the basis for uneven knitting: a row of tall stitches may alternate with one or more rows of short stitches for an interesting visual effect. Short and tall stitches may also alternate within a row, forming a fish-like oval pattern.

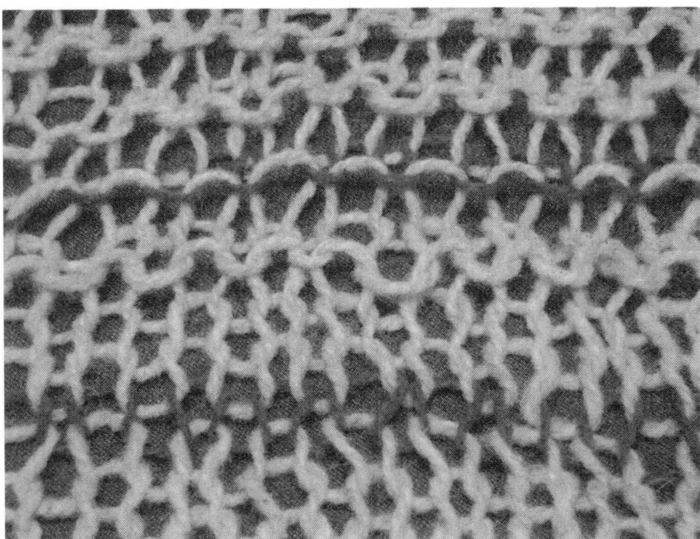

Figure: *Two courses of red yarn illustrating two basic fabric types. The lower red course is knit into the white row below it and is itself knit on the next row; this produces* stockinette *stitch. The upper red course is purled into the row below and then is knit, consistent with* garter *stitch.*

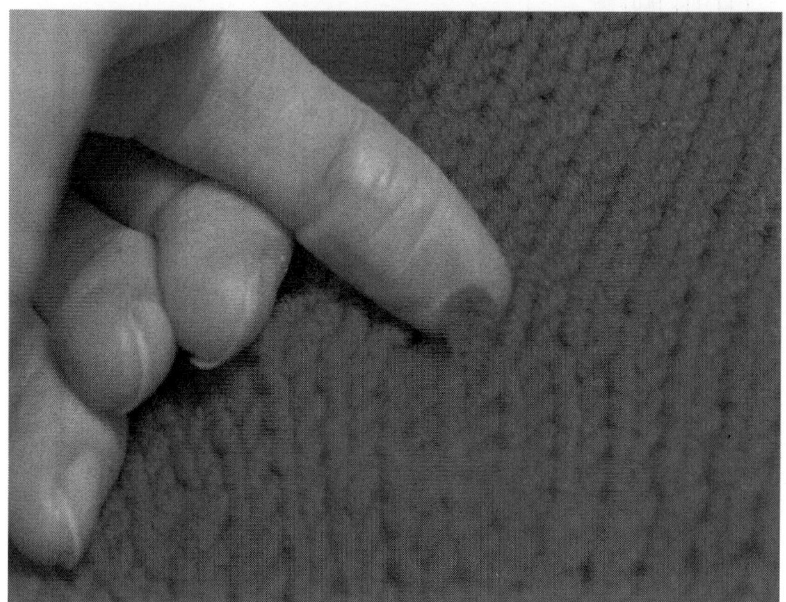

Figure: *A dropped stitch, or missed stitch, is a common error that creates an extra loop to be fixed.*

In the simplest knitted fabrics, all of the stitches are knit or purl; this is known as a garter stitch. Alternating rows of knit stitches and purl stitches produce what is known as a stockinette pattern. Vertical stripes (ribbing) are possible by having alternating wales of knit and purl stitches; for example, a common choice is 2x2 ribbing, in which two wales of knit stitches are followed by two wales of purl stitches, etc. Horizontal striping (welting) is also possible, by alternating *rows* of knit and purl stitches. Checkerboard patterns (basketweave) are also possible, the smallest of which is known as *seed stitch*: the stitches alternate between knit and purl in every wale and along every row.

Fabrics in which the number of knit and purl stitches are not the same, such as stockinette, have a tendency to curl; by contrast, those in which knit and purl stitches are arranged symmetrically (such as ribbing, garter stitch or seed stitch) tend to lie flat and drape well. Wales of purl stitches have a tendency to recede, whereas those of knit stitches tend to come forward. Thus, the purl wales in ribbing tend to be invisible, since the neighbouring knit wales come forward. Conversely, rows of purl stitches tend to form an embossed ridge relative to a row of knit stitches. This is the basis of shadow knitting, in which the appearance of a knitted fabric changes when viewed from different directions.

Typically, a new stitch is passed through a single unsecured ("active") loop, thus lengthening that wale by one stitch. However, this need not be so; the new loop may be passed through an already secured stitch lower down on the fabric, or even between secured stitches (a dip stitch). Depending on the distance between where the loop is drawn through the fabric and where it is knitted, dip stitches can produce a subtle stippling or long lines across the surface of the fabric, e.g., the lower leaves of a flower. The new loop may also be passed between two stitches in the *present* row, thus clustering the intervening stitches; this approach is often used to produce a smocking effect in the fabric. The new loop may also be passed through *two or more* previous stitches, producing a decrease and merging wales together. The merged stitches need not be from the same row; for example, a tuck can be formed by knitting stitches together from two different rows, producing a raised horizontal welt on the fabric.

Not every stitch in a row need be knitted; some may be left as is and knitted on a subsequent row. This is known as slip-stitch knitting. The slipped stitches are naturally longer than the knitted ones. For example, a stitch slipped for one row before knitting would be roughly twice as tall as its knitted counterparts. This can produce interesting visual effects, although the resulting fabric is more rigid, because the slipped stitch "pulls" on its neighbours and is less deformable.

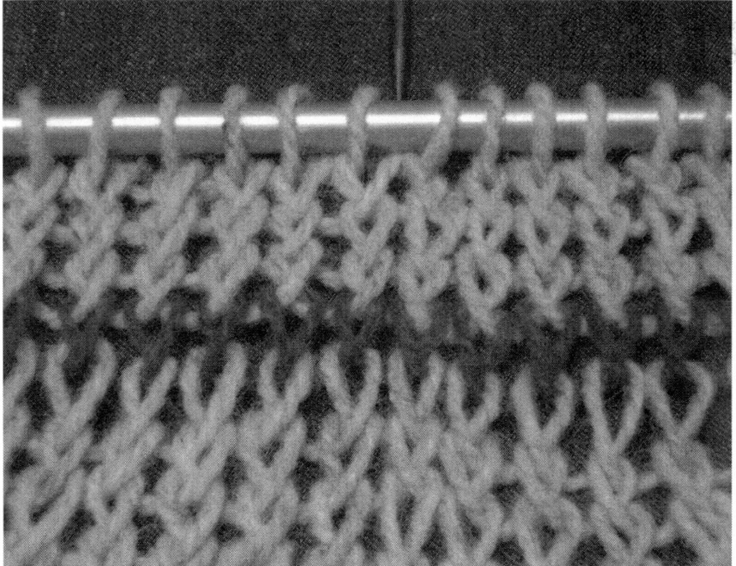

Figure: *The stitches on the right are right-plaited, whereas the stitches on the left are left-plaited.*

Slip-stitch knitting plays an important role in *mosaic knitting*, an important technique in hand-knitting patterned fabrics; mosaic-knit fabrics tend to be stiffer than patterned fabrics produced by other methods such as Fair-Isle knitting. In some cases, a stitch may be deliberately left unsecured by a new stitch and its wale allowed to disassemble. This is known as drop-stitch knitting, and produces a vertical ladder of see-through holes in the fabric, corresponding to where the wale had been.

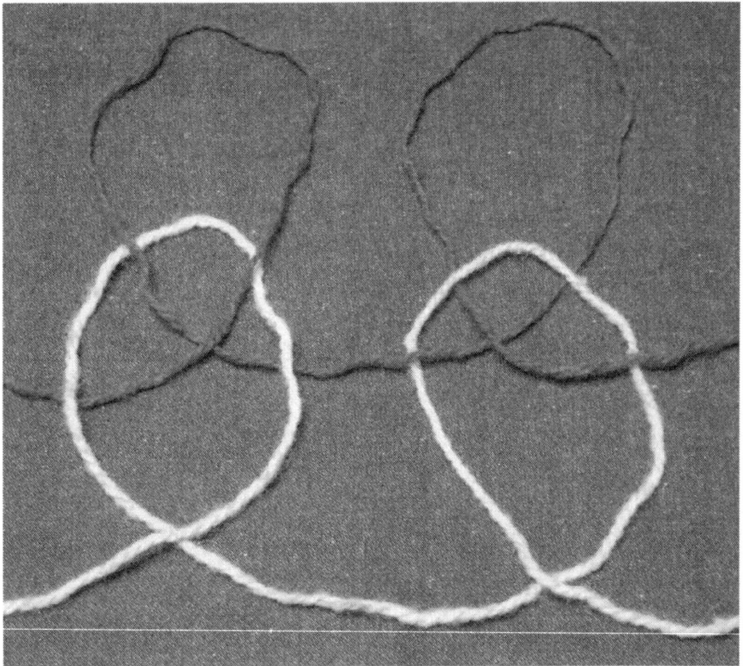

Figure: *Within limits, an arbitrary number of twists may be added to new stitches, whether they be knit or purl. Here, a single twist is illustrated, with left-plaited and right-plaited stitches on the left and right, respectively.*

Right- and Left-Plaited Stitches

Both knit and purl stitches may be twisted: usually once if at all, but sometimes twice and (very rarely) thrice. When seen from above, the twist can be clockwise (right yarn over left) or counterclockwise (left yarn over right); these are denoted as right- and left-plaited stitches, respectively. Hand-knitters generally produce right-plaited stitches by knitting or purling through the back loops, i.e., passing the needle through the initial stitch in an unusual way, but wrapping the yarn as usual. By contrast, the left-plaited stitch is generally formed by hand-knitters by wrapping the yarn in the opposite way, rather than by any change in the needle. Although they are mirror images in form, right- and left-plaited stitches are functionally equivalent. Both types of plaited stitches give a subtle but interesting visual texture, and tend to draw the fabric inwards, making it stiffer. Plaited stitches are a common method for knitting jewelry from fine metal wire.

Plaited Stitch (Knitting)

A plaited stitch is a single knitted stitch that is twisted clockwise (right over left) or counterclockwise (left over right), usually by one half-turn (180°) but sometimes by a full turn (360°) or more.

Plaited stitches can be produced in several ways. Knitting into the back loop produces a clockwise plaited stitch in the lower stitch being knitted (i.e., the loop that was on the left-hand needle.) The clockwise-plaited stitch is also called a left crossed stitch, since the left strand (i.e., the outgoing strand) of the loop crosses over the right incoming strand. Left-crossed stitches are sometimes called twisted stitches, although the latter term might be confused with similar terms from cable knitting.

Conversely, a counterclockwise plaited stitch can be produced if the yarn is wrapped around the needle in the opposite direction as normal while knitting a stitch. Such a stitch is also called a "right crossed stitch", since the right incoming strand crosses over the left outgoing strand. Here, the plait appears in the upper stitch being knitted, i.e., in the new loop being formed. In the "brute-force" approach, the knitter can produce any sort of plaiting by removing the stitch to be knitted from the left-hand needle, twisting it as desired, then returning it to the left-hand needle and knitting it.

Applications in Knitting

Both clockwise and counterclockwise plaited stitches are often repeated in wales, i.e., in columns of knitting, where they make attractive, subtly different ribbings. Fabrics made with plaited stitches are stiffer than normal and "draw in" sideways, i.e., have a smaller widthwise gauge.

Extra-long, full-turn clockwise plaited stitches can be made by knitting through the back loop and wrapping the yarn twice; this is an attractive stitch when repeated in a row, creating openness and a change in scale that enlivens even simple stockinette or garter stitch.

Plaited stitches are also useful in increases and decreases, both for drawing the fabric together and for covering potential "holes" in the fabric.

As a Method for Correcting Errors

As an aside, knitting through the back loop is a useful technique for untwisting stitches on the left-hand needle that "hang backwards". Such stitches are often produced when a knitted fabric is partially pulled out and some stitches are accidentally put back onto the needle with a backwards twist.

Edges and Joins between Fabrics

The initial and final edges of a knitted fabric are known as the *cast-on* and *bound-off* edges. The side edges are known as the *selvages*; the word derives from "self-edges", meaning that the stitches do not need to be secured by anything else. Many types of selvages have been developed, with different elastic and ornamental properties.

Vertical and horizontal edges can be introduced within a knitted fabric, e.g., for button holes, by binding off and re-casting on again (horizontal) or by knitting the fabrics on either side of a vertical edge separately.

Two knitted fabrics can be joined by embroidery-based grafting methods, most commonly the Kitchener stitch. New wales can be begun from any of the edges of a knitted fabric; this is known as picking up stitches and is the basis for entrelac, in which the wales run perpendicular to one another in a checkerboard pattern.

Cables, Increases, and Lace

Ordinarily, stitches are knitted in the same order in every row, and the wales of the fabric run parallel and vertically along the fabric. However, this need not be so, since the order in which stitches are knitted may be permuted so that wales cross over one another, forming a cable pattern. Cables patterns tend to draw the fabric together, making it denser and less elastic; Aran sweaters are a common form of knitted cabling. Arbitrarily complex braid patterns can be done in cable knitting, with the proviso that the wales must move ever upwards; it is generally impossible for a wale to move up and then down the fabric. Knitters have developed methods for giving the illusion of a circular wale, such as appear in Celtic knots, but these are inexact approximations. However, such circular wales are possible using Swiss darning, a form of embroidery, or by knitting a tube separately and attaching it to the knitted fabric.

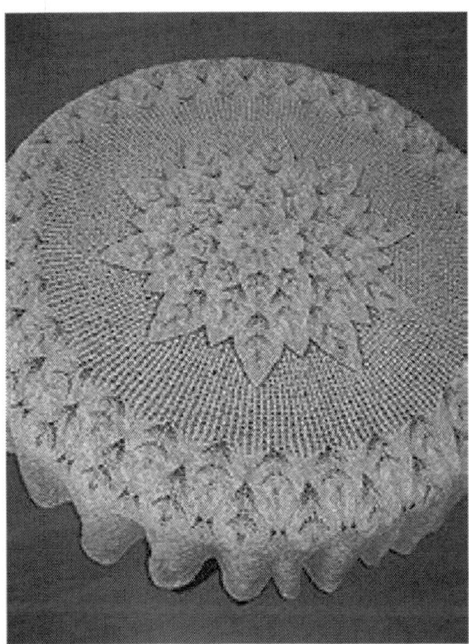

Figure: *In lace knitting, the pattern is formed by making small, stable holes in the fabric, generally with yarn overs.*

A wale can split into two or more wales using increases, most commonly involving a yarn over. Depending on how the increase is done, there is often a hole in the fabric at the point of the increase. This is used to great effect in lace knitting, which consists of making patterns and pictures using such holes, rather than with the stitches themselves. The large and many holes in lacy knitting makes it extremely elastic; for example, some Shetland "wedding-ring" shawls are so fine that they may be drawn through a wedding ring.

By combining increases and decreases, it is possible to make the direction of a wale slant away from vertical, even in weft knitting. This is the basis for bias knitting, and can be used for visual effect, similar to the direction of a brush-stroke in oil painting.

Ornamentations and Additions

Various point-like ornaments may be added to knitting for their look or to improve the wear of the fabric. Examples include various types of bobbles, sequins and beads. Long loops can also be drawn out and secured, forming a "shaggy" texture to the fabric; this is known as loop knitting. Additional patterns can be made on the surface of the knitted fabric using embroidery; if the embroidery resembles knitting, it is often called Swiss darning. Various closures for the garments, such as frogs and buttons can be added; usually buttonholes are knitted into the garment, rather than cut.

Ornamental pieces may also be knitted separately and then attached using applique. For example, differently coloured leaves and petals of a flower could be knit separately and attached to form the final picture. Separately knitted tubes can be applied to a knitted fabric to form complex Celtic knots and other patterns that would be difficult to knit.

Unknitted yarns may be worked into knitted fabrics for warmth, as is done in tufting and "weaving" (also known as "couching").

Types

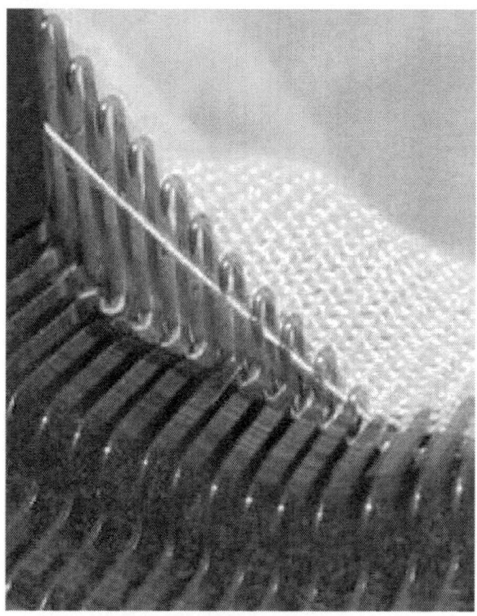

Figure: *A modern knitting machine in the process of weft knitting*

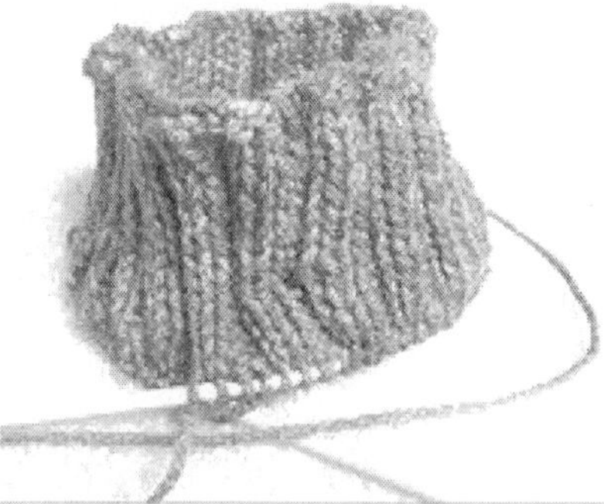

Figure: *Circular knitting on a circular needle*

Flat Knitting versus Circular Knitting

Circular knitting (also called "knitting in the round") is a form of knitting that can be used to create a seamless tube. Knitting is worked in rounds (the equivalent of rows in flat knitting) in a helix. Originally, circular knitting was done using a set of four or five double-pointed knitting needles. Later, circular needles were invented. A circular needle resembles two short knitting needles connected by a cable between them. Flat knitting, on the other hand, is used, in its most basic form, to make flat, rectangular pieces of cloth. It is done with two straight knitting needles and is worked in rows, horizontal lines of stitches. A circular knitting needle can also be used to create flat-knitted pieces that are too large for ordinary straight knitting needles, such as afghans and blankets.

Circular knitting is employed to create pieces that are circular or tube-shaped, such as hats, socks, mittens, and sleeves. Flat knitting is usually used to knit flat pieces like scarves, blankets, afghans, and the backs and fronts of sweaters. There is also such a thing as finger knitting. Instead of needles, fingers are used to produce a tube of knitted fabric.

Felting

Felting is the hand-knitters' term for fulling, a technique for joining knitted or woven wool fibres (only animal yarn fibres can be felted. Acrylic or any fibre that can be machine washed cannot be felted). The finished product is put in a hot wash and the yarn fibres become agitated until it starts to shrink. While the knitted project is in the washing machine, it is important to check the progress. Depending on the size of the project, some may felt faster than others. The end result typically has reduced dimensions. Bags, mittens, vests, socks, slippers and hats are just a few items that can be felted.

Needle Felting

Needle felting is a technique used to add decoration to a knitted or felted piece, where raw roving is applied using a very sharp barbed felting needle by repeatedly piercing the roving and background together. Once washed in hot water, the appliqued decoration is fused with the background. Felted knitting can be cut with scissors without concern about fraying. This is also a good method to use when attempting to give structure to what can be frail knitted fabrics.

History and Culture

The word is derived from *knot* and ultimately from the Old English *cnyttan,* to knot. One of the earliest known examples of knitting was cotton socks with stranded knit colour patterns, found in Egypt from the end of the first millennium AD. Originally a male-only occupation, the first knitting trade guild was started in Paris in 1527. With the invention of the knitting machine, however, knitting “by hand” became a useful but non-essential craft. Similar to quilting, spinning, and needlepoint, knitting became a leisure activity.

Hand-knitting has gone into and out of fashion many times in the last two centuries, and at the turn of the 21st century it is enjoying a revival. According to the industry group Craft Yarn Council of America, the number of women knitters in the United States age 25–35 increased 150% in the two years between 2002 and 2004. The latest incarnation is less about the “make-do and mend” attitude of the 1940s and early 50s and more about making a statement about individuality as well as developing an innate sense of community.

During the 1940s, English knitting rose in popularity while Continental knitting fell. This is due to the fact that continental knitting originated within Germany and was spread by immigrants. During World War II, continental knitting fell out of style due to its relationship with Germany. It wasn’t until Elizabeth Zimmermann publicized continental knitting in the 1980s that it again was popularized.

Additionally, many contemporary knitters have an interest in blogging about their knitting, patterns, and techniques, or joining a virtual community focused on knitting, such as the extremely popular Ravelry. There are also a number of popular knitting podcasts, and various other knitting websites. Contemporary knitting groups may be referred to in the U.S. as a “Stitch ‘N Bitch” where a group of knitters get together to work on projects, discuss patterns, troubleshoot their work and just socialize. In the UK, the term has been “knitting circle” since the early 20th century.

Properties of Fabrics

The topology of a knitted fabric is relatively complex. Unlike woven fabrics, where strands usually run straight horizontally and vertically, yarn that has been knitted follows a loopy path along its row, as with the red strand in the diagram at left, in which the loops of one row have all been pulled through the loops of the row below it.

Because there is no single straight line of yarn anywhere in the pattern, a knitted piece can stretch in all directions. This elasticity is unavailable from woven fabrics, which only stretch along the bias. Many modern stretchy garments, even as they rely on elastic synthetic materials for some stretch, also achieve at least some of their stretch through knitted patterns.

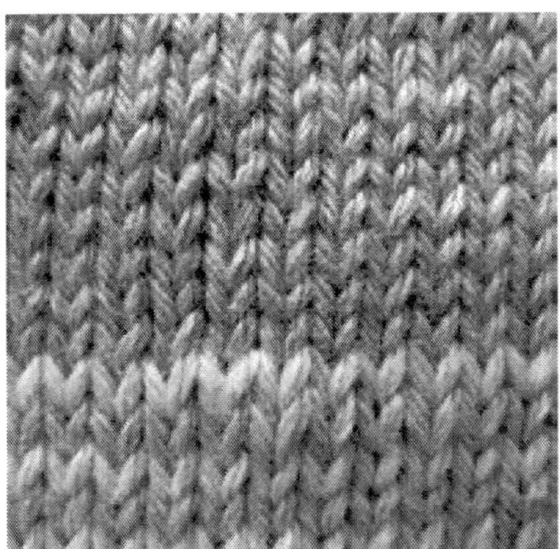

Figure: *Close-up of front of stockinette stitch*

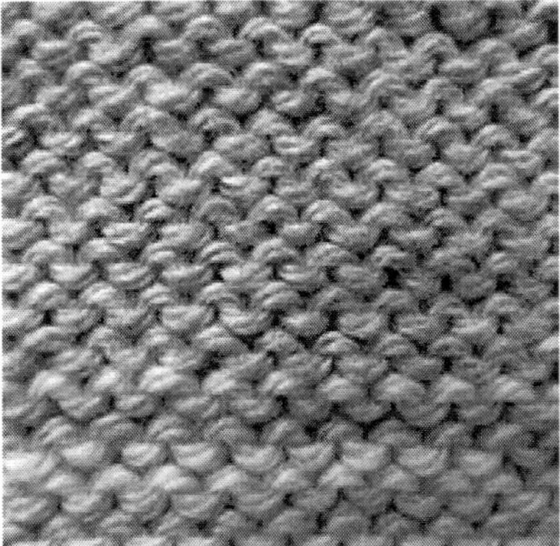

Figure: *Close-up of back of stockinette stitch, also same appearance as reverse stockinette stitch*

The basic knitted fabric (as in the diagram, and usually called a *stocking* or *stockinette* pattern) has a definite "right side" and "wrong side". On the right side, the visible portions of the loops are the verticals connecting two rows, arranged in a grid of *V* shapes. On the wrong side, the ends of the loops are visible, both the tops and bottoms, creating a much more bumpy texture sometimes called *reverse stockinette.* (Despite being the "wrong side," reverse stockinette is frequently used as a pattern in its own right.) Because the yarn holding rows together is all on the front, and the yarn holding side-by-side stitches together is all on the back, stockinette fabric has a strong tendency to curl toward the front on the top and bottom, and toward the back on the left and right side.

Stitches can be worked from either side, and various patterns are created by mixing regular knit stitches with the "wrong side" stitches, known as purl stitches, either in columns (ribbing), rows (garter, welting), or more complex patterns. Each such fabric has different properties: a garter stitch has much more vertical stretch, while ribbing stretches much more horizontally. Because of their front-back symmetry, these two fabrics have little curl, making them popular as edging, even when their stretch properties are not desired.

Different combinations of knit and purl stitches, along with more advanced techniques, generate fabrics of considerably variable consistency, from gauzy to very dense, from highly stretchy to relatively stiff, from flat to tightly curled, and so on.

Texture

The most common texture for a knitted garment is that generated by the flat stockinette stitch—as seen, though very small, in machine-made stockings and T-shirts—which is worked in the round as nothing but knit stitches, and worked flat as alternating rows of knit and purl. Other simple textures can be made with nothing but knit and purl stitches, including garter stitch, ribbing, and moss and seed stitches. Adding a "slip stitch" (where a loop is passed from one needle to the other) allows for a wide range of textures, including heel and linen stitches, and a number of more complicated patterns.

Some more advanced knitting techniques create a surprising variety of complex textures. Combining certain increases, which can create small eyelet holes in the resulting fabric, with assorted decreases is key to creating knitted lace, a very open fabric resembling lace. Changing the order of stitches from one row to the next, usually with the help of a cable needle or stitch holder, is key to cable knitting, producing an endless variety of cables, honeycombs, ropes, and Aran sweater patterning. Entrelac forms a rich checkerboard texture by knitting small squares, picking up their side edges, and knitting more squares to continue the piece.

The appearance of a garment is also affected by the *weight* of the yarn, which describes the thickness of the spun fibre. The thicker the yarn, the more visible and apparent stitches will be; the thinner the yarn, the finer the texture.

Colour

Plenty of finished knitting projects never use more than a single colour of yarn, but there are many ways to work in multiple colours. Some yarns are dyed to be either *variegated* (changing colour every few stitches in a random fashion) or *self-striping* (changing every few rows). More complicated techniques permit large fields of colour (intarsia, for example), busy small-scale patterns of colour (such as Fair Isle), or both (double knitting and slip-stitch colour, for example).

Yarn with multiple shades of the same hue are called *ombre*, while a yarn with multiple hues may be known as a given *colourway* — a green, red and yellow yarn might be dubbed the "Parrot Colourway" by its manufacturer, for example. *Heathered* yarns contain small amounts of fibre of different colours, while *tweed* yarns may have greater amounts of different coloured fibres.

Process

There are many hundreds of different knitting stitches used by knitters. A piece of knitting begins with the process of *casting on* (also known as "binding on"), which involves the initial creation of the stitches on the needle. Different methods of casting on are used for different effects: one may be stretchy enough for lace, while another provides a decorative edging — *Provisional* cast-ons are used when the knitting will continue in both directions from the cast-on.

There are various method employed to "cast on," such as the "thumb method" (also known as "slingshot" or "long-tail" cast-ons), where the stitches are created by a series of loops that will, when knitted, give a very loose edge ideal for "picking up stitches" and knitting a border; the "double needle method" (also known as "knit-on" or "cable cast-on"), whereby each loop placed on the needle is then "knitted on," which produces a firmer edge ideal on its own as a border; and many more. The number of active stitches remains the same as when cast on unless stitches are added (an increase) or removed (a decrease).

Most Western-style knitters follow either the English style (in which the yarn is held in the right hand) or the Continental style (in which the yarn is held in the left hand). There are also different ways to insert the needle into the stitch. Knitting through the front of a stitch is called Western knitting. Going through the back of a stitch is called Eastern knitting. A third method, called combination knitting, goes through the front of a knit stitch and the back of a purl stitch.

Once the knitted piece is finished, the remaining live stitches are "cast off". Casting (or "binding") off loops the stitches across each other so they can be removed from the needle without unravelling the item. Although the mechanics are different from casting on, there is a similar variety of methods. In knitting certain articles of clothing, especially larger ones like sweaters, the final knitted garment will be made of several knitted pieces, with individual sections of the garment knit separately and then sewn together. Seamless knitting, where a whole garment is knit as a single piece, is also possible. Elizabeth Zimmermann is probably the best-known proponent of seamless or circular knitting techniques. Smaller items, such as socks and hats, are usually knit in one piece on double-pointed needles or circular needles.

Mega Knitting

Mega knitting is a term recently coined and relates to the use of knitting needles greater than or equal to half an inch in diameter.

Mega knitting uses the same stitches and techniques as conventional knitting, except that hooks are carved into the ends of the needles. The hooked needles greatly enhance control of the work, catching the stitches and preventing them from slipping off.

It was the development of the knitting machine that introduced hooked needles and enabled faultless, automated knitting. Most knitters probably aren't even aware of the many processes that their fingers perform in the making of a single stitch. However, large gauge needles emphasise those actions and knitting becomes increasingly more awkward when the needle diameter is greater than the width of the knitters finger. On a one inch diameter (size 50) needle for instance, the shaft begins to taper one and three quarter inches from the tip. This means that the stitches are spread much further apart on mega knitting needles, making them more difficult to control. The hook catches the loop of yarn as each stitch is knitted, meaning that wrists and fingers don't have to work so hard and there is less chance of stitches slipping off the needle. The position of the hook is most important. Turn the left (non-working) hook to face away at all times; turn the right (working) hook toward you up whilst knitting (plain stitch) and away whilst purling.

Mega knitting produces a chunky, bulky fabric or an open lacy weave, depending on the weight and type of yarn used.

Materials

Yarn: Yarn for hand-knitting is usually sold as balls or skeins (hanks), although it may also be wound on spools or cones. Skeins and balls are generally sold with a *yarn-band,* a label that describes the yarn's weight, length, dye lot, fibre content, washing instructions, suggested needle size, likely gauge, etc. It is common practice to save the yarn band for future reference, especially if additional skeins must be purchased. Knitters generally ensure that the yarn for a project comes from a single dye lot. The dye lot specifies a group of skeins that were dyed together and thus have precisely the same colour; skeins from different dye-lots, even if very similar in colour, are usually slightly different and may produce a visible stripe when knitted together. If a knitter buys insufficient yarn of a single dye lot to complete a project, additional skeins of the same dye lot can sometimes be obtained from other yarn stores or online. Otherwise, knitters can alternate skeins every few rows to help the dye lots blend together easier.

The thickness or weight of the yarn is a significant factor in determining the gauge, i.e., how many stitches and rows are required to cover a given area for a given stitch pattern. Thicker yarns generally require thicker knitting needles, whereas thinner yarns may be knit with thick or thin needles. Hence, thicker yarns generally require fewer stitches, and therefore less time, to knit up a given garment. Patterns and motifs are coarser with thicker yarns; thicker yarns produce bold visual effects, whereas thinner yarns are best for refined patterns. Yarns are grouped by thickness into six categories: superfine, fine, light, medium, bulky and superbulky; quantitatively, thickness is measured by the number of wraps per inch (WPI). The related *weight per unit length* is usually measured in tex or dernier.

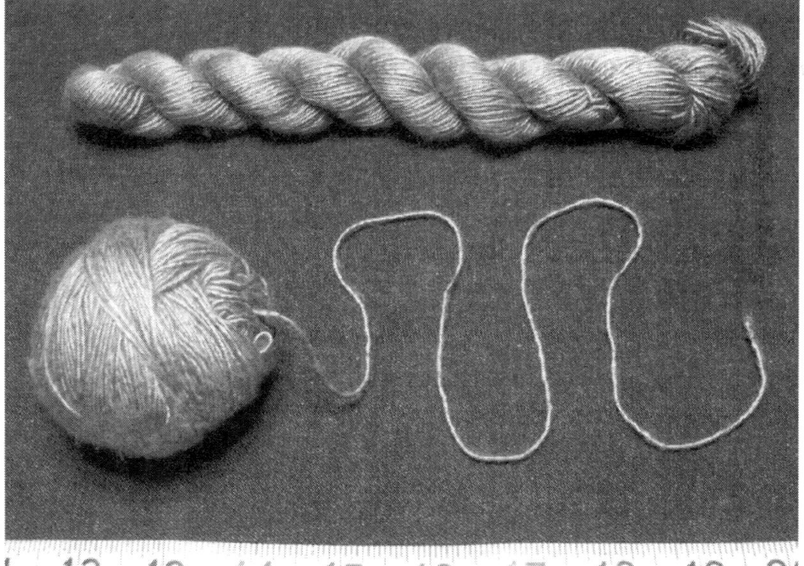

Figure: *Transformation of a hank of lavender silk yarn (top) into a ball in which the knitting yarn emerges from the centre (bottom). The latter is better for knitting, since the yarn is much less likely to tangle.*

Before knitting, the knitter will typically transform a hank into a ball where the yarn emerges from the centre of the ball; this making the knitting easier by preventing the yarn from becoming easily tangled. This transformation may be done by hand, or with a device known as a ballwinder. When knitting, some knitters enclose their balls in jars to keep them clean and untangled with other yarns; the free yarn passes through a small hole in the jar-lid.

A yarn's usefulness for a knitting project is judged by several factors, such as its *loft* (its ability to trap air), its *resilience* (elasticity under tension), its washability and colourfastness, its *hand* (its feel, particularly softness vs. scratchiness), its durability against abrasion, its resistance to pilling, its *hairiness* (fuzziness), its tendency to twist or untwist, its overall weight and drape, its blocking and felting qualities, its comfort (breathability, moisture absorption, wicking properties) and of course its look, which includes its colour, sheen, smoothness and ornamental features.

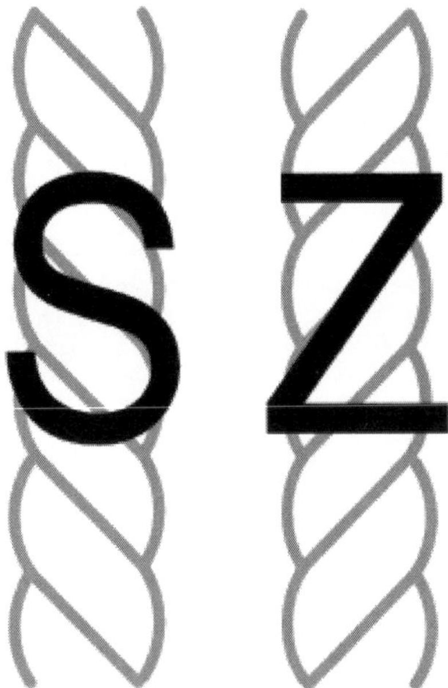

Figure: *The two possible twists of yarn*

Other factors include allergenicity; speed of drying; resistance to chemicals, moths, and mildew; melting point and flammability; retention of static electricity; and the propensity to become stained and to accept dyes. Different factors may be more significant than others for different knitting projects, so there is no one "best" yarn. The resilience and propensity to (un)twist are general properties that affect the ease of hand-knitting. More resilient yarns are more forgiving of irregularities in tension; highly twisted yarns are sometimes difficult to knit, whereas untwisting yarns can lead to split stitches, in which not all of the yarn is knitted into a stitch. A key factor in knitting is *stitch definition*, corresponding to how well complicated stitch patterns can be seen when made from a given yarn. Smooth, highly spun yarns are best for showing off stitch patterns; at the other extreme, very fuzzy yarns or eyelash yarns have poor stitch definition, and any complicated stitch pattern would be invisible.

Although knitting may be done with ribbons, metal wire or more exotic filaments, most yarns are made by spinning fibres. In spinning, the fibres are twisted so that the yarn resists breaking under tension; the twisting may be done in either direction, resulting in a Z-twist or S-twist yarn. If the fibres are first aligned by combing them, the yarn is smoother and called a *worsted*; by contrast, if the fibres are carded but not combed, the yarn is fuzzier and called *woolen-spun*. The fibres making up a yarn may be continuous *filament* fibres such as silk and many synthetics, or they may be *staples* (fibres of an average length, typically a few inches); naturally filament fibres are sometimes cut up into staples before spinning. The strength of the spun yarn against breaking is determined by the amount of twist, the length of the fibres and the thickness of the yarn. In general, yarns become stronger with more twist (also called *worst*), longer fibres and thicker yarns (more fibres); for example, thinner yarns require more twist than do thicker yarns to resist breaking under tension. The thickness of the yarn may vary along its length; a *slub* is a much thicker section in which a mass of fibres is incorporated into the yarn.

The spun fibres are generally divided into animal fibres, plant and synthetic fibres. These fibre types are chemically different, corresponding to proteins, carbohydrates and synthetic polymers, respectively. Animal fibres include silk, but generally are long hairs of animals such as sheep (wool), goat (angora, or cashmere goat), rabbit (angora), llama, alpaca, dog, cat, camel, yak, and muskox (qiviut). Plants used for fibres include cotton, flax (for linen), bamboo, ramie, hemp, jute, nettle, raffia, yucca, coconut husk, banana trees, soy and corn. Rayon and acetate fibres are also produced from cellulose mainly derived from trees. Common synthetic fibres include acrylics, polyesters such as dacron and ingeo, nylon and other polyamides, and olefins such as polypropylene. Of these types, wool is generally favoured for knitting, chiefly owing to its superior elasticity, warmth and (sometimes) felting; however, wool is generally less convenient to clean and some people are allergic to it. It is also common to blend different fibres in the yarn, e.g., 85% alpaca and 15% silk. Even within a type of fibre, there can be great variety in the length and thickness of the fibres; for example, Merino wool and Egyptian cotton are favoured because they produce exceptionally long, thin (fine) fibres for their type.

A single spun yarn may be knitted as is, or braided or plied with another. In plying, two or more yarns are spun together, almost always in the opposite sense from which they were spun individually; for example, two Z-twist yarns are usually plied with an S-twist. The opposing twist relieves some of the yarns' tendency to curl up and produces a thicker, *balanced* yarn. Plied yarns may themselves be plied together, producing *cabled yarns* or *multi-stranded yarns*. Sometimes, the yarns being plied are fed at different rates, so that one yarn loops around the other, as in bouclé. The single yarns may be dyed separately before plying, or afterwards to give the yarn a uniform look.

The dyeing of yarns is a complex art that has a long history. However, yarns need not be dyed. They may be dyed just one colour, or a great variety of colours. Dyeing may be done industrially, by hand or even hand-painted onto the yarn. A great variety of synthetic dyes have been developed since the synthesis of indigo dye in the mid-19th century; however, natural dyes are also possible, although they are generally less brilliant. The colour-scheme of a yarn is sometimes called its colourway. Variegated yarns can produce interesting visual effects, such as diagonal stripes; conversely, a variegated yarn may frustrate an otherwise good knitting pattern by producing distasteful colour combination.

Glass/Wax

Knitted Glass combines knitting, lost-wax casting, mold-making, and kiln-casting. The process involves

1. *knitting* with wax strands,
2. surrounding the knitted wax piece with a heat-tolerant refractory material,
3. removing the wax by melting it out, thus creating a mold;
4. placing the mold in a kiln where lead crystal glass melts into the mold;
5. after the mold cools, the mold material is removed to reveal the knitted glass piece.

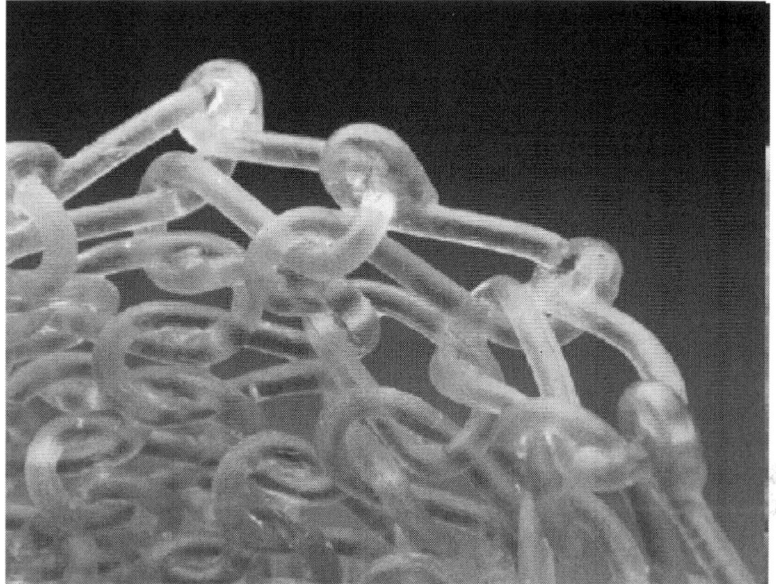

Figure: *Close-up of 'Jitterbug' - Knitted Glass*

Tools

The process of knitting has three basic tasks:

1. the active (unsecured) stitches must be held so they don't drop
2. these stitches must be released sometime after they are secured
3. new bights of yarn must be passed through the fabric, usually through active stitches, thus securing them.

In very simple cases, knitting can be done without tools, using only the fingers to do these tasks; however, knitting is usually carried out using tools such as knitting needles, knitting machines or rigid frames. Depending on their size and shape, the rigid frames are called knitting boards, knitting rings (also called knitting looms) or knitting spools (also known as knitting knobbies, knitting nancies, or corkers). There is also a technique of knitting with a crochet hook that has a cord attached to the end, to hold the stitches while they're being worked. This technique is called knooking. Other tools are used to prepare yarn for knitting, to measure and design knitted garments, or to make knitting easier or more comfortable.

Needles

There are three basic types of knitting needles (also called "knitting pins"). The first and most common type consists of two slender, straight sticks tapered to a point at one end, and with a knob at the other end to prevent stitches from slipping off. Such needles are usually 10–16 inches (250–410 mm) long but, due to the compressibility of knitted fabrics, may be used to knit pieces significantly wider. The most important property of needles is their diameter, which ranges from below 2 to 25 mm (roughly 1 inch). The diameter affects the size of stitches, which affects the gauge of the knitting and the elasticity of the fabric. Thus, a simple way to change gauge is to use different needles, which is the basis of uneven knitting.

Although the diameter of the knitting needle is often measured in millimetres, there are several different measurement systems, particularly those specific to the United States, the United Kingdom and Japan; a conversion table is given at knitting needle. Such knitting needles may be made out of any materials, but the most common materials are metals, wood, bamboo, and plastic. Different materials have different frictions and grip the yarn differently; slick needles such as metallic needles are useful for swift knitting, whereas rougher needles such as bamboo offer more friction and are therefore less prone to dropping stitches. The knitting of new stitches occurs only at the tapered ends. Needles with lighted tips have been sold to allow knitters to knit in the dark.

The second type of knitting needles are straight, double-pointed knitting needles (also called "DPNs"). Double-pointed needles are tapered at both ends, which allows them to be knit from either end. DPNs are typically used for circular knitting, especially smaller tube-shaped pieces such as sleeves, collars, and socks; usually one needle is active while the others hold the remaining active stitches. DPNs are somewhat shorter (typically 7 inches) and are usually sold in sets of four or five.

Cable needles are a special case of DPNs, although they usually are not straight, but dimpled in the middle. Often, they have the form of a hook. When cabling a knitted piece, a hook is easier to grab and hold the yarn. Cable needles are typically very short (a few inches), and are used to hold stitches temporarily while others are being knitted. Cable patterns are made by permuting the order of stitches; although one or two stitches may be held by hand or knit out of order, cables of three or more generally require a cable needle.

The third needle type consists of circular needles, which are long, flexible double-pointed needles. The two tapered ends (typically 5 inches (130 mm) long) are rigid and straight, allowing for easy knitting; however, the two ends are connected by a flexible strand (usually nylon) that allows the two ends to be brought together. Circular needles are typically 24-60 inches long, and are usually used singly or in pairs; again, the width of the knitted piece may be significantly longer than the length of the circular needle. A developing trend in the knitting world is interchangeable needles. These kits consist of pairs of needles with usually nylon cables or cords. The cables/cords are screwed into the needles, allowing the knitter to have both flexible straight needles or circular needles. This also allows the knitter to change the diameter and length of the needles as needed.

The ability to work from either end of one needle is convenient in several types of knitting, such as slip-stitch versions of double knitting. Circular needles may be used for flat or circular knitting. Cable needles are a specific design, and are used to create the twisting motif of a knitted cable. They are made in different sizes, which produces cables of different widths. When in use, the cable needle is used at the same time as two regular needles. It functions by holding together the stitches creating the cable as the other needles create the rest of the stitches for the knitted piece. At specific points indicated by the pattern, the cable needle is moved, the stitches on it are worked by the other needles, then the cable needle is turned around to a different position to create the cable twist.

Mega Needles

Mega knitting needles are generally considered to be any knitting needles larger than size 17 (half inch diameter). Mega needles may or may not have hooks carved in the ends. Hooks on large diameter needles help enormously to control the stitches whilst knitting.

Largest Circular Knitting Needles

The largest aluminum circular knitting needles on record are size US 150 and are nearly 7 feet tall. They are owned by Paradise Fibres and are currently on display in the Paradise Fibres retail showroom.

Record

The current holder of the Guinness World Record for Knitting with the Largest Knitting Needles is Julia Hopson of Penzance in Cornwall. Julia knitted a square of ten stitches and ten rows in stockinette stitch using knitting needles that were 6.5 centimetres in diameter and 3.5 metres long.

Ancillary Tools

Various tools have been developed to make hand-knitting easier. Tools for measuring needle diameter and yarn properties have been discussed above, as well as the yarn swift, ballwinder and "yarntainers". Crochet hooks and a darning needle are often useful in binding off or in joining two knitted pieces edge-to-edge.

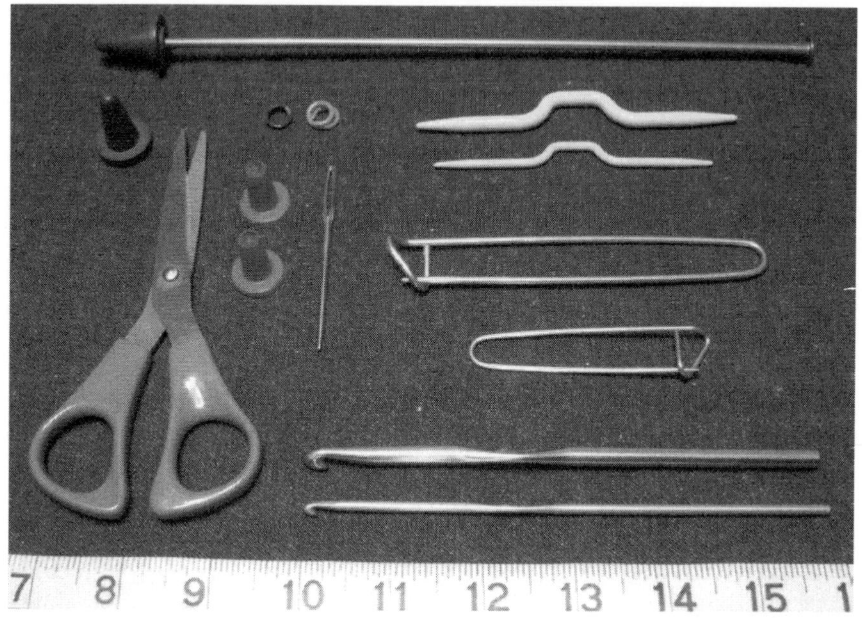

Figure: *Some ancillary tools used by hand-knitters. Starting from the bottom right are two crochet hooks, two stitch holders (quasi-safety pins), and two cable needles in pink and green. On the left are a pair of scissors, a yarn needle, green and blue stitch markers, and two orange point protectors. At the top left are two blue point protectors, one on a red needle.*

The darning needle is used in duplicate stitch (also known as Swiss darning), while the crochet hook is also essential for repairing dropped stitches and some speciality stitches such as tufting. Other tools are used to prepare specific ornaments include the pompom tree for making pompoms conveniently. For large or complex patterns, it is sometimes difficult to keep track of which stitch should be knit in a particular way; therefore, several tools have been developed to identify the number of a particular row or stitch, including circular stitch markers, hanging markers, extra yarn and row counters. A second potential difficulty is that the knitted piece will slide off the tapered end of the needles when unattended; this is prevented by "point protectors" that cap the tapered ends. Another problem is that too much knitting may lead to hand and wrist troubles; for this, special stress-relieving gloves are available. Finally, there are sundry bags and containers for holding knitting, yarns and needles.

Commercial Applications

Industrially, metal wire is also knitted into a metal fabric for a wide range of uses including the filter material in cafetieres, catalytic converters for cars and many other uses. These fabrics are usually manufactured on circular knitting machines that would be recognised by conventional knitters as sock machines. Many fashion designers make heavy use of knitting in their fashion collections. Gordana Gelhausen, who appeared in season six of the television show *Project Runway*, is primarily a knit designer. Other designers and labels that make heavy use of knitting include Michael Kors, Fendi, and Marc Jacobs. For individual hobbyists, websites such as Etsy, Liz and Ravelry have made it easy to sell patterns on a small scale, in a way similar to eBay.

Graffiti

In the last decade, a practice called knitting graffiti, guerilla knitting, or yarn bombing— the use of knitted or crocheted cloth to modify and beautify one's (usually outdoor) surroundings—emerged in the U.S. and spread worldwide. Magda Sayeg is credited with starting the movement in the US and Knit the City are a prominent group of graffiti knitters in the United Kingdom. Yarn bombers sometimes target existing pieces of graffiti for beautification. For instance, Dave Cole is a contemporary sculpture artist who practiced knitting as graffiti for a large-scale public art installation in Melbourne, Australia for the Big West Arts Festival in 2009. The work was vandalized the night of its completion. A new movie, shot by a Tasmanian filmmaker on a set made almost entirely out of yarn, was partially inspired by "knitted graffiti".

Charity

Knitting garments for free distribution to others has become common practice among knitting groups. Girls and women knitted socks, sweaters, scarves, mittens, gloves, and hats for soldiers in Crimea, the American Civil War, and the Boer Wars; this practice continued in World War I, World War II and the Korean War, and continues for soldiers in Iraq and Afghanistan. In the historical projects, yarn companies provided patterns approved by the various branches of the armed services; often they were distributed by local chapters of the American Red Cross. Modern projects usually entail the knitting of hats or helmet liners; the liners provided for soldiers must be of 100% worsted weight wool and be crafted using specific colours.

Clothing and afghans are frequently made for children, the elderly, and the economically disadvantaged in various countries. Pine Ridge Indian Reservation accepts donations for the Lakota people in the United States. Prayer shawls, or shawls in which the crafter meditates or says prayers of their faith while knitting with the intent on comforting the recipient, are donated to those experiencing loss or stress. Many knitters today knit and donate “chemo caps,” soft caps for cancer patients who lose their hair during chemotherapy. Yarn companies offer free patterns for these caps.

Penguin sweaters were knitted by volunteers for the rehabilitation of penguins contaminated by exposure to oil slicks. The project is now complete. Chicken sweaters were also knitted to aid battery hens that had lost their feathers. The organisation is not currently accepting donations, but maintains a list of volunteers.

Originally started after the 2004 Indonesian tsunami, Knitters Without Borders is a charity challenge issued by knitting personality Stephanie Pearl-McPhee that encourages knitters to donate to Médecins Sans Frontières (Doctors Without Borders). Instead of knitting for charity, knitters are encouraged to a week’s worth of disposable income, including money that otherwise might have been spent on yarn. Knitted items are occasional offered as prizes to donors. As of September 2011, Knitters Without Borders donors have contributed CAD$1,062,217.

Security blankets can also be made through the Project Linus organisation which helps needy children. There are organisations that help reach other countries in need such as afghans for Afghans. This outreach is described as, “afghans for Afghans is a humanitarian and educational people-to-people project that sends hand-knit and crocheted blankets and sweaters, vests, hats, mittens, and socks to the beleaguered people of Afghanistan.”

Health Benefits

Studies have shown that knitting, along with other forms of needlework, provide several significant health benefits. These studies have found the rhythmic and repetitive action of knitting can “help prevent and manage stress, pain and depression, which in turn strengthens the body’s immune system”, as well as create a relaxation response in the body which can decrease blood pressure, heart rate, help prevent illness, and have a calming effect. Pain specialists have also found that the brain chemistry is changed when one knits, resulting in an increase in “feel good” hormones (i.e. serotonin and dopamine), and a decrease in stress hormones. Knitting, along with other leisure activities has been linked to reducing the risk of developing Alzheimer's disease and dementia. Much like physical activity strengthens the body, mental exercise makes our brains more resilient.

Knitted fabrics are the third major class of fabric, after woven and nonwoven fabrics.

Structure of Knitted Fabrics

Knitted fabrics are divided into two basic types: warp-knit fabrics such as tricot and weft-knit fabrics such as a hand-knit sweater. Weft-knit items have the drawback that they *run* when cut. Warp-knit fabrics are often used in lingerie.

- knits can shrink but can also extend if a rib construction
- knits have nap
- ribs/wales versus courses
- generally more elasticity along the course than along the wale

Knitting Stitches

Over the long history of knitting across the world, hundreds of different knitting stitches have been created. The basic building blocks of all hand knitting are the following stitches: knit, purl, cast on, cast off (also known as bind off), increase and decrease stitches. Use of a combination of these methods can provide a vast number of different textures to knitted fabrics.

In order to save space in knitting patterns, the names of stitches are normally abbreviated.

Composition of Knitted Fabrics

The most common fibres used for knitted fabrics are cotton & viscose with or without elastane, these tend to be single jersey construction and are used for most t-shirt style tops.

History of Knitwear

Coco Chanel's 1916 use of jersey in her hugely influential suits was a turning point for knitwear, which became associated with the woman. Shortly afterwards, Jean Patou's cubist-inspired, colour-blocked knits were the sportswear of choice.

In the 1940s came the iconic wearing of body-skimming sweaters by sex symbols like Lana Turner and Jane Russell, though the 1950s were dominated by conservative popcorn knits. The swinging 1960s were famously manifested in Missoni's colourful zigzag knitwear. This era also saw the rise both of Sonia Rykiel, dubbed the "Queen of Knitwear" for her vibrant striped sweaters and her clingy dresses, and of Kennedy-inspired preppy sweaters.

In the 1980s, knitwear emerged from the realm of sportswear to dominate high fashion; notable designs included Romeo Gigli's "haute-bohemian cocoon coats" and Ralph Lauren's floor-length cashmere turtlenecks.

Chinese Knotting

Chinese knotting (Chinese: -NWP}; pinyin: *Zhôngguó jié*) is a decorative handicraft art that began as a form of Chinese folk art in the Tang and Song Dynasty (960-1279 AD) in China. It was later popularized in the Ming). The art is also referred to as *Chinese traditional decorative knots*. In other cultures, it is known as *"Decorative knots"*.

Chinese knots are usually lanyard type arrangements where 2 cords enter from the top of the knot and 2 cords leave from the bottom. The knots are usually double-layered and symmetrical.

History

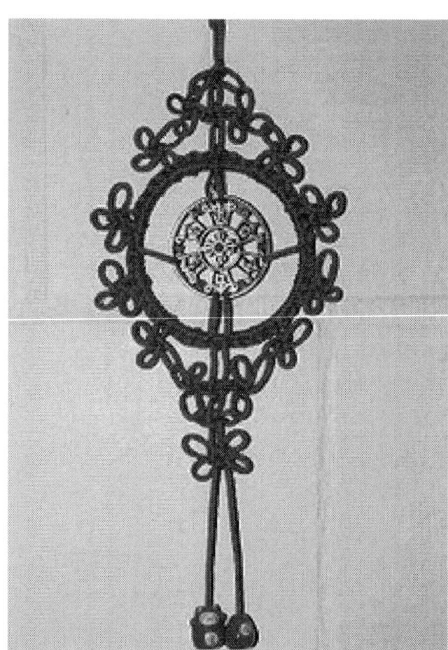

Figure: *A Chinese knot*

Archaeological studies indicate that the art of tying knots dates back to prehistoric times. Recent discoveries include 100,000-year old bone needles used for sewing and bodkins, which were used to untie knots. However, due to the delicate nature of the medium, few examples of prehistoric Chinese knotting exist today. Some of the earliest evidence of knotting have been preserved on bronze vessels of the Warring States period (481–221 BCE), Buddhist carvings of the Northern Dynasties period (317–581) and on silk paintings during the Western Han period (206 BCE–CE6).

Further references to knotting have also been found in literature, poetry and the private letters of some of the most infamous rulers of China. In the 18th century, one book that talked extensively about the art was *Dream of the Red Chamber*. The phenomenon of knot tying continued to steadily evolve over the course of thousands of years with the development of more sophisticated techniques and increasingly intricate woven patterns. During the Qing Dynasty (1644–1911) knotting finally broke from its pure folklore status, becoming an acceptable art form in Chinese society and reached the pinnacle of its success. Knotting continued to flourish up until about the end of imperial China and the founding of the Republic of China in 1911 AD when China began its modernisation period. From 1912 to the end of the Cultural Revolution in 1976, the art of Chinese knotting was almost lost.

In the late 1970s, a resurgence of interest occurred in Taiwan, largely due to the efforts of Lydia Chen (Chen Hsia-Sheng s–YÛv) of the National Palace Museum who founded the Chinese Knotting Promotion Centre. In the 1980s, Mrs. Chen focused her energies on the knotting artifacts preserved during the Qing Dynasty. Currently, Chinese knotting enjoys wide popularity in Taiwan with numerous speciality shops to be found.

Regional

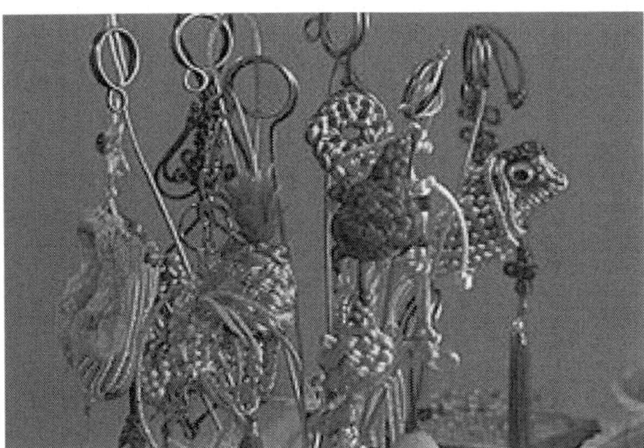

Figure: *Example of the different colours and designs used*

China: Historically knotwork are divided into cords and knots. In the dynastic periods, a certain number of craftsmen were stationed in the court and outside the court to produce cords and knots in order to meet the increasing demand for them at various places of the court. Cord, knot and tassels were made separated and combined later.

Hong Kong

Greatly influenced by western cultures, Chinese knotting crafts are almost invisible in the daily lives of Hong Kong Chinese. Yet, around the times of Chinese new year festival, you still can see Chinese knot decorations hanging on walls, doors of homes and as shop decorations to add some festival feel. Usually, these decorations are in red colour, which traditional Chinese regards it as a colour of "luck".

Korea

In Korea, decorative knotwork is known as *maedeup* (ä¹í´), often called *Korean knotwork* or *Korean knots.*

The origins of Maedeup date back to the Three Kingdoms of Korea in the first century CE. Maedeup articles were first used at religious ceremonies.

Inspired by Chinese knotwork, a wall painting found in Anak, Hwanghae Province, now in North Korea, dated 357 CE, indicates that the work was flourishing in silk at that time.

Decorative cording was used on silk dresses, to ornament swords, to hang personal items from belts for the aristocracy, in rituals, where it continues now in contemporary wedding ceremonies.

Korean Knotwork is differentiated from Korean embroidery. Maedeup is still a commonly practiced traditional art, especially amongst the older generations.

The most basic knot in Maedeup is called the *Dorae* or *double connection knot.* The Dorae knot is used at the start and end of most knot projects. There are approximately 33 basic Korean knots which vary according to the region they come from.

The Bong Sool tassel is noteworthy as the most representative work familiar to Westerners, and often purchased as souvenirs for macramé-style wall-hangings.

Japan

With greater emphasis on the braids that are used to create the knots, Japanese knotting (also known as *hanamusubi*) tends to focus on individual knots.

Types of Knots

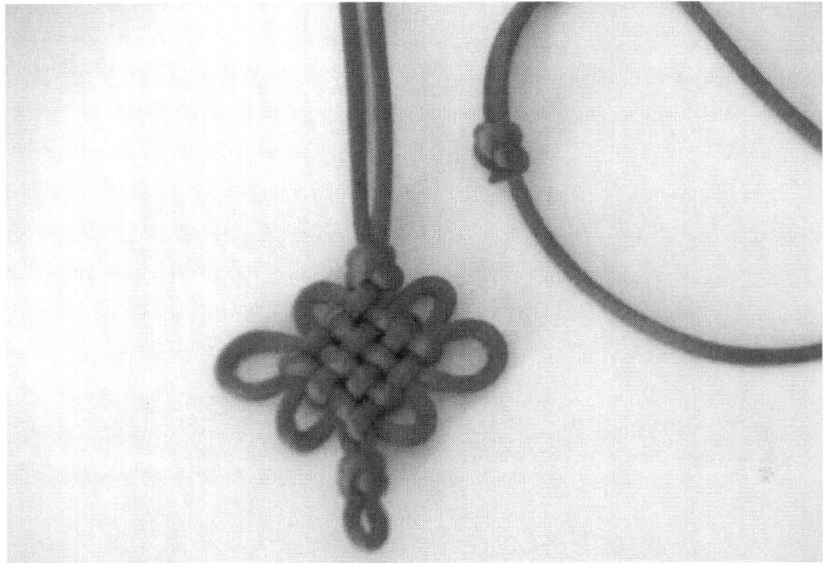

Figure: *A 4-row Pan Chang knot with cross knots*

Lydia Chen lists 11 basic types of Chinese decorative knotwork in her first book. More complex knots are then constructed from repeating or combining basic knots. They are:

Name	*Alternate Names*
Cloverleaf Knot	4 Flower Knot, Dragonfly Knot, Ginger Knot (Korean)
Round Brocade Knot	6 Flower Knot
Chinese Button Knot	Knife Lanyard Knot, Bosun Whistle Knot
Double Connection Knot	Matthew Walker knot
Double Coin Knot	Carrick Bend, Josephine Knot
Sauvastika Knot	Agemaki (Japanese)
Cross Knot	Friendship knot, Japanese crown knot
Square Knot	
Plafond Knot	Spectacle/Glasses Knot (Korean), Caisson Ceiling Knot
Pan Chang Knot	Coil Knot, Temple Knot, Chrysanthemum Knot (Korean), 2x2 Mystic Knot
Good Luck Knot	

One major characteristic of decorative knotwork is that all the knots are tied using one piece of thread, which is usually about one metre in length. However, finished knots look identical from both the front and back. They can come in a variety of colours such as; gold, green, blue or black, though the most commonly used colour is red. This is because it symbolizes good luck and prosperity.

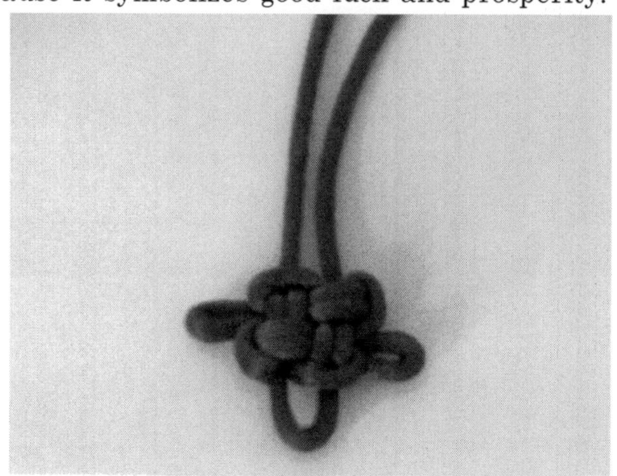

Figure: *An example of the "good luck" knot*

There are many different shapes of Chinese knots, the most common being butterflies, flowers, birds, dragons, fish, and even shoes. Culturally they were expected to ward off evil spirits similar to bagua mirrors or act as good-luck charms for Chinese marriages.

Modern Adaptations

In February 2008, Corra Liew from Malaysia was seeking possibilities outside traditional wire jewelry making techniques. She developed jewelry based on Chinese knotting made from wire. She calls the technique Wired Chinese Knot.

Other

Chinese knot also refers to a game in which the players hold their arms together in a complex pattern, while a bystander tries to give them directions to untie their arms.

4

Machine Embroidery

Machine embroidery is an embroidery process whereby a sewing machine or embroidery machine is used to create patterns on textiles. It is used commercially in product branding, corporate advertising, and uniform adornment. Hobbyists also machine embroider for personal sewing and craft projects.

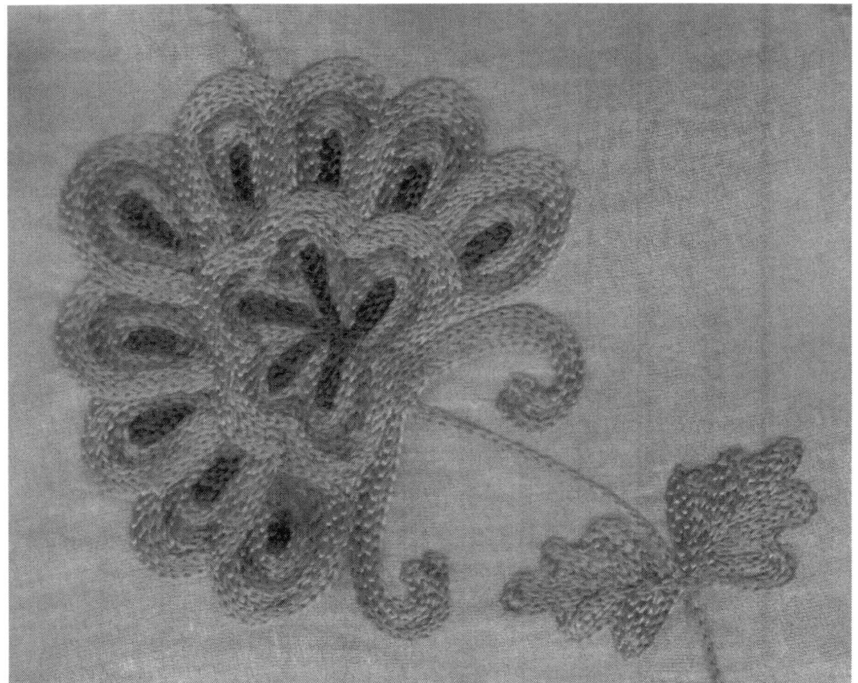

Figure: *Commercial machine embroidery in chain stitch on a voile curtain, China, early 21st century.*

There are multiple types of machine embroidery. These include *free-motion sewing machine embroidery*, this uses a basic zigzag sewing machine. Much commercial embroidery is still done with *link stitch embroidery* the patterns may be manually or automatically controlled. More modern *computerized machine embroidery*, uses an embroidery machine or sewing/embroidery machine that is controlled with a computer that will embroider stored patterns, these may have multiple heads and threads

Free-Motion Machine Embroidery

In free-motion machine embroidery, embroidered designs are created by using a basic zigzag sewing machine. As it is used primarily for tailoring, this type of machine lacks the automated features of a specialised machine.

To create free-motion machine embroidery, the embroiderer runs the machine and skillfully moves tightly hooped fabric under the needle to create a design. The operator lowers or covers the "feed dogs" or machine teeth and moves the fabric manually. The operator develops the embroidery manually, using the machine's settings for running stitch and fancier built-in stitches. In this way, the stitches form an image onto a piece of fabric. An embroiderer can produce a filled-in effect by sewing many parallel rows of straight stitching. A machine's zigzag stitch can create thicker lines within a design or be used to create a border. Many quilters and fabric artists use a process called thread drawing (or thread painting) to create embellishments on their projects or to create textile art.

Free-motion machine embroidery can be time-consuming. Since a standard sewing machine has only one needle, the operator must stop and re-thread the machine manually for each subsequent colour in a multi-colour design. He or she must also manually trim and clean up loose or connecting threads after the design is completed.

As this is a manual process rather than a digital reproduction, any pattern created using free-motion machine embroidery is unique and cannot be exactly reproduced, unlike with computerized embroidery.

With the advent of computerized machine embroidery, the main use of manual machine embroidery is in fibre art and quilting projects. Though some manufacturers still use manual embroidery to embellish garments, many prefer computerized embroidery's ease and reduced costs.

Computerized Machine Embroidery

Most modern embroidery machines are computer controlled and specifically engineered for embroidery. Industrial and commercial embroidery machines and combination sewing-embroidery machines have a hooping or framing system that holds the framed area of fabric taut under the sewing needle and moves it automatically to create a design from a pre-programmed digital embroidery pattern.

Depending on its capabilities, the machine will require varying degrees of user input to read and sew embroidery designs. Sewing-embroidery machines generally have only one needle and require the user to change thread colours during the embroidery process. Multi-needle industrial machines are generally threaded prior to running the design and do not require re-threading. These machines require the user to input the correct colour change sequence before beginning to embroider. Some can trim and change colours automatically.

A multi-needle machine may consist of multiple sewing heads, each of which can sew the same design onto a separate garment concurrently. Such a machine might have 20 or more heads, each consisting of 15 or more needles. A head is usually capable of producing many special fabric effects, including satin stitch embroidery, chain stitch embroidery, sequins, appliqué, and cutwork.

Before computers were affordable, most embroidery was completed by punching designs on paper tape that then ran through an embroidery machine. One error could ruin an entire design, forcing the creator to start over.

In 1980, Wilcom introduced the first computer graphics embroidery design system to run on a minicomputer. Melco, an international distribution network formed by Randal Melton and Bill Childs, created the first embroidery sample head for use with large Schiffli looms. These looms spanned several feet across and produced lace patches and large embroidery patterns. The sample head allowed embroiderers to avoid manually sewing the design sample and saved production time. Subsequently, it became the first computerized embroidery machine marketed to home sewers.

The economic conditions of the Reagan years, coupled with tax incentives for home businesses, helped propel Melco to the top of the market. At the Show of the Americas in 1980, Melco unveiled the Digitrac, a digitizing system for embroidery machines. The digitized design was composed at six times the size of the embroidered final product. The Digitrac consisted of a small computer, similar in size to a BlackBerry, mounted on an X and Y axis on a large white board. It sold for $30,000.

The original single-needle sample head sold for $10,000 and included a 1" paper-tape reader and 2 fonts. The digitizer marked common points in the design to create elaborate fill and satin stitch combinations.

Melco patented the ability to sew circles with a satin stitch, as well as arched lettering generated from a keyboard. An operator digitized the design using similar techniques to punching, transferring the results to a 1" paper tape or later to a floppy disk.

This design would then be run on the embroidery machine, which stitched out the pattern. Wilcom enhanced this technology in 1982 with the introduction of the first multi-user system, which allowed more than one person to work on the embroidery process, streamlining production times.

Brother Industries entered the embroidery industry after several computerized embroidery companies contracted it to provide sewing heads. Later, the Japanese company Tajima provided sewing heads that were capable of using multiple threads. Singer failed to remain competitive during this time. Melco was acquired by Saurer in 1989.

The major embroidery machine companies eventually adapted their commercial systems and marketed them to companies such as Janome for home use.

Since the late 1990s, computerized machine embroidery has grown in popularity as costs have fallen for computers, software, and embroidery machines. Many machine manufacturers sell their own lines of embroidery patterns. In addition, many individuals and independent companies also sell embroidery designs, and there are free designs available on the internet.

The Computerized Machine Embroidery Process

The basic steps for creating embroidery with a computerized embroidery machine are as follows:

- purchase or create a digitized embroidery design file
- edit the design and/or combine with other designs (optional)
- load the final design file into the embroidery machine
- stabilize the fabric and place it in the machine
- start and monitor the embroidery machine

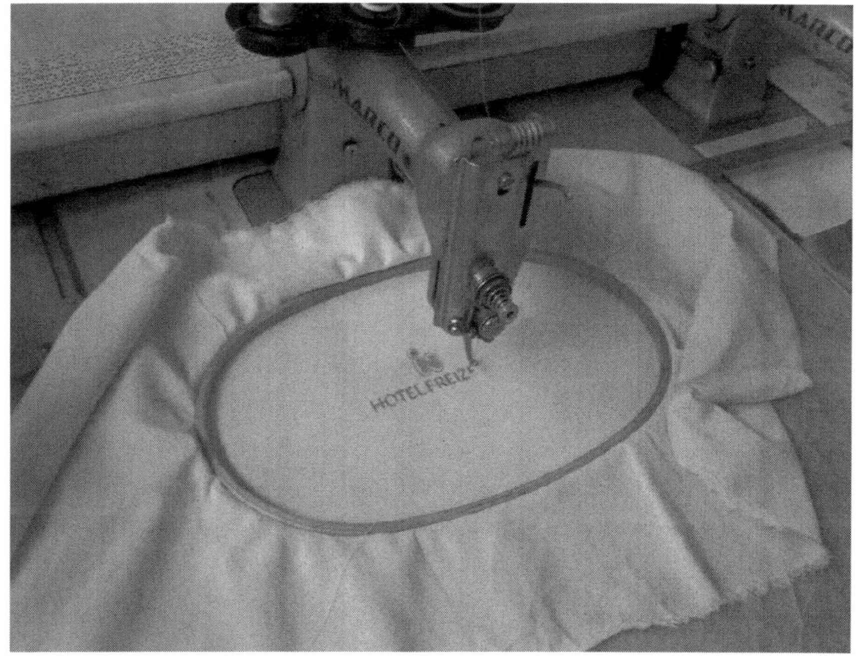

Figure: *Machine embroidery in progress.*

Design Files

Digitized embroidery design files can be either purchased or created with industry-specific embroidery digitizing software. Embroidery file formats broadly fall into two categories. The first, source formats, are specific to the software used to create the design. For these formats, the digitizer keeps the original file for the purposes of editing. The second, machine formats, are specific to a particular brand of embroidery machine. Here, the files are available for use with particular embroidery machines and are not easily edited or scaled.

Embroidery machines generally have one or more machine formats specific to their brand. However, some formats such as Tajima's .dst, Melco's .exp/.cnd and Barudan's .fdr have become so prevalent that they have effectively become industry standards and are often supported by machines built by rival companies.

Machine formats generally contain primarily stitch data (offsets) and machine functions (trims, jumps, etc.) and are thus not easily scaled or edited without extensive manual work.

Many embroidery designs can be downloaded in popular machine formats from embroidery web sites. However, since not all designs are available for every machine's specific format, some machine embroiderers use conversion programs to convert from one machine's format file to another, with various degrees of reliability.

A person who creates a design is known as an embroidery digitizer or puncher. A digitizer uses software to create an object-based embroidery design, which can be easily reshaped and edited. These files retain important information such as object outlines, thread colours, and original artwork used to punch the designs. When the file is converted to a stitch file, it loses much of this information, rendering editing difficult or impossible.

Software vendors often advertise auto-punching or auto-digitizing capabilities. However, if high quality embroidery is essential, then industry experts highly recommend either purchasing solid designs from reputable digitizers or obtaining training on solid digitization techniques.

Editing Designs

Once a design has been digitized, an embroiderer can use software to edit it or combine it with other designs. Most embroidery programs allow the user to rotate, scale, move, stretch, distort, split, crop, or duplicate the design in an endless pattern. Most software allows the user to add text quickly and easily. Often the colours of the design can be changed, made monochrome, or re-sorted. More sophisticated packages allow the user to edit, add, or remove individual stitches. Some embroidery machines have rudimentary built-in design editing features.

Loading the Design

After editing the final design, the file is loaded into the embroidery machine. Different machines require different formats that are proprietary to that company. Common design file formats for the home and hobby market include .ART, .HUS, .JEF, .PES, .SEW, and .VIP. Embroidery patterns can be transferred to the computerized embroidery machines through cables, CDs, floppy disks, USB interfaces, or special cards that resemble flash or compact cards.

File Type/Extension	*Company/Machine Compatibility*
.ART	Bernina artista, OESD
.ASD	Melco
.CND	Melco condensed
.CSD	POEM, Singer EU, Viking Huskygram

Contd...

File Type/Extension	*Company/Machine Compatibility*
.DST	Tajima
.EMB	
.EMD	Elna Expressive
.EXP	Bernina, Melco
.GNC	Great Notions Condensed
.HUS	Viking Husqvarna
.JEF/.JEF+	Janome, New Home
.OEF	OESD Condensed
.PCD, .PCS, .PCQ	Pfaff
.PEC, .PEL, .PEM, .PES	Baby Lock, Bernina Deco, Brother, Simplicity
.PHB, .PHC	Baby Lock, Bernina Deco, Brother
.SEW	Elna, Janome, New Home, Kenmore
.SHV	Viking Husqvarna
.STI	Toyota/Data Stitch
.STX	Toyota/Data Stitch
.VIP	VIP Customizing
.VP3	Pfaff
.XXX	Singer, Compucon

Stabilizing the Fabric

To prevent wrinkles and other problems, the fabric must be stabilized. The method of stabilizing depends on the type of machine, the fabric type, and the design density. For example, knits and large designs typically require firm stabilization. There are many methods for stabilizing fabric, but most often one or more additional pieces of material called stabilizers or interfacing are added beneath or on top of the fabric, or both. Stabilizer types include cut-away, tear-away, vinyl, nylon, water-soluble, heat-n-gone, peel and stick, and open mesh, sometimes in various combinations.

For smaller embroidered items, the fabric is placed in a hoop, which is attached to the machine. A mechanism called an arm moves the hoop under the needle.

Embroidering the Design

Finally, the embroidery machine is started and monitored. For commercial machines, this process is more automated than for the home machines. Many designs require more than one colour and may involve additional processing for appliqués, foam, or other special effects. Since home machines have only one needle, every colour change requires the user to cut the thread and change the colour manually. In addition, most designs have one or more jumps that need to be cut. Depending on the quality and size of the design, sewing a design file can require anywhere from a few minutes to over an hour

Embroidery Machines

Not all machines are solely used for embroidery; some are also used for sewing. Some of the more advanced features becoming available include a large colour touchscreen, a USB interface, auto threading, built-in design editing software, embroidery adviser software, and design file storage systems. Commercial embroidery machines can be purchased with a set number of heads (1, 2, 3, 4, 6, 12, 15,18 or more colours). Industrial embroidery machines are available with 1 to 56 heads.

Commercial and Contract Embroidery Factories

Factories can have a few small machines or many large machines, or any combination of machines. Contract embroidery is done on goods that the customer supplies to the embroidery house and is limited to the trade. A company offering contract embroidery sews designs onto wearable items for brokers, other embroiderers, speciality firms, and screen printers at a wholesale rates. The customer of a contract embroiderer usually supplies the items to the factory and only pays for the embroidery service.

Commercial embroiderers offer their services to the public and supply the wearable items, and know the latest designs available in market and top of foil.

Other Supplies

Almost any type of fabric can be embroidered, given the proper stabilizer. Base materials include paper, fabric, and lightweight balsa wood.

Machine embroidery commonly uses polyester, rayon, or metallic embroidery thread, though other thread types are available. 40 wt thread is the most commonly used embroidery thread weight. Bobbin thread is usually either 60 wt or 90 wt. The quality of thread used can greatly affect the number of thread breaks and other embroidery problems. Polyester thread is generally more colour-safe and durable. High quality embroidery thread is produced by Madeira and Robison-Anton.

Other associated costs are thread, stabilizer, purchased designs, needles, bobbins, and other miscellaneous tools and supplies.

Embroidery Glossary

Appliqué: French term meaning applying, usually by sewing, one piece of fabric to the surface of another. A cut piece of material stitched to another adds dimension and texture and reduces the stitch count.

Backer/Stabilizer: Backing and stabilizer are often used interchangeably to refer to materials, generally non-woven textiles, which are placed inside or under the item to be embroidered.

The backing provides support and stability to the garment which will improve the quality of the finished embroidered product. Backings come primarily in two types: cutaway and tear-away. With cutaway, the excess backing is cut with a pair of scissors. With tear-away, the excess is torn away after the item is embroidered. Additional types of stabilizer can be dissolved by water or heat.

Bobbin: A small spool of thread inside the rotary hook housing of a sewing machine. The bobbin thread forms the stitches on the underside of the garment. The bobbin on an embroidery machine works in the same manner and for the same purpose as on a standard sewing machine.

Digitize: The computerized technique of turning a design image into an embroidery program. Special software is used to create plotting commands for the embroidery machine. The commands are transferred to the machine's logic head by a designated embroidery language.

Fill Stitch: Fill stitches are a series of running stitches sewn closely together to form broad areas of embroidery with varying patterns and stitch directions.

Hoop: A clamping device used to hold the backing and fabric in place in the machine.

Running Stitch: One straight line of stitches, often used for fine details, outlining, and underlay.

Satin Stitch: Also known as zigzag stitch, a satin stitch is a line, border or edge produced by thread being alternately stitched to either side of a baseline. Satin stitches are generally limited to a maximum of 1/2" in stitch length before some alternate technique must be used, such as split stitching or fill stitching.

Underlay: A stabilizing pattern of embroidery which, if used, precedes the main body of satin or fill stitching. It consists of one or a combination of running stitches for centreing, edging, paralleling, or zigzagging the design area.

Styles

Assisi

Assisi embroidery is a form of counted-thread embroidery based on an ancient Italian needlework tradition in which the background is filled with embroidery stitches and the main motifs are outlined but not stitched. The name is derived from the Italian town of Assisi where the modern form of the craft originated.

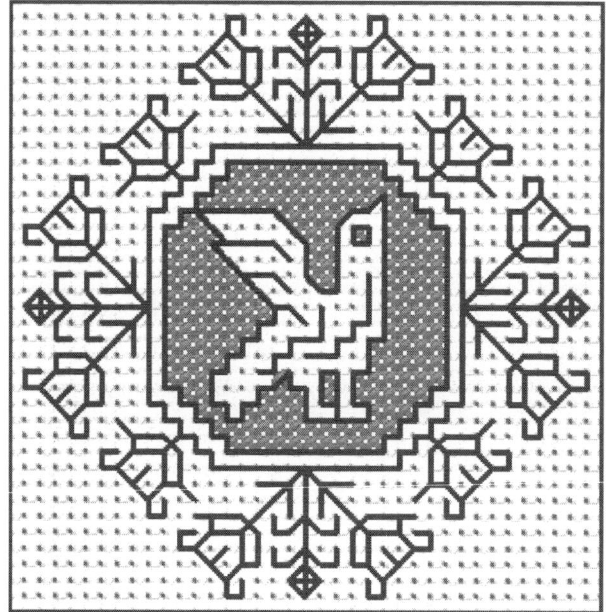

Figure: *Pattern for a simple Assisi bird motif*

Description of the Technique

Assisi work uses a method known as voiding in which cross-stitch fills the background while the motif itself is left blank. Holbein stitch, a style of linear blackwork, is used to outline and emphasize the motif and to create surrounding decorative scrollwork.

Traditionally, Assisi embroidery was rarely executed in cross-stitch but was most often in long-armed cross-stitch. Examples employing other stitches, such as Italian cross-stitch and Algerian plait stitch, are also known. The colours of thread used were red, blue, green or gold for the background and black or brown for the outlines. Traditional motifs were largely heraldic, especially heraldic beasts, and typically featured symmetrically arranged pairs of animals and birds surrounded by ornate filigree borders.

In the oldest pieces, the figures were drawn freehand on the fabric and surrounded with Holbein stitch. The background, often cream linen, was filled as well as possible. For more modern pieces the pattern was constructed carefully on a paper grid in much the same way as counted cross-stitch patterns are created. Today Assisi embroidery is nearly always done this way.

History

Historically, Italy has had a long tradition of bright and colourful embroidery. In the thirteenth and fourteenth centuries monastic embroideries developed a simpler style where designs and motifs were voided on fine linen cloth with the outlines and background embroidered in coloured silk. Motifs were strongly influenced by traditional designs of bird or animal pairs surrounded by elaborate scrollwork. These early articles were most often used for religious purposes, e.g., altar cloths and chasubles.

By the sixteenth century Assisi work had become more popular and employed a wider range of motifs, many based on Renaissance imagery of satyrs, demons and ancient mythical creatures.

In the eighteenth and nineteenth centuries, however, this form of embroidery fell into decline and many of the designs and motifs were lost. It was only at the turn of the twentieth century that the practice was revived in the Italian town of Assisi from which this form of embroidery gets its name. St. Anne's Convent in October 1902 established the Laboratorio Ricreativo Festivo Femminile San Francesco di Assisi. The aim of this handicrafts workshop was to revive traditional local handicrafts and provide employment to poor women to supplement their incomes. This cottage industry flourished and these designs using the counted thread technique quickly spread throughout Italy, Europe and further abroad.

Modern Assisi Work

A modern version of Assisi embroidery has been evolving in the twenty-first century. Many different colours and patterns are used for the background, and the motifs are extremely varied. However, the revived traditional version is still practised in the town of Assisi where one can see the local women sitting in front of their houses and embroidering Assisi work items for the local co-operative embroidery shop.

Bargello

Bargello is a type of needlepoint embroidery consisting of upright flat stitches laid in a mathematical pattern to create motifs. The name originates from a series of chairs found in the Bargello palace in Florence, which have a "flame stitch" pattern.

Traditionally, Bargello was stitched in wool on canvas. Embroidery done this way is remarkably durable. It is well suited for use on pillows, upholstery and even carpets, but not for clothing. In most traditional pieces, all stitches are vertical with stitches going over two or more threads.

Traditional designs are very colourful, and use many hues of one colour, which produces intricate shading effects.

The patterns are naturally geometric, but can also resemble very stylised flowers or fruits. Bargello is considered particularly challenging, as it requires very precise counting of squares for the mathematical pattern connected with the various motifs to accurately execute designs.

Alternate Names

A number of alternative names are used by different scholars, including:

- Florentine Work - After the fact that the Bargello Museum is in Florence.
- Hungarian Point (*punto unghero*) - In Italian, Bargello is known as "Hungarian Point" (Williams 1967: 5, Petschek 1997), indicating that the Florentines believed the technique originated in Hungary. However, English embroidery vocabulary also includes a diamond shaped stitch called the Hungarian Point, so few English language books use this term to refer to Bargello.
- Flame Stitch (*fiamma*) - A type of Bargello motif in which zig-zag or flames are created. The chairs in the Bargello museum do use flame stitch motifs, but curved motifs are also common. These curved Bargello motifs would normally not be "flame stitch", but would be called *Bargello*.

Because of the potential for confusion, most books written in English refer to the technique simply as "Bargello" (Williams 1969, Kaestner 1972, Petscheck 1997).

History

As with many traditional crafts, the origins of Bargello are not well documented. Although early examples are from the Bargello Museum in Florence, there does exist documentation that a Hungarian connection is possible. For one thing, the Bargello Museum inventory identifies the chairs in its inventory as "17th century with backs and seats done in *punto unghero* (Hungarian Point)." (Williams, 1967:5). In the 18th century, Queen Maria Teresa of Hungary stitched Bargello and her work has been preserved in the Hungarian National Museum

Petschek (1997:7) also cites additional "legends" of Hungarian noblewomen practicing the craft, including a Hungarian princess marrying into the de Medici family, and a princess Jadwiga (Hedwig) of Hungary who married into the Jagie[33]o dynasty of Poland. It is unknown if those were distinct developments or if they influenced each other. Both Bargello and Hungarian Point tend to be colourful and use many hues of one colour, which produces intricate shading effects. The patterns are naturally geometric, but can also resemble very stylized flowers or fruits.

Bargello Technique

Bargello refers not just a stitching technique, but also to motifs created by the change of colours in the stitches. This section describes the vertical stitch, and how it is combined with colour and "stepping" to create different motifs.

Vertical Stitches

Most agree that traditional Bargello pieces incorporate a series of all vertical stitches (vs. diagonal stitches). The basic unit is usually a vertical stitch of four threads, but other heights are possible. Some Bargello pieces use only one height of stitch, but even the earliest pieces (such as chairs in the Bargello museum) combine different heights of stitches.

Stepping

Bargello patterns are formed when vertical stitches are stepped or offset vertically, usually by two threads (i.e., halfway down a unit of four threads). The patterns in the steps combined with colour changes determines how the overall pattern will emerge.

Flame (Sharp) vs. Curved Motifs

If vertical stitches are stepped down quickly, the design forms sharp points or zig-zags. This type of Bargello motif is often known as “flame stitch”. Flame stitch can be found on the Bargello Museum chairs. If steps are gradual, then the design will appear to be curved. Traditional curved Bargello motifs include medallions and ribbons.

Examples of Bargello Motifs

There are many identified motifs possible (Williams 1967), but some common ones include:

Flame Zig Zag (Sharp)

Stitches step sharply across the design.

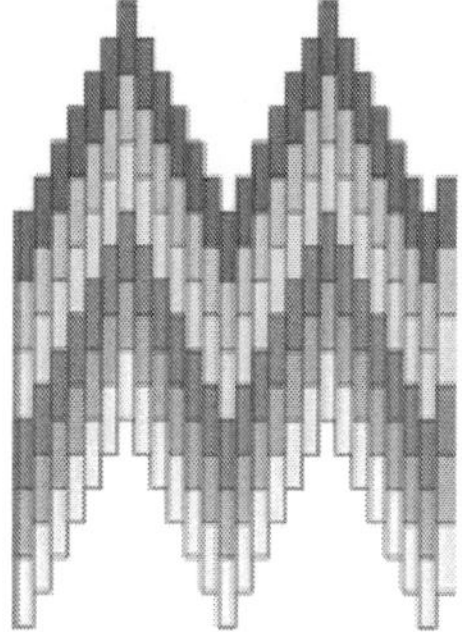

Figure: *Example of a flame stitch motif. Image created and licensed by Elizabeth Pyatt.*

Diamonds (Sharp)

Stitches step sharply across the designs and colour changes cause diamonds to appear.

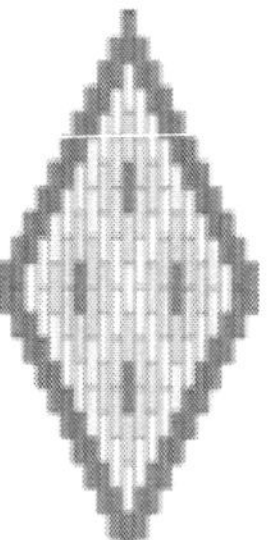

Figure: *Example of diamond motif formed with Bargello stitches. Image created and licensed by Elizabeth Pyatt.*

Ribbons (Curved)

Stitches are gradually stepped in different colours.

Medallions (Curved)

Stitches are gradually stepped and colour changes cause spheres or medallions to appear.

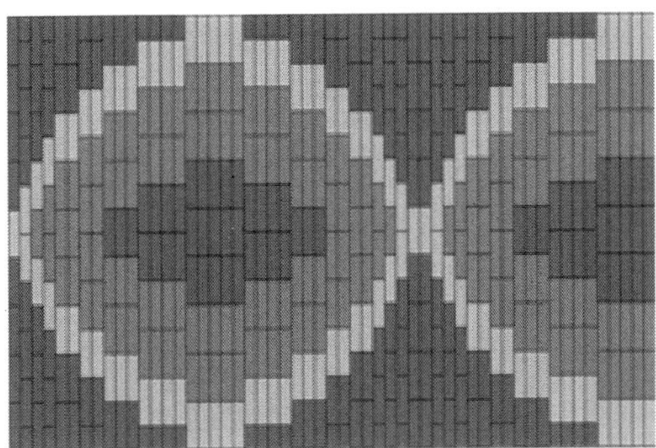

Figure: *Example Bargello Medallion design. Image created and licensed by Elizabeth Pyatt.*

Modern Day Bargello

Since the revival of Bargello in the 1960s, the technique has evolved in different directions. Although traditional Bargello is still stitched, modern designers have expanded the repertoire of design possibilities.

Four-Way and Eight-Way Bargello

Traditional Bargello is executed with just a vertical stitch in one direction, but Dorothy Kaestner (1972) created a style of Bargello called four-way Bargello. In this technique, the canvas is first divided into diagonally into quarters. Then the same motif is worked in horizontal stitches in two opposite areas, and vertical stitches in the remaining two areas. The resulting design frequently resembles a kaleidoscope effect.

Kaestner describes the origin of the technique:

My first piece of four-way Bargello was started approximately ten years ago [in the early 1960s]. I placed a mirror on a Bargello design in a way that showed me how it would look if I mitered [turned] a corner. This intrigued me so much, I graphed a design starting in the centre and mitering all four corners.

Some examples include

- *Cathy Decker -*
- *Stan Taylor -*
- *Stan Taylor -*

This concept has been expanded to eight-way Bargello, or Bargello stitches in eight directions (horizontal stitches, vertical stitches and diagonal stitches), by designers including Susan Kerndt:

- *Kaleidoscope* (Eight Way Bargello by Susan Kerndt)
- *Ice Crystals* (Eight Way Bargello by Susan Kerndt)

The two links above are broken try the alternative link below for samples of Susan Kerndt's work, including Kaleidoscope and Ice Crystals:

- "Sue Kerndt" -

Bargello Band Samplers

Designers of band samplers may include a band of a Bargello motif among other sampler stitches. Unlike traditional Bargello, these bands are stitched with the same stranded cotton, silk or linen embroidery thread used in band samplers.

- *Laura's Sampler (American Needlepoint Guild)* - first horizontal band is a Bargello motif
- *Lavendar Hearts* by Thea Dueck - bottom band is a Bargello motif

Bargello Quilts

In addition to Bargello embroidery, there are now Bargello quilts in which the patterns used in Bargello embroidery are constructed with strips of fabric of the same height but different widths.

In Bargello quilting, long strips of fabric are sewn together along their long sides. Then the first and last strip are sewn together, forming a loop. The loop is laid flat on a table, and then cut vertically (in the opposite direction from how the strips were sewn together) to make many narrow loops. The quilter then opens the loops by pulling out the stitching between two pieces of fabric, making a long, flat strip. Finally, all the strips are sewn together.

By opening the loops in between different pieces of fabric (for instance, between the first and second piece on one loop, then the second and third piece on the next loop), the artist can make the colours of the quilt appear to shift and wave. Slicing the loops very narrowly makes the waving and movement appear sharp and fast; cutting wide loops creates more gentle movement in the quilt.

Berlin Work

Berlin wool work is a style of embroidery similar to today's needlepoint. It was typically executed with wool yarn on canvas. It is usually worked in a single stitch, such as cross stitch or tent stitch although *Beeton's book of Needlework* (1870) describes 15 different stitches for use in Berlin work. It was traditionally stitched in many colours and hues, producing intricate three-dimensional looks by careful shading.

The design of such embroidery was made possible by the great progresses made in dyeing in the 1830s, especially by the discovery of aniline dyes which produced bright colours.

This kind of work created very durable and long-lived pieces of embroidery that could be used as furniture covers, cushions, bags, or even on clothing.

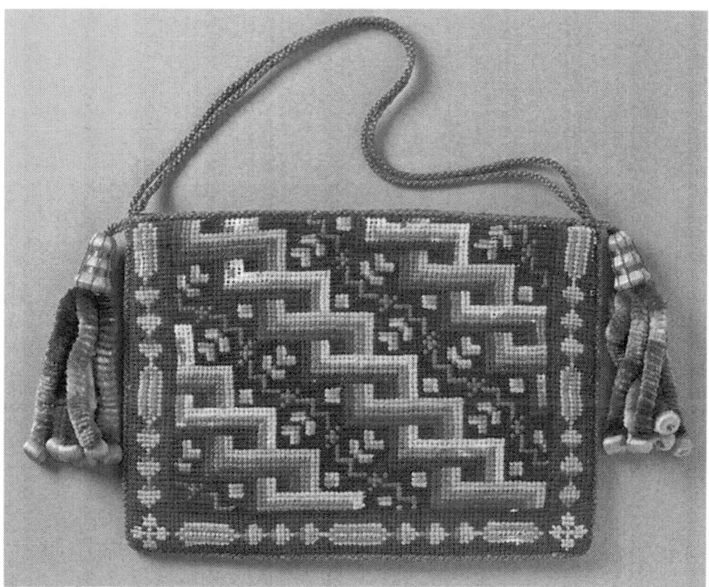

Figure: *Woman's purse, Berlin wool work, Europe, cotton canvas with wool needlepoint, silk-braided cord, and silk chenille tassels, c.* ***1840****, Los Angeles County Museum of Art*

History

Berlin wool work patterns were first published in Berlin, Germany, early in the 19th century. The first Berlin wool patterns were printed in black and white on grid paper and then hand-coloured. Previously, the stitcher was expected to draw the outlines on the canvas and then stitch following the colours on the pattern.

Counted stitch patterns on charted paper, similar to modern cross-stitch patterns, made it easier to execute the designs, because there was no need for translating the patterns into actual wool colours by the stitchers themselves. They were published mostly as single sheets which made them affordable for the masses.

Soon they were exported to Britain and the USA, where "Berlin work" became all the rage. Indeed, *Berlin work* became practically synonymous with *canvas work*. In Britain, Berlin work received a further boost through the Great Exhibition of 1851, and by the advent of ladies' magazines such as *The Englishwoman's Domestic Magazine.*

The popularity of Berlin work was due largely to the fact that, for the first time in history, a fairly large number of women had leisure time to devote to needlework. Subjects to be embroidered were influenced by Victorian Romanticism and included floral designs, Victorian paintings, biblical or allegorical motifs, and quotations such as "Home Sweet Home" or "Faith, Hope, Love".

In the late 1880s, the demand for Berlin wool work decreased dramatically, largely because the tastes had changed, but Berlin work publishers failed to accommodate new tastes. Other, less opulent styles of embroidery became more popular, such as the art needlework advocated by William Morris and his Arts and Crafts movement.

Berlin Wool Work Today

Original charted Berlin wool work patterns remain available in a number of books. Berlin wool work designs are still popular in trammed needlepoint canvases, printed canvas needlepoint kits and can be found as digitized charts on needlework enthusiasts' websites.

Blackwork

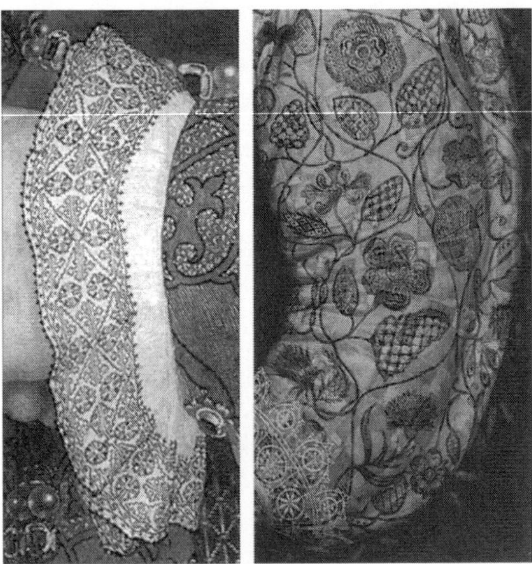

Figure: *Counted stitch Blackwork, 1530s (left), and free stitch Blackwork, 1590s (right).*

Blackwork is a form of embroidery using black thread. Sometimes it is counted-thread embroidery which is usually stitched on even-weave fabric. Any black thread can be used, but firmly twisted threads give a better look than embroidery floss. Traditionally blackwork is stitched in silk thread on white or off-white linen or cotton fabric. Sometimes metallic threads or coloured threads are used for accents.

Scarletwork is like blackwork, except it is sewn with red thread.

Technique

The stitches used for counted thread blackwork are double running or holbein stitch, *backstitch*, and sometimes *stem stitch*. Historically it was done on plain weave fabric. Modern stitchers often use even weave fabric made especially for counted thread work.

Historically, there are three common styles of blackwork:

- In the earliest blackwork, counted stitches are worked to make a geometric or small floral pattern. Most modern blackwork is in this style, especially the commercially produced patterns that are marketed for hobby stitchers.
- Later blackwork features large designs of flowers, fruit, and other patterns connected by curvilinear stems. These are frequently not counted thread work and are outlined with stem stitch, and the outlined patterns are filled with geometric counted designs.
- In the third style of blackwork, the outlined patterns are "shaded" with random stitches called *seed stitches*. This style of blackwork imitates etchings or woodcuts.

History

Historically, blackwork was used on shirts and chemises or smocks in England from the time of Henry VIII. The common name "Spanish work" was based on the belief that Catherine of Aragon brought many blackwork garments with her from Spain, and portraits of the later 15th and early 16th centuries show black embroidery or other trim on Spanish chemises. Black embroidery was known in England before 1500. Geoffrey Chaucer in the Canterbury Tales describes the clothing of the miller's wife, Alison: "Of white, too, was the dainty smock she wore, embroidered at the collar all about with coal-black silk, alike within and out."

Blackwork in silk on linen was the most common domestic embroidery technique for clothing (shirts, smocks, sleeves, ruffs, and caps) and for household items such as cushion covers throughout the reign of Elizabeth I, but it lost its popularity by the 17th century.

Historic blackwork embroidery is rare to find well-preserved, as the iron-based dye used was corrosive to the thread, and there are currently no conservation techniques that can stop the decay. Black embroidery silk from outside England, such as Spain, contained less iron in the black dye and so blackwork worked using non-English silk tends to survive in better condition.

Modern Blackwork

Blackwork remains popular. Common subjects among hobbyists include chessboards, maps, Tudor houses, roses and cats. Much of the success of a blackwork design depends on how tone values are translated into stitches.

Today, the term "Blackwork" is used to refer to the technique, rather than the colour combination.

Broderie Anglaise

Broderie anglaise (French, "English embroidery") is a whitework needlework technique incorporating features of embroidery, cutwork and needle lace that became associated with England, due to its popularity there in the 19th century.

History and Technique

Broderie anglaise is characterized by patterns composed of round or oval holes which are cut out of the fabric, called *eyelets,* which are bound with overcast or buttonhole stitches. The patterns, often depicting flowers, leaves, vines, or stems, are further delineated by simple embroidery stitches made on the surrounding material. Later broderie anglaise also featured small patterns worked in satin stitch.

The technique originated in 16th century eastern Europe—probably in what is now the Czech Republic—but remains associated with England because of its popularity there during the 19th century. In the Victorian era, broderie anglaise typically had open areas in many sizes. Transfers were used first to lay out the design on the material. In some cases, the holes were punched out with an embroidery stiletto before finishing the edge; in other cases, the fabric was embroidered first, and the hole was cut afterwards, with scissors. Beginning in the 1870s, the designs and techniques of broderie anglaise could be copied by the Swiss hand-embroidery machine. Today, most broderie anglaise is created by machine.

Madeira work is a popular form of broderie anglaise associated with artisans on the island of Madeira, a Portuguese territory off the coast of Africa.

Fashion and Popular Culture

Broderie anglaise was extremely popular in England between 1840-1880 for women's underclothing and children's wear. The 1950s saw a resurgence in popularity, when it was frequently used to trim dresses and underwear. In 1959, Brigitte Bardot wore a dress of gingham and broderie anglaise for her wedding to Jacques Charrier.

In contemporary western fashion, it has been featured on a wide variety of modern garments such as shorts and even t-shirts. It has been characterized as "lace, but scaled-up" making it more robust and suited to daytime wear, and less associated with the fine, lacy look of lingerie.

Broderie Perse

Broderie perse (French for "Persian embroidery") is a style of appliqué embroidery which uses printed elements to create a scene on the background fabric. It was most popular in Europe in the 17th century, and probably travelled from India, as there are some earlier findings there. The technique could be considered an early form of puzzle piecing.

Broderie perse can be done with any printed fabric on any ground, but it originally was worked with Chintz type fabrics. Chintz typically has clearly defined, separated motifs, which were cut out and invisibly applied onto the ground fabric. The typical intention was to create a scene from the motifs, but the decoration could also be random. The resulting fabric was often made into bedspreads, either unlined for summer or quilted for winter. They were typically saved for special occasions, such as guest beds.

Candlewicking

Candlewicking is a form of whitework embroidery that traditionally uses an unbleached cotton thread on a piece of unbleached muslin. It gets its name from the nature of the soft spun cotton thread, which was braided then used to form the wick for candles. Motifs are created using a variety of traditional embroidery stitches as well as a tufted stitch. Subject matter is usually taken from nature - flowers, insects, pine trees, and so on, Other traditional motifs resemble Pennsylvania Dutch or Colonial American designs. Modern designs include coloured floss embroidery with the traditional white on white stitching. Loom-woven or machine-made candlewicks of the early 19th century are white bedcovers with designs created during the weaving process by raising loops over a small twig or tool. Contemporary candlewicking is most commonly used as a cushion cover.

Canvas Work

Canvas work is a type of embroidery in which yarn is stitched through a canvas or other foundation fabric. Canvas work is a form of counted-thread embroidery. Common types of canvas work include needlepoint, petit point, and bargello.

History

Early canvas work or needlepoint used tent, continental or basketweave stitches, with each stitch covering one canvas intersection. Bargello, first developed in Europe, uses colours and stitches across multiple canvas intersections to create motion and patterns. Modern methods have incorporated crewel and other embroidery stitches to add depth and differences not only by shading but by texture.

Contemporary Materials

Several types of embroidery canvas are available: single thread and double thread embroidery canvas are open even-weave meshes, with large spaces or holes to allow heavy threads to pass through without fraying. Aida cloth or Hardanger fabric can also be used for canvas work, and plastic canvas is used in craft projects.

Canvas is measured by the number of squares per inch or centimetre. In canvas work the stitches may completely cover the canvas. Newer methods will use the canvas as part of the pattern. Yarns vary from knitting yarns and tapestry wools to pure silk, synthetic, or metallic threads. Fine ribbons, plastic thread, raffia and string can also be used in canvas work.

Examples

A famous example of a large carpet worked in canvas work is the Bradford carpet which is on display in the Victoria and Albert Museum, London.

Celtic Cross Stitch

Celtic cross stitch is a style of cross-stitch embroidery which recreates Celtic art patterns typical of early medieval Insular art using contemporary cross-stitch techniques. Celtic cross stitch typically employs rich, deep colours, intricate geometrical patterns, spirals, interlacing patterns, knotwork, alphabets, animal forms and zoomorphic patterns, similar to the decorations found in the Book of Kells.

Although they share design inspirations, today's Celtic cross-stitch differs from the embroidery of the Celtic Revival of the late 19th and early 20th century which employed freehand surface embroidery stitches in line with the principles of the Arts and Crafts Movement. Celtic cross stitch embroideries are very much part of the heritage found in Scotland, Isle of Man and Ireland. These cross stitch patterns are used to decorate everyday items, such as cushion covers, wall tapestries and decorations, tea cozies, eyeglass covers and clothing.

Counted-Thread

Counted-thread embroidery is any embroidery in which the fabric threads are counted by the embroiderer before inserting the needle into the fabric. Evenweave fabric is usually used; it produces a symmetrical image as both warp and weft fabric threads are evenly spaced. The opposite of counted-thread embroidery is free embroidery.

Crewel

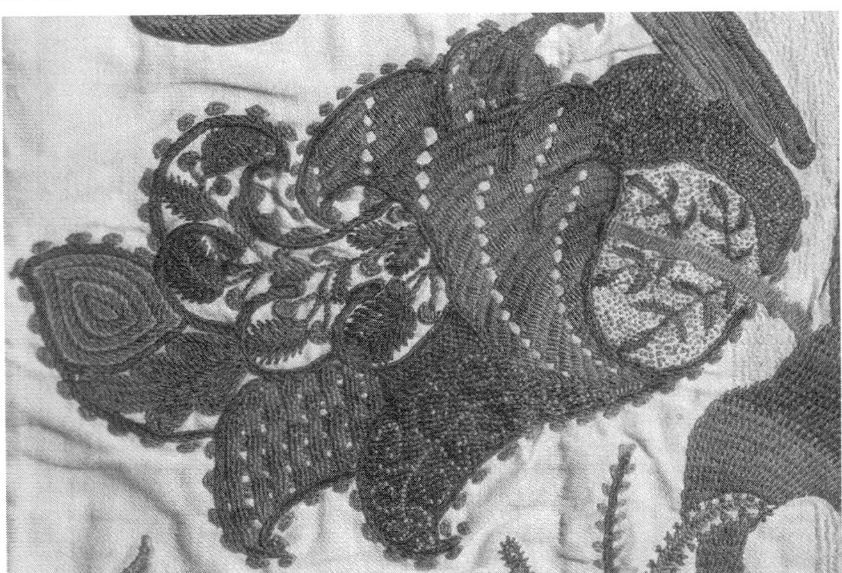

Figure: *Fanciful leaf in crewelwork, detail of a curtain, English, c. 1696. Victoria and Albert Museum T.166-1961.*

Crewel embroidery, or Crewelwork, is a decorative form of surface embroidery using wool and a variety of different embroidery stitches to follow a design outline applied to the fabric. The technique is at least a thousand years old. It was used in the Bayeux Tapestry, in Jacobean embroidery and in the Quaker Tapestry sewn in the 1980s.

The origin of the word crewel is unknown but is thought to come from an ancient word describing the curl in the staple, the single hair of the wool. Crewel wool has a long staple; it is fine and can be strongly twisted. Modern crewel wool is a fine, 2-ply or 1-ply yarn available in many different colours.

Description of the Technique

The crewel technique is not a counted-thread embroidery (like canvas work), but a style of free embroidery. It was in the 17th Century, its heyday, and now traditionally worked on a closely woven linen twill ground "Jacobean linen twill" fabric, typically linen or cotton. This linen is part of the design and many stitches allow the sight of the linen through and around the design. More recently commercially made crewel is being made on Matka silk, cotton velvet, rayon velvet, silk organza, net fabric and also jute. A firm fabric is required to support the weight of the stitching. Special crewel needles or [sewing needle] are required, with a wide body, large eye and a sharp point.

The outlines of the design to be worked are often screen printed onto the fabric or can be transferred to plain fabric using modern transfer pens, containing water soluble ink or air soluble ink, or iron-on designs applied using transfer sheets. The old fashioned "pinprick and chalk" or "prick and pounce" methods also work well. This is where the design outlines on paper are pricked with a needle to produce perforations along the lines. Powdered chalk or pounce material is then forced through the holes onto the fabric using a felt pad or stipple brush in order to replicate the design on the material.

Designs range from the traditional to more contemporary patterns. The traditional design styles are often referred to as Jacobean embroidery featuring highly stylized floral and animal designs with flowing vines and leaves.

Many different embroidery stitches are used in crewelwork to create a textured and colourful effect. Unlike silk or cotton embroidery threads, crewel wool is thicker and creates a raised, dimensional feel to the work. Some of the techniques and stitches include:

- Outlining stitches such as stem stitch, chain stitch and split stitch
- Satin stitches to create flat, filled areas within a design

- Couched stitches, where one thread is laid on the surface of the fabric and another thread is used to tie it down. Couching is often used to create a trellis effect within an area of the design.
- Seed stitches, applied randomly in an area to give a lightly shaded effect
- French knots are commonly used in floral and fruit motifs for additional texture
- Laid and Couched Work
- Long and Short "soft shading"

Crewel embroidery was, in the past, embroidered to create elaborate and expensive bed hangings and curtains. Now it is most often used to decorate cushions, curtains, clothing and wall hangings. Recently several other items such as Lamp Shades, Handbags, have been added to ever growing list of crewel home furnishings. A Tambour Work technique is also used for creating chain stitched rugs, and is sometimes referred to as crewel work.

Unlike canvas work, crewel embroidery requires the use of an embroidery hoop or frame on which the material is stretched taut and secured prior to stitching. This ensures an even amount of tension in the stitches, so that designs do not become distorted. Although nowadays, crewel and free embroidery is generally executed with a small portable hoop, early embroidery was executed on large free standing frames. Such free standing frames were common parlor furniture in most homes. The rectangular canvas mount could tilt and pivot over so that the needleworker could also access the back of the canvas with ease.

Cross-Stitch

Cross-stitch is a popular form of counted-thread embroidery in which X-shaped stitches in a tiled, raster-like pattern are used to form a picture. Cross-stitch is often executed on easily countable evenweave fabric called aida cloth. The stitcher counts the threads in each direction so that the stitches are of uniform size and appearance. This form of cross-stitch is also called counted cross-stitch in order to distinguish it from other forms of cross-stitch. Sometimes cross-stitch is done on designs printed on the fabric (stamped cross-stitch); the stitcher simply stitches over the printed pattern.

Fabrics used in cross-stitch include aida, linen, and mixed-content fabrics called 'evenweave'. All cross stitch fabrics are technically "evenweave", it refers to the fact that the fabric is woven to make sure that there are the same number of threads in an inch both left to right and top to bottom (vertically and horizontally). Fabrics are categorized by threads per inch (referred to as 'count'), which can range from 11 to 40 count. Aida fabric has a lower count because it is made with two threads grouped together for ease of stitching. Cross stitch projects are worked from a gridded pattern and can be used on any count fabric, the count of the fabric determines the size of the finished stitching.

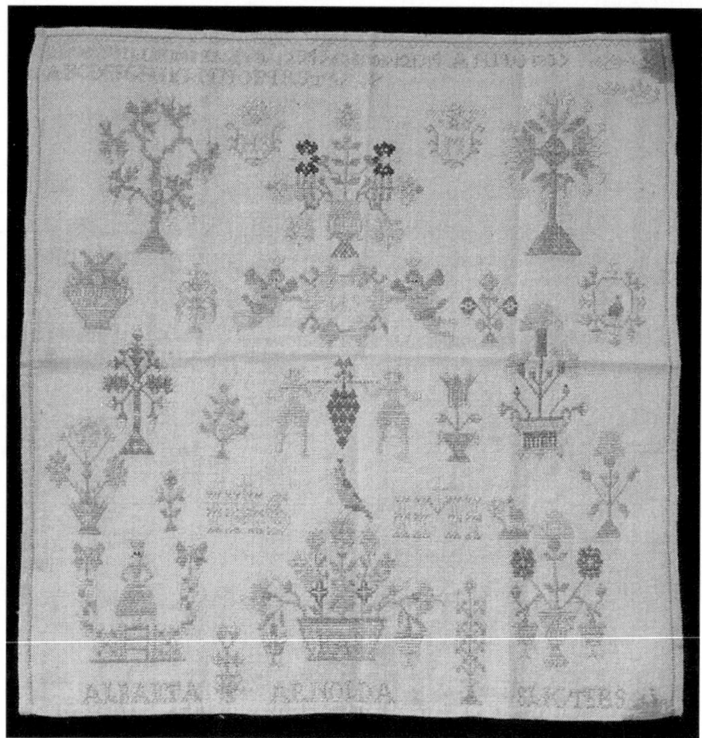

Figure: *Cross-stitch sampler, Germany*

History

Cross-stitch is one of the oldest forms of embroidery and can be found all over the world. Many folk museums show examples of clothing decorated with cross-stitch, especially from continental Europe and Asia. Two-dimensional (unshaded) cross-stitch in floral and geometric patterns, usually worked in black and red cotton floss on linen, is characteristic of folk embroidery in Eastern and Central Europe.

The cross stitch sampler is called that because it was generally stitched by a young girl to learn how to stitch and to record alphabet and other patterns to be used in her household sewing. These samples of her stitching could be referred back to over the years. Often, motifs and initials were stitched on household items to identify their owner, or simply to decorate the otherwise-plain cloth. In the United States, the earliest known cross-stitch sampler is currently housed at Pilgrim Hall in Plymouth, Massachusetts. The sampler was created by Loara Standish, daughter of Captain Myles Standish and pioneer of the Leviathan stitch, circa 1653.

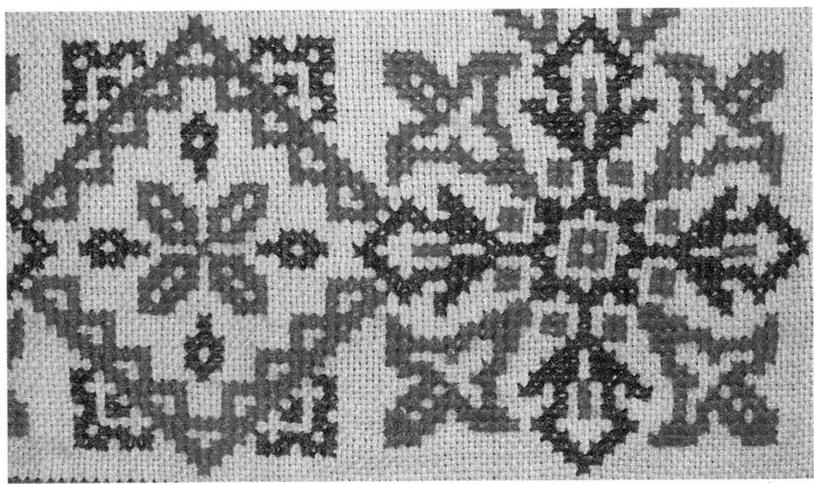

Figure: *Detail of floral border pattern in cotton. Tea cloth (small tablecloth), Hungary, mid-twentieth century*

Traditionally, cross-stitch was used to embellish items like household linens, tablecloths, dishcloths, and doilies (only a small portion of which would actually be embroidered, such as a border). Although there are many cross-stitchers who still employ it in this fashion, it is now increasingly popular to work the pattern on pieces of fabric and hang them on the wall for decoration. Cross stitch is also often used to make greeting cards, pillowtops, or as inserts for box tops, coasters and trivets.

Multicoloured, shaded, painting-like patterns as we know them today are a fairly modern development, deriving from similar shaded patterns of Berlin wool work of the mid-nineteenth century. Besides designs created expressly for cross stitch, there are software programs that convert a photograph or a fine art image into a chart suitable for stitching. One stunning example of this is in the cross stitched reproduction of the Sistene Chapel charted and stitched by Joanna Lopianowski-Roberts.

There are many cross-stitching "guilds" and groups across the United States and Europe which offer classes, collaborate on large projects, stitch for charity, and provide other ways for local cross-stitchers to get to know one another. Individually owned local needlework shops (LNS) often have stitching nights at their shops, or host weekend stitching retreats.

Today cotton floss is the most common embroidery thread. It is a thread made of mercerized cotton, composed of six strands that are only loosely twisted together and easily separable. While there are other manufacturers, the two most-commonly used (and oldest) brands are DMC and Anchor , both of which have been manufacturing embroidery floss since the 1800s.

Other materials used are pearl (or perle) cotton, Danish flower thread, silk and Rayon. Different wool threads, metallic threads or other novelty threads are also used, sometimes for the whole work, but often for accents and embellishments. Hand-dyed cross stitch floss is created just as the name implies - it is dyed by hand. Because of this, there are variations in the amount of colour throughout the thread. Some variations can be subtle, while some can be a huge contrast. Some also have more than one colour per thread, which in the right project, creates amazing results. Cross stitch is widely used in traditional Palestinian dressmaking.

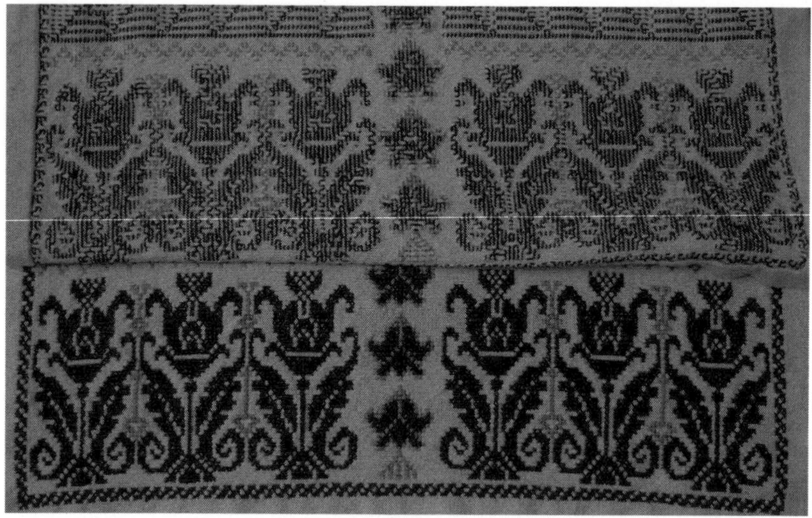

Figure: *Cross stitch from Surif. Top half of picture is the reverse side.*

Related Stitches and Forms of Embroidery

Other stitches are also often used in cross-stitch, among them ¼, ½, and ¾ stitches and backstitches. Cross-stitch is often used together with other stitches. A cross stitch can come in a variety of prostational forms. It is sometimes used in crewel embroidery, especially in its more modern derivatives. It is also often used in needlepoint.

A specialised historical form of embroidery using cross-stitch is Assisi embroidery. There are many stitches which are related to cross-stitch and were used in similar ways in earlier times. The best known are Italian cross-stitch, Celtic Cross Stitch, Irish Cross Stitch, long-armed cross-stitch, Ukrainian cross-stitch and Montenegrin stitch. Italian cross-stitch and Montenegrin stitch are reversible, meaning the work looks the same on both sides. These styles have a slightly different look than ordinary cross-stitch. These more difficult stitches are rarely used in mainstream embroidery, but they are still used to recreate historical pieces of embroidery or by the creative and adventurous stitcher.

The double cross-stitch, also known as a Leviathan stitch or Smyrna cross stitch, combines a cross-stitch with an upright cross-stitch. Berlin wool work and similar petit point stitchery resembles the heavily shaded, opulent styles of cross-stitch, and sometimes also used charted patterns on paper.

Cross-stitch is often combined with other popular forms of embroidery, such as Hardanger embroidery or blackwork embroidery. Cross-stitch may also be combined with other work, such as canvaswork or drawn thread work. Beadwork and other embellishments such as paillettes, charms, small buttons and speciality threads of various kinds may also be used.

Recent Trends in the UK

Cross-stitch has become increasingly popular with the younger generation of the United Kingdom in recent years. The Great Recession has also seen renewal of interest in home crafts. Retailers such as John Lewis experienced a 17% rise in sales of haberdashery products between 2009 and 2010. Hobbycraft, a chain of stores selling craft supplies, also enjoyed an 11% increase in sales over the past year. The chain is said to have benefited from the "make do and mend" mentality of the credit crisis, which has driven people to make their own cards and gifts.

Knitting and cross stitching have become more popular hobbies for a younger market, in contrast to its traditional reputation as a hobby for retirees. Sewing and craft groups such as Stitch and Bitch London have resurrected the idea of the traditional craft club. At Clothes Show Live 2010 there was a new area called "Sknitch" promoting modern sewing, knitting and embroidery.

In a departure from the traditional designs associated with cross stitch, there is a current trend for more postmodern or tongue-in-cheek designs featuring retro images or contemporary sayings. It is linked to a concept known as 'subversive cross stitch', which involves more risque designs, often fusing the traditional sampler style with sayings designed to shock or be incongruous with the old-fashioned image of cross stitch.

Stitching designs on other materials can be accomplished by using a Waste Canvas. This waste canvas is a temporary gridded canvas similar to regular canvas used for embroidery that is held together by a water soluble glue, this is removed after completion of stitch design.

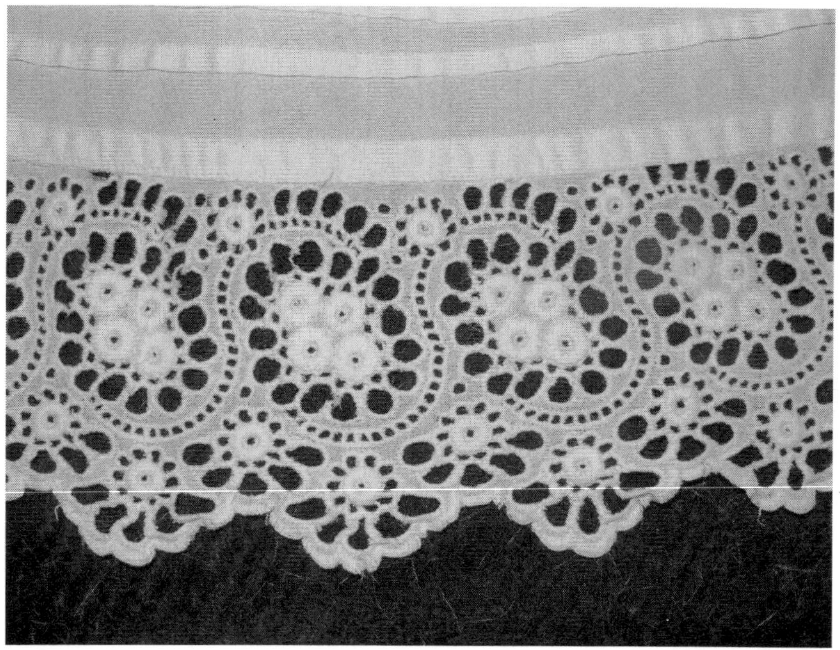

Cutwork

Cutwork or cut work is a needlework technique in which portions of a textile are cut away and the resulting "hole" is reinforced and filled with embroidery or needle lace.

Cutwork is related to drawn thread work. In drawn thread work, typically only the warp or weft threads are withdrawn (cut and removed), and the remaining threads in the resulting hole are bound in various ways. In other types of cutwork, both warp and weft threads may be drawn.

Needlework styles that incorporate cutwork include broderie anglaise, Carrickmacross lace, whitework, and early reticella.

Darning

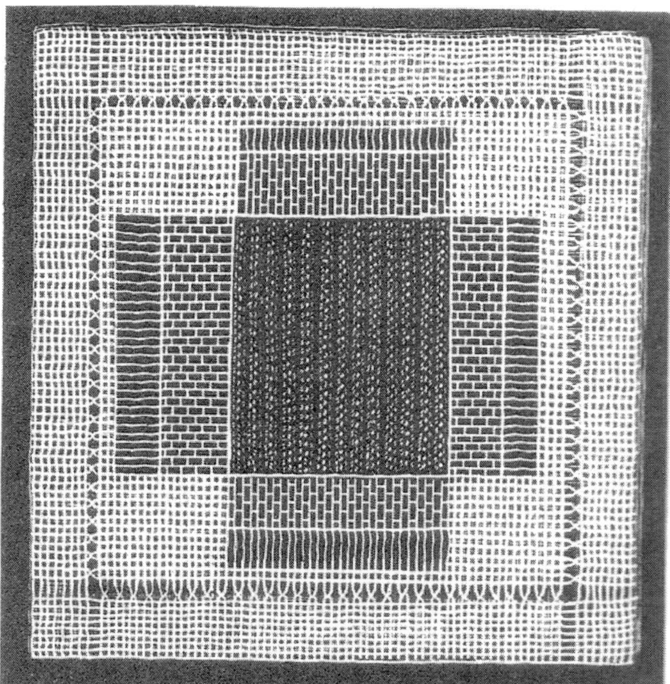

Figure: *"Cashmere darn", a fine darning technique for twill fabric, from* The Dictionary of Needlework, *1885.*

Darning is a sewing technique for repairing holes or worn areas in fabric or knitting using needle and thread alone. It is often done by hand, but it is also possible to darn with a sewing machine. Hand darning employs the darning stitch, a simple running stitch in which the thread is "woven" in rows along the grain of the fabric, with the stitcher reversing direction at the end of each row, and then filling in the framework thus created, as if weaving. Darning is a traditional method for repairing fabric damage or holes that do not run along a seam, and where patching is impractical or would create discomfort for the wearer, such as on the heel of a sock.

Darning also refers to any of several needlework techniques that are worked using darning stitches:

- Pattern darning is a type of embroidery that uses parallel rows of straight stitches of different lengths to create a geometric design.

- Net darning, also called filet lace, is a 19th century technique using stitching on a mesh foundation fabric to imitate lace.
- Needle weaving is a drawn thread work embroidery technique that involves darning patterns into barelaid warp or weft threads.

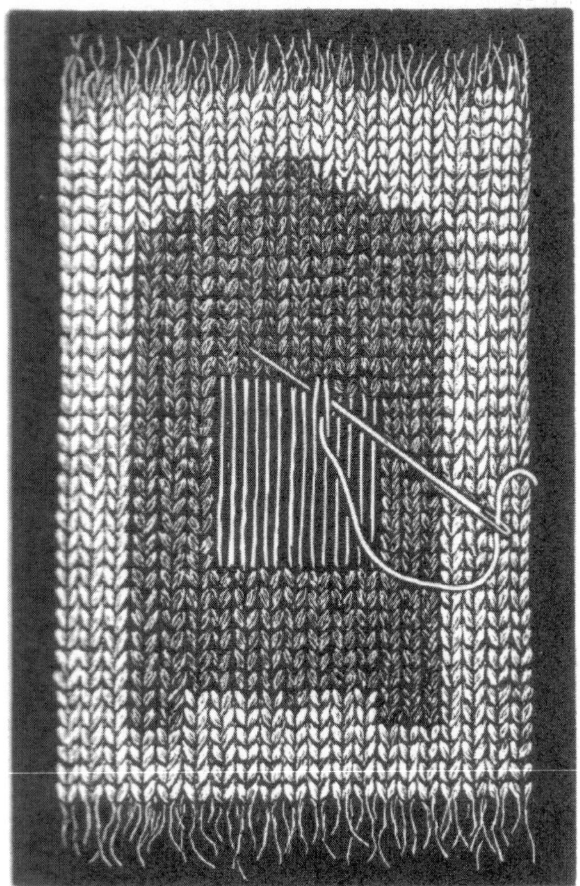

Figure: *"Swiss darning" to repair knits*

Darning Cloth

In its simplest form, darning consists of anchoring the thread in the fabric on the edge of the hole and carrying it across the gap. It is then anchored on the other side, usually with a running stitch or two. If enough threads are criss-crossed over the hole, the hole will eventually be covered with a mass of thread.

Fine darning, sometimes known as *Belgian darning*, attempts to make the repair as invisible and neat as possible. Often the hole is cut into a square or darn blends into the fabric.

There are many varieties of fine darning. Simple over-and-under weaving of threads can be replaced by various fancy weaves, such as twills, chevrons, etc., achieved by skipping threads in regular patterns.

Invisible darning is the epitome of this attempt at restoring the fabric to its original integrity. Threads from the original weaving are unravelled from a hem or seam and used to effect the repair. Invisible darning is appropriate for extremely expensive fabrics and items of apparel. In machine darning, lines of machine running stitch are run back and forth across the hole, then the fabric is rotated and more lines run at right angles. This is a fast way to darn, but it cannot match the effects of fine darning.

Darning Tools

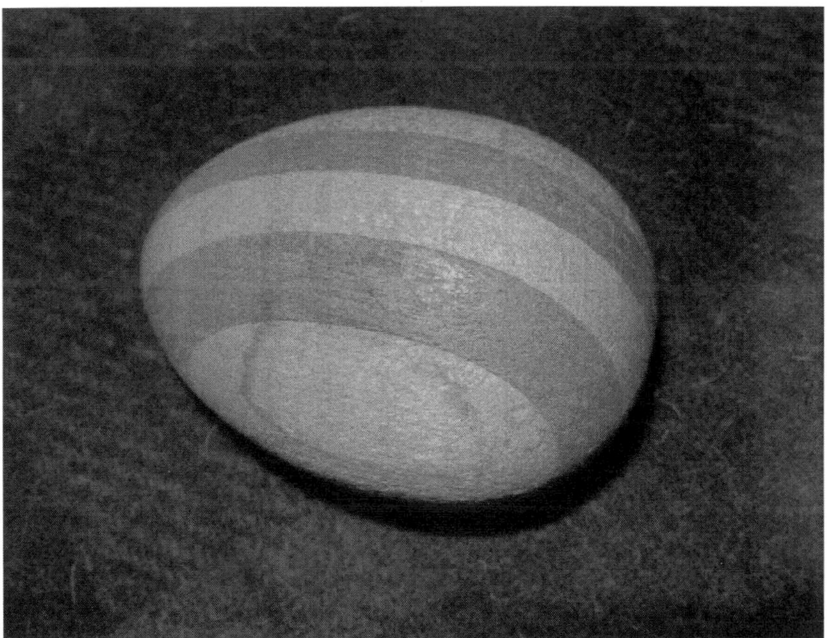

Figure: *Darning egg, early 20th century*

There are special tools for darning socks or stockings:

- A darning egg is an egg-shaped ovoid of stone, porcelain, wood, or similar hard material, which is inserted into the toe or heel of the sock to hold it in the proper shape and provide a firm foundation for repairs. When the repairs are finished, the darning egg is removed. A shell of the tiger cowry *Cypraea tigris*, a popular ornament in Europe and elsewhere, was also sometimes used as a ready-made darning egg.

- A darning mushroom is a mushroom-shaped tool usually made of wood. The sock is stretched over the curved top of the mushroom, and gathered tightly around the stalk to hold it in place for darning.
- A darning gourd is a hollow dried gourd with a pronounced neck. The sock can be stretched over the full end of the gourd and held in place around the neck for darning.
- A used light bulb can be used to hold a sock in place for darning.

Pattern Darning

Pattern darning is a simple and ancient embroidery technique in which contrasting thread is woven in-and-out of the ground fabric using rows of running stitches which reverse direction at the end of each row. The length of the stitches may be varied to produce geometric designs. Traditional embroidery using pattern darning is found in Africa, Japan, Northern and Eastern Europe, the Middle East, Mexico and Peru. Pattern darning is also used as a *filling stitch* in blackwork embroidery.

Drawn Thread Work

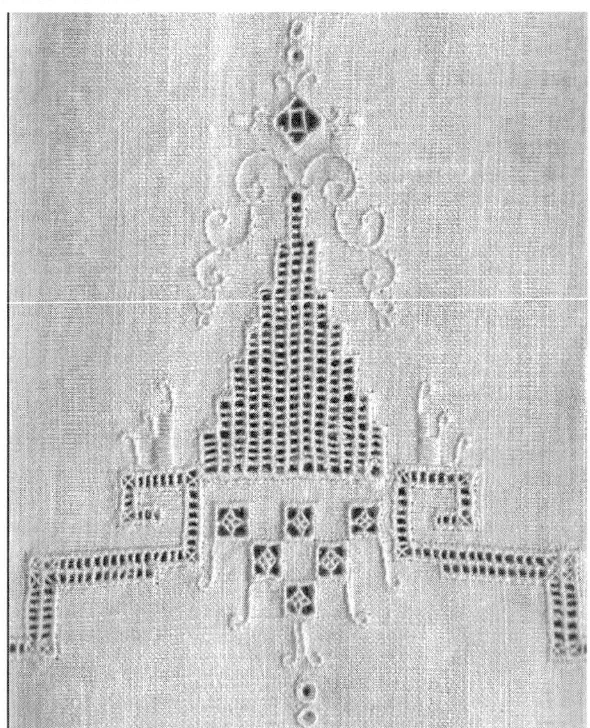

Figure: *Linen towel with drawn thread work accented with embroidery in stem and satin stitch*

Drawn thread work also known as pulled thread work, is a form of counted-thread embroidery based on removing threads from the warp and/or the weft of a piece of even-weave fabric. The remaining threads are grouped or bundled together into a variety of patterns. The more elaborate styles of drawn thread work use in fact a variety of other stitches and techniques, but the drawn thread parts are their most distinctive element. It is also grouped as whitework embroidery because it was traditionally done in white thread on white fabric and is often combined with other whitework techniques.

Styles

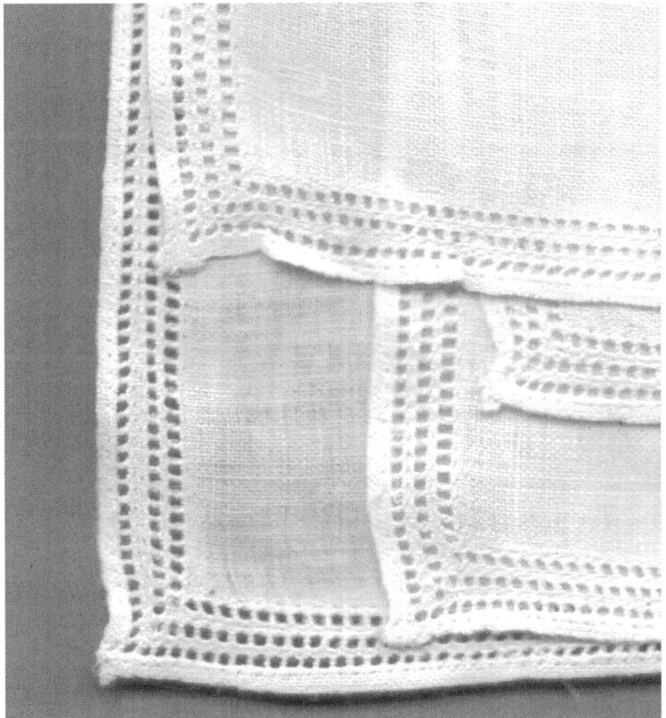

Figure: *Linen handkerchief decorated with three rows of hemstitching.*

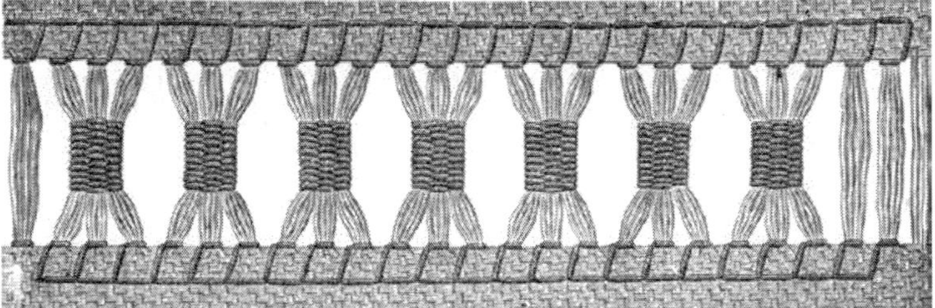

Figure: *Openwork insertion with needle-weaving.*

Basic Hemstitching

The most basic kind of drawn thread work is hemstitching. Drawn thread work is often used to decorate the trimmings of clothes or household linens. The border between hemstitching gone fancy and more elaborate styles of drawn thread work isn't always clear.

Needle-Weaving

This relatively easy type of drawn thread work is created by weaving (or darning) the embroidering thread into the barelaid warp or weft threads to create patterns of light-coloured threads and dark openings in the drawn-thread cloth. Needleweaving is most often used for decorative borders. It is nearly always used in combination with other types of embroidery stitches. Together they create a complete design and, historically, in ethnic embroidery, distinctive embroidery 'styles'.

Also known as "needle-darning".

Poltava-Style Drawnwork

In Ukrainian and some other Slavic languages, *merezhka* is the general term for "drawn-thread" work. "Merezhka", pronounced [meÈre*f*ka], includes all types of drawn-thread work including those mentioned in the paragraphs above. In recent years (199(?)-2005), the term "myreschka", a variant of "merezhka", began to be used in some circles for a specific Ukrainian drawn-thread technique that is traditionally used in the central lands of Ukraine, esp. in the regions of Poltava and Kyiv, and areas along the Dniepro (Dnieper) River, and some have come to call it "Poltava-style" merezhka. The technique has its own descriptive name in the Ukrainian language, which might be translated into English as "layerings".

The technique for doing Poltava-style 'layerings'-merezhka basically involves withdrawing sets of parallel threads of weft while leaving others in place, then using the antique hem-stitch (called "prutyk") and this special "layerings" technique to create both the openwork 'net' and the design of embroidering threads upon the "withdrawn" part of cloth. The designs which can be created in this way can be simple and narrow, or as complex and wide (high) as any one-coloured embroidery design.

"Prutyk" (may also be spelled "prutik") is the *bunch* (switch or stick) that is created when you pull together each bunch of three threads together using hem-stitch. In Ukrainian, "prutyk" is simply another name for 'simple hemstitch' (i.e.: "merezhka-prutyk"), or it can mean each tiny 'bunch' in the hemstitching.

Other Drawn-Thread

A form of double-drawnwork, where both warp and weft are removed at regular intervals, consists of wrapping the remaining threads into "bundles", using embroidery thread to secure them, thus creating something similar to a net. Then embroidery threads are woven in patterns into that net using needle weaving or needle darning. The result is a pattern of the design in white (or coloured, depending on ethnic region) embroidery on the "openwork" background of netted cloth.

Cutwork

Hardanger: Hardanger embroidery is a style of drawn thread work that is most popular today. It originally comes from Norway, and there from the traditional district of Hardanger. The backbone of Hardanger designs consists of satin stitches, in geometrical areas both warp and weft threads are removed and the remaining mesh is secured with simple weaving or warping, or with a limited number of simple filling patterns. The designs tend to be geometric, if they include flowers or such they are very stylized due to the nature of the technique. Hardanger never includes Buttonhole stitches, except for securing the edges of a piece of fabric. It is usually executed using rather coarse fabric and thread.

Ukrainian Cutwork

Much like Hardanger, Ukrainian cutwork belongs to the category of 'cut-and-drawn' work, since, unlike 'merezhka' (drawn-work), threads of the ground cloth are cut both vertically and horizontally, and thus create specifically larger cut-work openings in the body of the fabric, when compared with drawn-work. The Ukrainian word for cutwork embroidery is vyrizuvannya (pronounced *veree-zoo-van-nya* - translates into "cutwork"). There are several styles of Ukrainian cutwork, one of which closely resembles Hardanger cutwork.

Needlelace and Drawn-Thread Work

Reticella lace is a form of embroidery in which typical techniques of needlelace are used to embellish drawn thread work. It was first used in 16th century Italy. Needlelace evolved from this when the lacemakers realised that they can do the same things without any supporting fabric. High quality reticella is done with thread almost as thin as sewing silk. Ruskin lace is in fact a near-modern form of it. Warp and weft threads are removed, and the remaining threads are overcast with buttonhole stitches, as in needlelace.

Another embroidery style that combines drawn thread work with needlelace techniques is Hedebo from Denmark, which originates from the area around Copenhagen and Roskilde. It uses techniques that are clearly distinct from reticella and traditional Italian neddlelace on the one hand and Hardanger on the other. It does make extensive use of buttonhole stitches, but they are done slightly differently than in Italian embroidery.

Make safe and Dying Rewoven Threads Techniques of re-weaving drawn threads diverge from book to book. By Patricia Bage, the writer reveals the every-other-thread technique. But in neither book do they go into fact about how to make safe your threads after re-weaving. They on the whole declare that "trim the threads on the back"

Hardanger

Hardanger embroidery or "Hardangersøm" is a form of embroidery traditionally worked with white thread on white even-weave cloth, using counted thread and drawn thread work techniques. It is sometimes called whitework embroidery.

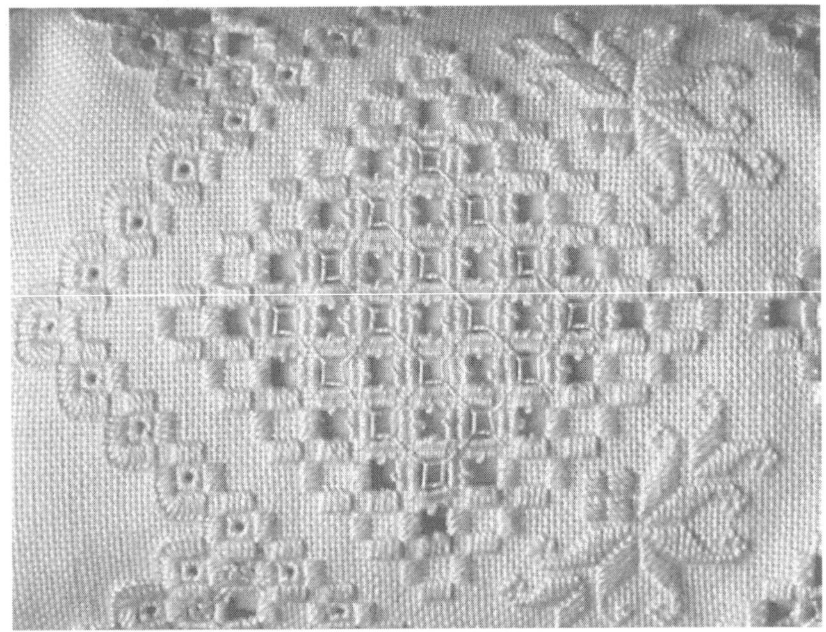

Figure: *Example of modern Hardanger embroidery work*

History

The exact origins of Hardanger embroidery are not known but it is thought to have its beginnings in ancient Persia and Asia. During the Renaissance this early form of embroidery spread to Italy where it evolved into Italian Reticella and Venetian lacework. By 1700 variations of this type of embroidery had spread to northern Europe where it developed further into Danish and Dutch Hedebo, Scottish Ayrshire work and Ruskin lacework as well as Norwegian Drawn Work, as it was then called.

In the period between 1650-1850 Hardangersom (meaning: *work from Hardanger area*) flourished in Norway. Flax was grown, carded, spun and woven into white fabric and thread which was used to make and decorate traditional Norwegian costume items called bunads (national costumes) as well as other items of clothing and household linens such as mats, curtains and bedspreads.

Materials and Technique

Fabric

Modern Hardanger fabric is an evenweave cotton material woven with pairs of threads, typically 22 pairs per linear inch in both directions, referred to as '22-count'. The weave gives a squared appearance to the fabric (similar to Aida cloth), with distinct holes, making it easy to count and work on. Other evenweave fabrics are also suitable for Hardanger embroidery but do not usually have the clearly defined block appearance. These include pure linen, cotton or mixed fibre fabrics that may also vary in count from 18-24 threads per inch to finer counts of 26 threads per inch or higher.

Threads

Traditional Hardanger embroidery is worked with a thread colour that matches the fabric, usually white or cream. Using self-coloured thread enhances both the sculptural nature of the stitches and the details in the intricate filling stitches. Many contemporary designs, however, do make use of coloured, variegated and overdyed threads to great effect. Two weights of Pearl (perlé) cotton are generally used. On normal 22-count Hardanger fabric this is usually Pearl cotton #5, a heavier weight used for satin stitch Kloster blocks and motifs, and Pearl cotton #8, a thinner thread used for more delicate filling stitches and other surface details. On finer, higher count fabrics the combination of #8 and #12 threads is often more suitable.

Stitches and Techniques

Hardanger embroidery uses satin stitch blocks known as Kloster blocks, consisting of 5 parallel satin stitches, worked over a group of

4 x 4 ground threads. These blocks enclose areas of fabric where a number of warp and weft threads are cut and withdrawn, leaving a network of loose threads and large holes within the shape defined by the Kloster blocks. Various decorative filling stitches are then worked over the remaining loose threads and holes to create a lacy effect.

Some of the stitches and special techniques used are:

- Simple satin stitch surface motifs, often resembling stars, ships, crescents and crosses.
- Other decorative surface stitches such as fly stitch, running stitch, cable stitch and French knots.
- Woven bars: weaving the needle over and under four threads until they are completely covered, and wrapped bars (overcast bars) where the thread is wound around groups of four threads.
- Filling stitches resembling wheels, spider's webs and dove's eyes.
- Picot: twisting the thread once round the needle before inserting the needle to produce a decorative loop.
- Edging stitches such as four-sided stitch, buttonhole stitch and fancy hemstitching techniques for finishing items.

Designs

The traditional style of Hardanger work is very geometrical in form and based on several basic shapes such as squares, rectangles, triangles, diamonds, hearts, zig-zags and crosses. The combination and placement of these elements allow an unlimited number of beautiful patterns of all sizes to be created.

A wide range of patterns are available today for the modern needleworker to try, in both traditional and contemporary styles. Hardanger is still used to decorate cushions, table linen and other household items as well as items for display on a wall. Several modern needlework designers have incorporated elements of Hardanger cut work into their embroidery designs and samplers, often combining them with other needlework techniques, stitches, speciality threads and other embellishments to great effect.

New Uses

Some Lutheran pastors of Norwegian descent in the United States have had stoles embroidered with Hardanger work made for their use. While altar paraments in Hardanger work have been traditional in Norwegian churches for a long time, their use in American Lutheran churches is becoming more common as an alternative to the more traditional machine-embroidered damask paraments. Even the traditional alternating cross and chalice motif of Norwegian Hardanger work is now found in American Lutheran churches.

Needlepoint

Needlepoint is a form of counted thread embroidery in which yarn is stitched through a stiff open weave canvas. Most needlepoint designs completely cover the canvas. Although needlepoint may be worked in a variety of stitches, many needlepoint designs use only a simple tent stitch and rely upon colour changes in the yarn to construct the pattern.

The degree of detail in needlepoint depends on the thread count of the underlying mesh fabric. Needlepoint worked on fine canvas is known as petit point. Due to the inherent stiffness of needlepoint, common uses include wall hangings, pillows, upholstery, holiday ornaments, purses and eyeglass cases.

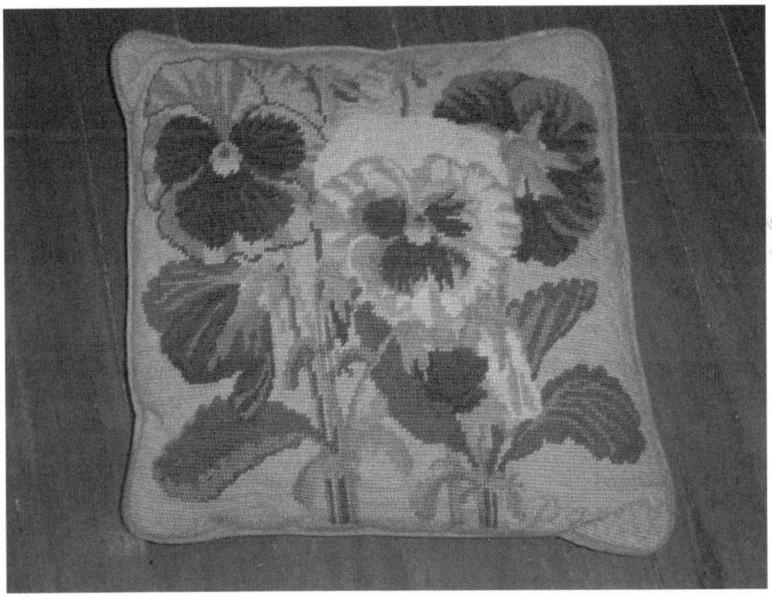

Figure: *Needlepoint cushion*

History

The roots of needlepoint go back thousands of years to the ancient Egyptians, who used small slanted stitches to sew up their canvas tents. Howard Carter, of Tutankhamen fame, found some needlepoint in the cave of a Pharaoh who had lived 1500 years before Christ.

Modern needlepoint descends from the canvas work in Tent Stitch, done on an evenly woven open ground fabric, that was a popular domestic craft in the 16th century.

The development of needlepoint was influenced in the 17th century by Bargello, and by shaded Berlin wool work in brightly coloured wool yarn in the 19th century. Upholstered furniture became fashionable in the 17th century, and this prompted the development of a more durable material to serve as a foundation for the embroidered works of art.

Terminology

Differences between Needlepoint and Other Types of Embroidery

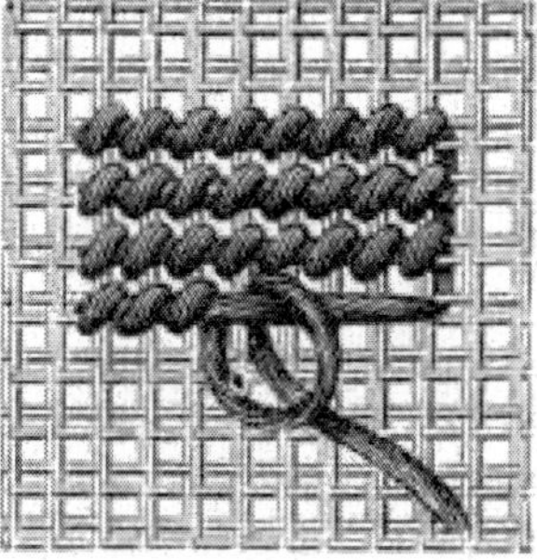

Figure: *Needlepoint is worked upon specialised types of stiff canvas that have openings at regular intervals.*

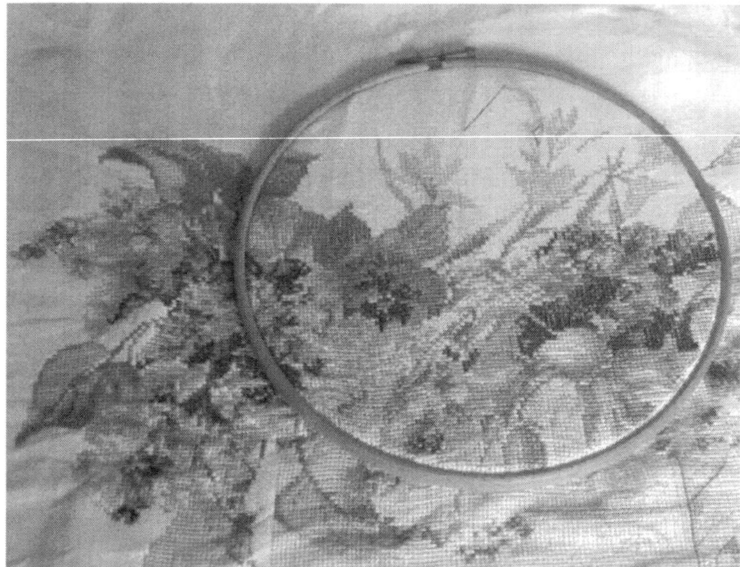

Figure: *Embroidery that is not needlepoint often uses soft cloth and requires an embroidery hoop.*

Needlepoint refers to a particular set of stitching techniques worked upon stiff openwork canvas. Because it is stitched on a fabric that is an open grid, needlepoint is not embellishing a fabric, as is the case with most other types of embroidery, but literally the making of a new fabric. It is for this reason that many needlepoint stitches must be of sturdier construction than other embroidery stitches.

"Needlepoint" is not synonymous with all types of embroidery. Needlepoint is often referred to as "tapestry" in the United Kingdom and sometimes as "canvaswork." Needlepoint differs from true tapestry, which is woven on a vertical loom. Needlepoint is stitched on canvas mesh. When worked on fine weave canvas in Tent Stitch it is also known as "Petitpoint". "Needlepoint lace" is also an older term for needle lace, a historic lacemaking technique. When referring to handcrafted textile arts which a speaker is unable to identify, the appropriate generalized term is "needlework".

Berlin Work (also spelled Berlinwork) refers to a subset of needlepoint, popular in the mid-19th Century that was stitched in brightly coloured wool on needlepoint canvas from hand-coloured charts.

Contemporary Techniques

Materials: The threads used for stitching may be wool, silk, cotton or combinations, such as wool-silk blend. Variety fibres may also be used, such as metallic cord, metallic braid, ribbon, or raffia. Stitches may be plain, covering just one thread intersection with a single orientation, or fancy, such as in bargello or other counted-thread stitches. Plain stitches, known as tent stitches, may be worked as basketweave, continental or half cross. Basketweave uses the most wool, but does not distort the rectangular mesh and makes for the best-wearing piece.

Several types of embroidery canvas are available: single thread and double thread embroidery canvas are open even-weave meshes, with large spaces or holes to allow heavy threads to pass through without fraying. Canvas is sized by mesh sizes, or thread count per inch. Sizes vary from 5 threads per inch to 24 threads per inch; popular mesh sizes are 10, 12, 14, 18, and 24 (Congress Cloth). The different types of needlepoint canvas available on the market are mono, penelope, interlock, rug and plastic

- Mono canvas comes in the widest variety of colours (especially 18 mesh) and is plain woven, with one weft thread going over and under one warp thread. This canvas has the most possibilities for manipulation and open canvas. It is used for hand-painted canvases as well as counted thread canvaswork.

- Penelope canvas has two threads closely grouped together in both warp and weft. Because these threads can be split apart, penelope sizes are often expressed with two numbers, such as 10/20.
- Interlock Mono Canvas is more stable than the others and is made by twisting two thin threads around each other for the lengthwise thread and "locking" them into a single crosswise thread. Interlock canvas is generally used for printed canvases. Silk gauze is a form of interlock canvas, which is sold in small frames for petit-point work. Silk gauze most often comes in 32, 40 or 48 count, although some 18 count is available and 64, 128 and other counts are used for miniature work.
- Rug canvas is a mesh of strong cotton threads, twisting two threads around each other lengthwise forms the mesh and locking them around a crosswise thread made the same way; this cannot be separated. Canvases come in different gauges, and rug canvas is 3.3 mesh and 5 mesh, which is better for more detailed work.
- Plastic Canvas is a stiff canvas that is generally used for smaller projects and is sold as "pre-cut pieces" rather than by the yard. Plastic canvas is an excellent choice for beginners who want to practice different stitches.

Frames and Hoops

Needlepoint canvas is stretched on a scroll frame or tacked onto a rectangular wooden frame to keep the work taut during stitching. Petit point is sometimes worked in a small embroidery hoop rather than a scroll frame.

Patterns

Commercial designs for needlepoint may be found in different forms: Hand-Painted Canvas, Printed Canvas, Trammed Canvas, Charted Canvas, and Free-form.

In Hand-Painted Canvas, the design is painted on the canvas by the designer, or painted to their specifications by an employee or contractor. Canvases may be stitch-painted, meaning each thread intersection is painstakingly painted so that the stitcher has no doubts about what colour is meant to be used at that intersection. Alternatively, they may be hand-painted, meaning that the canvas is painted by hand but the stitcher will have to use their judgment about what colours to use if a thread intersection is not clearly painted. Hand-painted canvases allow the stitcher to give free range to their creativity with threads and unique stitches by not having to pay attention to a separate chart. In North America this is the most popular form of needlepoint canvas.

Printed Canvas is when the design is printed by silk screening or computer onto the needlepoint canvas. Printing the canvas in this means allows for faster creation of the canvas and thus has a lower price than Hand-Painted Canvas. However, care must be taken that the canvas is straight before being printed to ensure that the edges of the design are straight. Designs are typically less involved due to the limited colour palette of this printing method. The results (and the price) of printed canvas vary extensively. Often printed canvases come as part of kits, which also dramatically vary in quality, based on the printing process and the materials used. This form of canvas is widely available outside North America.

On a Trammed Canvas the design is professionally stitched onto the canvas by hand using horizontal stitches of varying lengths of wool of the appropriate colours. The canvas is usually sold together with the wool required to stitch the trammed area. The stitcher then uses tent stitch over the horizontal lines with the tramme stitches acting as an accurate guide as to the colour and number of stitches required. This technique is particularly suited to designs with a large area of mono-colour background as such areas do not require tramming, reducing the cost of the canvas and allowing the stitcher to choose the background colour themselves. The Portuguese island of Madeira is the historic centre for the manufacture of trammed canvases.

Charted Canvas designs are available in book or leaflet form. They are available at book stores and independent needlework stores. Charted Canvas designs are typically printed in two ways: either in grid form with each thread intersection being represented with a symbol that shows what colour is meant to be stitched on that intersection, or as a line drawing where the stitcher is to trace the design onto his canvas and then fill in those areas with the colours listed. Books typically include a grouping of designs from a single designer such as Kaffe Fassett or Candace Bahouth, or may be centred around a theme such as Christmas or Victorian Needlepoint. Leaflets usually include one to two designs and are usually printed by the individual designer.

Free-form needlepoint designs are created by the stitcher. They may be based around a favourite photograph, stitch, thread colour, etc. The stitcher just starts stitching! Many interesting pieces are created this way. It allows for the addition of found objects, appliqué, computer-printed photographs, goldwork, or speciality stitches. While traditionally needlepoint has been done to create a solid fabric, more modern needlepoint incorporates open canvas, techniques which allow some of the unstitched, or lightly stitched, canvas to show through. Some of these techniques include "shadow" or "lite" stitching, blackwork on canvas, and pattern darning. Needlepoint continues to evolve as stitchers use new techniques and threads, and add appliqué or found materials. The line between needlepoint and other forms of counted-thread embroidery is becoming blurred as new stitchers adapt techniques and materials from other forms of embroidery to needlepoint.

Famous Needlepointers

Mary, Queen of Scots, Marie Antoinette, Queen Elizabeth I, Princess Grace, Martha Washington, American football player Roosevelt "Rosey" Grier, and actresses Mary Martin and Loretta Swit have all been avid stitchers. Martin released a book titled *Mary Martin's Needlepoint* in 1969 that cataloged her works and provided needlework tips.

Grier released a book titled *Rosey Grier's Needlepoint for Men* in 1973 that shows Grier stitching and samples of his work.

Swit published *A Needlepoint Scrapbook* in 1986. This book is said to include a design for Ms. Pac Man.

The American Needlepoint Guild has established a Princess Grace Award (Needlepoint) for needlepoint completed entirely in tent stitch. This award is not formally associated with the Princess Grace Foundation which presents the "Princess Grace Awards".

The American actress Sylvia Sidney sold needlepoint kits featuring her designs and she published two popular instruction books: *Sylvia Sidney's Needlepoint Book* (1968) and *The Sylvia Sidney Question and Answer Book on Needlepoint* (1975).

Needlepoint Stitches

Most commercial needlework kits recommend one of the variants of tent stitch, although Victorian cross stitch and random long stitch are also used. Authors of books of needlepoint designs sometimes use a wider range of stitches. Historically, a very wide range of stitches have been used including:

- Arraiolos stitch
- Brick Stitch
- (Victorian) Cross Stitch

- Encroaching Upright Gobelin stitch
- Gobelin stitch
- Hungarian Ground stitch
- Hungarian point stitch
- Mosaic stitch
- Old Florentine stitch
- Parisian stitch
- Random Long Stitch
- Smyrna stitch
- Tent stitches - Basketweave, Continental and Half cross variants
- Upright cross stitch
- Whipped flower stitch

There are many books that teach readers how to create hundreds, if not thousands, of stitches. Some were written by famous stitchers, such as Mary Martin and Sylvia Sydney. However, the most popular and long-lived is *The Needlepoint Book* by Jo Ippolito Christensen, Simon & Schuster. First published in 1976 by Prentice-Hall, the nearly 400-page text has been continuously in print and was revised in 1999; over 350,000 copies have been sold.

Quillwork

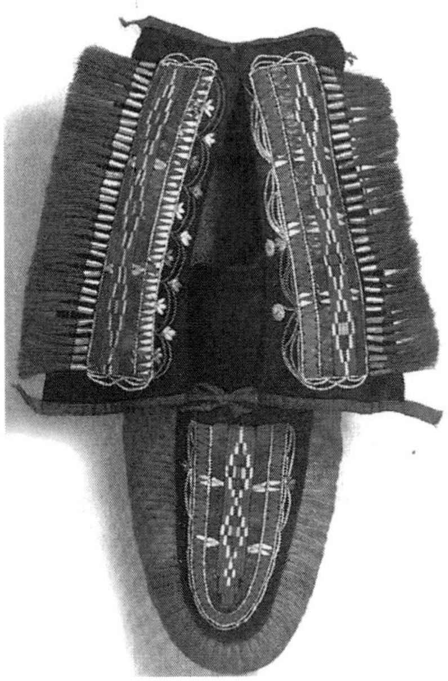

Quillwork is a form of textile embellishment traditionally practiced by Native Americans that employs the quills of porcupines as a decorative element.

History

Porcupine quillwork is an art form completely unique to North America. Before the introduction of glass beads, quillwork was a major decorative element used by the peoples who resided in the porcupine's natural habitat. The use of quills in designs spans from Maine to Alaska. The earliest known quillwork was found in Alberta, Canada and dates back to the 6th century CE.

Cheyenne oral history, as told by Picking Bones Woman to George Bird Grinnell, says quilling came to their tribe from a man who married a woman, who hid her true identity as a buffalo. His son was also a buffalo. The man visited his wife and son in their buffalo home, and, while among the buffalo, the man learned the art of quilling, which he shared with the women of his tribe. Joining the Cheyenne Quilling Society was a prestigious honour for Cheyenne women. Upon entering the Society, women would work first on quilling moccasins, then cradleboards, rosettes for men's shirts and tipis, and ultimately, hide robes and backrests.

Porcupine quills often adorned rawhide and tanned hides, but during the 19th century, quilled birch bark boxes were a popular trade item to sell to European-Americans among Eastern and Great Lakes tribes.

Technique

Quills suitable for embellishment are two to three inches long and may be dyed before use. In their natural state, the quills are pale yellow to white with black tips. The tips are usually snipped off before use. Quill readily take dye, which originally was derived from local plants and included colours such as black, yellow, red, and blue. By the 19th century, aniline dyes were available through trade and greatly expanded the quilling palette.

The four most common techniques for quillwork are appliqué, embroidery, wrapping, and loom weaving. Appliquéd quills are stitched into hide in a manner that covers the stitches. In wrapping, a single quill may be wrapped upon itself or two quills may be intertwined.

Quills can be appliquéd singly to form curvilinear patterns, as found on Odawa pouches from the 18th century. This technique lends itself to floral designs popularized among northeastern tribes by

Ursuline nuns. Huron women excelled at floral quillwork during the 18th and 19th centuries.

Plains quillwork is characterized by bands of rectangles creating geometrical patterns found also in Plains painting. Rosettes of concentric circles of quillwork commonly adorned historical Plains men's shirts, as did parallel panels of quillwork on the sleeves.

The Red River Ojibwe of Manitoba created crisp, geometric patterns by weaving quills on a loom in the 19th century.

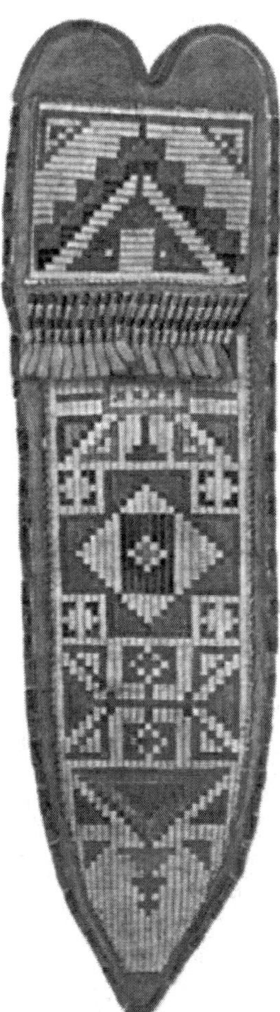

Figure: *A quillwork knife sheath.*

Today

Quillwork never died out as a living art form in the Northern Plains. Some communities that had lost their quillwork tradition have been able to revive the art form. For instance, no women quilled in the Dene community of Wha Ti, Northwest Territories by the late 1990s. The Dene Cultural Institute held two workshops there in 1999 and 2000, effectively reviving quillwork in Wha Ti.

The art form is very much alive today. Examples of contemporary, award-winning quillworkers include Juanita Growing Thunder Fogarty, (Sioux-Assiniboine) artist; Dorothy Brave Eagle (Oglala Lakota) of Denver, Colorado; Kanatiiosh (Akwesasne Mohawk) of St. Regis Mohawk Reservation; Cathy A. Smith of Galisteo, New Mexico; Leonda Fast Buffalo Horse (Blackfeet) of Browning, Montana; and Deborah Magee Sherer (Blackfeet) of Cut Bank, Montana.

Northern Lakes College of Alberta, Canada teaches a college-level course in quill work art.

Smocking

Smocking is an embroidery technique used to gather fabric so that it can stretch. Before elastic, smocking was commonly used in cuffs, bodices, and necklines in garments where buttons were undesirable. Smocking developed in England and has been practised since the Middle Ages and is unusual among embroidery methods in that it was often worn by laborers. Other major embroidery styles are purely decorative and represented status symbols. Smocking was practical for garments to be both form fitting and flexible, hence its name derives from *smock* — a farmer's work shirt. Smocking was used most extensively in the eighteenth and nineteenth centuries.

Materials

Smocking requires lightweight fabric with a stable weave that gathers well. Cotton and silk are typical fibre choices, often in lawn or voile. Smocking is worked on a crewel embroidery needle in cotton or silk thread and normally requires three times the width of initial material as the finished item will have. Historically, smocking was also worked in pique, crepe de Chine, and cashmere. According to *Good Housekeeping: The Illustrated Book of Needlecrafts*, "Any type of fabric can be smocked if it is supple enough to be gathered."

Fabric can be gathered into pleats in a variety of ways.

Early smocking, or gauging, was done by hand. Some embroiderers also made their own guides using cardboard and an embroidery marking pencil. By 1880, iron-on transfer dots were available and advertised in magazines such as Weldon's. The iron on transfers places evenly spaced dots onto the wrong side of the fabric, which were then pleated using a regular running stitch.

Since the early 1950s, pleating machines have been available to home smockers. Using gears and speciality pleater needles, the fabric is forced through the gears and onto the threaded needles. Pleating machines are typically offered in 16-row, 24-row and 32-row widths. Manufacturers include Read and Amanda Jane.

Method

Smocking refers to work done before a garment is assembled. It usually involves reducing the dimensions of a piece of fabric to one-third of its original width, although changes are sometimes lesser with thick fabrics. Individual smocking stitches also vary considerably in tightness, so embroiderers usually work a sampler for practice and reference when they begin to learn smocking.

Traditional hand smocking begins with marking *smocking dots* in a grid pattern on the wrong side of the fabric and gathering it with temporary running stitches. These stitches are anchored on each end in a manner that facilitates later removal and are analogous to basting stitches. Then a row of cable stitching stabilizes the top and bottom of the working area.

Smocking may be done in many sophisticated patterns. Standard hand smocking stitches are:

A. Cable stitch: a tight stitch of double rows that joins alternating columns of gathers.

B. Stem stitch: a tight stitch with minimum flexibility that joins two columns of gathers at a time in single overlapping rows with a downward slope.

C. Outline stitch: similar to the stem stitch but with an upward slope.

D. Cable flowerette: a set of gathers worked in three rows of stitches across four columns of gathers. Often organised in diagonally arranged sets of flowerettes for loose smocking.

E. Wave stitch: a medium density pattern that alternately employs tight horizontal stitches and loose diagonal stitches.

F. Honeycomb stitch: a medium density variant on the cable stitch that double stitches each set of gathers and provides more spacing between them, with an intervening diagonal stitch concealed on the reverse side of the fabric.

G. Surface honeycomb stitch: a tight variant on the honeycomb stitch and the wave stitch with the diagonal stitch visible, but spanning only one gather instead of a gather and a space.
H. Trellis stitch: a medium density pattern that uses stem stitches and outine stitches to form diamond-shaped patterns.
I. Vandyke stitch: a tight variant on the surface honeycomb stitch that wraps diagonal stitches in the opposite direction.
J. Bullion stitch: a complex knotted stitch that joins several gathers in a single stitch. Organised similarly to cable flowerettes.
K. Smocker's knot: (not depicted) a simple knotted stitch used to finish work with a thread or for decorative purposes.

Stumpwork

Stumpwork is a style of embroidery where the stitched figures are raised from the surface of the work to form a 3-dimensional effect. Stitches can be worked around pieces of wire to create individual forms such as leaves, insect wings or flower petals. This form is then applied to the main body of work by piercing the background fabric with the wires and securing tightly. Other shapes can be created using padding under the stitches, usually in the form of felt layers sewn one upon the other in increasingly smaller sizes. The felt is then covered with a layer of embroidery stitches.

A modern day subcategory of this art form used primarily in production embroidery on automated embroidery machines is referred to as puff embroidery. The process involves putting down, typically, a layer of foam rubber larger than the intended shape on top of the target material to be decorated. The shape is then embroidered on top of the foam rubber in such a way that the needle penetrations cut the foam rubber around the periphery of the shape.

When the embroidery is finished the excess foam rubber is weeded (pulled away or cleaned off) from the design area, leaving the underlying foam rubber shape trapped under the embroidery stitches resulting in a stumpwork effect. Puff embroidery generally lacks the intricate design characteristics obtainable with true stumpwork techniques and is primarily seen on leisure wear such as baseball caps, sweatshirts and jackets. Many times the designs are used to portray company logos or team mascots.

Surface

Surface embroidery is any form of embroidery in which the pattern is worked by the use of decorative stitches and laid threads *on top of* the foundation fabric or canvas rather than *through* the fabric; it is contrasted with canvas work.

Much free embroidery is also surface embroidery, as are a few forms of counted-thread embroidery such as cross stitch.

Suzani

Suzani is a type of embroidered and decorative tribal textile made in Tajikistan, Uzbekistan, Kazakhstan and other Central Asian countries. Suzani is from the Persian ÓæÒä *Suzan* which means needle. The art of making such textiles in Iran is called ÓæÒä˜ÇÑì *Suzankâri* (needlework).

Suzanis usually have a cotton (sometimes silk) fabric base, which is embroidered in silk or cotton thread. Chain, satin, and buttonhole stitches are the primary stitches used. There is also extensive use of couching, in which decorative thread laid on the fabric as a raised line is stitched in place with a second thread. Suzanis are often made in two or more pieces, that are then stitched together

Popular design motifs include sun and moon disks, flowers (especially tulips, carnations, and irises), leaves and vines, fruits (especially pomegranates), and occasional fish and birds.

The oldest surviving suzanis are from the late 18th and early 19th centuries, but it seems likely that they were in use long before that. In the early 15th century, Ruy Gonzáles de Clavijo, the Castilian ambassador to the court of Timur (Tamerlane), left detailed descriptions of embroideries that were probably forerunners of the suzani.

Suzanis were traditionally made by Central Asian brides as part of their dowry, and were presented to the groom on the wedding day.

Major Types of Suzani

- Bukhara Suzani
- Khodjent Suzani (Khodjent, Tajikistan)
- Lakai Suzani
- Nurata Suzani, made in the town of Nurata in Uzbekistan.
- Pskent Suzani
- Samarkand Suzani
- Shakhrisabz Suzani
- Tashkent Suzani
- Ura Tube Suzani (Istaravshan, Tajikistan)

Trianglepoint

Trianglepoint is a form of embroidery in which a series of equilateral triangles are stitched in different colours to create geometric designs, three-dimensional designs or pictures. The term was coined by needlepoint designer Sherlee Lantz.

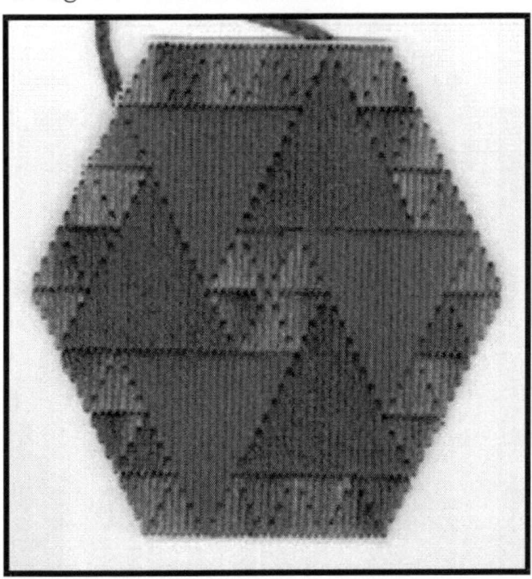

Figure: *Trianglepoint completed on plastic canvas with varigated and solid coloured yarn. The design is based on "Whirlygig" by Sherlee Lantz, but has been modified by the stitcher. Photograph and stitching by Elizabeth Pyatt.*

Basic Stitch

Sherlee Lantz created a system to create an equilateral triangle in needlepoint then put them together to create original designs.

It starts with a vertical stitch over two threads, then an adjacent vertical stitch over four threads, then a vertical stitch over six threads, then a vertical stitch over eight threads at the *apex* (highest point) After the apex, you place a stitch over six threads, then a stitch over four threads, then a final stitch over two threads. That is, for every stitch placed to the left or right, you increase or decrease the number of threads you stitch over by two.

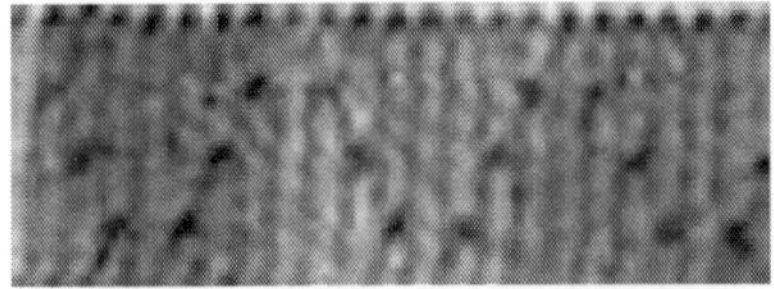

Figure: *Row of trianglestitch in variegated yarn. Each triangle is eight stitches high at the apex.*

Depending on how tall you make the apex (e.g. 6 threads, 10 threads, 12 threads, etc.) you can create triangles of different sizes.

Combining Triangles, Hexagons, Diamonds and Parallelograms

Although the design of the triangle is simple to execute, the power of this technique is the ability to combine triangles together to create patterns and other shapes including hexagons, diamonds and parallelograms. Note that shapes made of combined equilateral triangles are also called polyiamonds.

Note that where two short points of a triangle come together, Lantz uses an extra long stitch to join them two shapes.

These shapes along with the triangles can be combined to form a wide variety of geometric designs and tessellations or tilings.

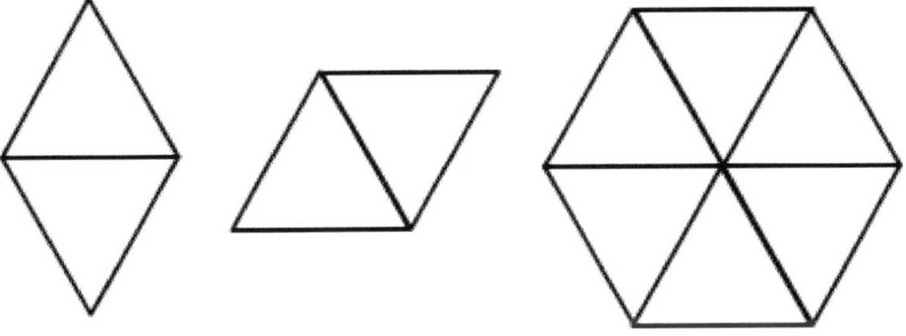

Figure: *Equilateral triangles combined to make a diamond (lozenge), a rhombus (parallellogram) and a hexagon.*

Development of Trianglepoint

Sherlee Lantz calls this a triangle stitch, but it simply a variation of basic satin stitch in canvas work. That is you create stitch patterns by covering different numbers of threads on the canvas with your fibre in different configurations.

Historical Sources

Lantz refers to Islamic and European sources as inspirations for trianglepoint designs, but tessellations based on triangles and regular hexagons can be found in a wide number of cultures Roman, Chinese and Byzantine cultures.

- Islamic Geometric Art (Dartmouth Geometry in Art)
- English Example (Tiling Plain & Fancy)
- Chinese Example (Tiling Plain & Fancy)
- Byzantine Example (Tiling Plain & Fancy)
- Roman Example (Tiling Plain & Fancy)

However, some might argue that the most recognised examples are associated with Islamic cultures.

Three Dimensional Illusions with Triangle Point

If you use a light, medium and dark value of fibre, you can easily create three dimensional effects with triangle point. A simple example is a cube illusion created by a six-triangle hexagon filled in with light values in two triangles, then a medium value in two areas, then two areas of darks. These cubes can be clustered together to form more intricate three-dimensional patterns. Below are some examples of three-dimensional effects created with triangles and diamonds.

- Pompeii Floor (Dartmouth Geometry in Art)
- Modern Isometric Design (Tiling Plain & Fancy)

Design How To

Isometric graph paper:

To create trianglepoint designs, Lantz suggests using triangular isometric graph paper, then colouring in the shapes to create different designs.

Sizing Triangles

In "classic" triangle point as envisioned by Lantz, you stitch one size of triangle for each triangle on your isometric graph paper. In Lantz's book the apex of each trianglular unit is usually 6, 8 or 10 stitches tall. However, it is possible to combine triangles of different sizes in one pattern. For instance a large triangle of one colour can replace a set of smaller ones. As long as each triangle is formed by stitches increasing or decreasing heights in increments of two, the patterns are usually workable.

5

Stitches

In the textile arts, a stitch is a single turn or loop of thread or yarn. Stitches are the fundamental elements of sewing, knitting, embroidery, crochet, and needle lace-making, whether by hand or machine. A variety of stitches, each with one or more names, are used for specific purposes.

Sewing, Embroidery, and Lace

All stitches made with a sewing needle with an "eye" or hole are variations on seven basic stitches:

- Running stitch
- Backstitch
- Overcast stitch
- Cross stitch
- Buttonhole or blanket stitch
- Chain stitch
- Knot stitch

These stitches and their variations are named according to the position of the needle and direction of sewing (*running stitch, backstitch*), the form or shape of the stitch (*chain stitch, feather stitch*) or the purpose of the stitch (tailor's tack, *hem stitch*).

Sewing machine stitches are classified by their structure:

- Chain stitch, made with one thread
- Lockstitch, made with two threads
- Overlock, made with one to four threads
- Coverstitch, made with two or four threads (a twine)

Fancy machine stitches mimic traditional hand stitches using variations on the basic stitches.

Crochet

In crochet, stitches are made by pulling a loop of thread through the work with a crochet hook. Crochet stitches are named based on their structure. In the English-speaking crochet world, basic stitches have different names that vary by country. The differences are usually referred to as UK/US or British/American.

Backstitch

Backstitch or back stitch and its variants stem stitch, outline stitch and split stitch are a class of embroidery and sewing stitches in which individual stitches are made backward to the general direction of sewing. These stitches form lines and are most often used to outline shapes or to add fine detail to an embroidered picture.

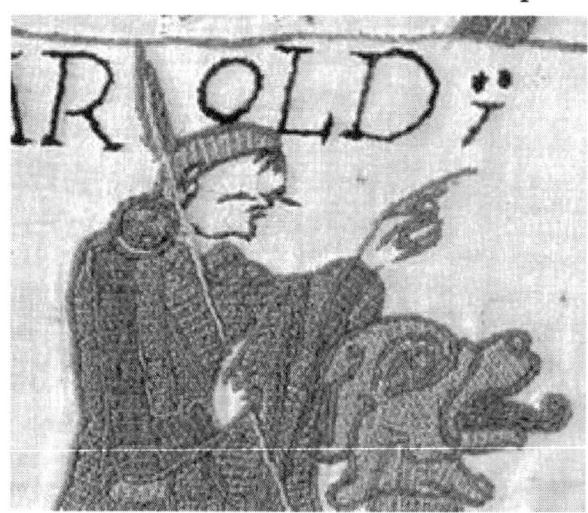

Figure: *Detail of the Bayeux Tapestry showing text and outlines in stem stitch.*

Applications

Basic backstitch is used to outline shapes in modern cross-stitch, in Assisi embroidery and occasionally in blackwork.

A versatile and easy to work stitch, backstitch is ideal for following both smooth and complicated outlines and as a foundation row for more complex embroidery stitches such as *Herringbone ladder filling stitch*. Although superficially similar to Holbein stitch, commonly used in Blackwork embroidery, backstitch differs in the way it is worked, requiring a single journey only to complete a line of stitching. Stem stitch is an ancient technique; surviving mantles embroidered with stem stitch by the Paracas people of Peru are dated to the first century BCE. Stem stitch is used in the Bayeux Tapestry, an embroidered cloth probably dating to the later 1070s, for lettering and to outline areas filled with couching or laid-work.

Split stitch in silk is characteristic of Opus Anglicanum, an embroidery style of Medieval England.

Description of the Technique

Backstitch is most easily worked on an even-weave fabric, where the threads can be counted to ensure regularity, and is generally executed from right to left. The stitches are worked in a 'two steps forward, one step back' fashion, along the line to be filled, as shown in the diagram.

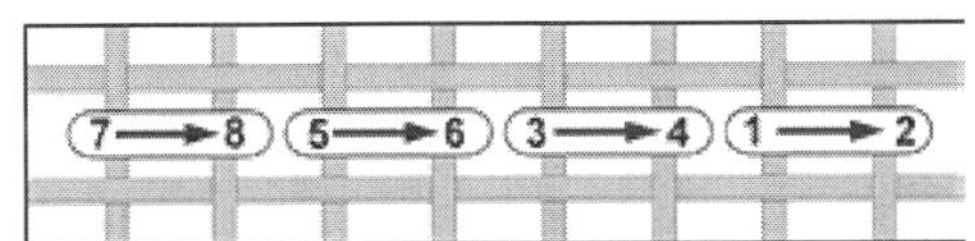

Figure: *Neatly worked in a straight line this stitch resembles machine stitching.*

The back stitch can also be used as a hand-sewing sewing utility stitch to attach two pieces of fabric together.

Variants

Variants of backstitch include:

- Basic backstitch or *point de sable.*
- Threaded backstitch
- Pekinese stitch, a looped interlaced backstitch
- Stem stitch, in which each stitch overlaps the previous stitch to one side, forming a twisted line of stitching, with the thread passing below the needle. It is generally used for outlining shapes and for stitching flower stems and tendrils.
- Whipped stem stitch
- Outline stitch, sometimes distinguished from stem stitch in that the thread passes above rather than below the needle.
- Split stitch, in which the needle pierces the thread rather than returning to one side.

Blanket

A blanket is a type of bedding, generally speaking, a large piece of cloth, intended to keep the user warm, especially while sleeping.

Blankets are distinguished from sheets by their thickness and purpose; the thickest sheet is still thinner than the lightest blanket.

Blankets are generally used for warmth, while sheets are for hygiene, comfort and aesthetics. Blankets are subdivided into many types, including quilts, duvets, and comforters, depending on their thickness, construction and/or fill material.

Blankets were traditionally made of wool because of wool's warmth, breathability and natural fire-retardant properties, while sheets were made of cotton or linen, which are less irritating to the skin. Nowadays, synthetic fibres are frequently used for both. Throw blankets are smaller blankets, often in decorative colours and patterns, that can be used for extra warmth outside of bed. Blankets are sometimes used as comfort objects by small children.

Blanket Stitch

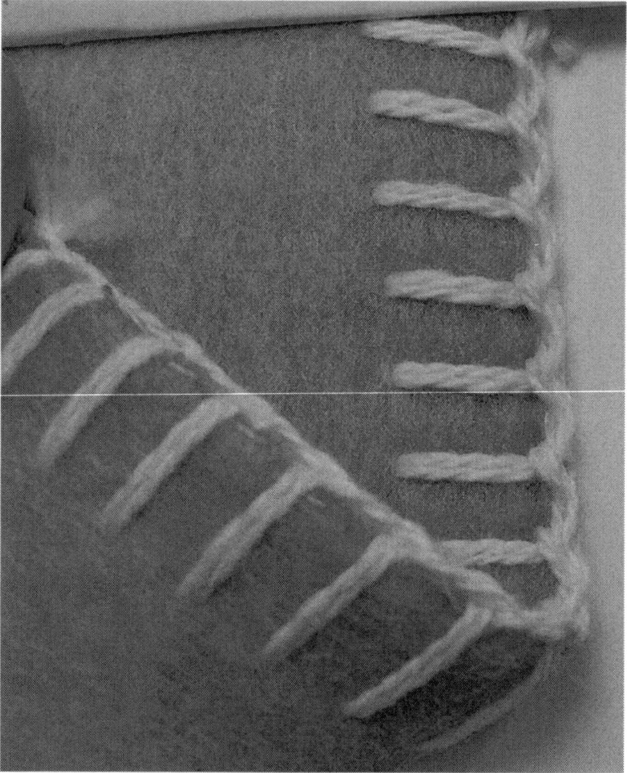

Figure: *A merrow blanket stitch*

The blanket stitch is a stitch used to reinforce the edge of thick materials. Depending on circumstances, it may also be called a *whip stitch* or a *crochet stitch*. It is defined as "A decorative stitch used to finish an unhemmed blanket. The stitch can be seen on both sides of the blanket."

History

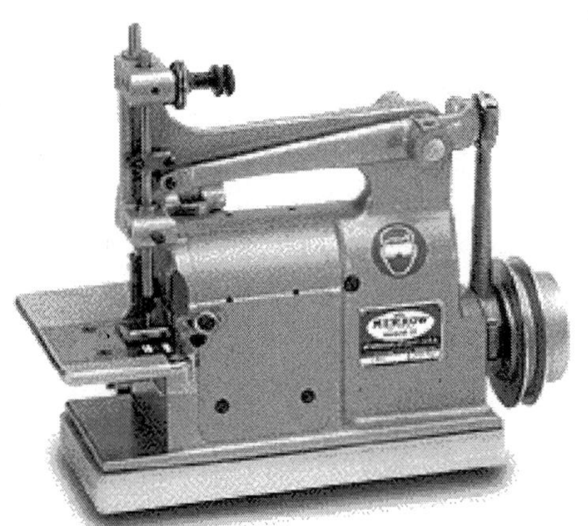

Figure: *A merrow industrial crochet machine*

This stitch has long been both an application by hand and as a machine sewn stitch. When done by hand, it is sometimes considered a crochet stitch, used to join pieces together to make a blanket or other larger item. It is used in sewing leather pieces together, as traditionally done by indigenous American cultures, and even for weaving basket rims. The whipstitch is also a type of surgical suturing stitch.

When done by machine, it may be called a whip stitch or, sometimes, a Merrow Crochet Stitch, after the first sewing machine that was used to sew a blanket stitch. This machine was produced and patented by the Merrow Machine Company in 1887. The defining characteristic of the crochet machine is its ability to sew with yarn and stitch thick goods with a consistent overlock edge. From 1877-1925 the machine evolved dramatically, and consequently so did the capacity of manufacturers to produce goods with the whip stitch. To this day, Merrow retains a patent on the mechanism that creates the blanket stitch, renewing it with each redesign, which has occurred hundreds of times since its introduction in 1877. The most recent patent renewal occurred in 1934

In the early 1990s Chinese manufacturers copied the design of the original crochet sewing machines; Merrow is currently involved in litigation with several Chinese firms who are accused of violating Merrow's intellectual property rights.

Style

The blanket stitch is commonly used as a decorative stitch on an array of garments. Besides blankets, it is used on sweaters, outerwear, swimsuits, home furnishings, and much more. There are many styles of production blanket stitching, including rolled, narrow, with elastic, and traditional.

Additionally, the term "blanket stitch" has become a verb, describing the application of the stitch.

Buttonhole

Buttonholes are holes in fabric which allow buttons to pass through, securing one piece of the fabric to another. The raw edges of a buttonhole are usually finished with stitching. This may be done either by hand or by a sewing machine. Some forms of button, such as a Mandarin button, use a loop of cloth or rope instead of a buttonhole. Buttonholes can also refer to flowers worn in the lapel buttonhole of a coat or jacket, which are referred to simply as "buttonholes" or *boutonnières*.

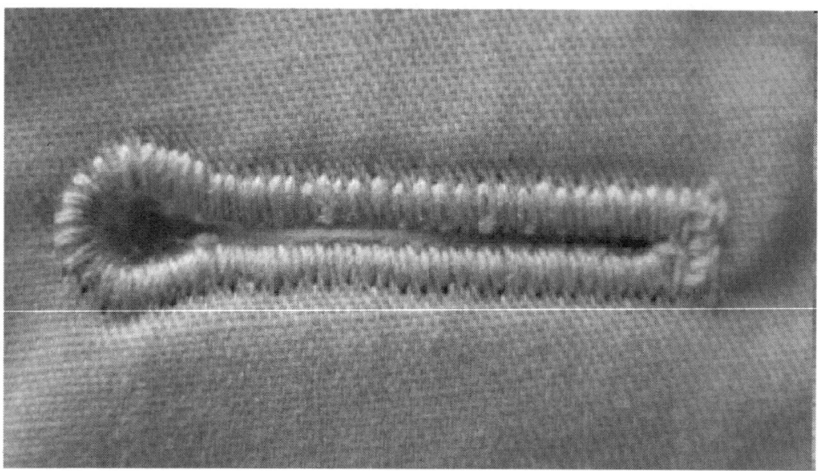

Figure: *Machine-stitched keyhole buttonhole with bar*

Buttonholes for fastening or closing clothing with buttons appeared first in Germany in the 13th century. However it is believed that ancient Persians used it first. They soon became widespread with the rise of snug-fitting garments in 13th- and 14th-century Europe.

Aspects of Buttonholes

Buttonholes often have a bar of stitches at either side of them. This is a row of perpendicular hand or machine stitching to reinforce the raw edges of the fabric, and to prevent it from fraying.

Traditionally, men's clothing buttonholes are on the left side, and women's clothing buttonholes are on the right. The lore of this 'opposite' sides buttoning is that the practice came into being as 'women of means' had chamber maids who dressed them. So as not to confuse the poor chamber maids, the wealthy began having women's garments made with the buttons and holes 'switched'; the birth of the modern ladies' blouse. It is interesting to note that the chamber maids themselves, as did most all the common class, both male and female, actually wore 'shirts' with buttons and holes placed as on men's clothing. There appears to be no concrete reference to prove or disprove this story, but its plausibility bears noting.

There is also the theory that if a man is driving his ox cart or carriage or car, he can see inside her blouse and she can see inside of his. (Of course this assumes the driver is on the left hand side.)

Types of Buttonholes

Hand stitching:

- A plain buttonhole, by far the most the most common type. In plain buttonholes, the raw (cut) edges of the textile are finished with thread in very closely spaced stitches (if made by hand, often the buttonhole stitch) with a gimp cord at the edges to act as a reinforcement. When stitched by hand, a slit is made in the fabric first and the result is called a worked buttonhole.

Machined Stitching

Sewing machines offer various levels of automation to creating plain buttonholes. When made by machine, the slit between the sides of the buttonhole is opened after the stitching is completed.

- A machine-made buttonhole is usually sewn with two parallel rows of machine sewing in a narrow zig-zag stitch, with the ends finished in a broader zig-zag stitch. (One of the first automatic buttonhole machines was invented by Henry Alonzo House in 1862.)
- A bound buttonhole, which has its raw edges encased by pieces of fabric or trim instead of stitches.
- A keyhole buttonhole is a special case of a thread-finished buttonhole that is normally machine-made due to the difficulty of achieving it by hand working. It is characterized by a round hole at the end of the slit to accommodate the button's shank without distorting the fabric.

Keyhole buttonholes are most often found on tailored coats and jackets.

Chain Stitch

Chain stitch is a sewing and embroidery technique in which a series of looped stitches form a chain-like pattern. Chain stitch is an ancient craft - examples of surviving Chinese chain stitch embroidery worked in silk thread have been dated to the Warring States period (5th – 3rd century BC).

Handmade chain stitch embroidery does not require that the needle pass through more than one layer of fabric. For this reason the stitch is an effective surface embellishment near seams on finished fabric.

Because chain stitches can form flowing, curved lines, they are used in many surface embroidery styles that mimic "drawing" in thread.

Chain stitches are also used in making tambour lace, needlelace, macramé and crochet.

Figure: *Traditional embroidery in chain stitch on a Kazakh rug, contemporary.*

History

The earliest archaeological evidence of chain stitch embroidery dates from 1100 BC in China. Excavated from royal tombs, the embroidery was made using threads of silk. Chain stitch embroidery has also been found dating to the Warring States period. Chain stitch designs spread to Iran through the Silk Road.

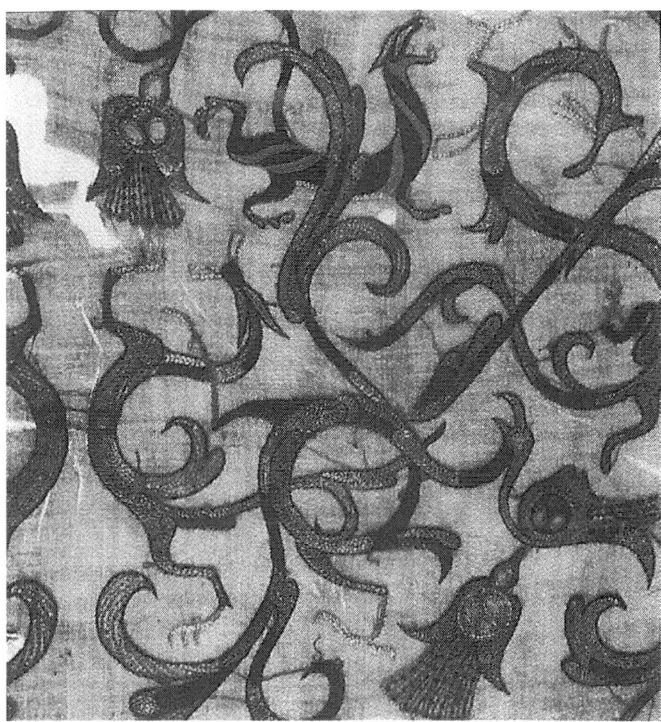

Figure: *Detail of an embroidered silk gauze ritual garment from a 4th-century BC, Zhou era tomb at Mashan, Hubei province, China. Rows of even, round chain-stitches are used both for outline and to fill in colour.*

Applications

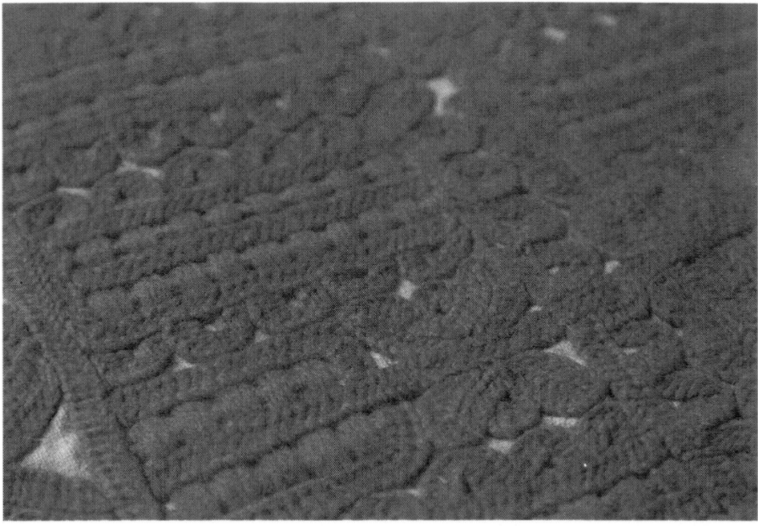

Figure: *Open chain stitch from Kalotaszeg, early 20th century.*

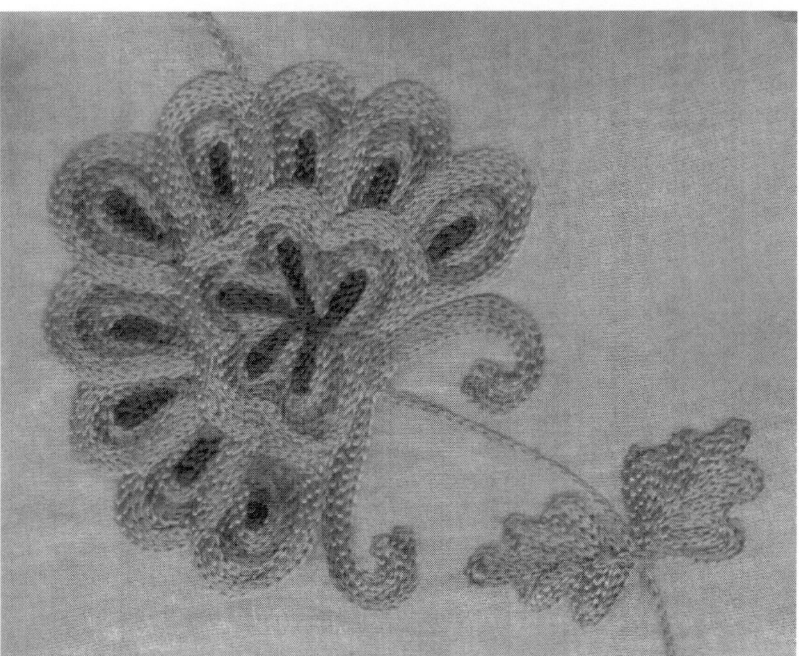

Figure: *Machine embroidery in chain stitch on a voile curtain, China, early 21st century.*

Hand Embroidery

Chain stitch and its variations are fundamental to embroidery traditions of many cultures, including Kashmiri *numdahs*, Iranian Resht work, Central Asian suzani, Hungarian Kalotaszeg "written embroidery", Jacobean embroidery, and crewelwork.

Machine Sewing and Embroidery

Chain stitch was the stitch used by early sewing machines; however, as it is easily unraveled from fabric, this was soon replaced with the more secure lockstitch. This ease of unraveling of the single-thread chain stitch, more specifically known as ISO 4915:1991 stitch 101, continues to be exploited for industrial purposes in the closure of bags for bulk products. Machine embroidery in chain stitch, often in traditional hand-worked crewel designs, is found on curtains, bed linens, and upholstery fabrics.

Variants

Hand variants: Variations of the basic chain stitch include:

- Back-stitched chain stitch
- Braided stitching

- Cable chain stitch
- Knotted chain stitch
- Open chain stitch
- Petal chain stitch
- Rosette chain stitch
- Singalese chain stitch
- Twisted chain stitch
- Wheat-ear stitch
- Zig-zag chain stitch

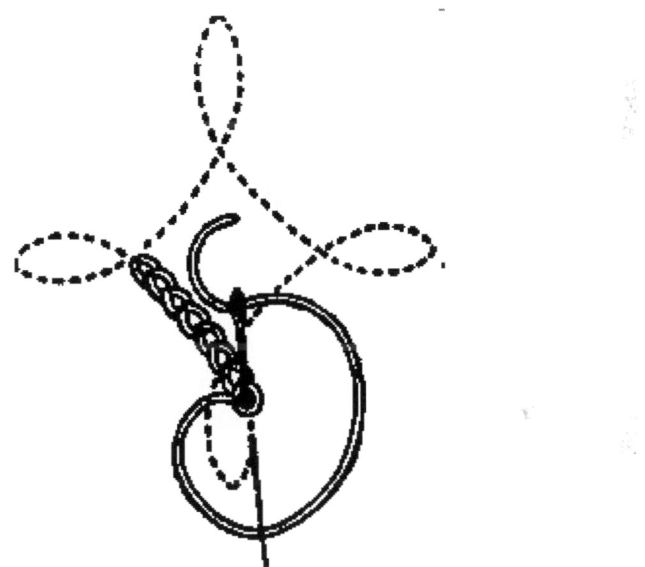

Figure: *"Drawing" or outlining in basic chain stitch*

Machine Variants

- The Basic Chain stitch is made by first sending the needle down through the material. Then, as the needle rises upward, the friction of the thread against the fabric is sufficient to form a small loop on the underside of the material. That loop is caught by a circular needle which is beneath the work.

  The machine then moves the material forward projecting the loop on the underside from the previous stitch. The next drop of the needle goes through the previous loop. The circular needle then releases the first loop and picks up the new loop and the process repeats.

- The Double chain stitch uses two threads. It is rarely used in today's machines except for ornamental purposes because it uses a lot of thread. It is found in bulk material packaging, where it is used to close big bags. In this case it is useful to allow an easy opening of the bag.

Couching and Laid Work

In embroidery, couching and laid work are techniques in which yarn or other materials are laid across the surface of the ground fabric and fastened in place with small stitches of the same or a different yarn.

The couching threads may be either the same colour as the laid threads or a contrasting colour. When couching threads contrast with laid threads, patterns may be worked in the couching stitches.

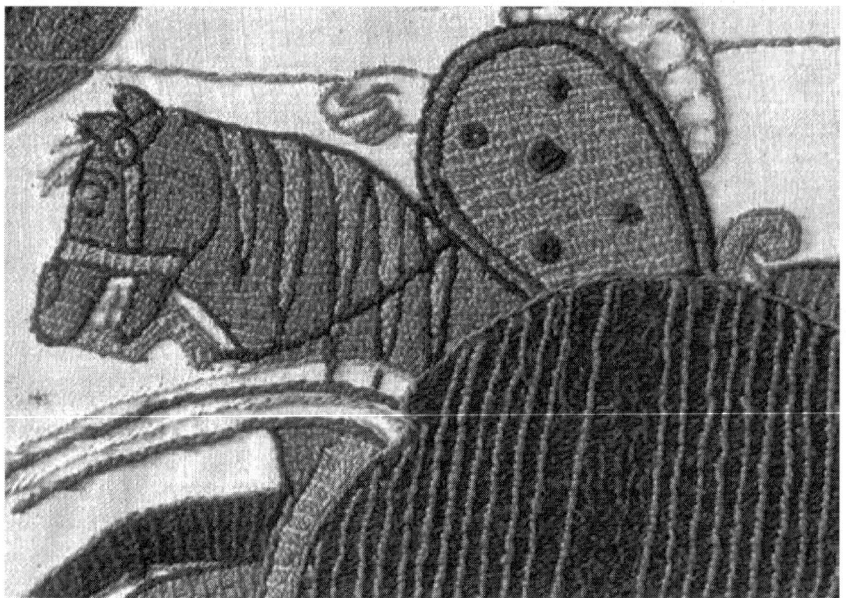

Figure: *Detail of the Bayeux Tapestry showing fillings in laid work.*

Applications

Laid work is one of two techniques used in the Bayeux Tapestry, an embroidered cloth probably dating to the later 1070s. (The other technique is stem stitch.)

Underside couching of metal thread was characteristic of earlier Opus Anglicanum in Medieval England and was also used historically in Sicily and rarely in other parts of Italy and France. Couching is also characteristic of Japanese metal-thread embroidery and Central Asian suzani work.

There is a strong tradition of couching stitch in Palestine. Production centred on Bethlehem and its two neighbouring villages Beit Sahour and Beit Jalla; it was used for wedding dresses and formal wear.

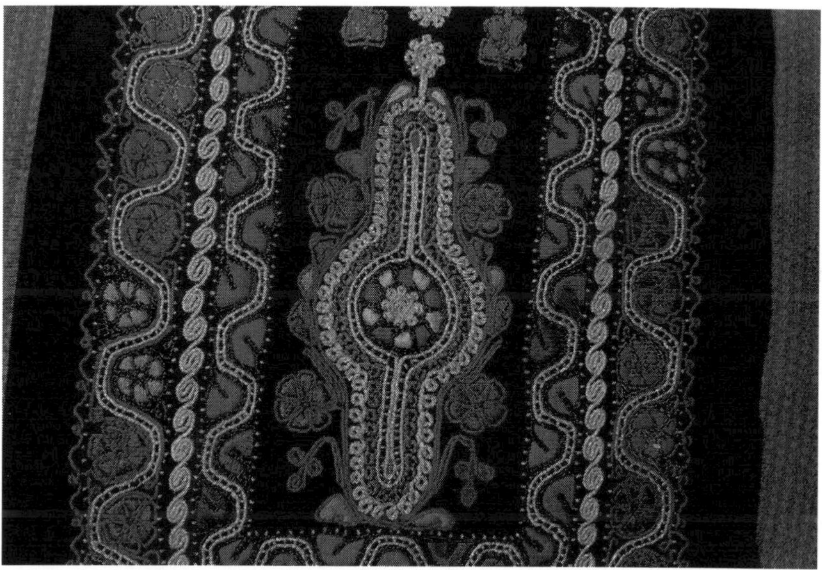

Figure: *Couching stitch from Beit Jalla.* ***2006.***

Variants

- In couching, one or more threads are laid on the fabric surface and sewn to the fabric at regular intervals.
- In couched filling, threads are laid on the surface in a trellis pattern and sewn to the fabric at the intersections.
- In laid work or Bayeux stitch, threads are laid side-by-side to fill a shape, then held in place with a thread at right angles to the laid threads. This crossing thread is then couched to the fabric to hold the laid threads in place.
- In Bokhara couching or Bokhara stitch, the couched threads are held in place with many tiny crossing stitches, which may be aligned from row to row to produce patterns.,
- In Roumanian stitch, long satin stitches are each held in place with a small diagonal stitch made in the centre
- In Roumanian couching, bundles of laid threads are held in place with Roumanian stitches

- In Underside couching, a heavy couching thread (historically, a stout linen) is brought up from the wrong side of the work, looped over the laid thread, and returned to the wrong side. The couching thread is then given a sharp pull which draws a small loop of laid thread through to the wrong side of the fabric. Underside couching has the advantages that the couching thread is completely concealed from the front and is not subject to wear.

Cross Stitches

The cross stitch sampler is called that because it was generally stitched by a young girl to learn how to stitch and to record alphabet and other patterns to be used in her household sewing. These samples of her stitching could be referred back to over the years. Often, motifs and initials were stitched on household items to identify their owner, or simply to decorate the otherwise-plain cloth. In the United States, the earliest known cross-stitch sampler is currently housed at Pilgrim Hall in Plymouth, Massachusetts. The sampler was created by Loara Standish, daughter of Captain Myles Standish and pioneer of the Leviathan stitch, circa 1653.

Traditionally, cross-stitch was used to embellish items like household linens, tablecloths, dishcloths, and doilies (only a small portion of which would actually be embroidered, such as a border). Although there are many cross-stitchers who still employ it in this fashion, it is now increasingly popular to work the pattern on pieces of fabric and hang them on the wall for decoration. Cross stitch is also often used to make greeting cards, pillowtops, or as inserts for box tops, coasters and trivets.

Multicoloured, shaded, painting-like patterns as we know them today are a fairly modern development, deriving from similar shaded patterns of Berlin wool work of the mid-nineteenth century. Besides designs created expressly for cross stitch, there are software programs that convert a photograph or a fine art image into a chart suitable for stitching. One stunning example of this is in the cross stitched reproduction of the Sistene Chapel charted and stitched by Joanna Lopianowski-Roberts.

There are many cross-stitching "guilds" and groups across the United States and Europe which offer classes, collaborate on large projects, stitch for charity, and provide other ways for local cross-stitchers to get to know one another. Individually owned local needlework shops (LNS) often have stitching nights at their shops, or host weekend stitching retreats. Today cotton floss is the most common embroidery thread. It is a thread made of mercerized cotton, composed of six strands that are only loosely twisted together and easily separable. While there are other manufacturers, the two most-commonly used (and oldest) brands are DMC and Anchor, both of which have been manufacturing embroidery floss since the 1800s.

Other materials used are pearl (or perle) cotton, Danish flower thread, silk and Rayon. Different wool threads, metallic threads or other novelty threads are also used, sometimes for the whole work, but often for accents and embellishments. Hand-dyed cross stitch floss is created just as the name implies - it is dyed by hand. Because of this, there are variations in the amount of colour throughout the thread. Some variations can be subtle, while some can be a huge contrast. Some also have more than one colour per thread, which in the right project, creates amazing results.

Cross stitch is widely used in traditional Palestinian dressmaking.

Related Stitches and Forms of Embroidery

Other stitches are also often used in cross-stitch, among them ¼, ½, and ¾ stitches and backstitches. Cross-stitch is often used together with other stitches. A cross stitch can come in a variety of prostational forms. It is sometimes used in crewel embroidery, especially in its more modern derivatives. It is also often used in needlepoint.

A specialised historical form of embroidery using cross-stitch is Assisi embroidery.

There are many stitches which are related to cross-stitch and were used in similar ways in earlier times. The best known are Italian cross-stitch, Celtic Cross Stitch, Irish Cross Stitch, long-armed cross-stitch, Ukrainian cross-stitch and Montenegrin stitch. Italian cross-stitch and Montenegrin stitch are reversible, meaning the work looks the same on both sides. These styles have a slightly different look than ordinary cross-stitch. These more difficult stitches are rarely used in mainstream embroidery, but they are still used to recreate historical pieces of embroidery or by the creative and adventurous stitcher.

The double cross-stitch, also known as a Leviathan stitch or Smyrna cross stitch, combines a cross-stitch with an upright cross-stitch. Berlin wool work and similar petit point stitchery resembles the heavily shaded, opulent styles of cross-stitch, and sometimes also used charted patterns on paper. Cross-stitch is often combined with other popular forms of embroidery, such as Hardanger embroidery or blackwork embroidery. Cross-stitch may also be combined with other work, such as canvaswork or drawn thread work. Beadwork and other embellishments such as paillettes, charms, small buttons and speciality threads of various kinds may also be used.

Recent Trends in the UK

Cross-stitch has become increasingly popular with the younger generation of the United Kingdom in recent years. The Great Recession has also seen renewal of interest in home crafts. Retailers such as John Lewis experienced a 17% rise in sales of haberdashery products between 2009 and 2010. Hobbycraft, a chain of stores selling craft supplies, also enjoyed an 11% increase in sales over the past year. The chain is said to have benefited from the "make do and mend" mentality of the credit crisis, which has driven people to make their own cards and gifts.

Knitting and cross stitching have become more popular hobbies for a younger market, in contrast to its traditional reputation as a hobby for retirees. Sewing and craft groups such as Stitch and Bitch London have resurrected the idea of the traditional craft club. At Clothes Show Live 2010 there was a new area called "Sknitch" promoting modern sewing, knitting and embroidery.

In a departure from the traditional designs associated with cross stitch, there is a current trend for more postmodern or tongue-in-cheek designs featuring retro images or contemporary sayings. It is linked to a concept known as 'subversive cross stitch', which involves more risque designs, often fusing the traditional sampler style with sayings designed to shock or be incongruous with the old-fashioned image of cross stitch. Stitching designs on other materials can be accomplished by using a Waste Canvas. This waste canvas is a temporary gridded canvas similar to regular canvas used for embroidery that is held together by a water soluble glue, this is removed after completion of stitch design.

Embroidery Stitch

In everyday language, a stitch in the context of embroidery or hand-sewing is defined as the movement of the embroidery needle from the backside of the fabric to the front side and back to the back side. The thread stroke on the front side produced by this is also called *stitch.* In the context of embroidery, an embroidery stitch means one or more *stitches* that are always executed in the same way, forming a figure of recognisable look. Embroidery stitches are also called *stitches* for short. Embroidery stitches are the smallest units in embroidery. Embroidery patterns are formed by doing many embroidery stitches, either all the same or different ones, either following a counting chart on paper, following a design painted on the fabric or even working freehand.

Common Stitches

Embroidery uses various combinations of stitches. Each embroidery stitch has a special name to help identify it. These names vary from country to country and region to region. Some embroidery books will include name variations. Taken by themselves the stitches are mostly simple to execute, however when put together the results can be extremely complex.

Straight Stitches

Straight stitches pass through the fabric ground in a simple up and down motion, and for the most part moving in a single direction. Examples of straight stitches are:

- Running or basting stitch
- Simple satin stitch
- Algerian eye stitch
- Fern stitch

Straight Stitches that have two journeys (generally forwards and backwards over the same path). Examples:

- Holbein stitch, also known as the double running stitch
- Bosnian stitch

Back Stitches

Back stitches pass through the fabric ground in an encircling motion. The needle in the simplest backstitch comes up from the back of the fabric, makes a stitch to the right going back to the back of the fabric, then passes behind the first stitch and comes up to the front of the fabric to the left of the first stitch. The needle then goes back to the back of the fabric through the same hole the stitch first came up from. The needle then repeats the movement to the left of the stitches and continues. Some examples of a back stitch are:

- Stem stitch or outline stitch
- Split stitch. The needle pierces the thread as it come back up.
- Crewel stitch

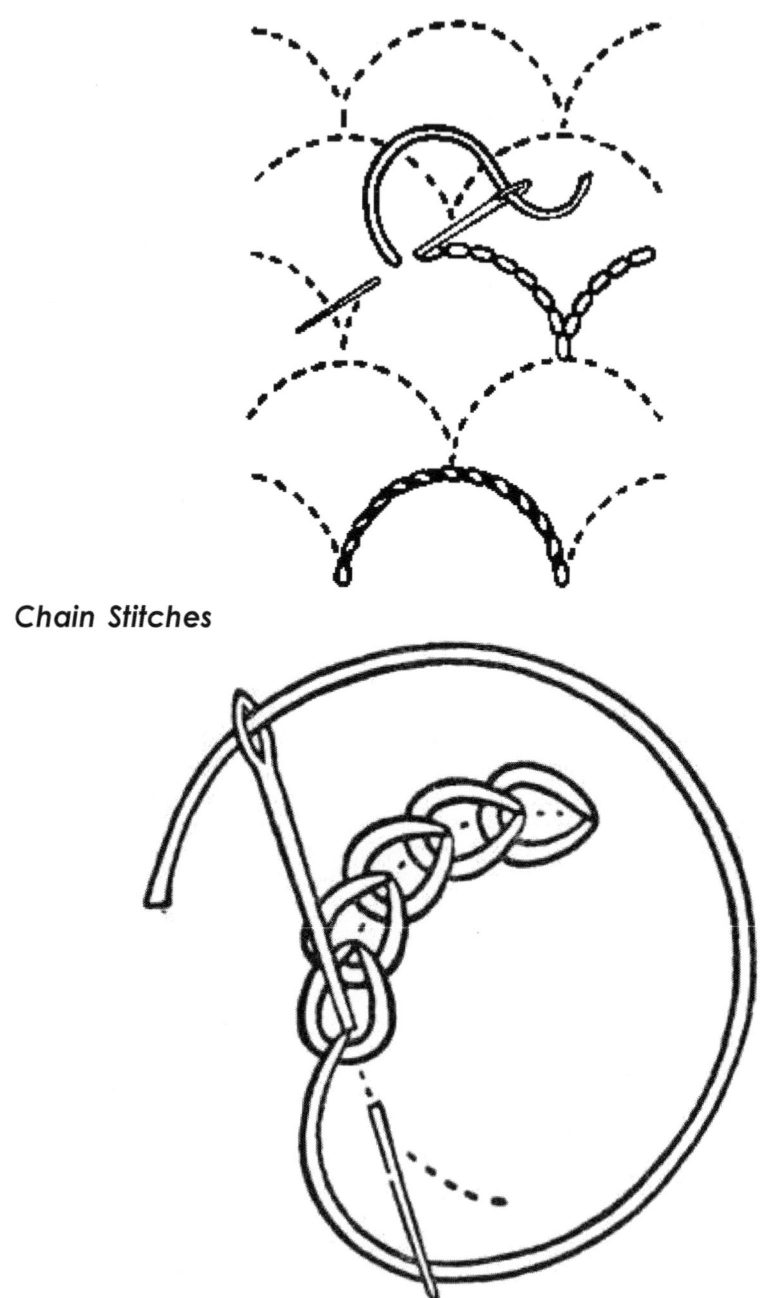

Chain Stitches

Chain stitches catch a loop of the thread on the surface of the fabric. In the simplest of the looped stitches, the chain stitch, the needle comes up from the back of the fabric and then the needle goes back into the same hole it came out of, pulling the loop of thread almost completely through to the back; but before the loop disappears, the needle come back up (a certain distance from the beginning stitch -the distance deciding the length of the stitch), passes through the loop and prevents it from being pulled completely to the back of the fabric.

The needle then passes back to the back of the fabric through the second hole and begins the stitch again. Examples of chain stitches are:

- Chain stitch
- Lazy Daisy stitch, or detached chain. The loop stitch is held to the fabric at the wide end by a tiny tacking stitch.
- Spanish Chain or Zig-zag Chain

Buttonhole Stitches

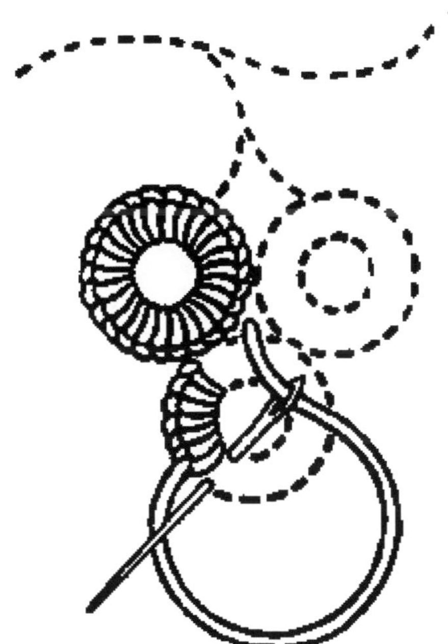

Buttonhole or blanket stitches also catch a loop of the thread on the surface of the fabric but the principal difference is that the needle does not return to the original hole to pass back to the back of the fabric. In the classic buttonhole stitch, the needle is returned to the back of the fabric at a right angle to the original start of the thread. The finished stitch in some ways resembles a letter "L" depending on the spacing of the stitches. For buttonholes the stitches are tightly packed together and for blanket edges they are more spaced out. The properties of this stitch make it ideal for preventing raveling of woven fabric. This stitch is also the basis for many forms of needle lace. Examples of buttonhole or blanket stitches.

- Blanket stitch
- Buttonhole stitch
- Closed buttonhole stitch, the tops of the stitch touch to form triangles
- Crossed buttonhole stitch, the tops of the stitch cross
- Buttonhole stitches combined with knots:
    - o Top Knotted Buttonhole stitch
    - o German Knotted Buttonhole stitch
    - o Tailor's buttonhole stitch

Feather Stitches

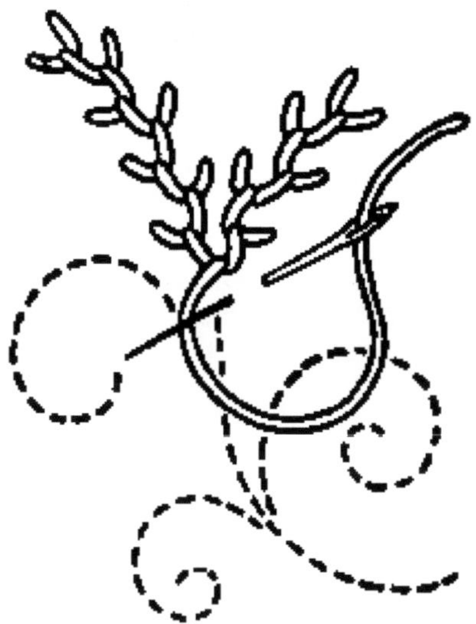

Feather or fly stitches also catch a loop of thread on the surface of the fabric but they differ from buttonhole stitches in that the catching of the loop is not at right angles or it alternates from side to side. The result is a very naturalistic looking stitch that is often used to make leaves and branches. Examples of fly stitches are:

- Fly stitch, or Y stitch
- Feather stitch
- Faggoting stitch, or Straight Open Cretan
- Cretan Stitch

Cross Stitches

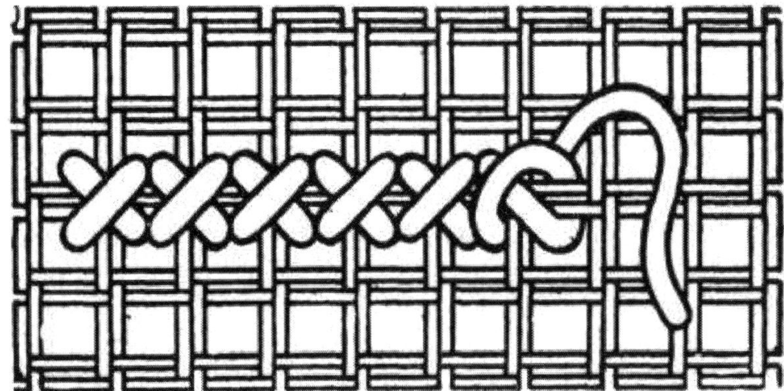

Cross stitches or cross-stitch have come to represent an entire industry of pattern production and material supply for the craft person. The stitch is done by creating a line of diagonal stitches going in one direction, usually using the warp and weft of the fabric as a guide, then on the return journey crossing the diagonal in the other direction, creating an "x". Also included in this class of stitches are:

- Herringbone stitches, including the hem stitch
- Breton stitch, here the threads of the "x" are twisted together
- Sprat's Head stitch
- Crow's Foot stitch, these last two stitches are often used in tailoring to strengthen a garment at a point of strain such as a pocket corner or the top of a kick pleat.

Many examples of cross stitches can be found here

Knotted Stitches

Knotted stitches are formed by wrapping the thread around the needle, once or several times, before passing it back to the back of the fabric ground. This is a predominate stitch in Brazilian embroidery, used to create flowers. Another form of embroidery that uses knots is Candlewicking, where the knots are created by forming a figure around the needle. Examples of knotted stitches are:

- French knot, or twisted knot stitch
- Chinese knot, which varies from the French knot in that it takes a tiny stitch in the background fabric while creating the knot
- Bullion knots
- Coral stitch

- There are also more complex knotted stitches such as:
  - o Knotted Loop stitch
  - o Plaited Braid stitch
  - o Sorbello stitch
  - o Diamond stitch
- Knotted edgings based on buttonhole stitches include:
  - o Antwerp edging stitch
  - o Armenian edging stitch

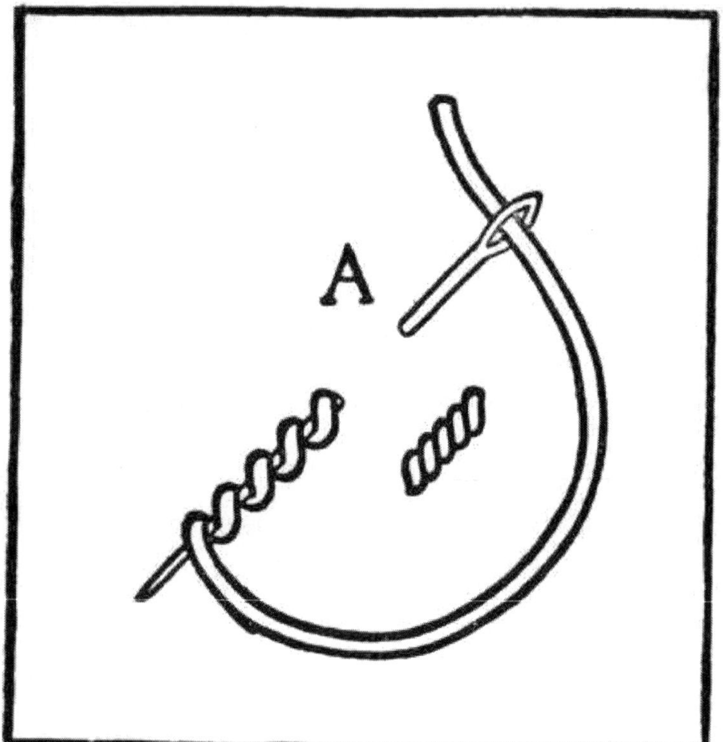

Figure: *Bullion knot*

Couching and Laid Work

Couching or laid stitches involve two sets of threads, the set that is being 'laid' onto the surface of the fabric and the set which attach the laid threads. The laid threads may be heavier than the attaching thread, or they may be of a nature that does not allow them to be worked like a regular embroidery thread, such as metal threads. The stitches used to attach the laid thread may be of any nature; cross stitch, buttonhole stitch, straight stitch; but some have specific names:

- Pendant couching,
- Bokhara couching
- Square laid work
- Oriental couching
- Battlement couching
- Klosterstitch
- Roumanian couching

Featherstitch

Featherstitch or feather stitch and Cretan stitch or faggoting stitch are embroidery techniques made of open, looped stitches worked alternately to the right and left of a central rib. Fly stitch is categorized with the featherstitches.

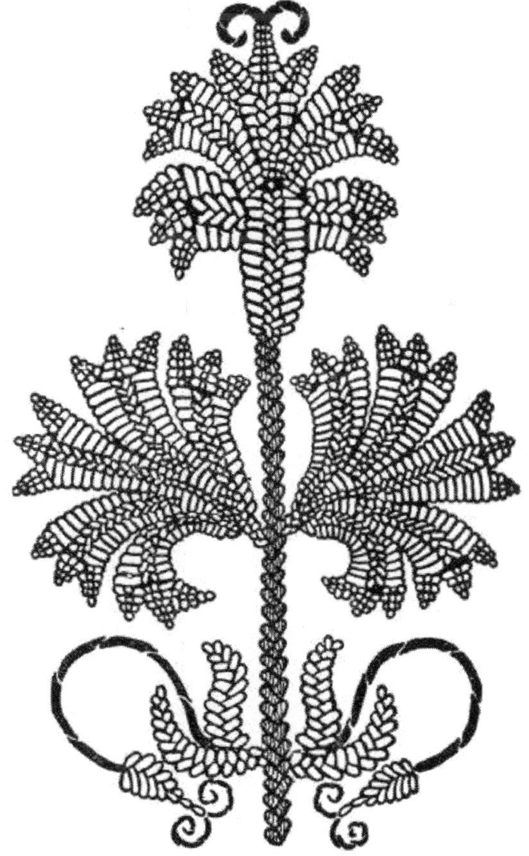

Figure: *Drawing of Cretan embroidery in closed Cretan stitch from* Embroidery and Tapestry Weaving, *1912*

Applications

Cretan stitch is characteristic of embroidery of Crete and the surrounding regions. Open Cretan stitch or faggoting is used in making open decorative seams and to attach insertions.

Featherstitch embroidery arose in England in the 19th century for decorating smock-frocks. It is also used to decorate the joins in crazy quilting. It is related to (and probably derives from) the older buttonhole stitch and chain stitch.

Featherstitch Variants

Common variants of featherstitch include:

- Basic featherstitch
- Long-armed featherstitch
- Double featherstitch
- Closed featherstitch
- Chained feather stitch
- Stitch gallery

Looped Stitches

Other looped stitches include:

- Cretan stitch or Open Cretan stitch or faggoting stitch
- Closed Cretan stitch
- Fishbone stitch
- Fly stitch, a filling stitch made of single, detached tacked loops.
- Loop stitch
- Scroll stitch

Parisian

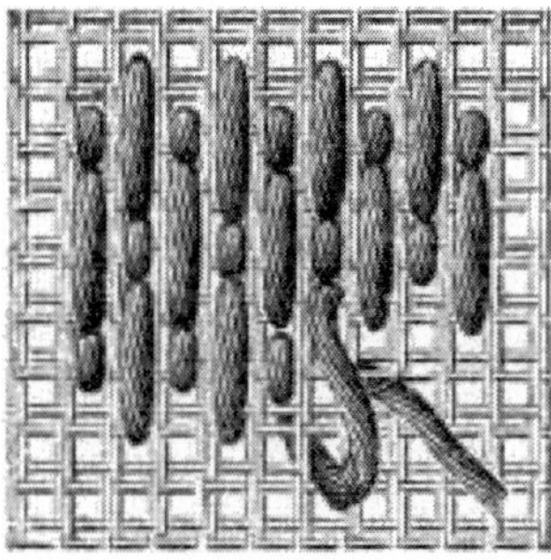

Figure: *Parisian stitch.*

Parisian stitch is a longer horizontal/vertical stitch used in needlepoint next to a smaller parallel stitch to create a basketweave pattern.

The end points on either end alternate in a staggered pattern. According to Thérèse de Dilmont in the *Encyclopedia of Needlework*:

This stitch, though it is generally worked on silk canvas, can also be worked on the different cotton and linen materials already referred to more than once in this Encyclopedia. It makes a very good grounding in cases where the material is not intended to be completely hidden. It consists of a long stitch over three threads, and a short stitch over one thread, alternately.

The case holding this thread is commonly known as an etu and is derived from the French word meaning fabric case.

Running

The running stitch or straight stitch is the basic stitch in hand-sewing and embroidery, on which all other forms of sewing are based. The stitch is worked by passing the needle in and out of the fabric. Running stitches may be of varying length, but typically more thread is visible on the top of the sewing than on the underside.

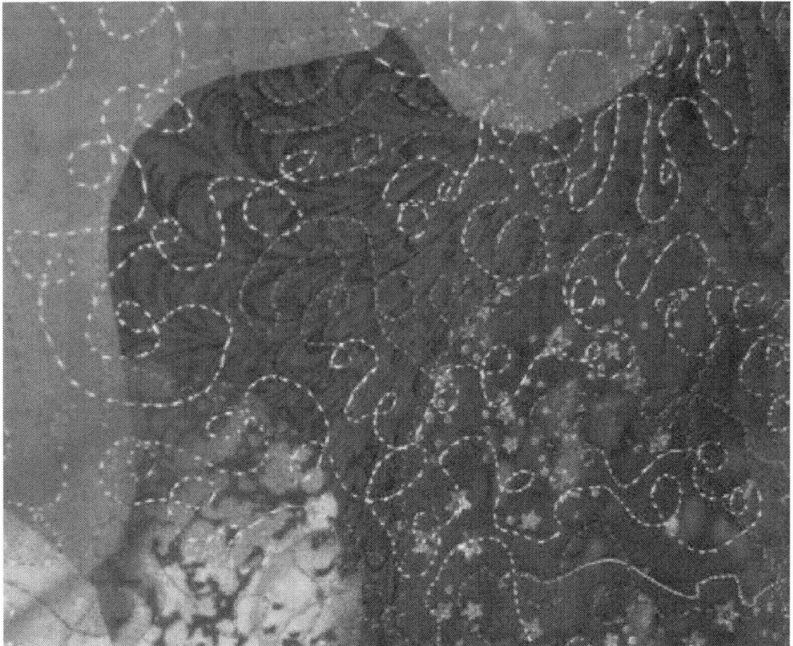

Figure: *Detail of a contemporary quilt with quilting in free-form white and coloured running stitches.*

Uses

Running stitches are used in hand-sewing and tailoring to sew basic seams, in hand patchwork to assemble pieces, and in quilting to hold the fabric layers and batting or wadding in place. Loosely spaced rows of short running stitches are used to support padded satin stitch. Running stitches are a component of many traditional embroidery styles, including kantha of India and Bangladesh, and Japanese sashiko quilting.

Related Stitches

- Basting stitches, also called *tailor's tack,* are long running stitches used to keep two pieces of fabric or trim aligned during final sewing, or to otherwise temporarily sew two pieces together.
- Darning stitches are closely spaced parallel rows of running stitches used to fill or reinforce worn areas of a textile, or as decoration.
- Double-running or Holbein stitches have a second row of running stitches worked in a reverse direction in between the stitches of the first pass, to make a solid line of stitching.
- Double darning stitches are closely spaced (but not overlapping) rows of Holbein stitches.

Satin Stitch

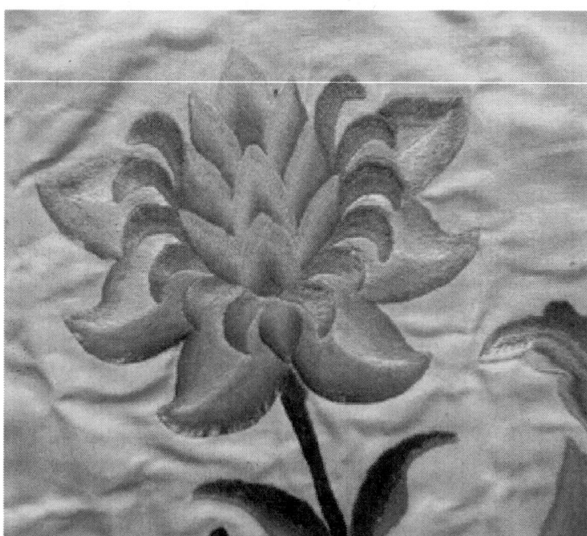

Figure: *Satin stitch in silk.*

In sewing and embroidery, a satin stitch or damask stitch is a series of flat stitches that are used to completely cover a section of the background fabric. Narrow rows of satin stitch can be executed on a standard sewing machine using a zigzag stitch or a special satin stitch foot.

In order to maintain a smooth edge, shapes can be outlined with back, split or chain stitch before the entire shape including the outline is covered with satin stitch. Machine-made satin stitch is often used to outline and attach appliques to the ground fabric.

Variants

Variants of the satin stitch include:

- Bourdon stitch - a tightly spaced, decorative stitch typically used for monograms and decorative purposes.
- Brick stitch, in which alternate rows of satin stitches are offset by half the stitch length. Worked in several related colours, brick stitch allows stepped shading. (Brick stitch is also the name of a beadwork technique.)
- Encroaching satin stitch, in which the top of each row of stitches is set between the bottom of the stitches on the previous row.
- Long-and-short stitch, used for fine shading; in the first row of satin stitches, every other stitch is half the length of its neighbours. Subsequent rows in related colours are all of the same length.
- Padded satin stitch, in which shapes are filled with rows of small running stitches which are then covered with satin stitches.

Thread

Satin stitch is frequently made with embroidery thread, which has less twist than standard sewing thread. This gives a more uniform effect, with the individual threads' filaments merging. While good sewing threads produce acceptable satin stitch, low quality threads usually do not sit straight, and produce an uneven result. The colour of each thread usually does not matter.

Shisha

Shisheh or Abhla Bharat embroidery, or mirror-work, is a type of embroidery which attaches small pieces of mirrors reflect metal to fabric. Mirror embroidery is spread throughout Asia, and today can be found in the traditional embroidery of Iran, India, Pakistan, Afghanistan, China, and Indonesia.

Straight Stitch

Straight or Flat stitch is a class of simple embroidery and sewing stitches in which individual stitches are made without crossing or looping the thread. These stitches are used to form broken or unbroken lines or starbursts, fill shapes, and create geometric designs.

Running stitch, Holbein or double-running stitch, satin stitch and darning stitch are all classed as straight or flat stitches. Backstitch is also sometimes included in this category.

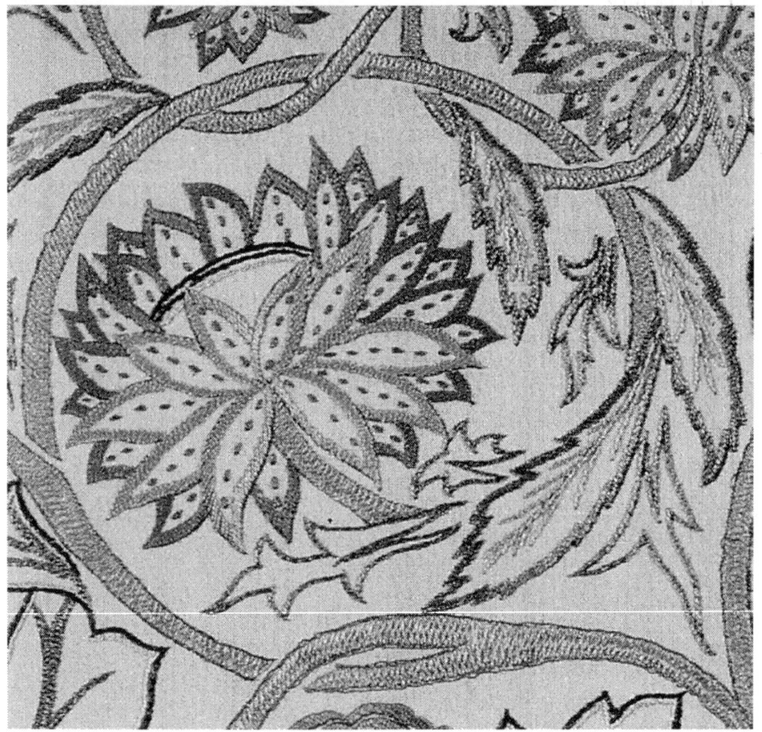

Figure: *Seed stitches (small, detached running stitches) are used on the centre ribs of these flower petals.*

Working Straight Stitch

Straight Stitch is a simple embroidery stitch created using a straight, long stitch individually or in groups to form patterns. This popular surface embroidery stitch can be worked on any type of embroidery fabric including plainweave.

Using straight stitches arranged in groups you can make simple leaves and flowers or geometric designs. Premark the fabric, or work the stitch freestyle, creating an infinite number of unique patterns.

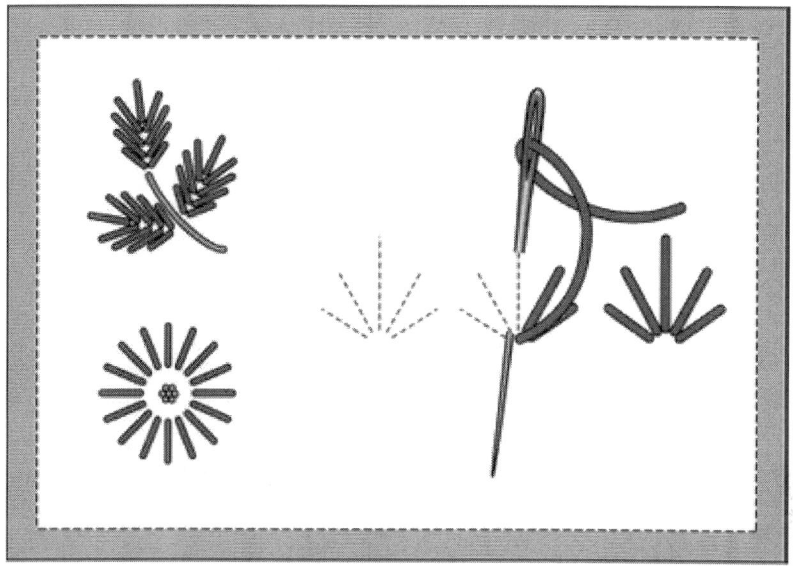

To work a straight stitch, bring the needle up through the fabric at the desired starting point and insert the needle into the fabric at the opposite end of the stitch where indicated on the pattern.

The diagram above shows how easy it is to work the straight stitch to make flowers, leaves or stems.

Tent Stitch

Tent stitch is a small, diagonal embroidery stitch that crosses over the intersection of one horizontal (weft) and one vertical (warp) thread of needlepoint canvas forming a slanted stitch at a 45-degree angle. It is also known as Needlepoint stitch and is one of the most basic and versatile stitches used in Needlepoint and other Canvas work embroidery. When worked on fine weave canvas over a single warp and weft thread it is known as Petit point in contrast to stitches, such as Gobelin, worked over multiple warp and/or weft threads.

"Petit point" comes from the French language, meaning "small point".

Tent Stitch Variants

There are three types of tent stitch, all producing the same appearance on the front of the canvas but each worked in a slightly different way and having particular characteristics, uses, benefits and drawbacks. These variants of tent stitch are known as basketweave, continental and half cross tent stitches:

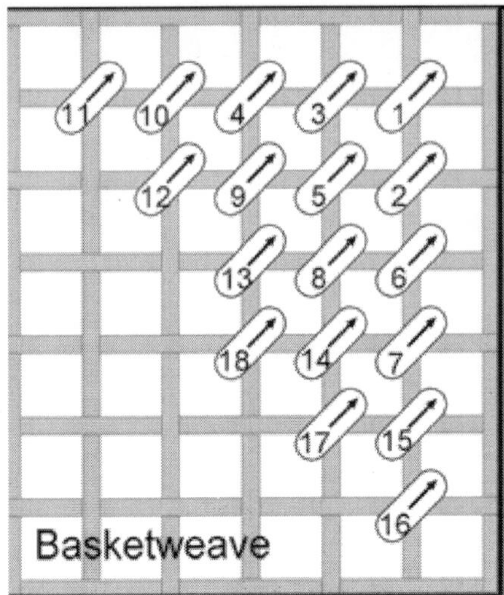

Figure: *Basketweave tent stitch*

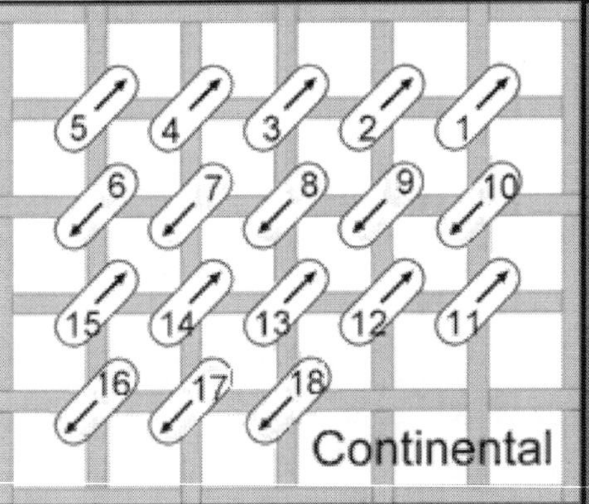

Figure: *Continental tent stitch*

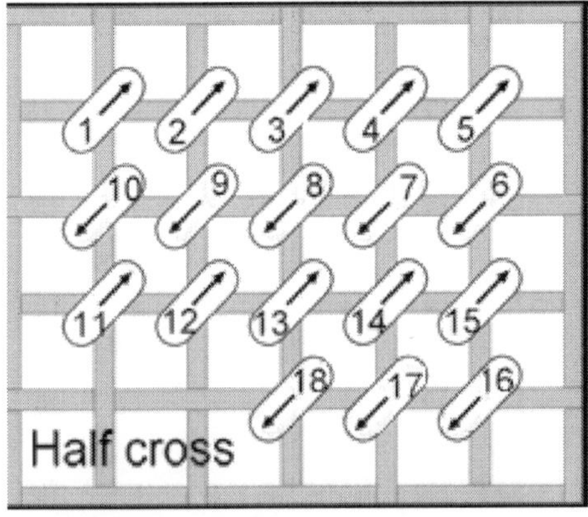

Figure: *Half cross tent stitch*

Basketweave Tent Stitch: The basketweave form of tent stitch is worked in diagonal rows up and down the canvas. The yarn on the back of the canvas has a typical basketweave appearance, with alternating horizontal and vertical stitches. Basketweave is the best stitch to use for covering large areas of canvas as it does not distort the canvas as the other two forms of tent stitch do.

Continental Tent Stitch: Continental stitch is worked horizontally or vertically across the canvas. On the back of the work, the stitches appear diagonally across two threads. This method uses more yarn than half cross stitch tent stitch but is more hardwearing.

Half Cross Tent Stitch: Half cross stitch is worked horizontally or vertically across the canvas. On the back of the work, the stitch appears vertical or horizontal, not diagonal, and crosses only one thread. This method uses less yarn than other stitches but is not very durable as coverage on the back of the canvas is a little thin.

6

Tools and Materials

Overview

Although embroidery doesn't have to be an expensive hobby, for those of us who get serious about our crafting there are certain techniques and equipment which help us embroider faster or fancier.

Laying Tools: When you work with multiple plies on a single needle, you'll need to keep the threads parallel, not twisted, as you stitch. (This is called "laying" the thread.) A variety of laying tools will help you achieve this. The simplest is a large tapestry needle or bodkin. Others specifically designed as laying tools include a stroking tool (also known as a tekobari); one end resembles an awl or stiletto, and the other end is square to prevent it from slipping from your fingers. A trolley needle has a point like a tapestry needle affixed to a metal band that fits on the end of your finger.

Pincushions: Pincushions are useful for stowing threaded needles if you must change colours often. Pincushions come in a variety of sizes and styles; select one that fits in your stitching bag or basket. Many stitchers like to make their own personalized models.

Many manufactured pincushions come with an emery, which looks like a very small pincushion filled with a gritty, sand-like material which keeps needles clean and sharp.

Needlebook or Needlecase: With "pages" of soft fabric, a needlebook keeps your pins and needles protected (and protects you from the needles, too) and organised. Each "open page" is designed to store a particular needle type in a range of sizes. As with pincushions, this is an item you can make yourself to show off your stitching talents.

Many stitchers like to store their needles in needlecases, which may be narrow and cylindrical or large and box-like; some of the latter have magnets to keep needles in place.

Thread Palette: These plastic wood or paper palettes have a series of holes along the edges to hold individual colours of threads, which you attach using half-hitch knots.

Thread Organiser: There are many products on the market for storing and identifying threads you accumulate. One of the simplest is small individual plastic bags held together on a metal binder ring. Storage boxes such as those used for hardware and fishing lurs work well for thread wound on bobbins. On the other end are wooden boxes or chests that resemble fine furniture.

Ruler and Tape Measure: Clear plastic rulers calibrated in inches are invaluable and come in a 6" length that fits easily into a stitching bag. For measuring a larger area, a tape measure is useful and takes up little space.

Thumbtacks and Tack Puller: Use these to attach fabric to stretcher bars. (Don't use staples to attach embroidery fabric; you'll risk pulling one of the fine threads and spoiling the appearance of the fabric.

Drafting Tape: This tape is less sticky than regular masking tape and helps keep your needlework cleaner. Use it for taping the cut edges of your fabric before mounting it in a stitching frame. Find it at art supply stores.

Lighting and Magnification Both your eyesight and your needlework deserve optimal lighting. Choose a light that directs a circle (not a spotlight) of light onto your entire stitching surface. Floor lamps and swivel-arm table lamps (such as an architect's light) are good choices. To avoid casting shadows over the work surface, right-handers will benefit from a light directed over the left shoulder, left-handers from the right.

For very fine work you may want to use a lamp that has a magnifier attached. Other possibilities include magnifiers that hang around the neck, attach to your eyeglasses, or are worn atop the head.

Embellishments. Small, decorative accents give your embroidery beauty, whimsy, and individuality. Look for buttons, beads, and charms at your local needlework shop, catalogs, consumer shows or online. Find them also in embroidery kits, often as the focus of a design theme.

Aida Cloth

Aida cloth (sometimes called Java canvas) is an open weave, even-weave fabric traditionally used for cross-stitch embroidery. This cotton fabric has a natural mesh that facilitates cross-stitching and enough natural stiffness that the crafter does not need to use an embroidery hoop.

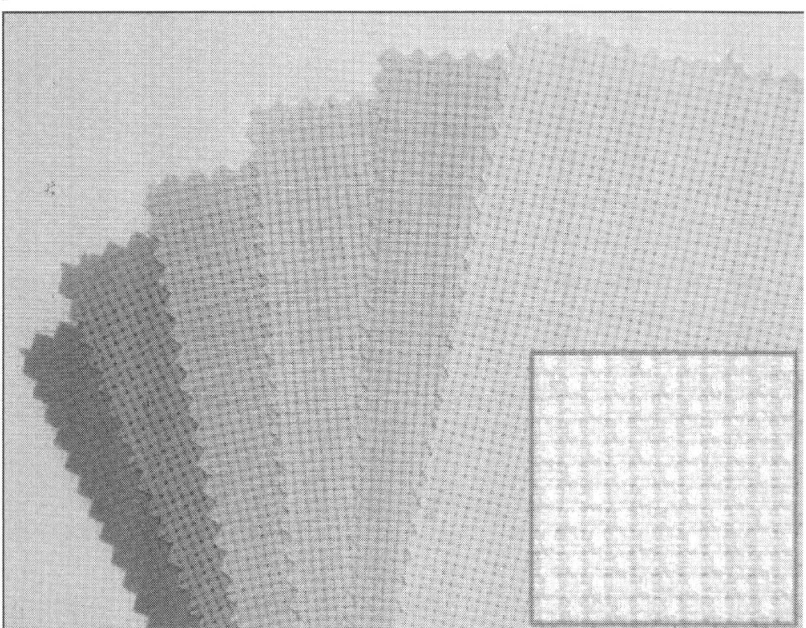

Figure: *Samples of Aida cloth with enlargement inset*

Characteristics

Aida cloth is manufactured with various size spaces or holes between the warp and weft to accommodate different thicknesses of yarn. These are described by the count. For example, a 10-count aida cloth would have 10 squares per linear inch. Typical sizes are 7, 10, 11, 12, 14, 16, 18 and 22 count, ranked from the coarsest to the finest count. Traditional colours are white, ecru, or shades of tan and brown, although brighter colours are also available. Aida cloth is sold in precut sheets or in bolts of 40" - 60" width.

Aida cloth has a tendency to fray and often needs hemming before use. It should never be laundered prior to craft work and tends to contract 1/2" to 1/4" when the finished item is washed in soap and water. Hand washing improves the appearance of finished cross-stitching because Aida cloth naturally contracts in specific areas where it is embroidered.

Pronunciation

The consensus from various discussions is that there are two ways to pronounce the word "Aida": either /QĐÈiĐdY/, as in the opera by Verdi, or /ÈejdY/. Since the name change occurred around the same time as Verdi's opera was first performed, there has been some speculation that the cloth was renamed after the opera to take advantage of the opera's publicity.

Embroidery Hoop

Embroidery hoops and frames are tools used to keep fabric taut while working embroidery or other forms of needlework.

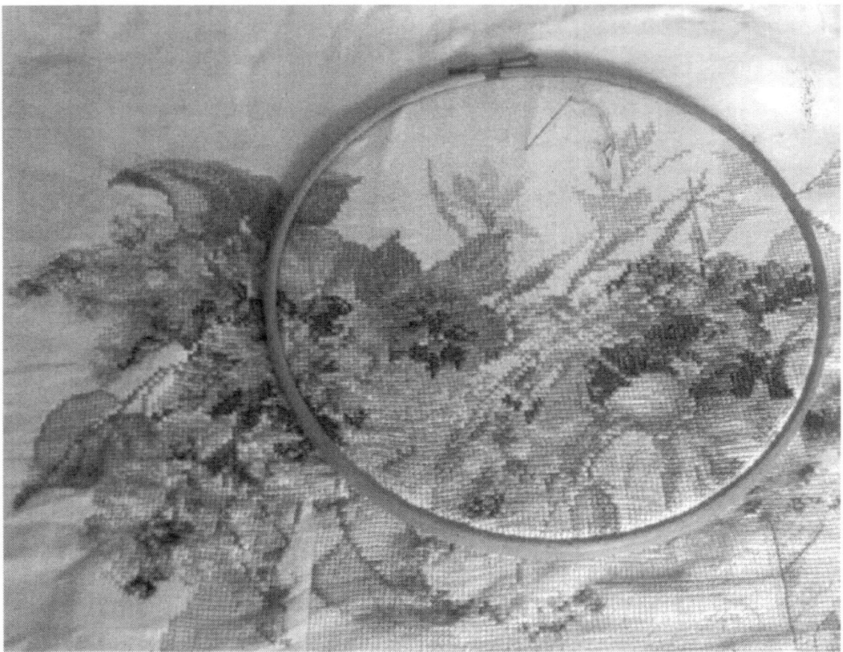

Figure: *An embroidery hoop.*

Hoops

An embroidery hoop or (earlier) tambour frame consists of a pair of concentric circular or elliptical rings. The larger ring has a tightening device, usually in the form of a metal screw. The artisan repositions the hoop as needed when working over a large piece of fabric. Embroidery hoops come in various sizes and are generally small enough to control with one hand and rest in the lap. Hoops were originally made of wood, bone, or ivory; modern hoops are made of wood or plastic. Hoops may be attached to a table-top or floor stand when both hands must be free for sewing, as in making tambour lace. Standing floor frames and lap frames allow the crafter to keep both hands free for working, which increases the speed and precision of work performed. Very thin plastic hoops are also used in machine embroidery.

Scroll Frames

A scroll frame or embroidery frame keeps the entire piece of fabric taut, rather than just the piece being worked. It is made of four pieces of wood: two rollers for the top and base, and two side pieces. Each of the rollers has a piece of fabric securely nailed or stapled along it and holes in its ends to hold the side pieces, which can be secured in place with wing nuts to adjust the width of the frame and the tautness of the stretched fabric. The ends of the ground fabric are sewn to the rollers, which are turned until the area of the fabric to be worked is stretched within the frame. Frames are used in needlepoint and other forms of canvas work as well as embroidery.

Embroidery Thread

Embroidery thread is yarn that is manufactured or hand-spun specifically for embroidery and other forms of needlework.

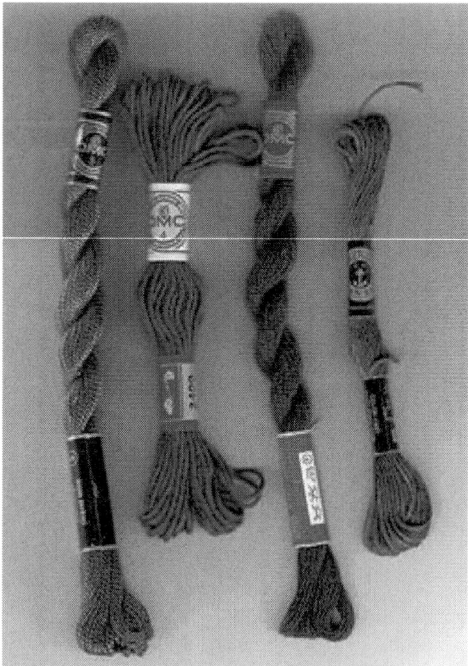

Figure: *Embroidery thread, left to right: No. 5 perle cotton (*coton perlé*), matte cotton embroidery yarn, tapestry wool, cotton stranded embroidery floss*

Threads for hand embroidery include:

- Crewel yarn is a fine 2-ply yarn of wool or, less often, a wool-like acrylic.
- Embroidery floss or stranded cotton is a loosely twisted, slightly glossy 6-strand thread, usually of cotton but also manufactured in silk, linen, and rayon. Cotton floss is the standard thread for cross-stitch. Extremely shiny rayon floss is characteristic of Brazilian embroidery. Historically, stranded silk embroidery threads were described as sleaved or sleided in the sixteenth century.
- Filoselle is a historical term for embroidery floss made using the left-over waste from reeled silk.
- Matte embroidery cotton or French *coton à broder* is a matte-finish (not glossy) twisted 5-ply thread.
- Medici or *broder medici* is a fine, light-weight wool thread formerly manufactured by DMC Group.
- Perle cotton, pearl cotton, or French *coton perlé* is an S-twisted, 2-ply thread with high sheen, sold in five sizes or weights (No. 3, 5, 8, 12 and 16 (Finca), with 3 being the heaviest and 16 the finest).
- Persian yarn is a loosely twisted 3-strand yarn of wool or acrylic, often used for needlepoint.
- Tapestry yarn or tapestry wool is a tightly twisted 4-ply yarn.

Threads for machine embroidery are usually of polyester or rayon (less often cotton or silk).

Threads, like textiles, can contain compounds that may be harmful to humans. Many dyes have been shown to be allergenic and in some cases carcinogenic. Testing for the presence of these dyes, and other additives can be done at many commercial laboratories.

Certification to the Oeko-tex standard may also be applied for. This tests the component for over 100 different chemicals and certifies the component according to human ecological safety.

Evenweave

Even-weave fabric or canvas is any woven textile where the warp and weft threads are of the same size.

Even-weave fabrics are typically required as foundations for counted-thread embroidery styles such as cross-stitch, needlepoint, and blackwork so that a stitch of the same "count" (that is, crossing the same number of fabric threads) will be the same length whether it crosses warp or weft threads.

Even-weave fabrics include even-weave linen, aida cloth, and needlepoint canvas.

Perforated Paper

Perforated paper is a craft material of lightweight card with regularly spaced holes in imitation of embroidery canvas. It is also sometimes referred to as *punched paper.*

Perforated paper is most commonly embroidered with cross stitch motifs and borders. When the stitching is complete the excess paper around the design can be cut away to create a regular or irregular shaped decorative item. Typical uses for such items include ornaments to decorate Christmas trees, bookmarks and greetings cards. It is also used in larger sized sheets to embroider motto sayings to frame and display on the wall. Since the paper is of a heavy weight, it does not require a hoop or frame when stitching.

Perforated paper is manufactured in a number of different colours and is typically sold as 14-count A4 size sheets. The *count* refers to the fact that there are 14 holes/perforations per linear inch.

History

This material, known as *Perforated card-board* at the time, first became available in the 1820s as plain sheets used for the creation of bookmarks and small mottoes and sayings, often taken from the Bible. By the 1870s the Victorian craze for this inexpensive and versatile craft material was at its peak. The invention of new printing processes made the pre-printing of mottoes and bookmarks on the perforated paper possible. These items were extremely popular and original examples, in good condition, can still be found today. The Victorian fad of embroidering mottoes on perforated paper died out around 1910 and was virtually lost as a needleart until recently being rediscovered. Perforated paper as we know it today was invented by Justin Ruble of Pennsylvania

Plainweave

plain weave, also called Tabby Weave, simplest and most common of the three basic textile weaves. It is made by passing each filling yarn over and under each warp yarn, with each row alternating, producing a high number of intersections. Plain-weave fabrics that are not printed or given a surface finish have no right or wrong side. They do not ravel easily but tend to wrinkle and have less absorbency than other weaves.

The visual effect of plain weave may be varied by combining yarns of different origins, thickness, texture, twist, or colour. Fabrics range in weight from sheer to heavy and include such types as organdy, muslin, taffeta, shantung, canvas, and tweed.

Variations of the plain weave include the rib weave, with either warp or filling yarns heavier, as in dimity and bengaline, and the basket weave, in which two or more filling yarns, or a single heavier yarn, pass alternately over and under two or more warp yarns, as in oxford shirting and monk's cloth.

Plastic Canvas

Plastic canvas is a craft material of lightweight plastic with regularly spaced holes in imitation of embroidery canvas. It is also commonly known as *vinyl weave*. Plastic canvas is typically used as a foundation for needlepoint or other canvas work embroidery, usually in acrylic or wool knitting yarn. Due to its rigidity, it is useful for creating 3-dimensional objects such as tissue box covers, small jewelry boxes, handbags, and other decorative objects.

Plastic canvas is manufactured in many colours and with various size holes for different thicknesses of yarn. As with textile canvas, these are described in *count* – that is, 10-count plastic canvas has 10 holes per linear inch. Typical sizes are 7-, 10-, and 14 count. It is most readily available in A4 size sheets but pre-made shapes such as circles, triangles as well as novelty shapes (e.g. dinosaur, bird, cross) are also available. Plastic canvas is also employed in teaching needlepoint and cross stitch to children, since its rigid structure does not require the use of a hoop or frame.

Other Uses

Plastic canvas is also used by some for making animal mascot heads as a frame to build faux fur upon to make the head of the mascot, some people stick the Plastic canvas together with glue but this is not the only method of construction or sticking together a frame of a mascot head.

Sampler

A (needlework) sampler is a piece of embroidery produced as a demonstration or test of skill in needlework. It often includes the alphabet, figures, motifs, decorative borders and sometimes the name of the person who embroidered it and the date. The word *sampler* is derived from the Latin 'exemplum' - an example.

History

The oldest surviving samplers were constructed in the 15th and 16th centuries. As there were no pre-printed patterns available for needleworkers, a stitched model was needed. Whenever a needlewoman saw a new and interesting example of a stitching pattern, she would quickly sew a small sample of it onto a piece of cloth - her 'sampler'. The patterns were sewn randomly onto the fabric as a reference for future use, and the woman would collect extra stitches and patterns throughout her lifetime.

16th Century English samplers were stitched on a narrow band of fabric 6–9 in (150–230 mm) wide. As fabric was very expensive, these samplers were totally covered with stitches. These were known as band samplers and valued highly, often being mentioned in wills and passed down through the generations. These samplers were stitched using a variety of needlework styles, threads, and ornament. Many of them were exceedingly elaborate, incorporating subtly shaded colours, silk and metallic embroidery threads, and using stitches such as Hungarian, Florentine, tent, cross, long-armed cross, two-sided Italian cross, rice, running, Holbein, Algerian eye and buttonhole stitches. The samplers also incorporated small designs of flowers and animals, and geometric designs stitched using as many as 20 different colours of thread.

The first printed pattern book was produced in 1523, but they were not easily obtainable and a sampler was the most common form of reference available to many women. The earliest dated surviving sampler, housed in the Victoria and Albert Museum in London, was made by Jane Bostocke who included her name and the date 1598 in the inscription on, with religious or moral quotations, while the entire sampler became more methodically organised. By the 18th century, samplers were a complete contrast to the scattered samples sewn earlier on. These samplers were stitched more to demonstrate knowledge than to preserve skill. The stitching of samplers was believed to be a sign of virtue, achievement and industry, and girls were taught the art from a young age.

Modern Samplers

Samplers are widely stitched today, some using kits purchased from needlework shops, some from chart-packs, and many from patterns available on the Internet or through e-mail from designers. Patterns range from simple using only one stitch, to complex, using 15 to 20 and more stitches. Designs range widely in style, from accurate reproductions of historic pieces to much more contemporary and modern styles. Many sampler reproductions are also available, copying colours and imperfect stitches from the originals.

The word "sampler" is sometimes inaccurately applied to any piece of needlework meant for display. Materials used include aida cloth, evenweave, and linen fabrics, in cotton, linen, and man-made materials combined in more and more ways; and fibres from cotton floss to silk, rayon, viscose, and metallic.

Slip

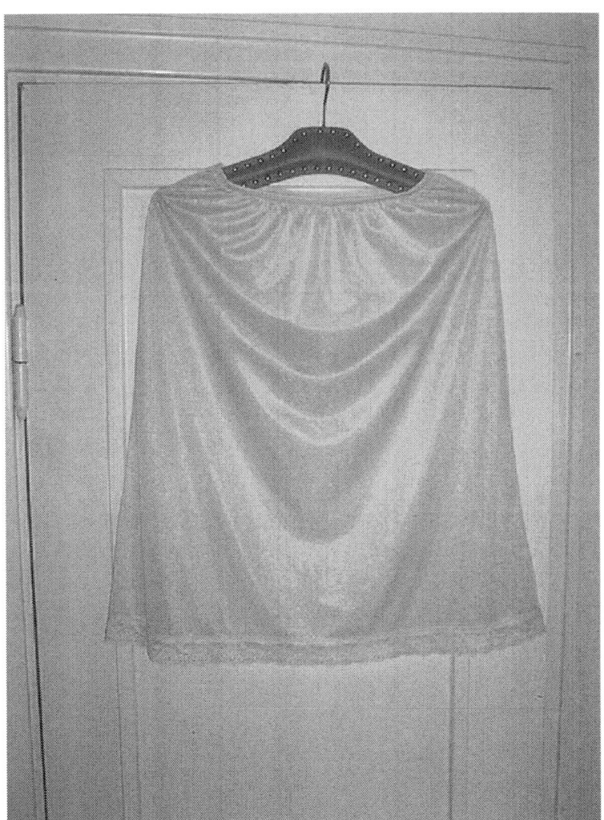

A slip is a woman's undergarment worn beneath a dress or skirt to help it hang smoothly and to prevent chafing of the skin from coarse fabrics such as wool. Slips are also worn for warmth, and to protect fine fabrics from perspiration. A full slip hangs from the shoulders, usually by means of narrow straps, and extends from the breast to the fashionable skirt length. A half slip hangs from the waist. It may also be called a waist slip or more rarely a petticoat.

Slips are often worn to prevent the show through of intimate undergarments such as panties or a brassiere. A slip may also be used to prevent a silhouette of the legs showing through clothing when standing in front of a bright light source. Other uses for slips are to make a dress or skirt hang properly, the prevention of chafing to the skin, to protect the outer garment from damage due to perspiration, or for warmth, especially if the dress or skirt is lightweight and thin. In very warm and/or humid climates a slip made from 100% cotton may be desired.

Types of Slips

Slips fall into two major categories. A full slip is hung from the shoulders by straps that extend down to the top of the breast area. Full slips come in a variety of lengths; some extend down to the upper thigh, some to just above the knees, or just below the knees, while others go down to just above the ankles. A waist slip, sometimes referred to as a "half slip", is held on to the body around the waist by means of an elastic waistband. The waist slip is also available in the same lengths as the aforementioned full slip. Waist slips that extend down to just above the ankle are often called "formal", or "maxi" slips. "Mini slips" are yet another size option for waist slips. They were first introduced in the 1960s to wear under a mini skirt. American Maid manufactured waist slips that had vents and a rear zipper in addition to the elastic waistband. These slips were made of 50% nylon and 50% dacron polyester. As an alternative to the full slip, a waist slip with a matching camisole can be worn. There is also a type of "slip" designed to be worn under pants known as "pettipants". In addition to pants, a pettipant may also be worn under a dress or skirt, and like slips, they are mainly made of nylon.

Decorations and Fabric

Many slips have floral lace at the hem and/or the "vents" or "sideslits". Some of the older slips have decorations, such as a butterfly or flowers sewn into the fabric of the slip, and a pillowtab was also added to the waistband of a waist slip. The vast majority of slips are made of 100% nylon, while others are made from polyester, rayon, acetate, silk or in some cases cotton. Still, there are others made of blends, and the label of the garment might read "40% nylon, 35% rayon, 25% polyester". Nylon slips are often shiny in appearance, and are very smooth to the touch, while polyester slips can even be more shiny with a real slippery feel, especially charmeuse or "satin" slips. Although charmeuse slips have very attractive eye appeal, they are not as durable as nylon slips, and often tear very easily, especially when wet.

History

Slips made in the 1940s were mainly made of 100% rayon due to the war effort. In the late 1940s, some nylon slips began to appear on the market, and the vast majority of slips made in the 1950s were nylon. In the 1960s, slips were offered in a much more variety of colours, including multi-coloured slips. Slips with a floral print design were also made available. Some of the most well known slip brand names of the past are: Lorraine, Dior, Velrose, Mel-Lin, Shadowline, Wonder Maid, Warner's, Kayser, Maidenform and Van Raalte. There are well established slip/lingerie manufacturers still in operation today such as Vanity Fair and Vassarette.

Modern Slips

Most of the slips made today are very plain, and are lacking in detail. Intricate decorations and lace designs are almost completely absent from modern day slips. As far as popularity, slips are not worn nearly as much as a few decades ago. Most transparent skirts and dresses now come with a lining making slips redundant. In German and French the word "slip" is commonly used for panties. Since the late 20th century, dresses closely based on slips have become very popular.

7

Regional and Historical

Art needlework was a type of surface embroidery popular in the later nineteenth century under the influence of the Pre-Raphaelites and the Arts and Crafts Movement.

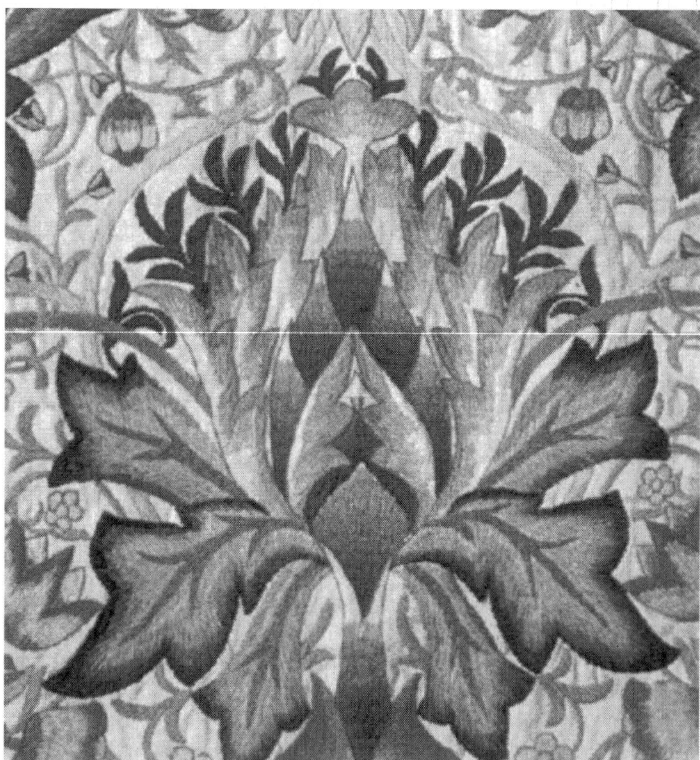

Figure: *Detail of an art needlework panel in wool on linen, designed by William Morris in 1877*

Artist and designer William Morris is credited with the resurrection of the techniques of freehand surface embroidery based on English embroidery styles of the Middle Ages through the eighteenth century, developing the retro-style which would be termed *art needlework*.

Art needlework emphasized delicate shading in satin stitch with silk thread accompanied by a number of novelty stitches, in sharp contrast with the counted-thread technique of the brightly coloured Berlin wool work needlepoint craze of the mid-nineteenth century.

In embroidery as in other crafts, Morris was anxious to encourage self-expression via handcrafts. His shop Morris & Co. sold both finished custom embroideries and kits in the new style, along with vegetable dyed silks in which to work them. Art needlework was considered an appropriate style for decorating artistic dress.

The Royal School of Art Needlework (now Royal School of Needlework) was founded as a charity in 1872 under the patronage of Princess Helena to provide apprenticeships in the new/old style. Morris's daughter May, an accomplished needlewoman and designer in her own right, was active in the School from its inception. Art needlework was introduced to America at the 1876 Centennial Exposition in Philadelphia.

Bunka Shishu

Bunka shishu (‡eS:RM~), in English often shortened to bunka, is a form of Japanese embroidery originating around the turn of the 20th century. Bunka artists use a specialised embroidery needle and rayon threads to create very detailed pictures that some liken to oil paintings. Typical subjects include people, living things (traditionally fish), and traditional Japanese scenes.

Unlike some other forms of embroidery, bunka is fragile and is usually presented as artwork rather than as clothing adornment. Bunka has gained in popularity since the advent of numbered kits, which provide a step-by-step guide to producing artwork.

Jacobean

The Jacobean style is the second phase of Renaissance architecture in England, following the Elizabethan style. It is named after King James I of England, with whose reign it is associated.

The reign of James VI of Scotland (or James I of England (1603–1625)), a disciple of the new scholarship, saw the first decisive adoption of Renaissance motifs in a free form communicated to England through

German and Flemish carvers rather than directly from Italy. Although the general lines of Elizabethan design remained, there was a more consistent and unified application of formal design, both in plan and elevation. Much use was made of columns and pilasters, round-arch arcades, and flat roofs with openwork parapets. These and other classical elements appeared in a free and fanciful vernacular rather than with any true classical purity. With them were mixed the prismatic rustications and ornamental detail of scrolls, straps, and lozenges also characteristic of Elizabethan design. The style influenced furniture design and other decorative arts.

Jacobean embroidery refers to embroidery styles that flourished in the reign of King James I of England in first quarter of the 17th century.

The term is usually used today to describe a form of crewel embroidery used for furnishing characterized by fanciful plant and animal shapes worked in a variety of stitches with two-ply wool yarn on linen. Popular motifs in Jacobean embroidery, especially curtains for bed hangings, are the Tree of Life and stylized forests, usually rendered as exotic plants arising from a landscape or *terra firma* with birds, stags, squirrels, and other familiar animals.

Kaitag

Kaitag textiles are an unusual embroidered textile art form from the Kaitag district of southwest Daghestan, Russia, inhabited mainly by Dargins. Kaitag textiles are of simple construction, being laid and couched silk-floss embroidery on a cotton ground. The designs are often in the style of classical Safavid Persian art, sometimes illustrating horsemen and hunting scenes. Abstract Kaitag designs have been compared to those of Matisse and Paul Klee, though it is unlikely that either artist ever saw a Kaitag textile. Surviving examples are mostly from the 17th and 18th centuries. These embroideries were apparently made for local use in weddings, funerals, and for cradle trappings. The traditional Kaitag art of embroidery was reportedly stamped out under Soviet rule.

Situated between the Black Sea and the Caspian Sea, Daghestan is an inaccessible and mountainous part of the Caucasus, an autonomous region first of the Soviet Union and now of Russia, flanked by the mighty Russian and Persian empires. Kaitag art, from a small region in the south of Daghestan, is the creation of a multi-ethnic people, incorporating Zoroastrian, Muslim, Christian, Jewish and pagan symbolism. This remarkably vibrant and beautiful tradition is found mostly in the rectangular panels embroidered with vividly coloured silks that are the subject of this book. Examples are attributed to the 16th through to the 19th centuries. The geography of the region and the self-contained and inward-looking pattern of living of the Kaitag people were major factors in the confinement of such a distinct art to such a small group of villages.

The Designs

The vast repertoire of designs is the legacy of the history of the region and the multi-religious society that produced them. Byzantine, Fatimid, Mongolian, Timurid, Mamluk, Chinese, Ottoman and Celtic forms, many of great antiquity, combined with local animist art in a glorious diversity: hieroglyphic motifs, sun signs, birds signs, sun bursts, octagons, cosmic columns, horns, crosses, fantastic crab-like beasts, elk, reindeer, fat swordfish, dragons, amoebae-like shapes, masks and even foetuses can be identified. Many ancient talismanic symbols occur, for these panels were used in rituals associated with birth, marriage and death - to wrap cradles or as dowry covers, for example. A number of the motifs can also be found on local tombstones.

The design bravado of the embroideries, with their shimmering colour density and the assured juxtapositioning of colour and texture gives them a contemporary significance. The designs have a confidence and verve which evoke a sense of recognition and pleasure in an audience far removed in history and culture from their original owners, to whom they were evidently of powerful totemic significance. Indeed, the more abstract among the embroideries stand on a par with the work of 20th-century Western masters such as Klee, Miro and Matisse.

Kantha

Kantha is a type of embroidery popular in West Bengal. The use of kantha is popular in "Kantha saris" traditionally worn by women in Bengal.

Kantha stitching is also used to make simple quilts, commonly known as Nakshi Kantha. Women in Bengal typically use old saris and cloth and layer them with kantha stitch to make a light blanket, throw or bedspread, especially for children. Kantha is very popular with tourists visiting Bengal and is a speciality of Bolpur

Weave

Kantha is still the most popular form of embroidery practised by rural women. The traditional form of Kantha embroidery was done with soft dhotis and saris, with a simple running stitch along the edges. Depending on the use of the finished product they were known as *Lepkantha* or *Sujni Kantha.*

The embroidered cloth has many uses including women's shawls and covers for mirrors, boxes, and pillows. In the best examples, the entire cloth is covered with running stitches, employing beautiful motifs of flowers, animals birds and geometrical shapes, as well as themes from everyday activities. The stitching on the cloth gives it a slight wrinkled, wavy effect. Contemporary Kantha is applied to a wider range of garments such as sarees, dupatta, shirts for men and women, bedding and other furnishing fabrics, mostly using cotton and silk.

Closeup of a kantha. In the left and bottom *Paar* is shown, also the running stitches (white) are seen

Other Uses of the Word

Kantha also means "throat". The name Nilakanth is given to Lord Shiva, literally meaning "blue throat" after he swallowed the poison that resulted from the churning of the ocean, or "Throat chakra". Kantha is also used as an adjective to describe a style of necklace that lies close to the throat, open at the back.

Nakshi Kantha

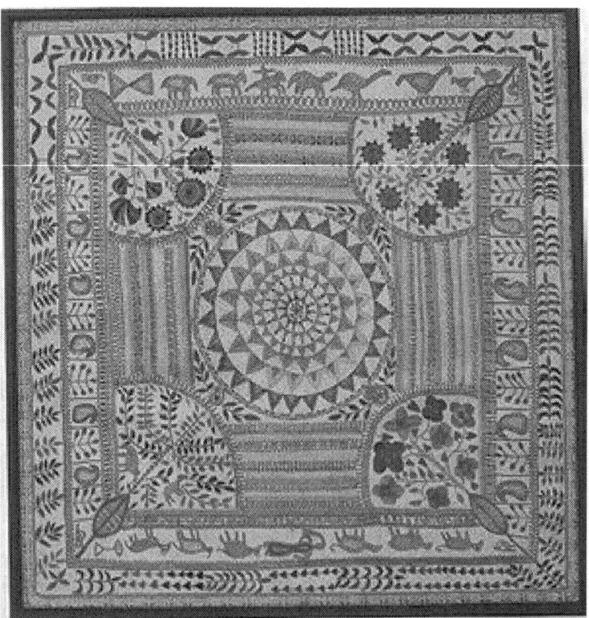

Figure: *Traditional nakshi kantha*

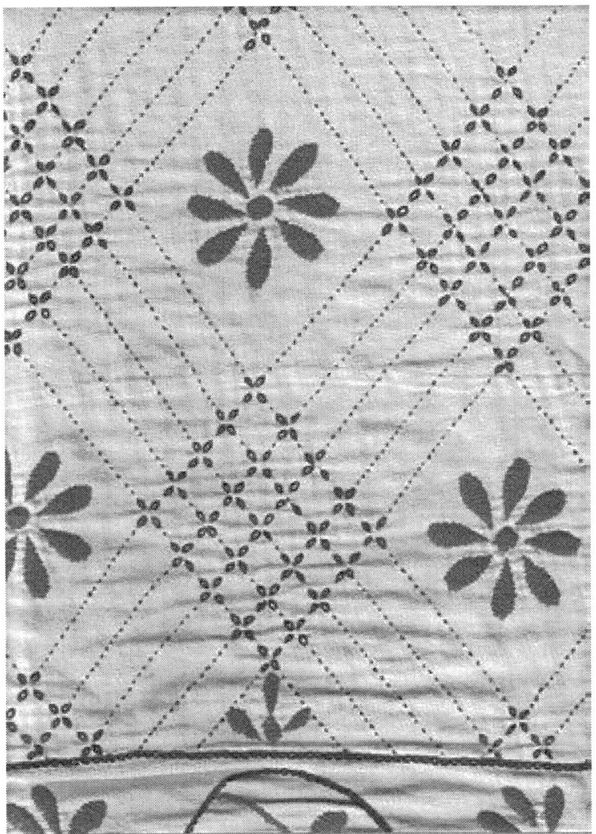

Figure: *Close view of a contemporary Nakshi kantha with flower motif*

Nakshi kantha, a type of embroidered quilt, is a type of folk art of Bangladesh and West Bengal, India. The art has been practiced in rural Bengal for centuries. The basic material used is thread and old cloth. Kanthas are made throughout Bangladesh, but the greater Mymensingh, Rajshahi, Faridpur and Jessore areas are most famous for this craft.

The colourful patterns and designs that are embroidered resulted in the name "Nakshi Kantha", which was derived from the Bengali word "naksha", which refers to artistic patterns. The early kanthas had a white background accented with red, blue and black embroidery; later yellow, green, pink and other colours were also included. The running stitch called "kantha stitch" is the main stitch used for the purpose. Traditionally, kantha was produced for the use of the family. Today, after the revival of the nakshi kantha, they are produced commercially.

Tradition

Like any other folk art, kantha making is influenced by factors such as materials available, daily needs, climate, geography, and economic factors. Probably the earliest form of kantha was the patchwork kantha, and the kanthas of the decorative applique type evolved from this.

In Literature

The earliest mention of Bengal Kantha is found in the book "Sri Sri Chaitanya Charitamrita" by Krishnadas Kaviraj, which was written some five hundred years ago.

Making

Traditionally old sarees, lungis and dhotis were used to make kanthas. Kantha making was not a full-time job. Women in almost every household were expert in the art. Rural women worked at leisure time or during the lazy days of the rainy season, so taking months or even years to finish a kantha was normal. At least five to seven sarees were needed to make a standard-size kantha. Today the old materials are replaced by new cotton cloths. Traditionally the thread was collected from the old sarees. That is rarely done today.

When a kantha is being made, first the sarees are joined together to attain the required size, and then layers are spread out on the ground. The cloths are then smoothed, and no folds or creases are left in between. During the process, the cloth is kept flat on the ground with weights on the edges. Then the four edges are stitched and two or three rows of large running stitches are done to keep the kantha together. At this stage, the kantha can be folded and stitched at leisure time.

Originally, designs and motifs were not drawn on the cloth. The design was first outlined with needle and thread, followed by focal points, and then the filling motifs were done. In a kantha with a predominant central motif the centre was done first, followed by corner designs and the other details. In some types of kanthas (carpet, lik and sujni, etc.) wooden blocks were used to print the outline. The blocks are replaced today by patterns drawn in tracing papers.

Types

The following is how kanthas are categorized, according to the stitch type:

Running Stitch

The Running stitch kantha is truly the indigenous kantha. They are subdivided into Nakshi (figured) and par tola (patterned). Nakshi (figured) kanthas are further divided into motif or scenic kanthas.

Lohori Kantha

The name was derived from Persian word 'lehr', which means wave. This type of kantha is particularly popular in Rajshahi. These kanthas are further divided into soja (straight or simple), Kautar khupi (pigeon coop or triangle), borfi or diamond (charchala, atchala or barachala).

Lik or Anarasi

The Lik or Anarasi (pine apple) type of kantha is found in the Chapainawabgonj and Jessore areas. The variations are lik tan, lik tile, lik jhumka, and lik lohori.

Cross Stitch or Carpet

This type of kantha was introduced by the English during the British Rule in India. The stitch employed in these kanthas is the cross stitch.

Sujni Kantha

This type of kantha is found only in Rajshahi area. The popular motif used is the undulating floral and vine motif.

Influence of Religion and Folk Belief

Stitches

The earliest and most basic stitch found in kanthas is the *running stitch*. The predominant form of this stitch is called the *phor* or kantha stitch. The other forms of stitches used are the Chatai or *pattern darning*, Kaitya or *bending stitch, weave running stitch darning stitch, Jessore stitch* (a variation of darning stitch), *threaded running stitch,* Lik phor or anarasi or ghar hasia *(Holbein) stitches*. The stitches used in modern day kantha are the *Kasmiri stitch* and the *arrow head stitch*. Stitches like the *herring bone stitch, satin stitch, back stitch* and *cross stitch* are occasionally used.

Types

Kanthas generally denote quilts used as wrappers; however, all articles made by quilting old cloth may also be referred to by the same generic name. However, depending on the size and purpose, kanthas may be divided into various articles, each with its specific names. The various types of kantha are as follows:

Quilt (Lep in Bengali): A light quilted covering made from the old sarees/dhotis/lungis and sometimes from sheet cloths.

Large Spread (Naksi Kantha in Bengali): An embellished quilt embroidered in traditional motifs and innovative style

Puja Floor Spread (Ason in Bengali): Cloth spread for sitting at a place of worship or for an honoured guest.

Cosmetic Wrapper (Arshilota in Bengali): A narrow embroidered wrapper to roll and store away a woman's comb, mirror, eye kohl, vermilion, sandal paste, oil bottle, etc. Often, a tying string is used to bind the wrap, as in later day satches.

Wallet (Batwa Thoiley in Bengali): Small envelop shaped bag for keeping money, betel leaves, etc.

Cover for Quran (Ghilaf in Arabic and Bengali): Envelope shaped bag to cover the Quran.

Prayer Mats (Jainamaz in Bengali): Mats used by Muslims to say prayers.

Floor Spread (Galicha in Bengali): Floor coverings.

Cloths Wrapper (Bostani, Guthri in Bengali): A square wrapper for books and other valuables.

Cover (Dhakni in Bengali): Covering cloths of various shapes and sizes.

Ceremonial Meal Spread (Daster Khan in Bengali): A spread for eating place, used at meal time.

Pillow Cover (Balisher Chapa or Oshar in Bengali): A flat single piece pillow cover.

Handkerchief (Rumal): Small and square in shape.

Modern Day Articles: Today newer uses are found for nakshi kanthas, such as bedspreads, wall hangins, cushion covers, ladies' purses, place mats, jewellery boxes, dress fronts, skirts border, shawls and sharees.

Motifs

Motifs of the nakshi kantha are deeply influenced by religious belief and culture. Even though no specific strict symmetry is followed, a finely embroidered naksi kantha will always have a focal point. Most kanthas will have a lotus as focal point, and around the lotus there are often undulating vines or floral motifs, or a shari border motif. The motifs may include images of flower and leaves, birds and fish, animals, kithen forms even toilet articles.

While most kantas have some initial pattern, no two naksi kantas are same. While traditional motifs are repeated, the individual touch is used in the variety of stitches, colours and shapes. The notable motifs found in naksi kantha are as follows:

Lotus Motif

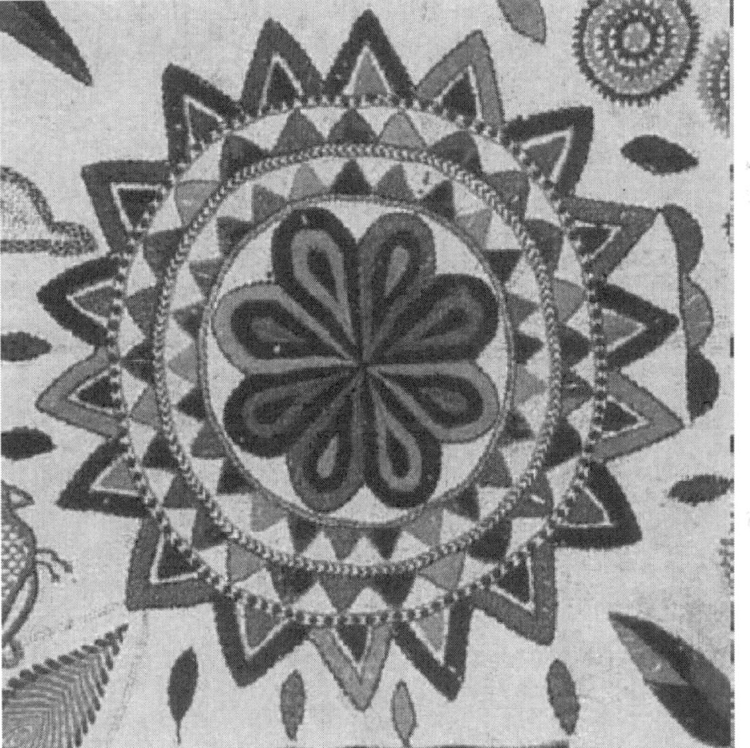

Figure: *Lotus motif*

The lotus motif is the most common motif found in kanthas. This motif is associated with Hindu iconography and thus is also very popular in the kantha. The lotus is the divine seat. It is also symbolic of cosmic harmony and essential womanhood. The lotus is also the symbol of eternal order and of the union of earth, water and, sky. It represents the life-giving power of water, and is also associated with the sun for the opening and closing of the petals. It is also the symbol of the recreating power of life. With the drying up of water, the lotus dies and with the rain it springs to life again. The lotus is associated with purity and the goddess Laksmi, the goddess of good fortune and abundance. There are various forms of lotus motifs, from the eight-petaled *astadal padma* to the hundred petaled *satadal*. In the older kanthas, the central motif is almost always a fully bloomed lotus seen from above.

Solar Motif

The solar motif is closely associated with the lotus motif. Often, the lotus and the solar motifs are found together at in the centre of a nakshi kantha. The solar motif symbolizes the life giving power of the sun. The sun is associated with the fire which plays a significant part in Hindu rites, both religious and matrimonial.

Moon Motif

The moon motif has a religious influence, and is popular amongst the Muslims. Mostly it is in the form of a crescent moon accompanied by a star. This motif is particularly found in *jainamaz* kanthas.

Wheel Motif

The wheel is a common symbol in Indian art, both Hindu and Buddhist. It is the symbol of order. The wheel also represents the world. The wheel is a popular motif in kanthas even when the maker has forgotten the significance of the symbol. The motif is relatively easy to make with *chatai phor*.

Swastika Motif

Su asti in Sanskrit means it is well. As a motif in Indian art, it dates back to the Indus Valley civilization. It is symbol of good fortune. It is also known as *muchri* or *golok dhanda*. With the passage of time, the design is more curvilinear than the four armed swastika of the Mohenjodaro seal. The symbolic design has significant influence in Hinduism, Buddhism, and Jainism.

Tree of Life Motif

The influence of this motif in Indian Art and Culture (as with kantha) may be traced back to the Indus Valley civilization. *It is likely that the Indus people conceived the pipal as the Tree of Life...with the devata inside embodying the power of fecundity*. During the Buddhist times, the cult of the tree continued.

Pipal is sacred to the Buddha because he received enlightenment under its shade. It reflects the fecundity of nature and is very popular in Bengal. Vines and creepers play an important role in kanthas and they contain the same symbolisation as that of tree of life. A popular motif in Rajshahi lohori is the betel leaf.

Kalka Motif

This is a latter day motif, dating from Mughal times. The kalka or paisley motif originated in Persia and Kashmir and has become an integral image of the subcontinental decorative motif. It can be compared with a stylized leaf, mango or flame. The kalka is an attractive motif and number of varieties are experimented. Similar motifs can be found in traditional kashmiri Shawls.

Other Motifs

- The Water Motif:
- The Mountain Motif:
- The Fish Motif:
- The Boat Motif:
- The Footprint Motif:
- The Rath Motif:
- The Mosque Motif:
- The Panja or Open Palm Motif:
- Agricultural Implements:
- Animal Motifs:
- Toilet Articles:
- Kithen Implements:
- The Kantha Motif:
- The Palanquin Motif:

Borders

Most nakshi kanthas have some kind of border. Either a sari border is stitched on or a border pattern is embroidered around the kantha. The common border found in kanthas are as follows:

- The Paddy stalk or date branch (dhaner shish or khejur chari)
- The Scorpion border(Biche par in Bengali)
- The Wavy or bent Border (Beki in Bengali)
- The Diamond border (Barfi)
- The Eye border (chok par in Bengali)
- The Amulet border (Taabiz par in Bengali)
- The Necklace border (mala par in Bengali)

- The Ladder Border (Moi taga)
- The Gut taga
- The Chick taga
- The nolok taga
- The Fish border (Maach par in Bengali)
- The panch taga
- The Bisa taga
- The Anaj taga
- The shamuk taga
- The wrench border
- The anchor (grafi par in Bengali)
- The pen border (kalam par in Bengali)

Korean

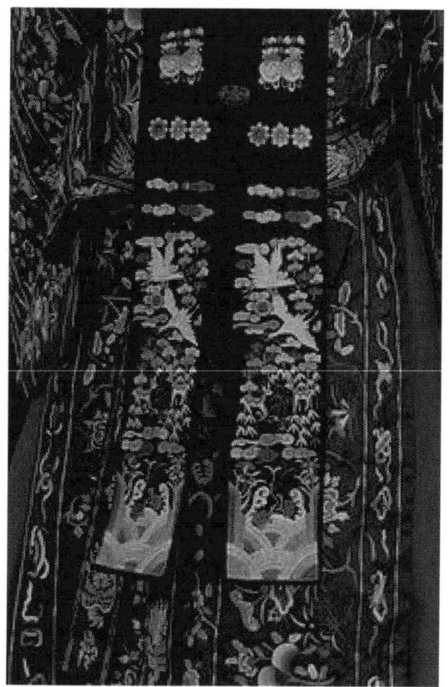

Figure: *Detail of colourful Korean embroidery.*

Korean embroidery techniques and artifacts have a long history, but there is the most evidence from the Joseon Dynasty, after the 14th century in Korea. This article talks about the history, styles, preservation, artists, and examples of screens, costumes, and domestic wares of this exacting and beautiful art form. People used needles made out of bones of fish or animals to sew and weave animal skins and the bark or leaves of trees.

Chasu, the Korean word for embroidery, was a method of cultivating beauty in every corner of daily life. *Pokshik chasu*, *kiyong chasu*, *kamsang chasu* and Buddhist *chasu* are the four types of Chasu.

- Pokshik chasu is the embroidery on clothes.
- Kiyong chasu is the embroidery decorated on various materials used in the king's palace.
- Kamsang chasu represented a type of artistic piece.
- Buddhist chasu came from Buddhism. Buddhist chasu was used in the statues of Buddha or various temples. Chasu has begun from the prehistoric era when the humans first started to make clothes.

Embroidery appears to have begun from the prehistoric era when the human race first started to make clothing and Korean *chasu* has a long history. As times changed, it has been a way of expressing the people's concept of beauty. Along with weaving and sewing, *chasu* was a method of cultivating beauty in very corner of daily life.

During the Chosun Dynasty, the *subang* (embroidery room) was exclusively responsible for the embroidery of clothing and miscellaneous objects for the royal family. Once they had completed a certain level of training and demonstrated a high level of expertise, women were selected to enter the palace to work in the *subang*. Interrelations among various artisan organisations and the *subang* provided the cornerstone of the palace *chasu*, which is also called *kungsu*.

The *kungsu* tradition produced delicate and perfectly executed embroidery. In contrast with *kungsu*, there was the embroidery produced by the common people called *minsu*. *Minsu* was a domestic skill passed down through the family. It was in the charge of women and reflected the characteristics of the individuals who created it.

Persian

Persian embroidery is one of the many forms of the multi-faceted Persian arts. The motifs used in the Persian embroidery are mostly floral, especial Persian figures, animals, and patterns related to hunting.

The Persian embroidered women's trouserings have rich patterns. They were very much in vogue up till the end of the 18th century. With a survival of Victorian modesty, these are usually known as

"Gilets Persans". The designs are always of diagonal parallel bands filled with close floral ornamentation and are very effective.

History

Sassanid Era: We know that the Persian embroidery existed from the ancient times and at least from the time of the Sassanids. Numerous designs are visible on the dresses of the personages on the rock-sculptures and silverware of that period, and have been classified by Professor Ernst Herzfeld. Also the patterns on the coat of Chosroes II at Taq-e Bostan are in such high relief that they may represent embroidery. Roundels, confronted animals and other familiar motives of Sassanid art were doubtless employed. It is probable that the famous Garden Carpet of Chosroes II was a piece of embroidery.

Later

The Persian embroideries we possess of the sixteenth and seventeenth centuries are almost exclusively divan-coverings or ceremonial cloth for present-trays, while in the eighteenth century and later we have the addition of rugs for the bathing-rooms, prayer-mats, and women's embroidered trousers, known as 'naghshe'.

Peculiarities

The earlier embroideries of Iran are almost all of a type in which the entire ground is covered by the design, while the reverse is true, in the main, of the later pieces, in which the background of one plain colour is made to play its part equally with the varied silks of the needlework. The earlier pieces are almost all closely allied in design to one or other of the many types of carpets. They are worked chiefly in darning-stitch on cotton or loosely woven linen, while occasionally examples in cross- or tent-stitch are met with.

It is perhaps reasonable to assume that the more important class of work, that of carpet-weaving, supplied the original design and that the embroiderer adopted it from a type familiar to her. Also it must be remembered that the carpet-weaving was mainly done by men, embroidery by women, so that members of the same family worked at both trades.

Opus Anglicanum

Opus Anglicanum or English work is fine needlework of Medieval England done for ecclesiastical or secular use on clothing, hangings or other textiles, often using gold and silver threads on rich velvet or linen grounds. Such English embroidery was in great demand across Europe, particularly from the late 12th to mid 14th centuries and was a luxury product often used for diplomatic gifts.

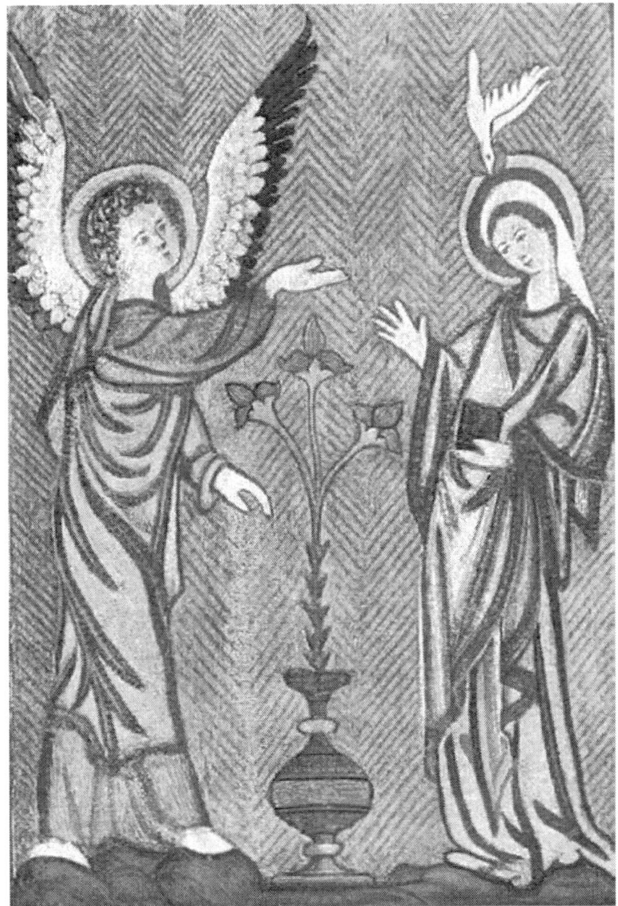

Figure: *Embroidered bookbinding for the Felbrigge Psalter in couched gold thread and split stitch, likely worked by Anne de Felbrigge, a nun in the convent of Minoresses at Bruisyard, Suffolk, during the latter half of the fourteenth century.*

Uses

Most of the surviving examples of Opus Anglicanum were originally designed for liturgical use. These exquisite and expensive embroidery pieces were often made as vestments, such as copes, chasubles and orphreys, or else as antependia, shrine covers or other church furnishings. Secular examples, now known mostly just from contemporary inventories, included various types of garments, horse-trappings, book covers and decorative hangings.

Manufacture

Opus Anglicanum was usually embroidered on linen or, later, velvet, in split stitch and couching with silk and gold or silver-gilt thread. Gold-wound thread, pearls and jewels are all mentioned in inventory descriptions. Although often associated with nunneries, by the time of Henry III (reg. 1216-72), who purchased a number of items both for use within his own court and for diplomatic gifting, the bulk of production was in lay workshops, mainly centred on London. The names of various (male) embroiderers of the period appear in the Westminster royal accounts.

Reputation

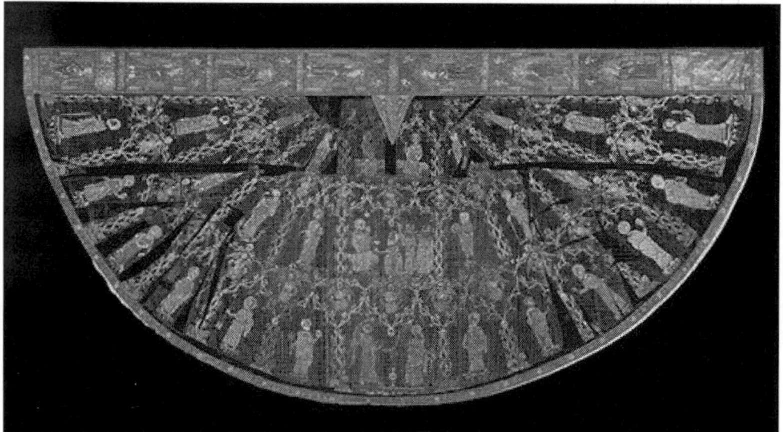

Figure: *The Butler-Bowden Cope, 1330-1350, V&A Museum*

English needlework had become famous across Europe during the Anglo-Saxon period (though very few examples survive) and remained so throughout the Gothic era. A Vatican inventory of 1295 lists over 113 pieces from England, more than from any other country; a request by Pope Martin IV, who had envied the gold-embroidered copes and mitres of English priests, that Cistercian religious houses send more is reported by the Benedictine chronicler Matthew Paris of St Albans:

"This command of my Lord Pope did not displease the London merchants who traded in these embroideries and sold them at their own price." The high water mark of style and refinement is normally conisdered to have been reached in the work of the 13th and early 14th centuries. An influential exhibition at the Victoria and Albert Museum from September–November 1963 displayed several examples of Opus Anglicanum from this period alongside contemporary works of wood and stone sculpture, metalwork and ivories.

Examples

Survival rates for Opus Anglicanum are low (especially for secular works) as is clear from comparing the large number listed in contemporary inventories with the handful of examples still existing. Sometimes ecclesiastical garments were later modified for different uses, such as altar coverings or book covers. Others were buried with their owners, as with the vestments of the mid-13th century Bishops, Walter de Cantilupe and William de Blois, fragments of which were recovered when their tombs in Worcester Cathedral were opened in the 18th century. The majority however were lost to neglect, destroyed by iconoclasts or else unpicked or burnt to recover the precious metals from the gold and silver threads. Although fragmentary examples can be found in a number of museums, the most important specialised collections of Opus Anglicanum garments are at the Cloisters Museum in New York, the Victoria and Albert Museum in London and in the Treasury of Sens Cathedral.

Only a few Anglo-Saxon pieces have survived, including three pieces at Durham that had been placed in the coffin of St Cuthbert, probably in the 930s, after being given by King Athelstan; they were however made in Winchester between 909 and 916. These are works "of breathtaking brilliance and quality", according to Wilson, including figures of saints, and important early examples of the Winchester style, though the origin of their style is a puzzle; they are closest to a wall-painting fragment from Winchester, and an early example of acanthus decoration. The earliest group of survivals, now re-arranged and with the precious metal thread mostly picked out, are bands or borders from vestments, incorporating pearls and glass beads, with various types of scroll and animal decoration. These are probably 9th century and now in a church in Maaseik in Belgium. A further style of textile is a vestment illustrated in a miniature portrait of Saint Aethelwold in his Benedictional, which shows the edge of what appears to be a huge acanthus "flower" (a term used in several documentary records) covering the wearer's back and shoulders. Other written sources mention other large-scale compositions.

One particularly fine example is *The Adoration of the Magi* chasuble from c.1325 in red velvet embroidered in gold thread and pearls at the Metropolitan Museum of Art in New York. It depicts a nativity scene with emphasis on decorative motifs, flowers, animals, birds, beasts, and angels. The Butler-Bowden Cope at the Victoria and Albert Museum is another surviving example; the same collection has a late cope made for a set of vestments given by Henry VII to Westminster Abbey.

Rushnyk

Rushnyk is a ritual cloth embroidered with symbols and cryptograms of the ancient world. They have been used throughout Eastern Europe in sacred rituals, religious services and ceremonial events such as weddings and funerals. Each region has its own designs and patterns with hidden meaning, passed down from generation to generation and studied by ethnographers. A permanent Rushnyk collection is housed at the Hermitage Museum.

The Rushnyk Museum is located in Pereiaslav-Khmelnytskyi, Ukraine as part of The Museum of Folk Architecture and Way of Life of Central Naddnipryanshchyna.

Meaning

The rectangular shape of the fabric indicates a life's journey and the ornamentation captures the cultural ancestral memory of the region. The material used is either linen or hemp. The act of spinning thread and the process of weaving linen embodies spiritual power dating back to the ancient deity Mokosh who is often represented in embroidery. The needle has its own energy, an idea similar to acupuncture, and the colour of the thread has sacred meaning. Red represents life and is the main colour used. A rushnyk is given to a baby at birth, it follows the person throughout life and used in the funeral service after death.

Uses

A Rushnyk has many uses. The very basic rushnik is colloquially called the *utyralnyk* or wiper and serves as a towel. The utyralnyk either has no designs on it or it has very narrow strip on the edges. In contrast, a *nabozhnyk* is a highly decorated Rushnyk composing of embroidery and of lace. *Nabozhnyks*, also called *nabraznyks* or *nakutnyks* are used to decorate icons and icon corners in homes.

Wedding Rushnyks

Colour plays a very important symbolic role in traditional Slavic embroidery. Red is the colour of life, the sun, fertility and health. The majority of rushnyks are embroidered with red threads. The very word "red" means "beautiful" and "splendid" in Ruthenian: a red girl, a red sun or a red spring. The diamond-shaped design of the rushnyk is an ancient agricultural symbol, which means a sown field, or the sun, and expresses the idea of fertility and protection against evil. Ducks, in the centre of the rushnyk, symbolize the element of life-giving water. In wedding folklore a duck and a drake symbolize a bride and a groom, in other words a pair of ducks is a symbol of family life.

During a wedding ceremony, the bride and groom are standing on a Rushnyk called a *pidnozhnyk,* which translates as step-on towel. What happens to the pidnozhnyk is that the bride will drag the towel behind her, and her bridesmaids follow behind her. Tradition has it that when the bridesmaids follow behind the pidnozhnyk, they are following the path of the bride and hopefully be married

Ukrainian

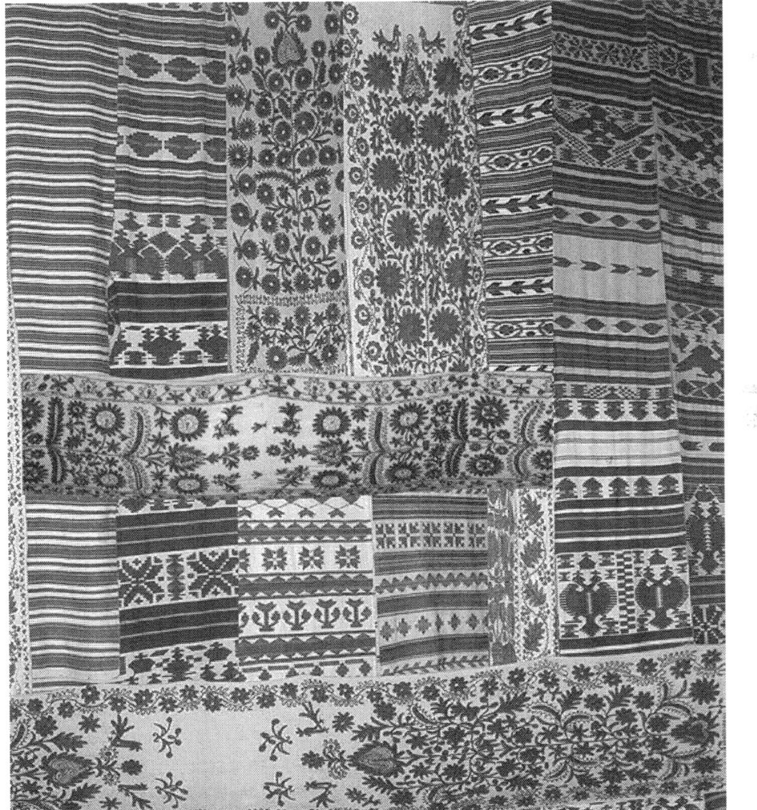

Figure: *Rushnyks - Ukrainian embroidered decorative towels. Pereyaslav-Khmelnytsky, Ukraine.*

Ukrainian embroidery occupies an important place among the various branches of Ukrainian decorative arts. Embroidery has a rich history in Ukraine, and has long appeared in Ukrainian folk dress as well as played a part in traditional Ukrainian weddings and other celebrations. Appearing all across the country, Ukrainian embroidery varies depending on the region of origin. From Poltava, Kiev, and Chernihiv in the east, to Volyn and Polissia in the northwest, to Bukovyna, and the Hutsul area in the southwest, the designs have a long history which defines its ornamental motifs and compositions, as well as its favourite choice of colours and types of stitches.

History

Embroidery is an ancient and symbolic tradition in Ukraine. In 513 BC, Herodotus, the famous Greek historian, in describing the invasion of Darius, mentioned that the Thracian-Dacian people who lived in what is now the Balkans and western Ukraine used embroidery to decorate their clothes. Excavations of sites from the 1st century AD have revealed examples of embroidered clothing in the territory of Ukraine. Other early examples of embroideries include pre-Christian goddess motifs, such as Berehynia. There are eleventh-century examples of embroidery in the Saint Sophia Cathedral in Kiev on frescos and miniatures. Many of these early examples have distinct similarities to the local embroidery throughout history. Ukrainian embroidery was an everyday art in the common people's lives until the 19th century, when it became more of a craft.

Embroidery was mostly used for the decoration of clothing and fabrics and for the decoration of homes and churches. Embroidered products, especially towels, are greatly symbolic for a series of ceremonies and rituals of Ukraine.

Most embroidery was used for clothing. The primary object of clothing that was decorated with embroidery was the shirt or vyshyvanka. The shirt was mostly decorated with embroidery on the sleeves, and also on the neck, bosom, and the cuffs. Other elements of clothing are also embroidered, including scarves, skirts, aprons, men's caps and trousers, sleeveless jackets, kozhukh and kozhushanka (sheepskin coats), sashes, ochipok, etc. In some areas, bed linens were also embroidered. Aside from clothing, other items decorated with embroidery are towels, tablecloths, bench covers, veils and kerchiefs, and pillowcases. Many of these items are used to decorate the interior of churches, for example a cover for the sacraments or a shroud for icons.

According to Mary Doliszny, a Ukrainian-Canadian activist, the Soviet Union's attempts at Russification took a toll on the embroidery of Ukrainians. Because of attempts to destroy the art of Ukrainian embroidery, diaspora Ukrainians worked to document patterns and revive the art. Much of this research was done at the institutes of Ukrainian studies at Harvard University and the University of Toronto.

Folk embroidery was symbolic and connected with a great number of beliefs, myths, and superstitions, including beliefs regarding protection and fertility. The lozenge shape is a common motif and represents a sown field and female fertility.

In Ukraine, embroidery was developed by women and typically a women's activity and remains one to this day. There was scarcely a woman who did not master it to some extent. It is popular in both Ukraine and her diaspora, where many embroidery clubs exist.

Embroidery is remembered as a national pastime and is a part of the Ukrainian cultural and national identity.

Variations

Ukrainian embroidery has many variations from region to region, or even village to village. However, most embroidery is generally similar overall for most Ukrainians. Even with these variation, the styles of needlework found throughout Ukraine, when taken together, represent a definite Ukrainian national style of embroidery. Red and black were the most common colours of Ukrainian embroidery. Ukrainian folk embroidery is notable for great variety of its techniques.

Central and Eastern Ukraine

In the Central and Eastern parts of Ukraine, embroidery usually consists of geometric forms and plant ornaments. The colour range of the motifs is very delicate and very diverse as to individual details. In the Poltava Region, the colours usually include pale blue, white, light ochre, pale green and gray tones. Poltava products are especially famed for their "white-on-white" and openwork embroidery. The red, red-blue (or red-black) colour scheme plays an important role in Central- and Eastern-Ukrainian embroidery, as it did throughout almost the whole of Ukraine.

Western Ukraine

In Western Ukraine, especially the Hutsul region, embroidery uses geometric ornament and a sharply contrasting palette. Besides the now widely used cross-stitch, there is still the ornamental needle-weaving stitch called "nyzynka", which is executed predominantly on the reverse of the fabric and gives a sort of "tweed" effect. This is one of the most archaic of traditional Ukrainian stitches that, in combination with the predetermined areas of white background material that peek through the densely laid threads, emphasizes the clear-cut silhouette of the main patterns.

In the Lemko region, the oldest embroideries were executed in red and red-blue linear motifs. Over time, other colours, such as blue, green and yellow, were added.

In the Boiko region, embroideries varied from simple red-blue geometric motifs in the western reaches of their territory, to wide, densely worked geometric and/or floral patterns in the eastern and southern reaches. Boikos were also well known for their finely embroidered pleated smocking work called "bryzhky", which were found mainly around the collars and sleeve cuffs of women's and men's shirts, but also along the top hems of women's aprons.

The embroideries of Bukovyna are among the richest in all of Ukraine, often combining as many as nine or more colours, including silver and gold metallic thread as well as coloured glass beads. It also uses a number of stitches.

The needlework of Pokuttya was also rich and intricately executed, and also quite varied. Red was the predominant colour in many of the styles of embroidery in this region, usually being worked in thick home-processed wool threads, sometimes with accents of yellow, green and blue added. Although cross-stitch was not uncommon, the older and more traditional technique was that of the so-called "curly stitch" (quite popular, in fact, throughout many areas of Southwestern Ukraine). In some parts of Pokuttya and neighbouring Podillya, wide motifs of intricately worked white-on-white embroidery combined with open work were popular. The embroideries of Podillya were similar in many respects to that of both Bukovyna and Pokuttya, with discreet yet recognisable differences in colour scheme, motifs and placement that nonetheless set them apart.

In Halychyna, there is a variety of embroidery styles that were specific for individual localities, such that when one sees a piece of embroidery there is no mistaking its origin.

Northern Ukraine

In the northwest and north of Ukraine (including the Ukrainian ethno-historic territory of Poland) needlework traditions have been preserved relatively intact from the oldest of times. Red, as well as red-blue and red-black were the predominant colour schemes in the archaic geometric embroideries of these northern regions of Ukraine, executed primarily in dense rows of a horizontal needle-weaving stitch (called "zavolikannia") that created horizontal bands of patterns reminiscent of weaving. Floral motifs are also popular in the North, using red, red-blue or red-black palette as the needle-woven bands, but in the much more recent technique of cross-stitch.

Vietnamese

Vietnamese hand embroidery is a 700-year-old tradition. Usually, tiny threads are used to create brightly coloured pictures on cloth. It is a popular extracurricular activity for young girls in high school together with cooking and cloth sewing. It was a part of Vietnamese culture; traditionally, girls are expected to know how to decorate pillowcases, curtains and tablecloths with hand embroidery.

Since the 1960s, hand embroidery in Vietnam has been raised to the level of an art. Many large pictures in different sizes, some as large as 2.5 × 2 yards, have been made. Popular topics include Vietnamese history, landscapes, animals, flowers, and religious scenes.

The History of Traditional Embroidery Art

In Vietnam, embroidery work is a handcraft that existed long time in the past. The history of this traditional work connected closely with the spiritual history of the Vietnamese women in the past.

From the first century, beside the flag embroidered "to requite country's debt and home's revenge" by the rising up in arms of Hai Ba Trung, women of Vietnam also embroider in order to decorate the house, move over to show the confidence, sentiment and to make beautiful for themselves.

However, up to now, nobody knows the embroidery work of Vietnam that created from which period. Who is the first person created and change the normal sewing work to be an embroidery art?

The legend said that, from the beginning of the century 17, the embroidery of Vietnam had marked a turning-point of development. At that time, Mr. Le Cong Hanh (born on 18/01/1606- died on 12/06/1661) lived at Quat Dong hamlet, Quat Dong village, Thuong Tin Dist., Ha Tay province had collected experience and technique of folk embroidery art of Vietnam to disseminate widely the handicraft art.

Material used for embroidery at the time included natural dyes, such as : " Tinctorial yam, Indigal plant, Indian almond pod, paletuvier water, leaves of phrynium, grinstone, multicoloured stone...". Many foreigners have admired Vietnamese embroidery : "In seeing the dyes that looked dirty and ugly, it was quite amazing the tranformation after the tinting process was complete. "Traditionally, the art of embroidery had been done by Vietnamese women according to Confucianist concept that Vietnamese have to have four virtues; "labour, appearance, speech and behaviour." As ourancestors often said:

"Men read books and declare poems.

Women have to do embroidery and sewing."

Almost women know how to embroider; however, concentration and professional character for long time started in Hue, when the regime of Nguyen King constructed at Hue, Mrs. Hoang Thi Cuc, mother of King Bao Dai, she accompanied with Nam Phuong Queen coordinated the advantages of embroidery technique of Europe with genius of Asia to establish embroidery work to become an embroidery art of the Imperial palace, related to charming, fine, detailed characters of the Hue women.

Gabrielle, a female French scholar specialising in the studing of Orieltal Cultures, wrote "In many place, people have transmitted, through generation , an extraordinary art, which was to draw in threads, making lotus flower open on silk, butterflies on blue water surface. Vietnamese embroiderers are more skillful than the Chinese in their use of sewing with the fine lines and their methods of mix colours...."

Hocquard , an author, said about the embroidery at the end of 19th century: "The Vietnamese embroiderers were very clever in distributing colour on silk to harmonise embroidered pieces without any contrast."

The risen and fallen century passed by, the embroidery work was up and down but it kept the cultural character of country.

In the early 1990s of the 20 century, the silk embroidered paintings of Vietnam come over and develop to the top of embroidery art.

When XQ company established, a couple of artists, Vo Van Quan and Hoang Le Xuan had scheduled a new way for the field by coordinating characters of painting with fine characters of traditional embroidery art that Mrs. Hoang Le Xuan – come from family of Hue city – had inherited and created.

Nowadays, XQ Vietnam silk hand embroidery pictures that are connected with kind of music, poem, painting. Through by the subjects about the living – the death – hope – the hidden things and characters of human condition, embroidery art has created the view of our world, through the images of musical world and it is performed by the traditional art of country.

Vyshyvanka

Vyshyvanka is the Ukrainian traditional clothing which contains elements of Ukrainian ethnic embroidery. Many variations of its design were created. Usually, it was made of homemade linen which was produced by loom. Local features are usually represented in the shirt's ornamental pattern.

History

The art of embroidery in Ukraine traces its roots back to the pre-Christian period, it has centuries-old history. It is proved by results of archaeological dig and travellers' documentary evidence. As a whole, embroidery is dated from the epoch primeval.

Kosovorotka

A kosovorotka is a Russian, skewed-collared shirt. The word is derived from *koso* - askew, and *vorot* collar.

Description

A *kosovorotka* is a traditional Russian shirt, long sleeved and reaching down to the mid-thigh. The shirt is not buttoned all the way down to the hem, but has several buttons at the collar (unfastened when the garment is pulled over the wearer's head), though these are positioned off to one side (regional styles vary between left and right), instead of centrally, as is customary with a typical Western 20th and 21st century man's shirt. If left unbuttoned the collar appears skewed, which accounts for the garment's name. The collar and sleeves of kosovorotka were often decorated with a traditional Slavic ornament.

Today kosovorotka are perceived mostly as men's shirts. However, the shirts for women and children are not too much different from the men's variant, and the word *kosovorotka* in fact is often used to denote just any kind of shirt. The men's garment was worn loose and was not tucked into the trousers, but instead belted either with a conventional belt, a rope, or a rope-like tie. The tails of the garment hung over the trousers. Women's shirts were tucked into the skirt or worn under the sarafan, and indeed tended to have a straighter collar. Children's shirts were often too long for those who wore them, and was the only piece of clothing on little boys and girls in the ancient times.

Generally associated with Russian peasants, the *kosovorotka* was worn by peasants and townsmen of various social categories into the early 20th century, when it was rapidly displaced as an everyday garment by more efficient and less elaborate clothing after the Bolshevik Revolution of 1917. The garment is also known as a *tolstovka,* or the Tolstoy-shirt, because the writer Count Leo Tolstoy customarily wore one in his later years. Since the late 20th century *kosovorotkas* appear mostly as souvenirs and as scenic garments of Russian folk music, song and dance ensembles. The *kosovorotka* is also seen worn by Omar Sharif as Yuri Zhivago in David Lean's 1965 film *Doctor Zhivago.*

Zardozi

Zardozi or Zar-douzi work is a type of embroidery in Iran, India and Pakistan.

Zardozi is a Persian word that means *Sewing with gold string.*

Iran

Zardozi is one of the most important elements of Persian cultural signs and Handicrafts. It is named around the country by names such Zar-douzi, Kam-douzi, Gol-douzi and Kaman-douzi. Today it is more popular in Hormozgan, especially in Bandar-e Lenge and Bandar-e Abbas and Minab that known as the centre of that. Persian Zardozi's are three kinds:

- Some are completely sewing the basic fabric with Bakhie (Persian: ÈÎÌåý) in order to make a new sight of pattern and colours, such as Baloch's Souzan-douzi, Rasht's Qollab-douzi and Kerman's Pate-douzi.
- Some are in different way sewing with less density of work on original fabric. In this way they cross the strings throughout the woof of the original fabric and sew this string to each other to made a lattice and colourful pattern. Such as Sekke-douzi and Qollab-douzi in Isfahan.
- Another way is sewing a variety of patterns on original fabric with golden and silver strings. Such as Dah-Yek-Douzi (1 of 10 sewing which today is demode), Naqade-douzi, Tafte-douzi, Kous-douzi Zari-douzi or Golabatoun-douzi.

India

It prospered during the Mugal Emperor, Akbar, but later a loss of royal patronage and industrialization led to its decline. Today, it is popular in the Indian cities of Lucknow, Farrukhabad and Chennai. In 2013 the Geographical Indication Registry (GIR) accorded the Geographical Indication (GI) registration to the *Lucknow Zardozi* – the world renowned textile embroidery from Lucknow. The Zardozi products manufactured in areas in Lucknow and six surrounding districts of Barabanki, Unnao, Sitapur, Rae Bareli, Hardoi and Amethi became a brand and can carry a registered logo to confirm their authenticity.

History of the Craft

The magnificent metallic embellishment of India —dates back to ancient times. It finds mention in Vedic literature, the Ramayana and the Mahabharata, and all accounts of the Sultanate period. The country, from very early times, was known for the use of gold embroidery on a variety of objects including furnishings, trappings, parasols, and equestrian ornaments. The more aesthetic and evolved embroideries were used on court costumes and especially on accessories such as shoes.

The historical accounts of this craft are shrouded in the usual romantic stories and inaccurate data. But the only certainty is that zarkas—a Persian word meaning zarior gold embroidery —was widely used in all the accounts. History says that from the 13th century, the craftspeople who worked with this medium, setting seed pearls and precious stones with fine gold and silver wire, were known as zardos workers.

Done with metal wire and metal pieces or sequins on velvet, satin and heavy silk bases, Zardozi is one of the most famous and elaborate techniques in metal embroidery. The original embroidery of

Zardozi was done with pure silver wires coated with real gold, and was known as Kalabatun. Though silver and gold wires have now been replaced with synthetic threads, the art remains the same. The use of metal embroidery in Indian textiles and costumes, especially those used for ritual or ceremonial purposes, demonstrates the importance of gold and silver within the culture.

Of all the crafts of the country, Zardozi seems to have flourished and survived to the present day like few others.

Regions Known for Zardozi Work in India

- Hyderabad
- Lucknow
- Jammu, Kashmir
- Kolkata

- Varanasi
- Agra
- Delhi

Producer Communities: Zardozi embroidery is the glitteringly ornate, heavily encrusted gold thread work practiced in various parts of the country. An imperial craft brought to India by Delhi's first Turko-Afghan sultans in the 12th century,

Zardozi became equally popular with the wealthy Hindu, Muslim and European elite down the ages. Today several families in Varanasi, Agra, Lucknow, Rampur, Bareilly and Farukkabad have revived this old craft to supply exquisite zari embroidered bridal outfits and salwar kameezes to boutiques around the country. In recent years, Zardozi has seen a renewed interest in Hyderabad.

Zardozi is also combined with Dabka work and is originally said to be from Lucknow.

Traditionally, only men did Zardozi work, and mostly in Lucknow and Kolkata. But now, Hyderabad is growing as a major Zardozi centre. Today, 10-15 per cent of the thousands of Zardozi workers in Hyderabad are women.

Raw Material

Metal Wire: Metal ingots are melted and pressed through perforated steel sheets, to be converted into wires. They are then hammered to the required thinness. Plain wire is called badla, and when wound round a thread, it is called kasav. Smaller spangles are called sitara, and tiny dots made of badla are called mukaish.

Embellishments: The original Zardozi thread was made from an alloy of silver and gold. The wire that came out of the furnace, although containing a lot of silver in it, glittered like gold. This flattened wire was then twisted around silk threads to form the spring like Zardozi. Zardozi uses dabka (a spring type of thread), kora, katori, tikena, and sitara (sequins) and also glass and plastic beads at times. All these are usually purchased from the local markets or from wholesale markets like Kinari and Sadar Bazaar. Heavy and grand to look at, garments made with Zardozi embroidery can weigh a lot in terms of pounds and kilos.

Dabka is bought at the rate of Rs 500/kg, sequins at an average rate of Rs 300-400/kg; the cost could vary depending on the size of the sequins. Small beads are purchased at a rate of Rs 20-100/pound (1 pound = 450 gms), again depending upon the size.

Of late, the coloured threads available in the market are replacing zari and go ld threads. Anchor threads are most commonly used. A box consisting of 25 skeins (lacchis) costs Rs 80/-.

Cheaper brands like Dolly and Magica offer lower prices of Rs 60/-per box.

Raw Material Procurement

The Zardozi thread comes in long curled strips of shiny gold wire and is sold by weight. It has to be cut to size depending on the design. A variety of materials are used for the embroidery: zari, sequins, cowries, beads, shiny stones that look like diamonds, dabka, sitara. They are all purchased from the local market.

All these embellishments are usually bought in bulk and stored for later use.

Tools Used

Frame / Adda: This is a wooden or metal frame over which the cloth is pulled tightly, so that it does not move while the artisans are at work. This also enables faster movement and clear vision.

Needle: The embroidery is done with a needle. A hooked awl kind of needle called Ari can be used, or a simple stitching needle.

The needle used is the smallest available, generally numbered nine. But it could depend on the design and the thread used.

Scissors: A pair of scissors is an essential tool of the workers involved in the embroidery. It is required time and again to cut the threads and loose ends.

The Process of Zardozi Embroidery

Zardozi is sheer magic of nimble fingers and imaginative designs.

Designing: Earlier the designs used to be very Mughal in nature, comprising of floral and leaf patterns derived from that era. With modern influences, the patterns have changed.

More and more geometric designs are used but flowers, petals and leaves still find their place. Clients specify patterns and motifs to suit their budget and choice.

The design is first traced on a tracing sheet and holes are made along the traced pattern using a needle.

Tracing: The fabric on which the embroidery is to be done is placed on a flat table and the tracing sheet is placed in position. A solution of kerosene and Robin Blue is made. A wad of cloth is dipped into this solution and wiped against the tracing so that the ink seeps through the holes to trace the design on to the fabric. This is then sent to the embroidery workers.

Setting the Adda/Frame: The fabric to be embroidered is stretched taut over a frame called the adda. This concept has evolved from a knockdown camp bed called the khatia used in rural areas.

The adda follows the assembly and tightening principles of the khatia, and gives the cloth a uniform tension. It consists of four wooden spars (sometimes, bamboo is used for the end members) resting on wooden posts. The frame can be made to fit any size of fabric.

The artisan sits on the floor behind the wooden frame working on the piece of cloth.

The frame itself is quite large, and can comfortably accommodate five to seven artisans working together on the pre-traced designs.

The Embroidery: A simple needle or a crochet like hook fixed to a wood en stick called the ari are used for the embroidery. The ari greatly enhances the speed of the work, as it enables the artisan to pass the threads both above and below the fabric. The ari has its disadvantages, though. One tug at a loose thread can spell disaster to the entire design as it can unravel in a matter of minutes. The needle and thread method is far more dependable, but is very time and labour consuming, and hence far more expensive.

All kinds of combinations are used to add to the grandeur of Zardozi. A little bit of thread work here or a few sequins or semi precious stones added there, can make the fabric appealing while giving it a unique exclusivity.

If the design is smaller, then a smaller metal frame can also be used instead of the wooden planks. This is much more comfortable when the embroidery is to be focused in a particular area of the fabric.

The smallest work takes a day to be completed and the most exclusive one can take up to ten days. Each piece is charged per design and material used. For bridal wear, the embroidery is usually very intricate and neatly done with the finest dabka, cowries and stones. For such work, the embroidery could cost as much as Rs 10,000-15,000/-.

Uses of the Product

These days Zardozi is used to make exquisite evening dresses, coats; fashion accessories like purses, handbags, belts, shoes; ceremonial adornments like badges and insignia; furnishing accessories like cushion covers, wall hangings table covers and boxes etc.

A few European and American designers have set up workshops in India, which specialise in Zardozi work on cushion covers, table linen and even curtains.

Marketing

Zardozi embellished outfits have always been 'en vogue' especially for weddings and special ceremonies.

During the last fifty years, the revival of Zardozi has been phenomenal. Not only is it found in the latest designer outlets, but it is being used yet again for interiors of mega weddings and grand ceremonies. Today the Indian ramp is ablaze with products of the craftspeople —the materials may not have the same aesthetic of the Mughals, but they do cater to the demand for highly ornamented garments with glittering beads and sequins.

With the change in times and demand, the Zardozi craftsman has become vital to the garments' en vogue' in Hollywood and Bollywood.

Changes in Recent Years

By the end of the Mughal era, the art declined because of its high cost and the lack of precious metals for the purpose of embroidery. It was again revived in the 20th century.

Today, like everything else, Zardozi too has its limitations: being sold in the market at a much cheaper cost, made out of copper and brass wires plated with gold. The latest additions are coloured Zardozi with a plastic base. Far more pocket friendly, this new Zardozi lasts longer and is lighter to wear.

At times the base fabrics have plastic replacements in place of what was formerly pure gold and the motifs are so far removed from the original, that the product does not resemble what had at one time bedazzled visitors to the royal courts of India. The days of using real gold and silver thread are now history. What one can get, however, is synthetic or 'tested' zari embroidery.

The richness of gold may no longer grace the work of Zardozi craftsman, but the glitter and glamour endures -hopefully it will for years to come. Zardozi is as tenacious as the wires the craftsmen work with.

8

Plain Sewing

Position of the Body and Hands

Before describing different kinds of stitches, a word should be said as to the position of the body and hands when at work. Long experience has convinced me that no kind of needlework necessitates a stooping or cramped attitude. To obviate which, see that your chair and table suit each other in height, and that you so hold your work as hardly to need to bend your head at all. The practice of fastening the work to the knee, besides being ungraceful, is injurious to the health.

Needles

These should be of the best quality. To test a needle, try to break it; if it resist, and then break clean in two, the steel is good; if it bend without breaking, or break without any resistance, it is bad. Never use a bent needle, it makes ugly and irregular stitches, and see that the eye, whether round or egg-shaped, be well-drilled, that it may not fray or cut the thread. Long or half-long needles are the best for white work, long ones for dress-making, and longer ones still, with long eyes, for darning. A stock of each, from No 5 to 12, is advised. The needle should always be a little thicker than the thread, to make an easy passage for it through the stuff.

To keep needles from rusting, strew a little stone alum in the packets, and workers whose hands are apt to get damp, should have a small box of it handy, to powder their fingers with. Blackened needles can be made quite bright again by drawing them through an emery cushion.

Scissors

Scissors are a very important accessory of the work-table, and two varieties are indispensable; a pair of large ones for cutting-out, with one point blunt and the other sharp, the latter to be always held downwards; and a pair of smaller ones with two sharp points. The handles should be large and round; if at all tight, they tire and disfigure the hand.

Thimble

Steel thimbles are the best; bone are very liable to break, and silver ones are not deeply enough pitted, to hold the needle. A thimble should be light, with a rounded top and flat rim.

The Thread

Except for tacking, your thread should never be more than from 40 to 50 c/m. long. If the thread is in skeins, it does not matter which end you begin with, but if you use reeled cotton, thread your needle with the end that points to the reel, when you cut it; as the other end will split, and unravel, when twisted from left to right, which is generally done, to facilitate the process of threading. The cotton should always be cut, as it is weakened by breaking.

Knotting the thread into the needle —When the thread becomes inconveniently short, and you do not want take a fresh one, it may be knotted into the needle, thus: bring it round the forefinger close to the needle, cross it on the inside next to the finger, hold the crossed threads fast, with the thumb draw the needle out through the loop thus formed, and tighten the loop round both ends.

Materials

For tacking, use Coton à coudre D.M.C qualité supérieure (black and gold stamp) Nos. 2 to 6.[A] For hand-sewing, Fil d'Alsace D.M.C Nos. 30 to 700,[A] and Fil à dentelle D.M.C, balls or reels, Nos. 25 to 100[A] will be found most useful. For machine-work: Câblé 6 fils pour machines D.M.C, Nos. 30 to 300,[A] black and white, or white and blue stamp. These can also be used for hand-work. Both these and the lace-thread (Fil à dentelle) on reels, are superfine in quality. The medium sizes are the most useful; but the only suitable ones for very fine and delicate fabrics are the Fil à dentelle D.M.C, and Fil d'Alsace, and the latter only is manufactured in the higher numbers.

All these threads are to be had, wound in balls, or on reels, the buyer may make his own choice; balls are apt to get tangled, but the cotton preserves its roundness better than when it is wound on reels. Linen is generally sewn with linen-thread, but Fil à dentelle and the Fil d'Alsace are very good substitutes.

Position of the Hands

The stuff, fastened to a cushion, must be held with the left hand, which should neither rest on the table, nor on the cushion, the needle must be held between the thumb and forefinger, of the right hand, and the middle finger, armed with the thimble, pushes the needle far enough through the stuff, for the other fingers to take hold of it and draw it out; the thread then comes to lie between the fourth and fifth fingers in the form of a loop, which must be tightened gradually to avoid its knotting.

Position of the Hands without Cushion

When the work cannot be fastened to a cushion it should be held between the forefinger and the thumb, and left hanging down, over the other fingers. If it need to be more firmly held, draw it between the fourth and fifth fingers, which will prevent it from getting puckered or dragged.

Stitches

Plain-Sewing comprises 4 varieties of stitches,

(1) running,

(2) back-stitching,

(3) hemming and

(4) top or over-sewing.

(1) *Running-stitch* : This is the simplest and easiest of all. Pass the needle in and out of the material, at regular intervals, in a horizontal direction, taking up three or four threads at a time. If the stuff allow, several stitches may be taken on the needle at once, before the thread is drawn out. Running-stitch is used for plain seams, for joining light materials, for making gathers and for hems.

(2) *Back-stitch*: Insert the needle, and draw it out six threads further on, carry your thread back, from left to right, and insert the needle three threads back from the point at which it was last drawn out, and bring it out six threads beyond. Stitching and back-stitching are better and more quickly done by machine than by hand.

Stitching: The production of a row of back-stitches, that exactly meet one another, constitutes what is called stitching. Only one stitch can be made at a time, and the needle must be put in, exactly at the point where it was drawn out to form the preceding back-stitch, and brought out as many threads further on as were covered by the last back-stitch. The beauty of stitching depends on the uniform length of the stitches, and the straightness of the line formed, to ensure which it is necessary to count the threads for each stitch, and to draw a thread to mark the line. If you have to stitch in a slanting line across the stuff, or the stuff be such as to render the drawing of a thread impossible, a coloured tacking thread should be run in first, to as a guide.

Stitched hem: Make a double turning, as for a hem, draw a thread two or three threads above the edge of the first turning, and do your stitching through all three layers of stuff; the right side will be that on which you form your stitches.

(3) *Hemming-stitch*: To make a good hem, your stuff must be cut in the line of the thread. Highly dressed stuffs, such as linen and calico; should be rubbed in the hand, to soften them, before the hem is laid. Your first turning should not be more than 2 m/m. wide; turn down the whole length of your hem, and then make the second turning of the same width, so that the raw edge is enclosed between two layers of stuff.

Narrow hems do not need to be tacked, but wide ones, where the first turning should only be just wide enough to prevent the edge from fraying, ought always to be. In hemming you insert the needle and thread directed in a slanting position towards you, just below the edge of the hem, and push it out two threads above, and so on to the end, setting the stitches, two or three threads apart, in a continuous straight line. To ensure the hem being straight, a thread may be drawn to mark the line for the second turning, but it is not a good plan, especially in shirt-making, as the edge of the stuff, too apt in any case, to cut and fray, is, thereby, still further weakened. Hems in woollen materials, which will not take a bend, can only be laid and tacked, bit by bit. In making, what are called rolled hems, the needle must be slipped in, so as only to pierce the first turning, in order that the stitches may not be visible on the outside.

Flat seam: Lay your two edges, whether straight or slanting, exactly even, tack them together with stitches 2 c/m. long, distant 1 to 2 c/m. from the edge, and then back-stitch them by machine or by hand, following the tacking-thread. Cut off half the inner edge, turn the outer one in, as for a hem and sew it down with hemming-stitches.

Smooth the seam underneath with the forefinger as you go, to make it lie quite flat. Beginners should flatten down the seam with their thimbles, or with the handle of the scissors, before they begin to hem, as the outer and wider edge is very apt to get pushed up and bulge over, in the sewing, which hides the stitches.

Rounded seam: Back-stitch your two edges together, as above directed, then cut off the inner edge to a width of four threads, and roll the outer one in, with the left thumb, till the raw edge is quite hidden, hemming as you roll. This kind of seam, on the wrong side, looks like a fine cord, laid on, and is used in making the finer qualities of underclothing.

Fastening threads off, and on: Knots should be avoided in white work. To fasten on, in hemming, turn the needle backwards with the point up, take one stitch, and stroke and work the end of the thread in, underneath the turning. To fasten on, in back-stitching or running, make one stitch with the new thread, then take both ends and lay them down together to the left, and work over them, so that they wind in, and out of the next few stitches.

(4) *Top or over-sewing stitch*: This stitch is used for joining selvedges together. To keep the two pieces even, it is better, either to tack or pin them together first. Insert the needle, from right to left, under the first thread of the selvedge, and through both edges, and sew from right to left, setting your stitches not more than three threads apart. The thread must not be drawn too tightly, so that when the seam is finished and flattened with the thimble, the selvedges may lie, side by side.

Another Kind of Sewing-stitch

For dress-seams and patching; sew left to right, tacking or pinning the edges together first, and holding them tightly with the thumb and finger, to keep perfectly even.

Antique or Old

German Seam: Tack or pin the selvedges together as above, then, pointing your needle upwards from below, insert it, two threads from the selvedge, first on the wrong side, then on the right, first through one selvedge, then through the other, setting the stitches two threads apart. In this manner, the thread crosses itself, between the two selvedges, and a perfectly flat seam is produced. Seams of this kind occur in old embroidered linen articles, where the stuff was too narrow to allow for any other. A similar stitch, only slanting, instead of quite straight is used in making sheets.

French double seam : For joining such stuffs as fray, use the so-called French-seam.

Run your two pieces of stuff together, the wrong sides touching, and the edges perfectly even, then turn them round just at the seam, so that the right sides come together inside, and the two raw edges are enclosed between, and run them together again. See that no threads are visible on the outside. This seam is used chiefly in dress-making, for joining slight materials together which cannot be kept from fraying by any other means.

Hemmed double seam: Turn in the two raw edges, and lay them one upon the other, so that the one next the forefinger, lies slightly higher than the one next the thumb. Insert the needle, not upwards from below but first into the upper edge, and then, slightly slanting, into the lower one. This seam is used in dress-making, for fastening down linings. Figure depicted earlier, shows another kind of double seam, where the two edges are laid together, turned in twice, and hemmed in the ordinary manner, with the sole difference, that the needle has to pass through a sixfold layer of stuff.

Gathering

Gathers are made with running-stitches of perfectly equal length; take up and leave three or four threads, alternately, and instead of holding the stuff fast with your thumb, push it on to the needle as you go, and draw up your thread after every four or five stitches.

Stroking gathers: When you have run in your gathering thread, draw it up tight, and make it fast round the finger of your left hand, and then stroke down the gathers with a strong needle, so that they lie evenly side by side, pushing each gather, in stroking it, under your left thumb, whilst you support the stuff at the back with your other fingers.

Running in a second gathering thread: This is to fix the gathers after they have been stroked, and should be run in 1 or 2 c/m. Below the first thread, according to the kind of stuff, and the purpose it is intended for: take up five or six gathers at a time, and draw your two threads perfectly even, that the gathers may be straight to the line of the thread.

Sewing on gathers: To distribute the fullness equally, divide the gathered portion of material, and the band, or plain piece, on to which it is to be sewn, into equal parts, and pin the two together at corresponding distances, the gathered portion under the plain, and hem each gather to the band or plain piece, sloping the needle to make the thread slant, and slipping it through the upper threads only of the gathers.

Whipping

Whipping is another form of gathering, used for fine materials. With the thumb and forefinger of the left hand, roll the edge over towards you, into a very tight thin roll, insert the needle on the inside of the roll next the thumb, and bring it out on the outside next the forefinger, at very regular distances, and draw up the thread slightly, from time to time, to form the gathers.

Ornamental hem: For an ornamental hem, make a turning, 2 or 3 c/m deep, and run in a thread, with small running-stitches up and down. By slightly drawing the thread, the straight edge will be made to look as if it were scalloped.

Sewing on cord: For sewing on cord, use strong thread, either Fil d'Alsace D.M.C, Fil à dentelle D.M.C or Câblé 6 fils D.M.C No. 25, 30, 35 or 40. Be careful not to stretch the cord, but to hold it in, as you sew it, as it invariably shrinks more than the stuff in the first washing. Fasten it with hemming stitches to the edge of the turning, taking care that it does not get twisted.

Sewing on flaps: These should be back-stitched on to the right side of the article they are to be affixed to, quite close to the edge, then folded over in half, and hemmed down on the wrong side. Like the cord, the flap must, in the process, be held in very firmly with the left hand. Though the back-stitching could be more quickly done by machine, hand-work is here preferable, as the holding in cannot be done by machine.

Sewing on tape-loops: These, in the case of the coarser articles of household linen, are generally fastened to the corners. Lay the ends of your piece of tape, which should be from 15 to 17 c/m. long, side by side, turn in and hem them down, on three sides: the loop should be so folded as to form a three-cornered point, shewn in the illustration. Join the two edges of the tape together in the middle with a few cross-stitches, and stitch the edge of the hem of the article to the loop, on the right side.

Strings and loops for fine under-linen: Sew these on, likewise, on the wrong side of the article, hemming down the ends, and fastening them on the right side, with two rows of stitching crossing each other, and a third row along the edge.

Button-holes in linen: Cut your hole perfectly straight, and of exactly, the diameter of the button, having previously marked out the place for it, with two rows of running-stitches, two or three threads apart. Put in your needle at the back of the slit, and take up about three threads, bring the working thread round, from right to left under the point of the needle, and draw the needle out through the loop, so that the little knot comes at the edge of the slit, and so on to the end, working from the lower left-hand corner to the right. Then make a bar of button-hole stitching across each end, the knotted edge towards the slit.

Button Holes in Dress Materials

Mark out and cut them as above described; if however, the material be liable to fray, wet the slit as soon as you have cut it, with liquid gum, and lay a strand of strong thread along the edge to make your stitches over; one end of dress button-holes must be round, the stitches diverging like rays from the centre, and when you have worked the second side, thread the needle with the loose strand, and pull it slightly, to straighten the edges; then fasten off, and close the button-hole with a straight bar of stitches across the other end.

Sewing on Buttons

To sew linen, or webbed buttons on to underclothing, fasten in your thread with a stitch or two, at the place where the button is to be; bring the needle out through the middle of the button, and make eight stitches, diverging from the centre like a star, and if you like, encircle them by a row of stitching. This done, bring the needle out between the stuff and the button, and twist the cotton six or seven times round it, then push the needle through to the wrong side, and fasten off.

Binding Slits

Nothing is more apt to tear than a slit whether it be hemmed or merely bound. To prevent this, make a semicircle of button-hole stitches at the bottom of the slit, and above that, to connect the two sides, a bridge of several threads, covered with button-hole stitches.

In under-linen, it often so happens that two selvedges meet at the slit, which renders binding unnecessary; in that case take a small square of stuff, turn in the raw edges, top-sew it into the slit on two sides, turn in the other two, fold over on the bias, and hem them down over the top-sewing. Such little squares of material, inserted into a slit or seam, to prevent its tearing, are called gussets.

Sewing on Piping

Piping is a border, consisting of a cord or bobbin, folded into a stripe of material, cut on the cross, and affixed to the edge of an article to give it more strength and finish. It is a good substitute for a hem or binding on a bias edge, which by means of the cord, can be held in, and prevented from stretching. Cut your stripes diagonally, across the web of the stuff, and very even; run them together, lay the cord or bobbin along the stripe, on the wrong side, 5 m/m, from the edge, fold the edge over, and tack the cord lightly in. Then lay it on the raw edge of the article, with the cord towards you, and with all the raw edges turned away from you. Back-stitch the piping to the edge, keeping close to the cord. Then turn the article round, fold in the raw outside edge over the others, and hem it down like an ordinary hem.

Fixing Whale-bones

Before slipping the whale-bone into its case or fold of stuff, pierce holes in it, top and bottom, with a red hot stiletto. Through these holes, make your stitches, diverging like rays or crossing each other.

Herring-boning

This stitch is chiefly used for seams in flannel, and for overcasting dress-seams, and takes the place of hemming, for fastening down the raw edges of a seam that has been run or stitched, without turning them in. Herring-boning is done from left to right, and forms two rows of stitches. Insert the needle from right to left, and make a stitch first above, and then below the edge, the threads crossing each other diagonally.

Crochet Work

Crochet work, so called from the hook, French *croche* or *croc*, with which it is done, is not only one of the easiest but in comparison with the cost and labour, one of the most effective kinds of fancy-work. It is also one of the most useful, as it can be applied to the domestic requirements of every-day life, to wearing apparel, house-linen and upholstery; and we are sure that the patterns contained in this chapter, which have in addition to their other merits that of novelty, will meet with a favourable reception.

Hooks, or needles, as they are generally called, made of wood, bone or tortoise-shell are used for all the heavier kinds of crochet work in thick wool or cotton, and steel ones for the finer kinds. The Tunisian crochet is done with a long straight hook, which is made all in one piece. The points should be well polished inside and not too sharp, the backs slightly curved, and the handles, whether of bone, steel or wood, so light as not to tire the hand. Those represented here, we consider the best, as regards shape. As it is most essential that the needle should be suited to the cotton in size, we subjoin a comparative table of the numbers of the D.M.C threads and cottons and of the different needles.

Explanation of the Signs *

In crochet, as in knitting, you frequently have to repeat the same series of stitches. Such repetitions will be indicated, by the signs *, **, ***, etc., as the case may be.

Crochet Stitches

In point of fact, there is only one, because all crochet work consists of loops made by means of the hook or needle, and connected together by being drawn the one through the other.

Crochet work may however, be divided into two kinds, German crochet, and Victoria or Tunisian crochet; the latter is known also under the name of *tricot-crochet.*

In German crochet there are eight different kinds of stitches:

(1) chain stitch,

(2) single stitch,

(3) plain stitch,

(4) treble stitch,

(5) knot stitch,

(6) bullion stitch,

(7) cluster or scale stitch,

(8) double stitch.

The rows are worked, according to the kind of stitch, either to and fro, or all from one end. In the former case, the work has to be turned at the end of each row, and the subsequent row begun with 1, 2 or 3 chain stitches to prevent the contraction of the outside edge.

When the rows are all worked one way, the thread must be fastened on afresh each time, which is done by putting the needle into the first chain stitch of the preceding row, drawing the thread through it so as to form a loop, and making one or more chain stitches according to the height required. At the end of each row, cut the thread and draw the end through the last loop; in this manner all crochet work is finished off. Some crochet workers make a few extra chain stitches with the ends of the thread at the beginning and end of each row, or fasten them off with a few stitches on the wrong side.

They can also, when the occasion requires, be formed into a fringe or tassels as a finish to the work.

Position of the hands and explanation of

(1) *Chain stitch:* Take the thread in the left hand between the finger and thumb, hold the needle between the thumb and first finger of the right hand, letting it rest on the second finger, in the same manner in which you hold your pen, and put it into the loop, which you hold between the finger and thumb of the left hand. Take up the thread, lying on your finger, with the needle and make your first stitch as you do in knitting, tightening the loop just enough to leave an easy passage through it for the needle. The end of the thread must be held by the thumb and forefinger. The next stitches are made by taking up the thread with the needle and drawing it through the loop. The throwing of the thread round the needle by a jerk of the wrist is called an 'over'.

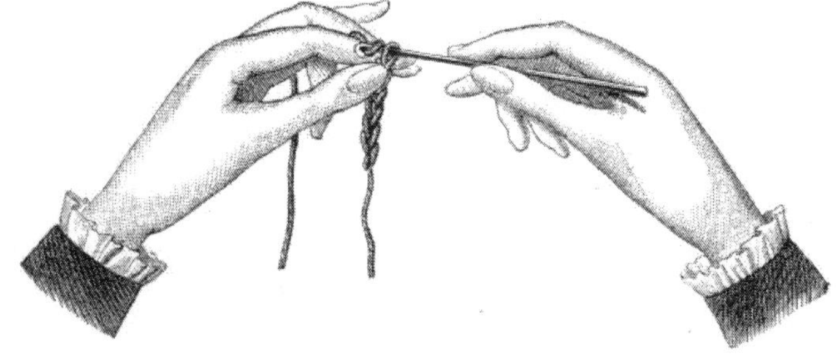

Figure: *Position of the hands and explanation of chain stitch.*

(2) *Single stitch:* Put the needle in from the right side of the work, into the uppermost loop of the preceding row, take up the thread on the needle and draw it through both loops.

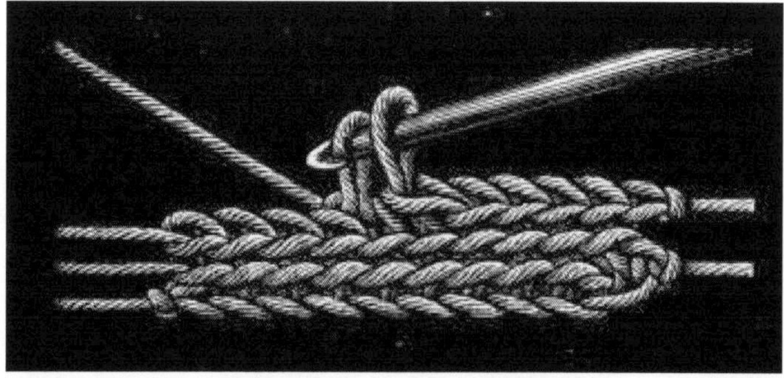

Figure: *Single stitch.*

(3) *Plain stitch:* Put the needle through, from the right side to the wrong, under the upper side, either of a chain, or of a stitch of the preceding row, draw the thread through it in a loop, turn the thread round the needle and draw it through both loops on the needle. By making the rows of plain stitches follow each other in different ways, a great variety of stitches can be produced, as the illustrations and written instructions here given will show.

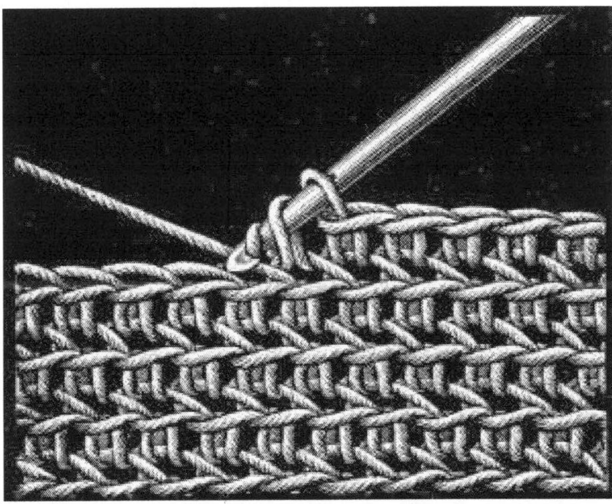

Figure: *Plain stitch.*

Rose stitch —This consists of rows of plain stitches, worked backwards and forwards. Insert the needle from the right side, under both the horizontal loops of the preceding row.

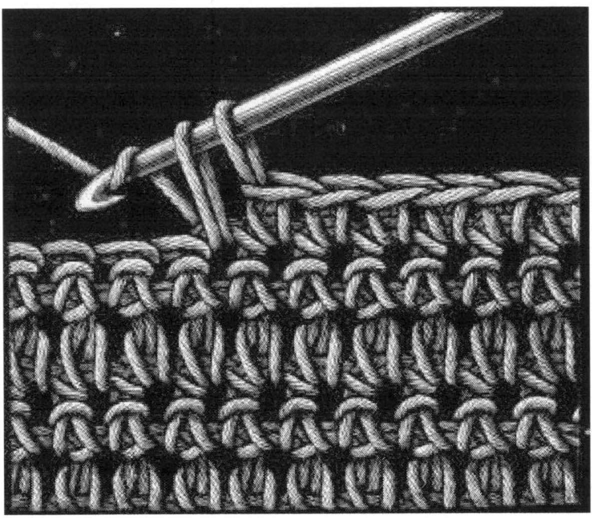

Figure: *Rose stitch.*

Russian stitch —This is worked like the foregoing, only that all the rows have to be begun from the same end, and the thread has to be cut off at the end of each row.

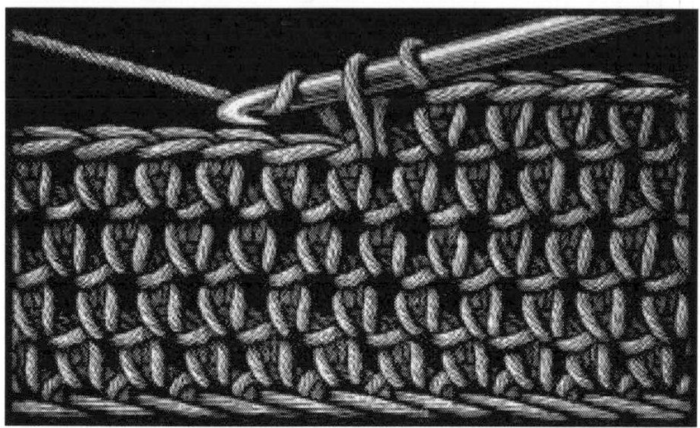

***Figure:** Russian stitch.*

Ribbed stitch —Worked backwards and forwards, the hook being passed through the back part only of the stitches of the preceding row.

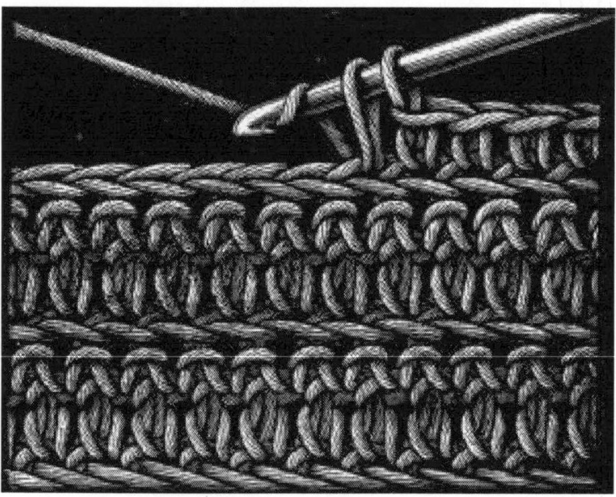

***Figure:** Ribbed stitch.*

Chain stitch.—Worked like, but on one side only.

Piqué stitch.—This stitch also is only worked on one side. Put the needle in under one of the vertical threads of a stitch and complete the plain stitch. This is a stitch that looks very well on the wrong side; the bars of the loop lie quite close together, which makes it particularly suitable for unlined articles of clothing. It requires a large-sized needle to do this stitch well, especially if the material be a heavy one.

Slanting stitch —Worked entirely on the right side. Take up the back thread of a stitch in the preceding row, take hold of the crochet thread without turning it round the needle and draw it through in a loop, and then finish the stitch like a plain stitch.

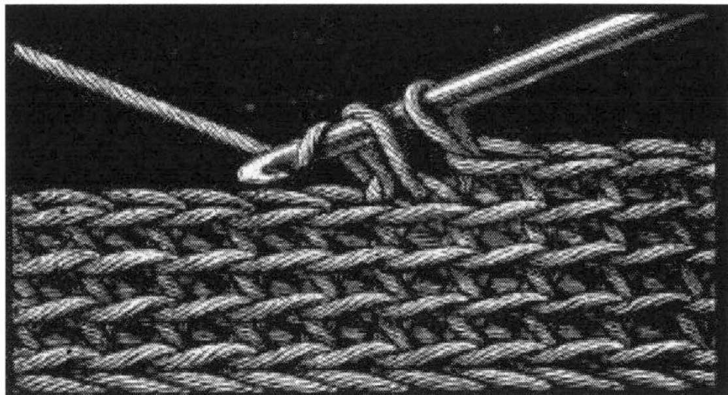

Figure: *Slanting stitch.*

Crossed stitch.—The name which is given to the preceding stitch when both the threads of the stitches in the row before, are taken up together, instead of the back one only.

Russian crossed stitch —To work this stitch which runs in slanting lines, put the needle in between the vertical threads of the stitches and underneath the two horizontal ones.

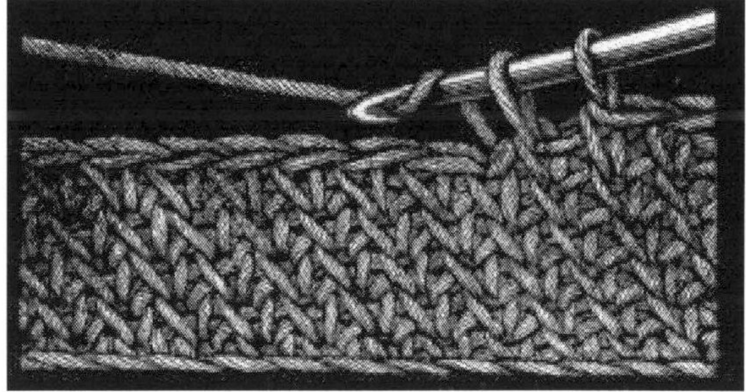

Figure: *Russian crossed stitch.*

Counterpane stitch —Counterpanes can be made in a less close stitch than those just described.

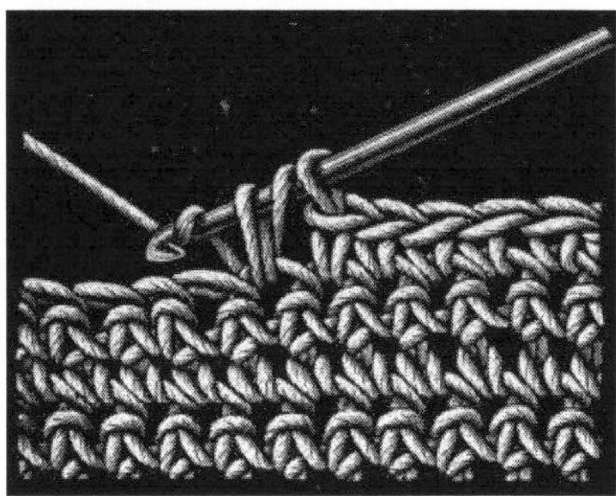

Figure: *Counterpane stitch.*

To produce a soft and elastic fabric turn the thread round the needle and insert it under both the horizontal threads of a loop, take up the thread without turning it round the needle, draw it through in a loop, make an over, and draw the thread through all the three loops, that you have on the needle.

Knotted stitch —This stitch likewise is composed of plain stitches, which, however differ in a slight degree from those we have described hitherto.

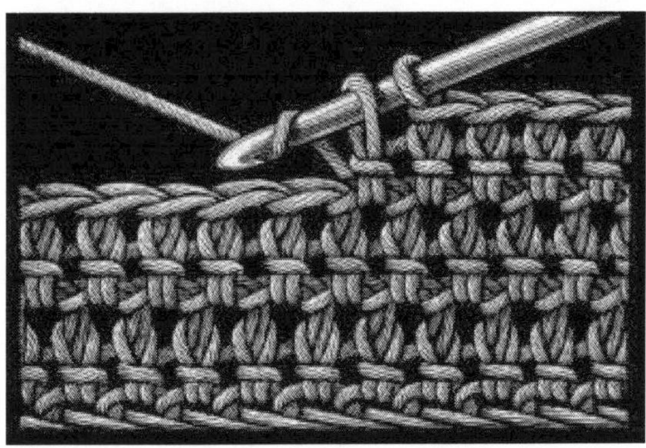

Figure: *Knotted stitch.*

Make an over, put the needle through the two horizontal threads of the stitch below, make another over and draw it back through the two loops and the first over, make another over, and draw the thread through the last two loops.

Loop stitch —Worked as follows: when you have put the needle into the loop of a stitch below, carry the thread, downwards from above, round a stripe of cardboard or a flat wooden ruler, then finish the stitch in the usual way. These long loops, each about 2 c/m. in length, can also be made over the forefinger and held fast by the thumb as you work, but it is more difficult to make them regular in this way.

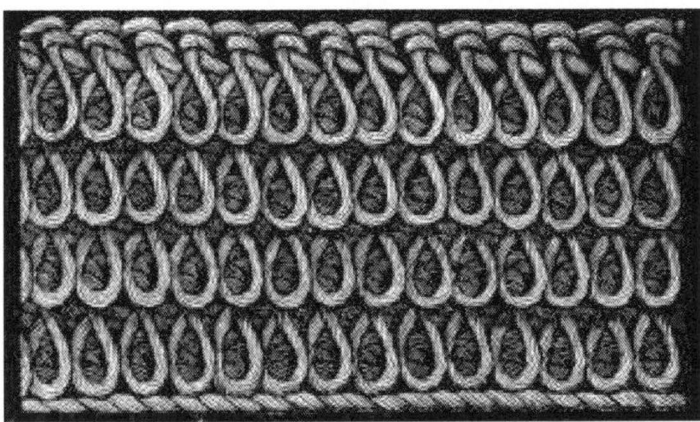

Figure: *Loop stitch.*

Each row of long stitches is followed by a row of plain stitches. The side, where the long loops lie, becomes the right side. If you wish this stitch to be very thick and handsome, wind the thread three times round the ruler, or finger, and secure it with a plain stitch; in this case, you should make one plain stitch between every two clusters. A loose, fleecy thread is generally used for this stitch, and for washing articles more especially, we recommend Coton à repriser D.M.C.

Plain stitches for a chain —Begin with two chain stitches, put the needle in between the two threads of the first chain stitch, turn the thread round the needle and draw it through in a loop, turn it round again and draw it through the two loops; then, put the needle into the left part of the stitch that was just made, turn the thread round the needle, draw it through the two loops and so on, to the end.

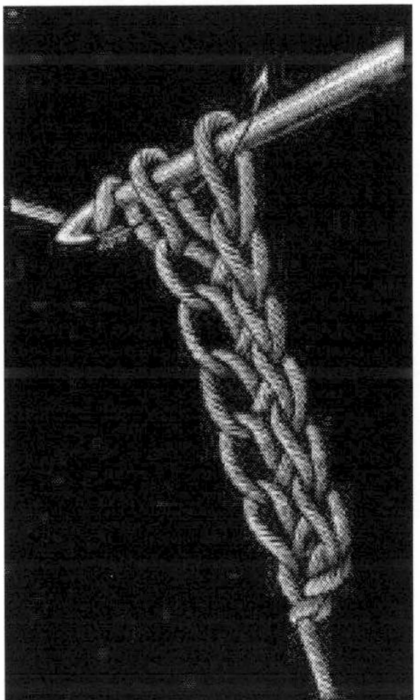

Figure: *Plain stitches for a chain.*

A chain of this kind makes a very good substitute for *mignardise* when that can not be got of the right size and colour for the required purpose.

(4) *Trebles:* Trebles are little columns, or bars made of loops or stitches. They can be worked, like all other crochet, either to and fro, or all one way. There are different kinds of trebles; half or short trebles, trebles, double trebles, called also 'long stitch', and quadruple and quintuple trebles, called 'extra long stitch', connected trebles and crossed trebles.

Half trebles —Turn the cotton round the needle from behind, put the needle in between the trebles of the preceding row, or into one edge of a chain stitch; make an over, bring the needle forward again with the thread, make another over and draw the needle through all three loops.

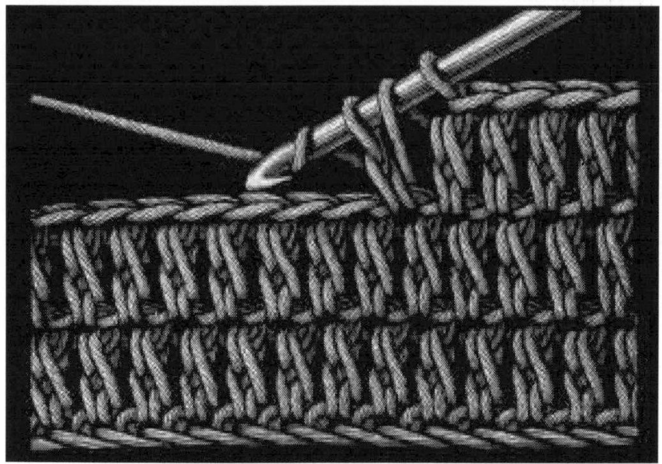

Figure: *Half trebles*

Trebles —Begin, as for the half treble, by turning the thread round the needle, and putting it in under one edge of the stitch beneath, then take up the thread on the needle and bring it through two of the loops, take it up again, and draw it through the two remaining loops.

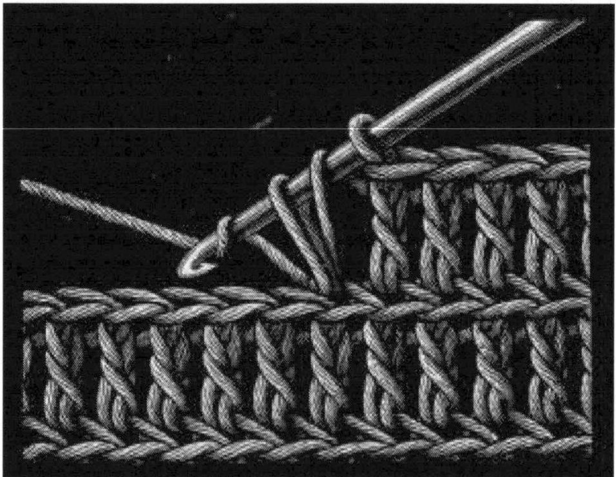

Figure: *Trebles made directly above one another.*

We have trebles made in the same manner, only that instead of putting the needle under one edge of the stitch beneath, you put it under both, and between the trebles of the last row.

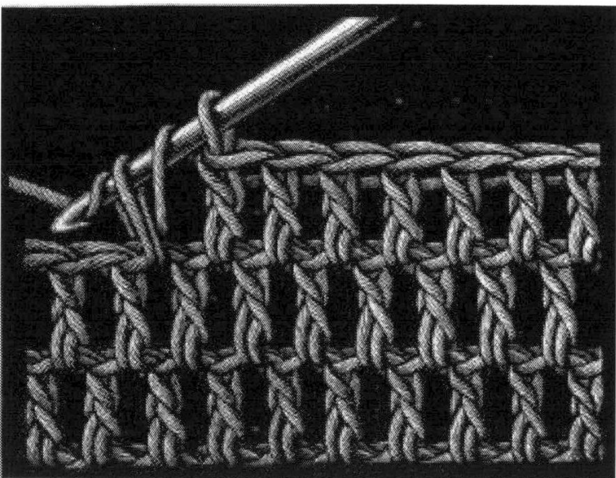

Figure: *Trebles set between those of the preceding row.*

Double trebles or 'long stitch' —Turn the thread twice round the needle, put it into a stitch of the work and bring the thread through in a loop, then take up the thread on the needle and bring it through two of the loops, three times in succession.

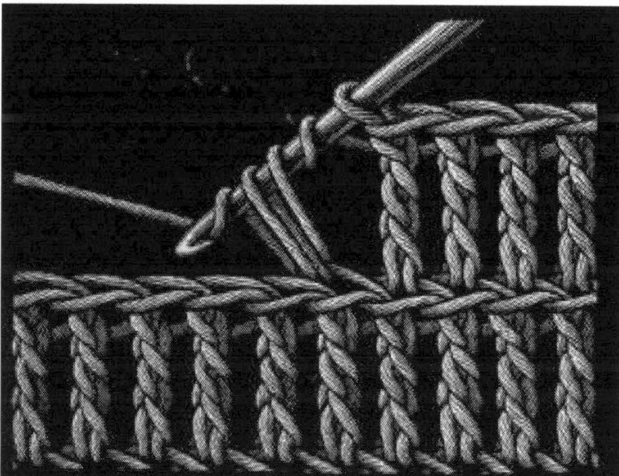

Figure: *Double trebles or 'long stitch'.*

Triple and quadruple trebles or 'extra long stitch' —For a triple treble, twist the cotton three times round the needle, for a quadruple one, four times, then form the treble in the usual way by bringing the needle through two of the loops at a time. To make a series of trebles, of gradually increasing length, bring the needle, at every other treble, through the last three loops, so that before making a triple treble you will have to make columns, respectively, 1 treble, 1½ treble, 2 trebles and 2½ trebles long. Columns like these, of different lengths, are often required in crochet work, for leaves and scalloped edgings.

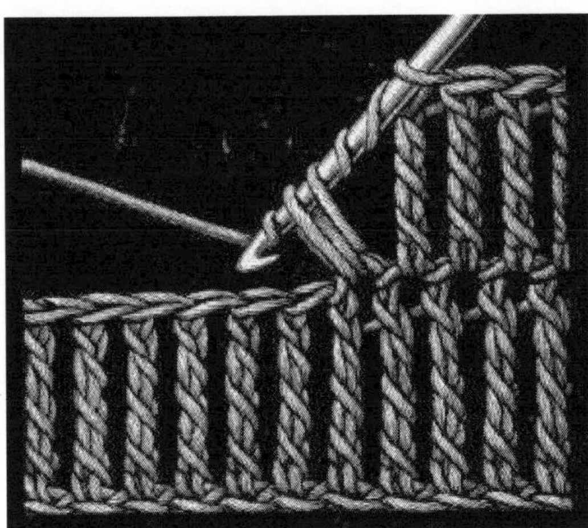

Figure: *Triple and quadruple trebles or 'extra long stitch'.*

Connected trebles —Trebles, connected together, can be worked to and fro, and take the place of plain stitches. Begin with a chain, then make a treble of the required height, form as many loops as you made overs for the treble, take up the upper thread of the stitch nearest the treble, turn the thread round the needle, bring it back to the right side and draw the needle through the trebles, two at a time.

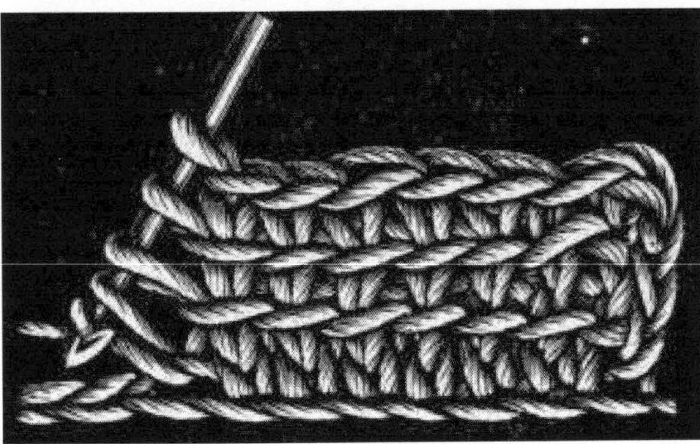

Figure: *Connected trebles.*

Crossed trebles —Trebles of this sort produce an open stitch, which is often used for the footing of lace, or for an insertion. Make a foundation of chain, or other stitches, and proceed as follows: 3 chain, miss 2 stitches of the row beneath, make 1 treble in the third stitch, 5 chain, 1 over, put the needle in between the loops of the connected trebles and finish with a treble. Then make a double over, put the needle into the next loop of the preceding row, make another over, draw the needle through the loops, make another over and join the two next loops. This leaves 3 loops on the needle. Make an over, put the needle into the third stitch of the row beneath, make an over, and bring the needle back to the right side.

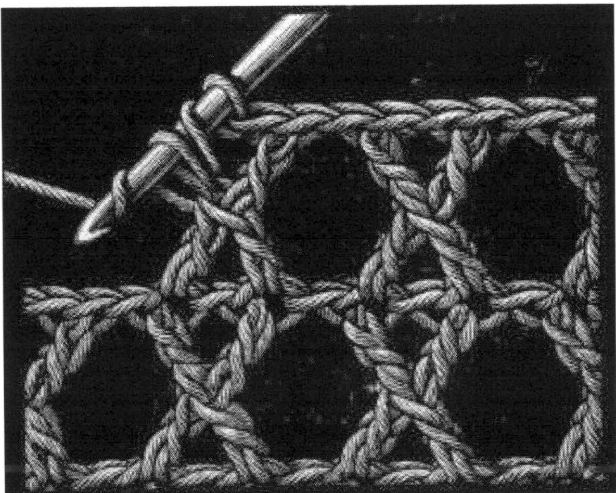

Figure: *Crossed trebles.*

Join the 5 loops on the needle together, 2 and 2, make 2 chain, 1 over, put the needle into the upper parts of the connected trebles and finish with a treble, and so on.

These trebles also can be lengthened if necessary, but in that case, the width of the crossed treble must correspond with the height. Generally speaking you make the trebles over the same number of stitches as you made overs on the needle, which should always be an even number.

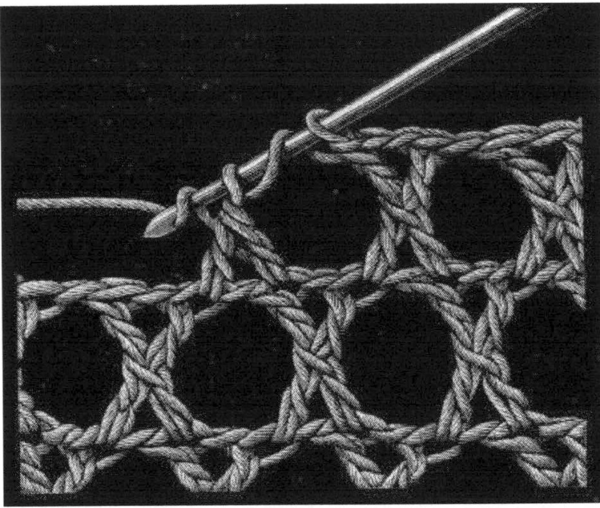

Figure: *Crossed trebles, set between those of the preceding row.*

Trebles for a chain.—A quicker way of making a wide footing for a crochet lace is to make the trebles in the following manner.

Make 4 chain stitches, 2 overs, put the needle into the first of the 4 chain, 1 over, draw the thread through the stitch *, 1 over, draw the thread through the next 2 loops and repeat twice from * = ** 2 overs, put the needle into the left bottom part of the treble, close the treble as before and repeat from **.

(5) *Knot stitch:* This stitch which is composed of several loops forming a tuft, can only be worked from one side, consequently all one way. It looks best in a coarse material to show the interlacing of the threads.

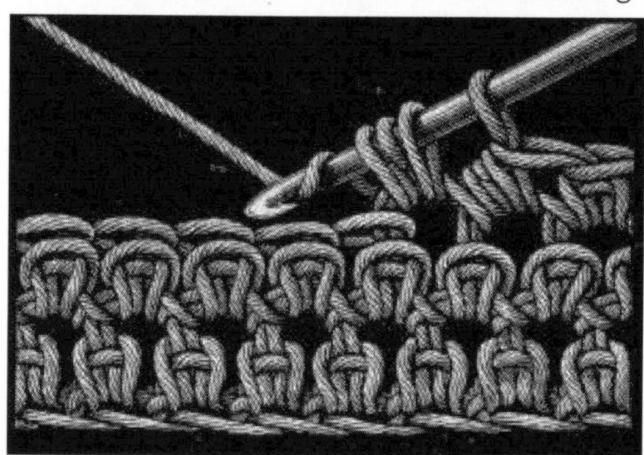

Figure: *Knot stitch.*

Enter the needle through the two loops of the stitches of the bottom row, turn the thread round the needle, but away from you towards the back; bring it forward to the right side, put the needle again through one of the bottom stitches, make another over like the first and draw the needle through all the bars at once.

(6) *Bullion Stitch:* For bullion stitch, select a needle, a little thicker towards the handle, and finer than you would use for any other crochet stitch.

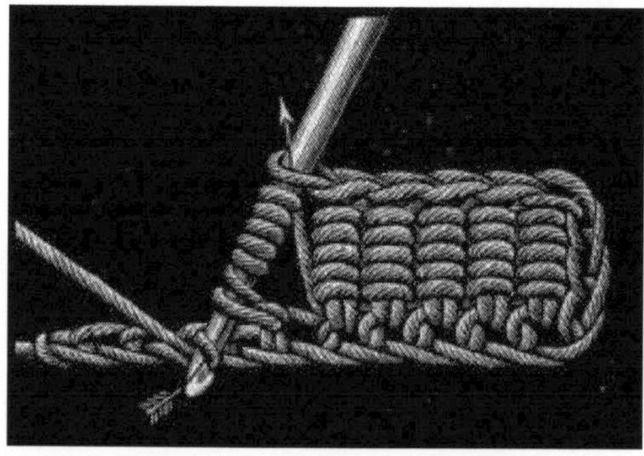

Figure: *Bullion stitch.*

Begin by making a chain of very loose stitches, then wind the thread several times, very evenly, round the needle. Insert the needle into a loop of the chain, make a single over, and draw it with the last over upon it, through all the other overs.

Trebles in bullion stitch, are worked in just the same manner, only that you have to turn the thread, at least 10 or 12 times round the needle and draw it through all the overs at once. To facilitate the passage of the needle, keep the overs in their place with the thumb and forefinger of the left hand.

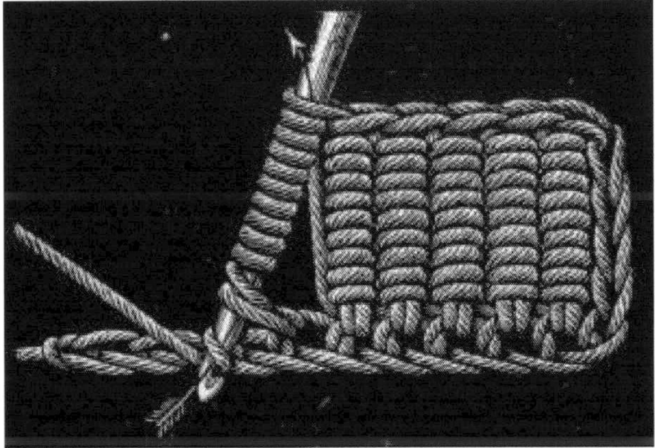

Figure: *Bullion stitch.*

Bullion stitch can only be worked with wool or a very fleecy thread, such as Coton à repriser D.M.C,[A]but trebles in bullion stitch can be worked in any of the D.M.C threads and cottons.

(7) *Cluster stitch:* Generally used as an insertion between rows of plain crochet.

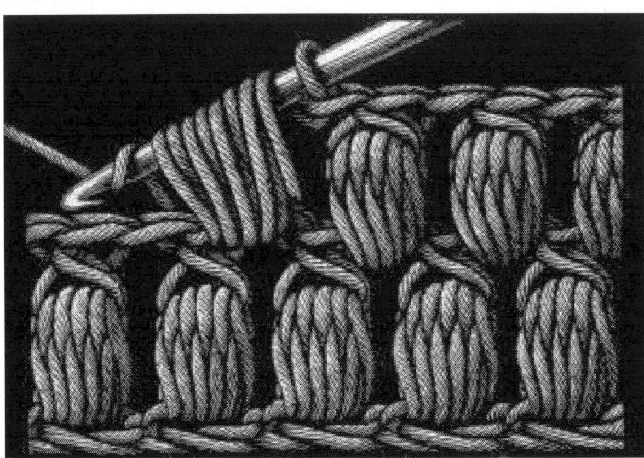

Figure: *Cluster stitch.*

Put the needle under one stitch of the preceding row, make an over, draw the thread through in a loop, make another over, put the needle in again under the same stitch, bring it back, make a third over, and pass a third time under the same stitch; bring the needle back, make a fourth over and pass the needle through all the loops that are upon it.

Then, after making a chain stitch, begin the same stitch over again, placing it in the second stitch of the lower row.

Cluster stitch may also be finished off by retaining the two last loops on the needle, making an over, and ending with a plain stitch.

(8) *Double stitch*: A rather coarse thread, such as Coton à tricoter D.M.C Nos. 6 to 12, Cordonnet 6 fils D.M.C Nos. 3 to 10, or Fil à pointer D.M.C Nos. 10 to 30[A] is better for this stitch than a loose fleecy thread which is apt to render it indistinct.

Take up a loop right and left of a stitch of the preceding row, so that counting the loop of the last stitch, you have 3 loops on the needle, make an over and draw it through the 3 loops.

Then take up a loop again by the side of the one you made on the left, and which now lies on the right. Take 2 loops in the next stitch, make an over and draw it through all the loops.

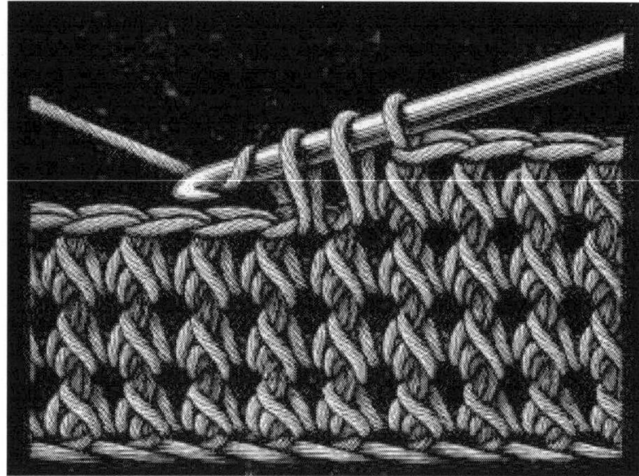

Figure: *Double stitch.*

Raised stitch —All the stitches that come under this heading require a foundation of a few plain rows for the raised trebles.

You will observe that the fourth stitch in the fourth row is a double treble, connected with a loop of the fourth stitch of the first row.

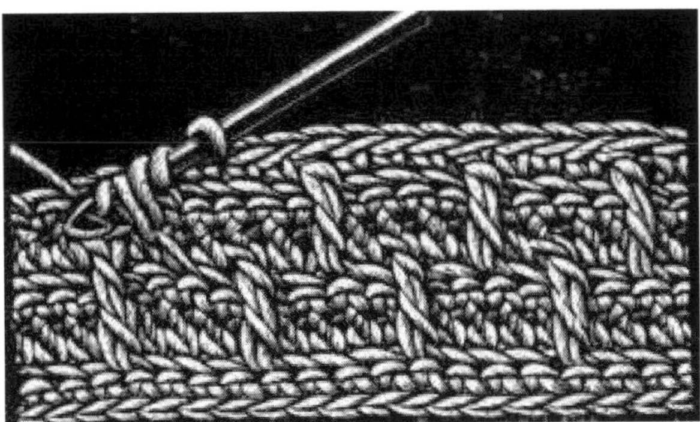

Figure: *Raised stitch.*

Miss the stitch of the preceding row, which is hidden under the treble, make 3 plain stitches, 1 double treble, and so on. Having finished this row, turn the work and make a plain row. In the next row begin with 4 plain stitches, then make 1 double treble between the 3 stitches that are between the first trebles, 3 plain stitches, 2 double trebles and so on.

In the 8th row of plain stitches, the trebles must be placed in the same order as in the 4th. Raised stitch with crossed trebles —Begin, by 3 rows of plain stitches. The 4th row begins with 2 plain stitches followed by: * 1 double treble joined to the upper part of the 1st stitch of the 1st row; keep the 2 last loops of this treble on the needle; make a double over for the next treble, pass the needle through the fourth stitch of the first row, make an over, turn the thread round the needle, bring it back, finish the treble all but the last 3 loops, which you crochet together. Miss the stitch behind the treble, make 3 plain stitches and repeat from *.

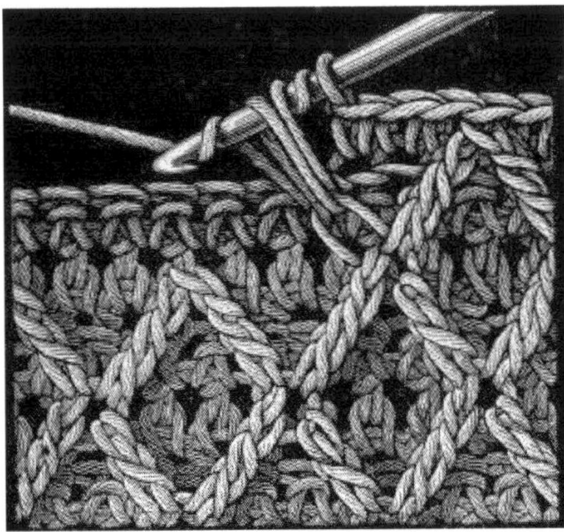

Figure: *Raised stitch, with crossed trebles.*

Then turn the work, make one plain row, and turn the work back to the right side.

The second row of trebles begins with a plain stitch. The way in which the trebles are to be crossed is shewn in the illustration.

Raised stitch with dots —After making 3 plain rows, begin the 4th with 3 plain stitches, and proceed as follows: * 6 trebles into the 4th plain stitch of the preceding row, leaving the last loop of each treble on the needle, so that altogether you have 7 loops upon it; then you turn the thread once round the needle and draw it through the loops; miss the stitch that is underneath the dot, make 3 plain stitches and repeat from *.

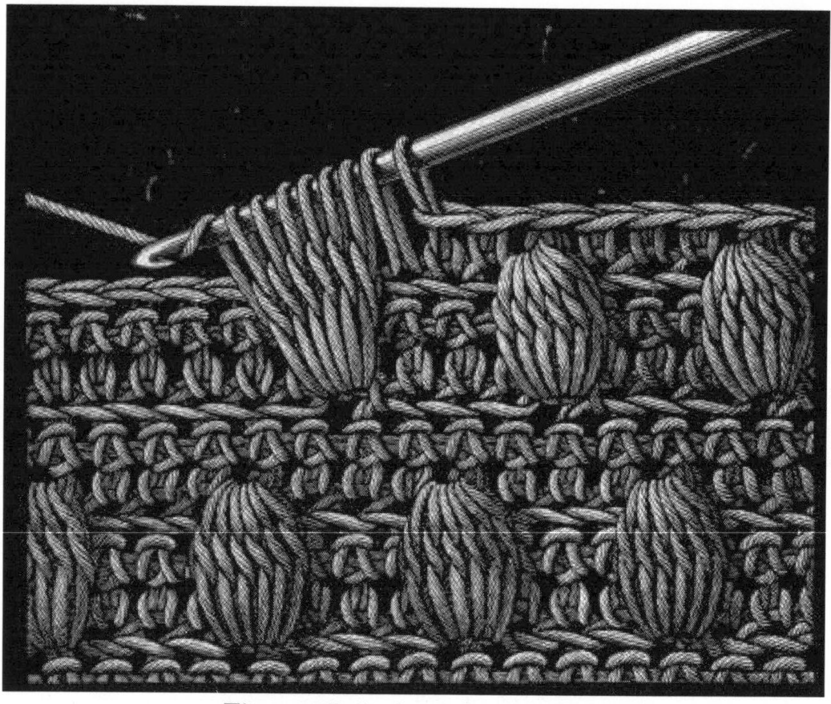

***Figure:** Raised stitch with dots.*

Then make 3 rows of plain stitches; in the 4th row, the 1st dot is made in the 4th stitch, so that the dots stand out in relief.

Raised dots with trebles —Turn the work after making 3 rows of plain stitches, make 3 stitches more in the 4th stitch of the 1st row, * 6 trebles, drop the last stitch of the 6th treble, put the needle into the stitch between the last plain stitch and the 1st treble, take the dropped loop of the last treble and draw it through the one on the needle; miss the stitch under the dot, make 5 plain stitches and repeat from *.

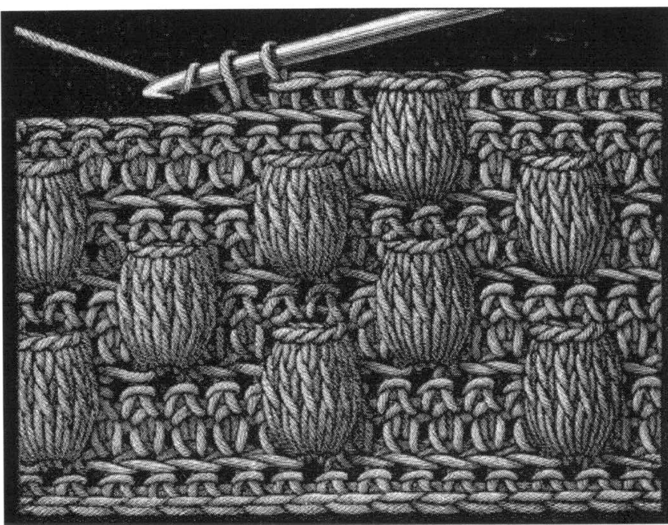

***Figure:** Raised dots with trebles.*

Raised dots in slanting lines —On the rows of stitches that have been previously prepared, make, for the 4th stitch of the 4th row, a cluster stitch, with 1 quadruple over and then 4 plain stitches, 1 cluster stitch and so on. The next row is plain; in the second you have to make 1 plain stitch more, and fasten the cluster stitches into the loops to the left of the second of the 3 covered rows. In this way you have to make each raised stitch, one stitch, in advance and to the left of the last, so that they run in slanting lines over the surface.

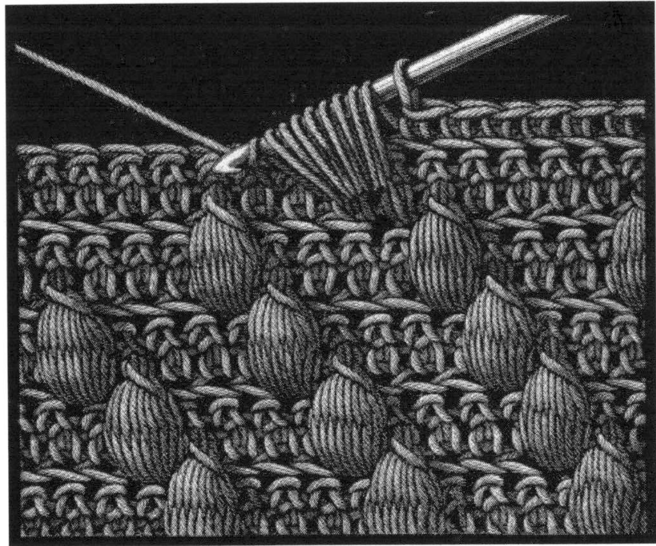

***Figure:** Raised dots in slanting lines.*

Close shell stitch —This pretty stitch which can only be worked in rows, all one way, is more especially suitable for children's jackets and petticoats; it is easy, and has the merit of being quickly done. On a foundation of chain, or other stitches, make: 2 chain, 7 trebles on the 4th stitch, * 1 chain, 7 trebles on the 5th stitch of the last row and repeat from *.

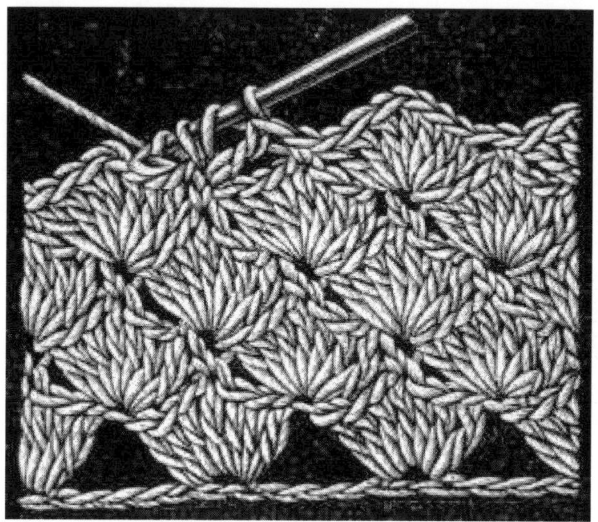

Figure: *Close shell stitch.*

2nd row—** 7 trebles on the chain stitch of the last row which connects 7 bars, 1 plain stitch on the 4th of the 7 trebles of the first row and repeat from **.

Picots.—The edges of most crochet work are ornamented with picots, or small points of different shapes, called severally close picots, chain picots and lace picots.

Close picots may be subdivided into, large and small, pointed, and rounded, picots with rounded leaves and picots with pointed leaves.

Small rounded picots.—These may either be made separately and then sewn on, or made at once, on to a crochet border. In the first case, begin with 3 chain, then coming back, make 1 plain stitch on the second and on the first chain stitch. In the second case make: 1 chain, take the needle out of the stitch and put it in from the right side, under both edges of the last stitch, take up the dropped stitch, bring it to the right side, * 3 chain; then returning: 1 plain stitch on each chain, draw the needle out, put it in from the right side into the second stitch of the row beneath, take up the loop, bring it back to the right side, and repeat from *.

Large rounded picots.—5 chain, miss 3, 1 treble on the 2nd and 1 treble on the 1st chain stitch.

When you want to attach these picots at once to an existing piece of work, drop the last loop and bring it back again with the needle from the wrong side to the right and miss 2 stitches, instead of one, as in the case of the small picots.

Pointed picots.—Cast on 6 chain, then returning, and missing the 6th stitch: 1 single stitch, 1 plain stitch, 1 half treble, 1 treble, 1 double treble.

Picots with rounded leaves.—* 4 chain, and 3 trebles on the first stitch, and 1 single on the same stitch on which the trebles were, **, or 6 chain and repeat from * to **.

When these picots serve as a finish to a straight edge, make 2 single stitches in the preceding row instead of 2 chain.

Picots with pointed leaves.—6 chain, on the first chain stitch: 3 double trebles, of which you retain the two last loops on the hook, 1 over, draw the thread through the 4 loops, 5 chain, 1 single on the stitch on which the trebles are.

Chain picots.—For the small chain picots, make: 5 chain and 1 plain stitch on the first of these 5 stitches. For the large ones: 5 chain and 1 treble on the first stitch.

Picots in bullion stitch —5 chain, 1 treble in bullion stitch drawn up into a ring, and joined to the 5th chain stitch.

Drooping picots —5 chain, drop the loop, put the needle into the first of the 5 chain, take up the dropped loop, and draw it through the stitch.

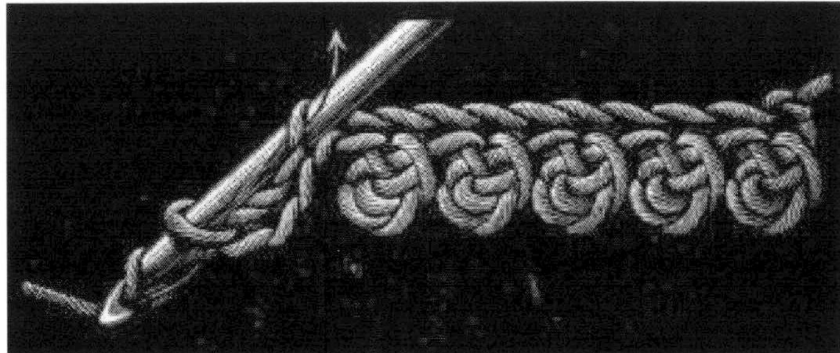

Figure: *Drooping picots.*

Lace picots —Represents picots formed of chain stitches, as follows: 2 chain, put the needle into the first, 1 over, bring the thread back to the front, 2 chain: * put the needle into the two loops, and at the same time, into the second loop and the first chain, draw the thread through in a loop, make 2 chain and repeat from *.

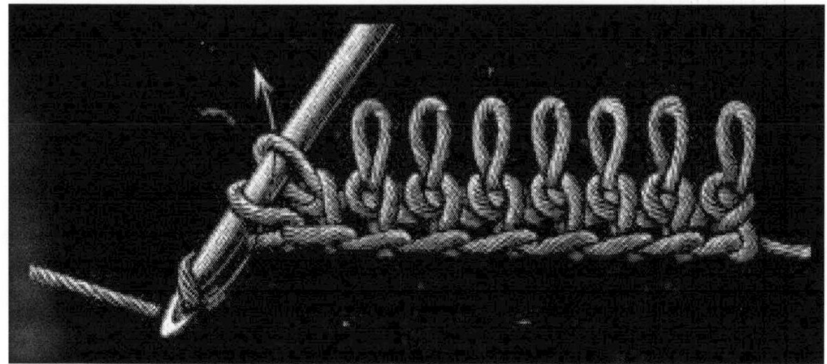

Figure: *Empty lace picots, worked in crochet.*

In order to make the picots more even and regular, it is advisable to form them over a coarse knitting needle or mesh.

Represents picots attached by plain stitches to the edge of a finished piece of work; this is done as follows: 1 plain stitch, draw out the loop to the proper length for a picot, and slip it on a mesh: put the needle into the horizontal parts of the last stitches, turn the thread round the needle, draw it through in a loop, and make 1 plain stitch on the next stitch and so on.

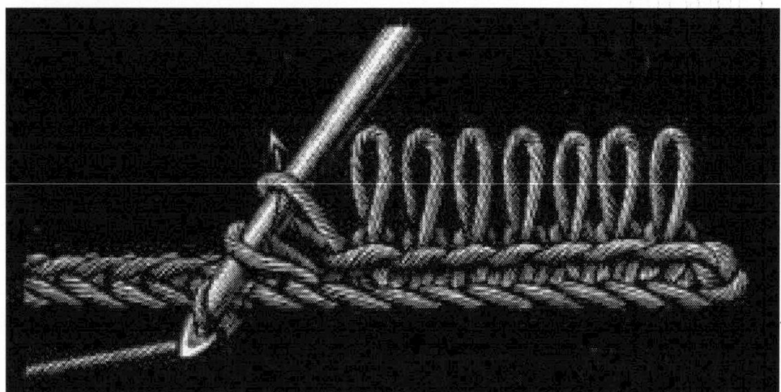

Figure: *Lace picots attached to a row of stitches made before hand.*

Method for copying tapestry patterns in crochet work —Printed cross stitch and embroidery patterns can very well be copied in crochet work especially when they are in two colours only, or rather, are drawn in one colour, on a plain ground.

The way in which such patterns are copied in crochet is by means of chain stitches and trebles, which, rising one above the other in rows, form little squares. For each square marked on the pattern, you must count, in the grounding, 1 treble and 2 chain stitches; in the solid parts, 3 trebles.

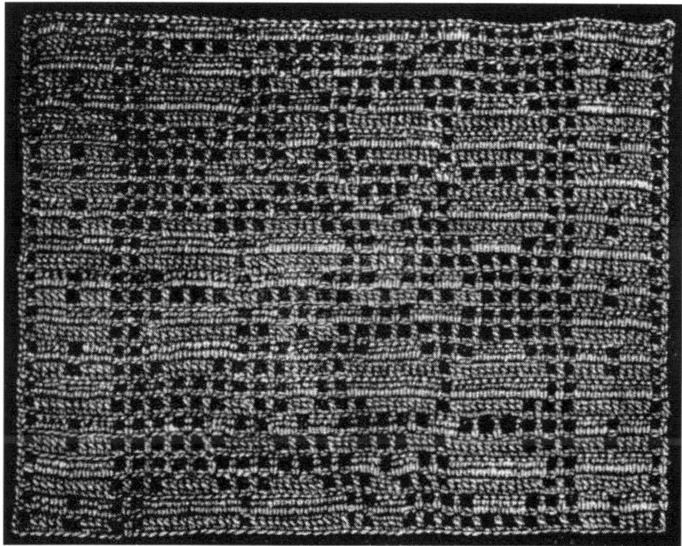

Figure: *Open-work crochet made after a tapestry pattern.*

The squares formed by the chain stitches should always begin and end with a treble. When, therefore, a solid square comes between empty or foundation squares, count 4 trebles for the solid square, because the last treble of the last empty square touches the third treble of the solid one.

Thus for 2 solid squares, side by side, count 7 trebles, and for 3 squares, 10. Embroidery patterns worked in several colours can be reproduced in crochet either by trebles and rows worked one way only, cutting off the thread at the end of each row, or by plain stitches, worked in rows to and fro.

When only three colours are used, pass two threads under the stitches; when more than two, leave those which are not in use, at the back of the work and only bring them to the front as they are wanted. The thread, you lay aside, takes at the back the place of the one in use. Of course, the threads not in use can only can be disposed of in this way when the work has a wrong side, otherwise they must be passed underneath the stitches. The colours should alternate in the order the pattern prescribes; moreover, the last stitch before you take another colour cannot be finished with the same thread, you must pass the new thread through the last loop and draw it up with that.

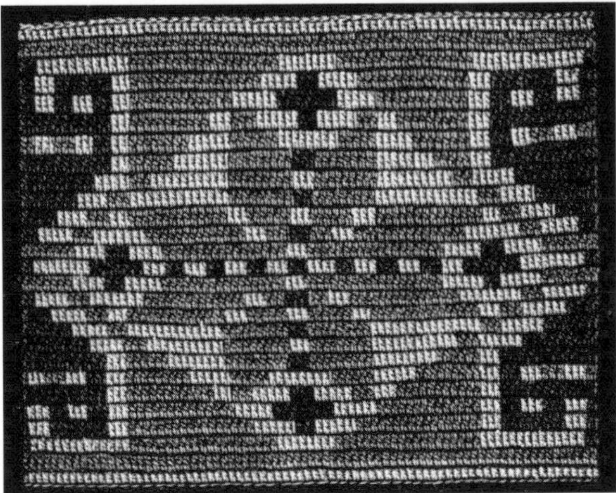

Figure: *Plain crochet made after a tapestry pattern.*

Crochet with Soutache or Lacet (braid)

These are two patterns of crochet, worked with the ordinary crochet cottons and with Soutache or Lacet D.M.C, a material which has not been used for crochet work before.

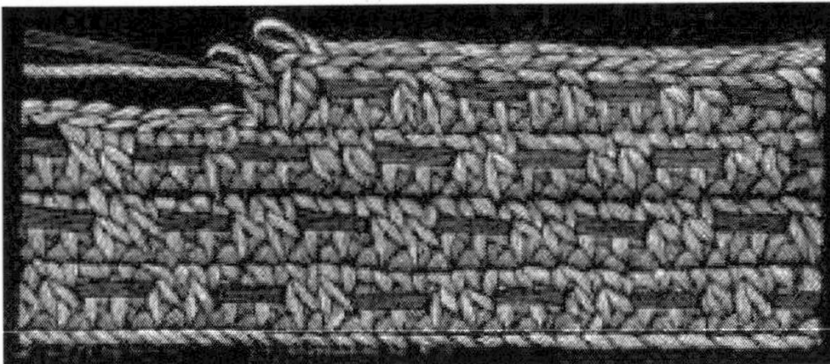

Figure: *Crochet with soutache or lacet (braid).*

Both patterns are worked entirely with trebles, the red braid passes over and under 2 trebles, it is brought, it will be observed, from the wrong side to the right after every 2 trebles, and passed between them, in such a manner as to form a slanting stitch between the rows of stitches.

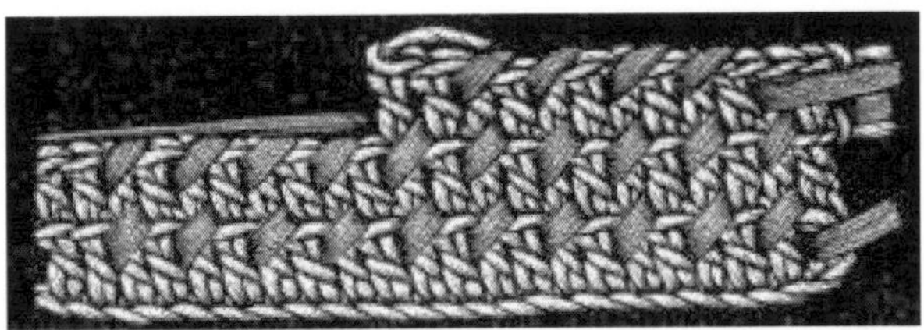

Figure: *Crochet with soutache or lacet (braid).*

Materials: Coton à tricoter D.M.C Nos. 6 to 12 or Cordonnet 6 fil D.M.C Nos. 3 to 10. Soutache D.M.C No. 2 or 3 or Lacets superfins D.M.C Nos. 2 to 5.

Colours: The cotton, white or écru. The Soutache or Lacet: Rouge-Cardinal 347, or Rouge-Grenat 326, or Bleu-Indigo 312.[A]

Crochet Square

Begin with 4 chain stitches, and work 1 single on the 1st chain, to make a round. Work, 1 chain and 2 plain on the next chain, 3 plain on each of the next 3 chain, 1 plain on the stitch on which the two first plain are worked.

Slip the next stitch, that is, put the needle in between the horizontal bars of the 1st plain stitch of the previous row, and draw the thread out without making a stitch.

Then make 1 chain and 2 plain on the slipped stitch.

After which, you make 3 plain on the second of the 3 plain that form the corner, and 1 plain on all the other stitches of the last row. The beginning and end of each row, are worked as described above.

Fig rerepresents a square, worked in consecutive rows. In making a crochet square, the rows may end in the middle of a side.

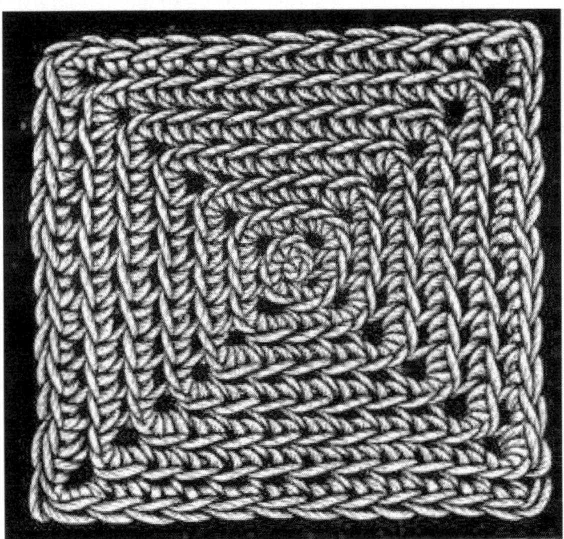

Figure: *Crochet square.*

When you use a stitch that has to be worked to and fro, you turn your work at the end of every row and work back along the stitches you have just made.

Crochet Hexagon

Make a foundation chain of 6 stitches, join the round; 12 plain on the 6 chain; finish the row as indicated for the previous figure == turn the work == * 1 plain, 3 plain on the second plain of the last row; repeat 5 times from *. Finish the row with 1 single == turn the work == 2 plain, 3 plain on the second of the first 3 plain; 3 plain and so on. These hexagons can be made of any size.

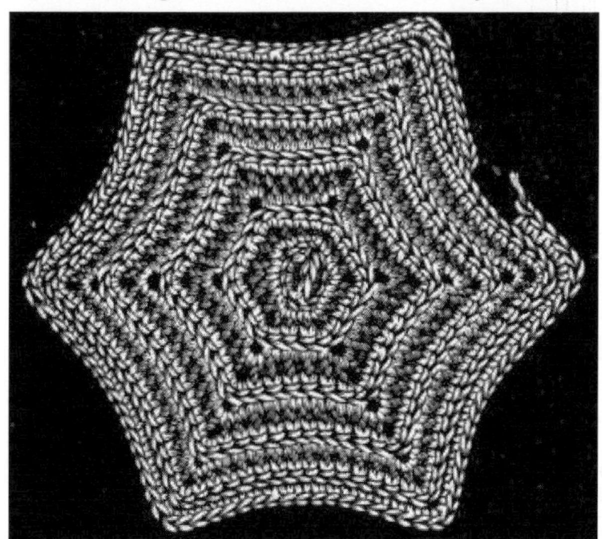

Figure: *Crochet hexagon.*

Coloured star worked into a light ground—Begin with 3 chain, join the ring = 2 plain on each of the 3 chain; then for the foundation, 1 plain with the dark thread, and 1 with the light on each of the 6 plain.

In each subsequent row, make one dark stitch more, increasing regularly, that is, making 2 stitches on the last light stitch that comes before the dark ones. Proceed in this manner until you have 6 or 8 dark stitches, in all and then begin to decrease in every row by one, until there is at last only one dark stitch remaining.

These stars are used in the making of purses, cap-crowns and mats for lamps, etc.

Tunisian Crochet

Tunisian crochet is also called crochet-knitting because, you have to cast on all the first row of stitches, as in knitting.

Materials—Every kind of cotton, as well as wool and silk, can be used for Tunisian crochet: the stitches look equally well in all these materials, but for things that require frequent washing or cleaning, a good washing material should be selected, such as Coton à tricoter D.M.C and Cordonnet 6 fils D.M.C[A], both strong and suitable in all ways.

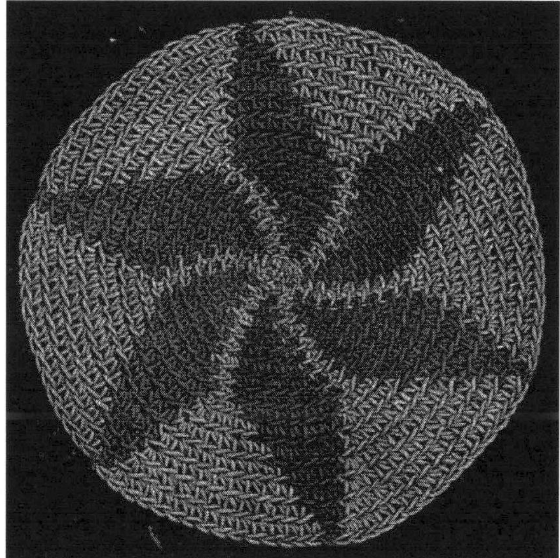

Figure: *Coloured star worked into a light ground.*

As we have already said, Tunisian crochet requires to be done with a long straight needle, with a knob at one end and it can only be worked on the right side.

Plain Tunisian Crochet

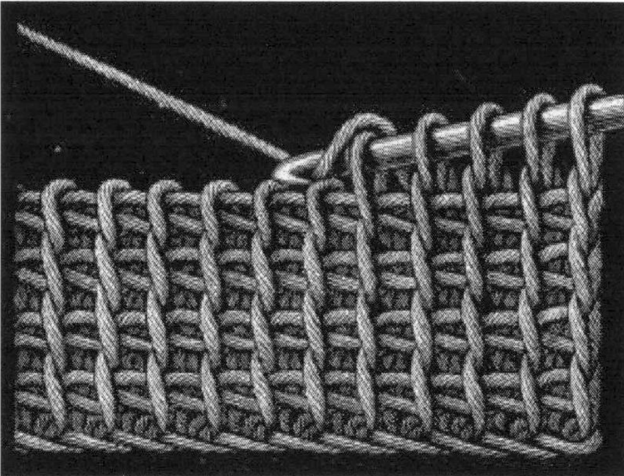

Figure: *Plain tunisian crochet.*

After making a foundation chain of the required length, begin the first, or loop row as it is called. Put the needle into the 2nd chain stitch, draw a loop through and so on, until you have taken up all the chain stitches on the needle. After having made the last stitch of the loop row, make 1 chain stitch and then pass to the second row that completes the stitch. Turn the thread round the needle, draw it through two loops, turn the thread round again, and again draw it through two loops, and so on to the end.

Straight Plaited Tunisian Stitch

Worked thus: miss the first loop in the 1st row, take up the second, and come back to the first, so that the 2 loops are crossed. Work the second row in the same manner as the second row of the preceding figure.

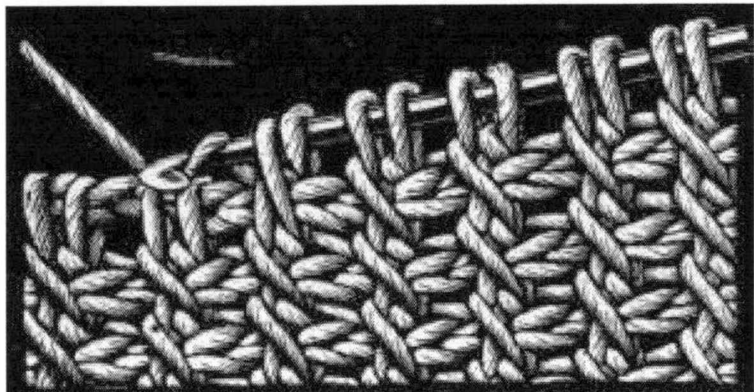

Figure: *Straight plaited tunisian stitch.*

Diagonal Plaited Tunisian Stitch

Worked like the preceding, taking up first the second loop and then the first: the second row also, in the same way as before. In the third row, take up the first stitch, and draw the third through the second, so as to produce diagonal lines across the surface of the work.

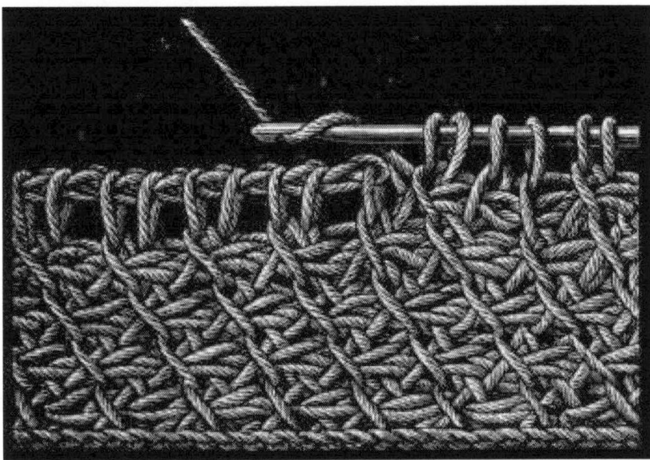

Figure: *Slanting plaited tunisian stitch.*

Open Tunisian Stitch

This is an easy kind of Tunisian crochet. The first row is worked. In the row of plain stitches, you alternately join 2 and 3, or 3 and 4 loops of the preceding row together, and replace them by as many chain stitches.

Decreasing and increasing in Tunisian crochet. Our illustration shows how to decrease on both sides and by that means form scallops.

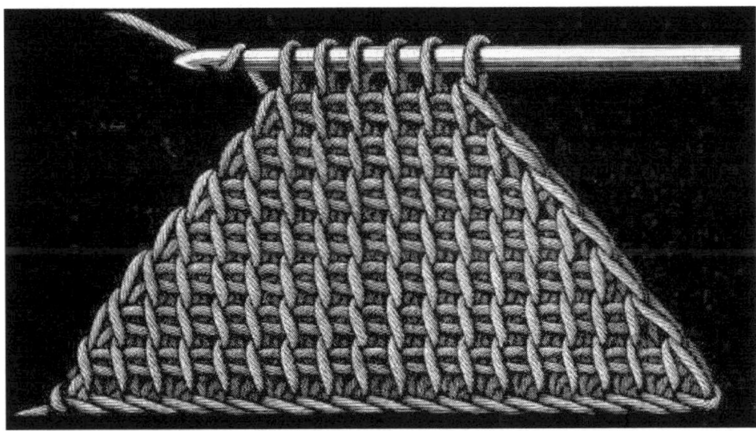

Figure: *Decreasing in tunisian crochet.*

You miss a stitch alternately on the right and left. On the right you crochet the first two stitches together, and at the end of the row, the last two, and so on, to the end. You increase in the same order, first on the right and then on the left.

Hairpin crochet: So called because it is worked on a kind of large steel hairpin or fork with two or more prongs. Wooden and nickel varieties of this implement, which are patented by Mme Besson, of Paris, are also used.

Very pretty laces, fringes, gimp headings and the like can be made in this kind of crochet work. It is often used in combination with ordinary crochet and plain and scalloped braids and gimps, or as a heading for fringes made of tufts and pendant balls. There are a great many stitches which can be worked in hairpin-crochet. We shall only describe those here that will best teach our readers how the work is done.

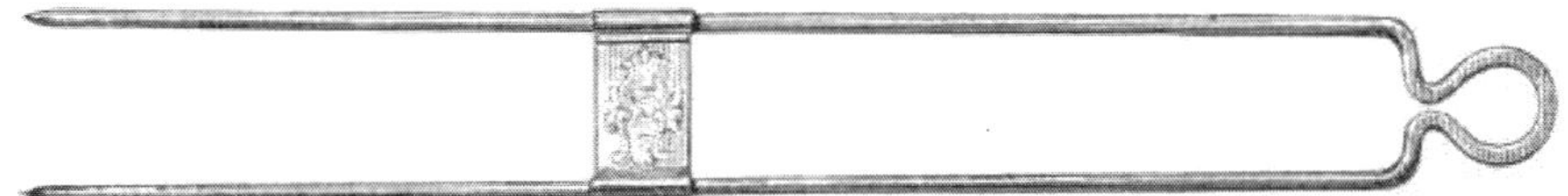

Figure: *Steel hairpin for crochet.*

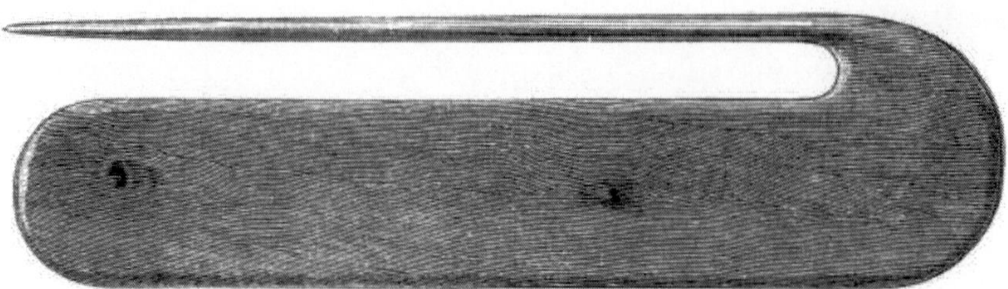

Figure: *Wooden fork for crochet.*

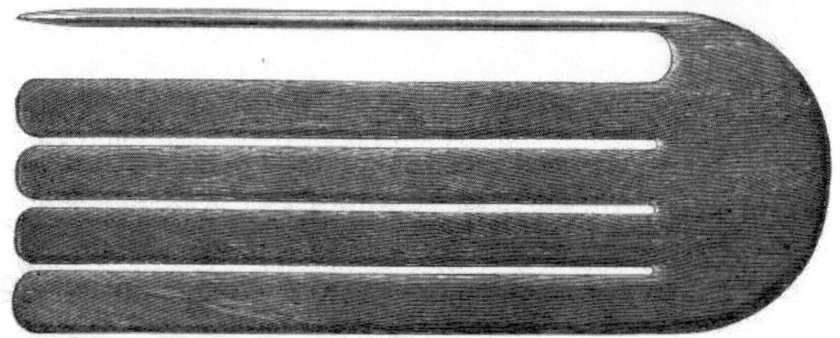

Figure: *Fork with several prongs for crochet.*

Materials:For washing laces, Cordonnet 6 fils D.M.C is the best; for furniture fringes, the lower numbers of Coton à tricoter D.M.C, and for producing the appearance of filoselle, the lower numbers of Coton à repriser D.M.C are to be taken.

Stitches: Begin by a chain stitch, made with an ordinary crochet needle, take the needle out of the loop, and insert the left prong of the fork upwards from below, holding the fork between the thumb and finger of the left hand. The thread should always be in front. Then put the thread over the right prong and the needle into the loop on the left prong, take up the thread, draw it through the loop, put the thread over the needle and draw it through the loop that is on the needle, twist the loop round the left prong, turn the needle round to the right (the thread will now be wound round the right prong); put the needle into the loop on the left prong, throw the thread over the needle, draw it through, tighten the loops and so on.

These stitches may be doubled, or you may make several trebles on each loop, or arrange the plain stitches in different ways.

Hairpin Insertion

Begin by making stripes with the fork, covering each thread with two plain stitches. Then join the stripes together by the loops, drawing the left loop over the right one and the right one over the left. When you come to the end of the stripes fasten off the last loops by a few stitches. To strengthen the edges, join two loops together by 1 plain, 2 chain, 1 plain and so on.

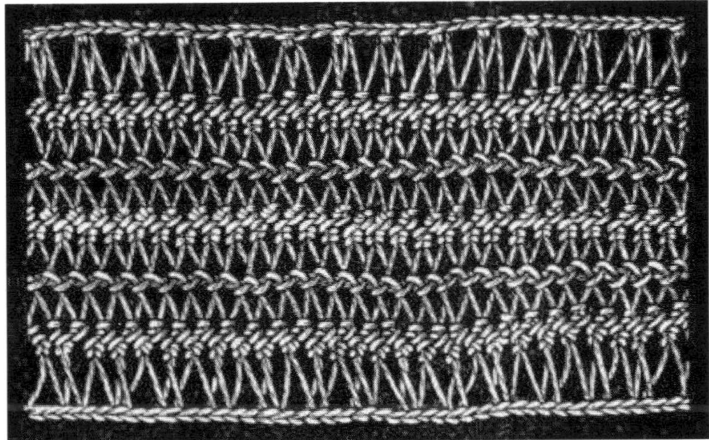

Figure: *Hairpin insertion.*

Materials: Fil à pointer D.M.C No. 20 or 30, or Cordonnet 6 fils D.M.C Nos. 4 to 15, white or écru.[A]

Hairpin lace

When, by making two half trebles in each loop, you have got the necessary length of hairpin crochet, join the loops two and two, by means of a coloured thread which makes a good contrast with the thread of which the hairpin crochet is made. Work 1 plain stitch joining 2 loops on the right, 2 chain, 1 plain joining the 2 loops on the left; then 2 chain and come back to the right, and so on, until you have taken up all the loops. This forms the zig-zag in the middle.

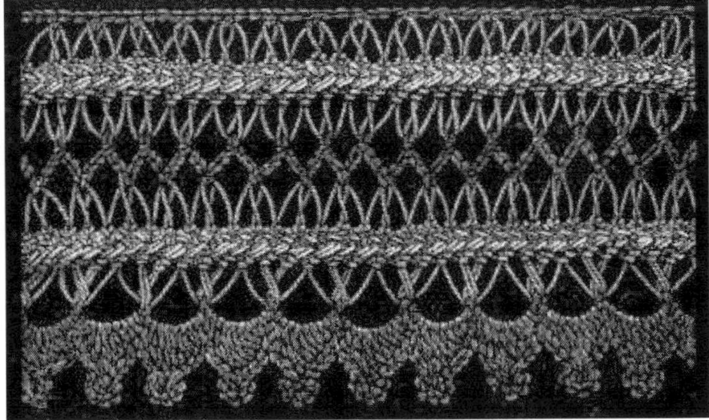

Figure: *Hairpin lace.*

Materials: For the hairpin work: Fil à pointer D.M.C Nos. 20 to 30, or Cordonnet 6 fils D.M.C Nos. 3 to 10, white or écru. For the edge. Coton à tricoter D.M.C Nos. 16 to 30.

Colours: Rouge-Cardinal 347, or Jaune-Rouille 364, or Brun-Marron 406.[A]

1st row—join 3 loops by: 1 plain, 5 chain.

2nd row—on the 5 chain stitches: 1 plain, 1 half-treble, 3 trebles, 1 picot, made with 5 chain (for the chain picots), 1 half-treble, 1 plain. The footing of this lace is made like the one in figure.

Hairpin Fringes

Figure depicted earlier, is made with a fork composed of one branch and 3 or 4 rulers, round which the thread is wound in succession, so as to form loops of different lengths. You may use for this, either a single very coarse thread, or else several fine ones, used together as one.

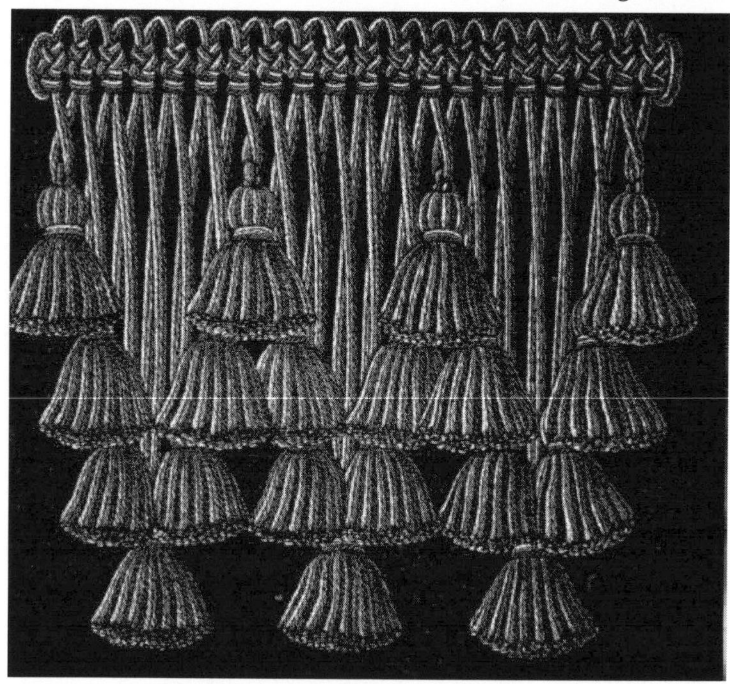

Figure: *Hairpin fringe with tassels.*

The heading of the fringe is plain, and heavy tassels are fastened into the loops. The tassels are made as follows: take a thick skein of the same thread the fringe is made of, pass it through the loop, leaving just the length required for the tassel, at one end, thread a needle with the same thread and twist it round the skein, the right distance from the top to form the head of the tassel and then cut the ends even, at the bottom. As the loops are of different lengths, the tassels will hang in steps and the fuller and heavier they are, the handsomer the fringe will be.

Figure represents another pattern of fringe, the first part of which is made with the same fork as the preceding one. Instead however of winding the thread round the several prongs in succession, you pass it alternately round the two first and the fourth, thus making loops of two lengths only. Tassels of a length, suited to the purpose the fringe is intended for, depend from these loops and may be varied in the second row by balls made to issue from the middle, or by long meshes, which are made over the whole width of the fork and affixed to the loops.

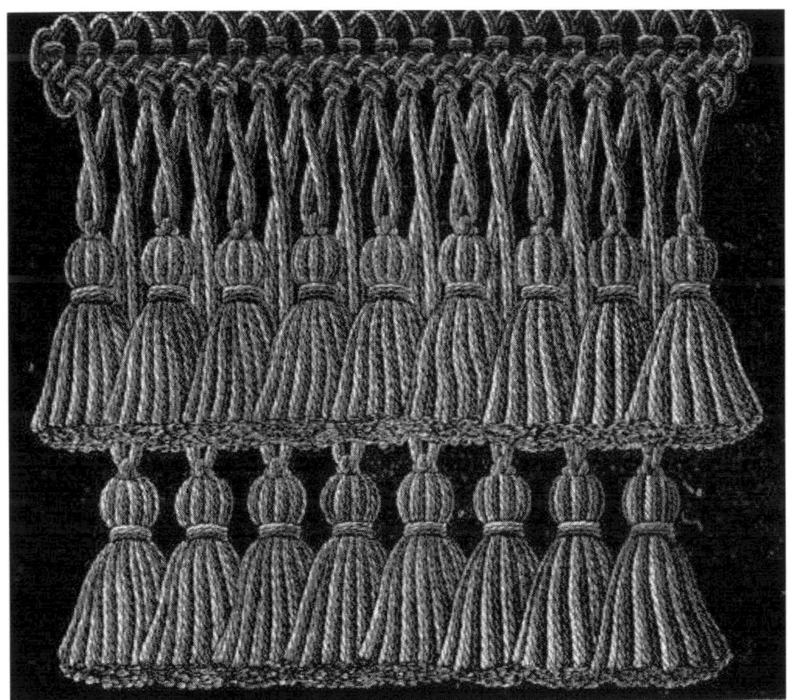

Figure: *Hairpin fringe with tassels.*

Materials: Coton à tricoter D.M.C Nos. 6 to 16.[A]

Colours: Écru and Jaune-Rouille 363, 368, or Gris-Tilleul 331 and Rouge-Cornouille 449 and 450, or three other shades.[A]

Figures represent two pretty patterns of fringes made of écru cotton with a strong twist. These are very suitable for washing articles, as the cotton balls wash perfectly.

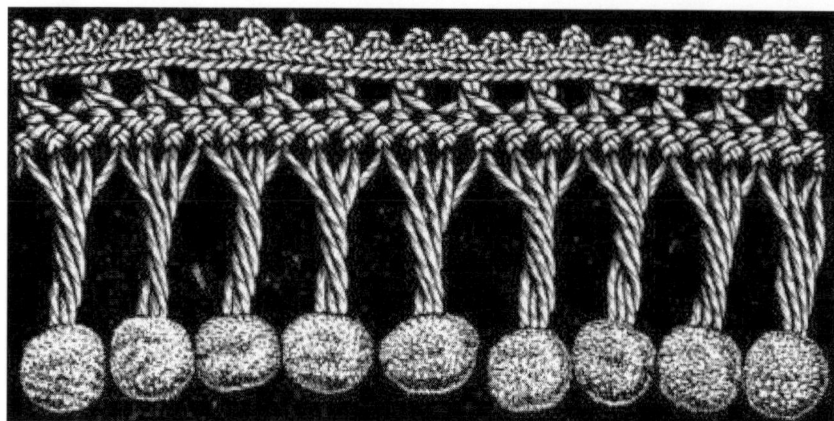

Figure: *Hairpin fringe with one line of balls.*

The loops are all of one length and a ball hangs from every third. In the last chapter but one, a minute description is given of the way in which these balls are made. The heading of the loops is formed by a row of chain stitches, varying in number from four to six, according to the size of the cotton. The edge is ornamented with little picots. The fringe consists of three long and three short loops alternately, which causes, the balls that are made to depend from them, to form two parallel lines.

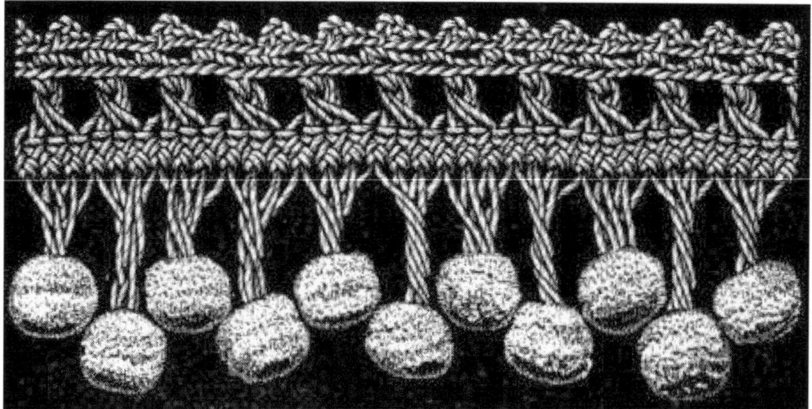

Figure: *Hairpin fringe with two lines of balls, one above the other.*

Materials: For the crochet-work: Cordonnet 6 fils D.M.C Nos. 3 to 10, or Fil à pointer D.M.C Nos. 10 to 30. For the balls: Coton à repriser D.M.C Nos. 8 to 16.

If you join the loops of the heading together, three and three, you will have to make enough chain stitches to cover the space that is to be filled.

The picots are made with 6 chain stitches, you put the needle back into the fifth stitch after closing the picot, make 1 chain, 2 plain, in the preceding row, 1 picot and so on.

Fringe Made with Lacet or Braid

This is an easy fringe to make and a very effective trimming for table-cloths, curtains etc., which are embroidered on coarse stuffs.

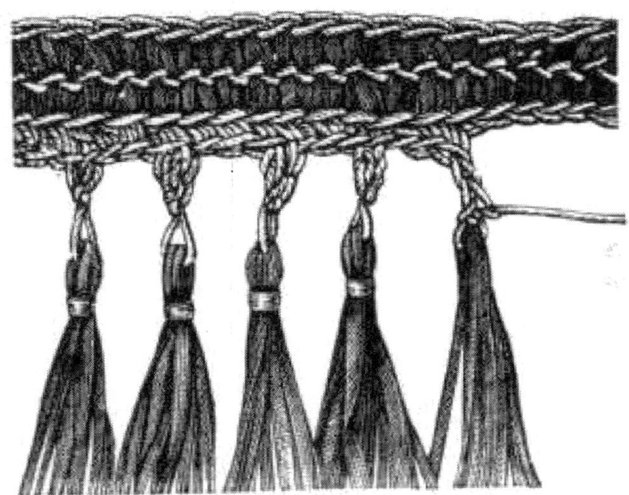

Figure: *Fringe made with lacet or soutache (braid).*

Materials: Lacet D.M.C No. 4 or Soutache D.M.C NO. 2½ in red. Cordonnet 6 fils D.M.C Nos. 3 to 10. Fil à pointer D.M.C Nos. 10 to 30, écru.[A]

Begin with a foundation chain, in coarse écru twist, the light stitch in the middle of the heading of the fringe being also made of the same material.

In the next row, you use the twist and the braid together, as follows—with the twist = 1 chain stitch, put the needle into the first stitch of the foundation chain, take up the braid, draw it through, turn the twist round the needle, draw it through the braid and the chain stitch.

To make the braid loops longer, they may be made over a wooden ruler. To the two rows of braid stitches, represented in the pattern, you may add as many other rows as you please. On the fringed side make: 4 plain, 3 chain, draw out one very long loop and fasten into it a cluster of lengths of braid from 10 to 12 c/m. long, and draw the loop tightly round it to secure the tassel; 3 plain on the chain stitches. Repeat from *.

Lace made on Point Lace braid —For the rounds: 1 plain on the braid, 10 chain, then coming back, 1 single on the 4th chain.

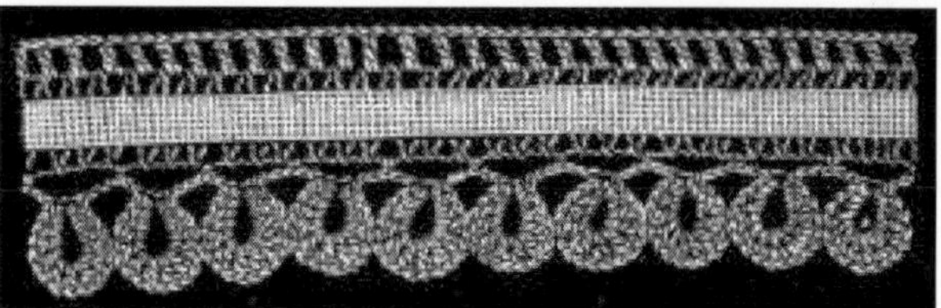

Figure: *Lace made on point lace braid.*

Materials: Fil d'Alsace D.M.C Nos. 30 to 50, or Cordonnet 6 fils D.M.C No. 80, white[A] and Point Lace braid.

In this first round you make: 1 chain, 1 half-treble, 12 trebles *, 1 half-treble, 1 chain, 1 single on the 4th chain; 3 chain, 1 single on the braid, far enough from the 1st chain for the rounds not to overlap each other. Then 10 chain, 1 single on the 4th chain, 1 single, 1 half-treble, 4 trebles, join to the first round between the 8th and 9th trebles, 8 trebles and repeat from *. For the footing: 1 treble, 1 chain, miss a few threads of the edge of the braid, 1 treble.

Bibliography

Adrosko, Rita J.: *Natural Dyes and Home Dyeing,* Dover Publications, New York, 1971.

Amir, Ziva: *Arabesque,* Van Nostrand Reinhold, New York, 1977.

Bahouth, Candace: *Flowers, Birds, and Unicorns: Medieval Needlepoint,* Harry Abrams, New York, 1993.

Barbara Snook: *English Embroidery,* Bell & Hyman, London, 1974.

Bath, Virginia Churchill: *Embroidery Masterworks*, Henry Regnery Co., Chicago, 1997.

Collingwood, Peter: *The Techniques of Tablet Weaving,* Watson-Guptill, New York, 1982.

Crockett, Candace: *Cardweaving,* Watson-Guptill, New York, 1973.

Don, Sarah: *Traditional Embroidered Animals,* Sterling Publishing Co., New York, 1990.

Drysdale, Rosemary. *The Art of Blackwork Embroidery*. New York: Charles Scribner's Sons, 1975.

Elizabeth Geddes and Moyra McNeill: *Blackwork Embroidery,* Dover Books, New York, 1976.

Freeman, Margaret B.: *The Unicorn Tapestries,* Dutton, New York, 1996.

Geddes, Elisabeth and Moyra McNeill: *Blackwork Embroidery*. Dover, New York, 1976.

George Wingfield Digby: *Elizabethan Embroidery,* Thomas Yoseloff, New York, 1964.

Gillow, John, and Bryan Sentance: *World Textiles*, Bulfinch Press/Little, Brown, NJ, 1999.

Jane Ashelford: *Dress in the Age of Elizabeth I,* B.T. Batsford Ltd., London. 1988.

Jane Zimmerman: *The Development of Western European Needlework: Thirteenth Century Through Eighteenth Century,* Self-published. Richmond, California. 1982.

Janet Arnold: *Queen Elizabeth's Wardrobe Unlock'd,* W.S. Maney & Son., London. 1988.

Karen Hearn: *Dynasties: Paiting in Tudor and Jacobean England 1530-1630.* Rizzoli, 1996.

King, Donald and Santina Levey: *Embroidery In Britain From 1200 to 1750,* Victoria & Albert Museum, London, 1993.

Lanto Synge: *The Royal School of Needlework Book of Needlework and Embroidery,* William Collins Sons and Company, London, 1986.

Lemon, Jane: *Metal Thread Embroidery,* Sterling, NY, 2004.

Liles, J.N.: *The Art and Craft of Natural Dyeing: Traditional Recipes for Modern Use,* University of Tennessee Press, Knoxville, TN, 1990.

Linn Skinner: *100 Blackwork Charts* and *Another 100 Blackwork Charts,* Self-published, 1997.

Margaret Pascoe: *Blackwork Embroidery,* B.T. Batsford ltd., London. 1986.

Marguerite Fawdry and Deborah Brown: *The Book of Samplers,* Cameron and Tayleur, London, 1980.

Mary Gostelow: *Blackwork,* Van Nostrand Reinhold, New York, 1976.

McRae, Bobbi A.: *Nature's Dyepot: A Resource guide for Spinners, Weavers & Dyers,* Fiberworks Publications, Austin, 1991.

Netherton, Robin, and Gale R. Owen-Crocker, editors: *Medieval Clothing and Textiles,* Boydell Press, London, 2005.

O'Steen, Darlene: *The Proper Stitch,* Symbol of Excellence Publishers, Birmingham, AL, 1994.

Patricia Wardle: *Guide to English Embroidery. Victoria and Albert Museum,* Her Majesty's Stationery office, London, 1970.

Quinault, Marie-Jo: *Filet Lace, Introduction to the Linen Stitch,* Trafford Publishing, 2003.

Rosemary Drysdale: *The Art of Blackwork Embroidery,* Charles Scribner's Sons, New York, 1975.

Roy Strong: *The English Icon: Elizabethan and Jacobean Portraiture,* The Paul Meloon Foundation for British Art, Routledge and Kegan Paul, London, 1969.

Simmons, Max: *Dyes and Dyeing,* Van Nostrand Reinhold, Melbourne, Australia, 1978.

Synge, Lanto: *Antique Needlework.* Blandford Press, London, 1982.

Therle Hughes: *English Domestic Needlework,* Abbey Fine Arts, London, 1998.

Thomasina Beck: *The Embroiderer's Flowers.* David and Charles, Newton Abbott, Devon, 1992.

Warner, Pamela: *Embroidery: A history,* B.T. Batsford, London, 1991.

Weir, Shelagh and Serene Shahid: *Palestinian Embroidery,* The British Museum, London, 1988.

Wilson, David M.: *The Bayeux Tapestry,* Thames and Hudson, US, 1985.

Index

K

L

M

N

O

P

R

S

T

V

W

❑❑❑